Lecture Notes in Computer Scien

Commenced Publication in 1973
Founding and Former Series Editors:
Gerhard Goos, Juris Hartmanis, and Jan van Leeuwen

Editorial Board

Luca Breveglieri Israel Koren
David Naccache Jean-Pierre Seifert (Eds.)

Fault Diagnosis and Tolerance in Cryptography

Third International Workshop, FDTC 2006
Yokohama, Japan, October 10, 2006
Proceedings

 Springer

Volume Editors

Luca Breveglieri
Politecnico di Milano, Dipartimento di Elettronica e Informazione
Piazza Leonardo Da Vinci n. 32, 20133 Milano, Italy
E-mail: luca.breveglieri@polimi.it

Israel Koren
University of Massachusetts, Department of Electrical and Computer Engineering
Amherst, MA 01003, USA
E-mail: koren@ecs.umass.edu

David Naccache
École normale supérieure, Département d'Informatique
45 rue d'Ulm, 75230 Paris Cedex 05, France
E-mail: david.naccache@ens.fr

Jean-Pierre Seifert
University of Haifa, Faculty of Science and Science Education
The Center for Computational Mathematics and Scientific Computation
31905 Haifa, Israel
E-mail: jeanpierreseifert@yahoo.com

Library of Congress Control Number: 2006933937

CR Subject Classification (1998): C.2.0, D.4.6, E.3, H.2.0, K.4.4, K.6.5

LNCS Sublibrary: SL 4 – Security and Cryptology

ISSN   0302-9743
ISBN-10   3-540-46250-3 Springer Berlin Heidelberg New York
ISBN-13   978-3-540-46250-7 Springer Berlin Heidelberg New York

Springer is a part of Springer Science+Business Media

springer.com

© Springer-Verlag Berlin Heidelberg 2006
Printed in Germany

Typesetting: Camera-ready by author, data conversion by Scientific Publishing Services, Chennai, India
Printed on acid-free paper   SPIN: 11889700   06/3142   5 4 3 2 1 0

Preface

In recent years applied cryptography has developed considerably to satisfy the increasing security requirements of various information technology disciplines, such as telecommunications, networking, database systems, mobile applications and others. Cryptosystems are inherently computationally complex and in order to satisfy the high throughput requirements of many applications, they are often implemented by means of either VLSI devices (cryptographic accelerators) or highly optimized software routines (cryptographic libraries) and are used via suitable (network) protocols.

The sophistication of the underlying cryptographic algorithms, the high complexity of the implementations, and the easy access and low cost of cryptographic devices resulted in increased concerns regarding the reliability and security of crypto-devices. The effectiveness of side channel attacks on cryptographic devices, like timing and power-based attacks, has been known for some time. Several recent investigations have demonstrated the need to develop methodologies and techniques for designing robust cryptographic systems (both hardware and software) to protect them against both accidental faults and maliciously injected faults with the purpose of extracting the secret key. This trend has been particularly motivated by the fact that the equipment needed to carry out a successful side channel attack based on fault injection is easily accessible at a relatively low cost (for example, laser beam technology), and that the skills needed to use it are quite common. The identification of side channel attacks based on fault injections and the development of appropriate counter-measures have therefore become an active field of scientific and industrial research.

Following this trend, the first workshop devoted to Fault Diagnosis and Tolerance in Cryptography (FDTC) was organized in June 2004, in Florence, Italy, to promote the exchange of ideas within the community of researchers who have been active in this field. The workshop has since then become an annual event with the second one held in Edinburgh, Scotland, in September 2005, and the third one in Yokohama, Japan, in October 2006. FDTC 2006 included 12 regular presentations plus two invited talks that provided an overview of the state of the art in this field.

The FDTC workshops aim at covering all aspects of fault injection-based side channel attacks on cryptographic devices and the corresponding counter-measures. This includes topics such as: modelling the reliability of cryptographic systems and protocols; inherently reliable cryptographic systems and algorithms; fault models for cryptographic devices (hardware and software); fault-injection-based attacks on cryptographic systems and protocols; adapting classical fault diagnosis and tolerance techniques to cryptographic systems; novel fault diagnosis and tolerance techniques for cryptographic systems; case studies of attacks, reliability and fault diagnosis and tolerance techniques in cryptographic systems.

FDTC 2006 has for the first time official proceedings as a Springer LNCS volume. The present volume contains all the papers presented at FDTC 2006, plus selected FDTC 2004 and 2005 papers that have undergone a second review process, which have been co-chaired for this Springer volume by David Naccache and Jean-Pierre

Seifert. The main goal of this volume is to provide the reader with a comprehensive introduction to the issues faced by designers of robust cryptographic devices and to the currently available methodologies and techniques for protecting these devices against fault injection attacks.

The papers contained in this volume are organized as follows. Section 1 includes new fault-injection-based attacks on public key systems, namely, RSA and ECC. Section 2 contains several proposed counter-measures, mainly at the algorithmic level, that are based on the use of fault diagnosis methods. Section 3 is dedicated to fault injection-based attacks on symmetric key systems and the related fault-diagnosis counter-measures. Section 4 focuses on models for evaluating the reliability and security of cryptographic systems that are subject to fault injection-based attacks. Section 5 is dedicated to counter-measures at the arithmetic level, which complement those at the algorithmic level mentioned above. Section 6 contains a miscellanea of topics demonstrating the connection between fault injection-based attacks and other security side channel threats, e.g., power attacks.

The interested reader may also wish to read the papers that have appeared in the "Special Section on Fault Diagnosis and Tolerance in Cryptography" of the September 2006 issue of the *IEEE Transactions on Computers*. This special section includes the extended version of several FDTC 2004 presentations (and consequently do not appear in this volume). Also worth mentioning is the February 2006 *Special Issue of the Proceedings of the IEEE* which is devoted to cryptography and contains a tutorial paper focusing on fault injection-based side channel attacks that was originally presented at FDTC 2004.

This workshop would not be possible without the involvement of many people, in particular the members of the Program Committee who reviewed all the submitted manuscripts. Their names are listed below. Thanks are also due to Alfred Hofman, who accepted our proposal to publish an LNCS volume dedicated to FDTC. We also wish to thank Akashi Satoh, Natsume Matsuzaki and Tsutomu Matsumoto for their tremendous help with the local arrangements in Yokohama. Last but not least, we would like to thank all the authors who have submitted their papers and greatly contributed to the success of the FDTC workshops.

August 2006   Luca Breveglieri
                                                               Israel Koren
                                                               David Naccache
                                                               Jean Pierre Seifert

Organization

Organizing Committee

Luca Breveglieri (volume contact editor)
Politecnico di Milano
Dipartimento di Elettronica e Informazione
Piazza Leonardo Da Vinci n. 32
Milan 20133
Italy
luca.breveglieri@polimi.it

Israel Koren
University of Massachusetts at Amherst
Department of Electrical and Computer Engineering
Amherst, MA 01003
USA
koren@ecs.umass.edu

David Naccache
École Normale Supérieure de Paris
Département d'Informatique
45 rue d'Ulm
75230 Paris Cedex 05
France
david.naccache@ens.fr

Jean-Pierre Seifert
Applied Security Research Group
The Center for Computational Mathematics and Scientific Computation
Faculty of Science and Science Education
University of Haifa
Haifa 31905, Israel

and

Institute for Computer Science
University of Innsbruck
6020 Innsbruck, Austria
jeanpierreseifert@yahoo.com

Program Committee of FDTC 2006

Bao Feng	I2R Corporation, France
Luca Breveglieri	Politecnico di Milano, Italy
Ernie Brickell	Intel Corporation, USA
Hervé Chabannes	Sagem Défense Sécurité, France
Christophe Clavier	Gemplus Corporation, France
Wieland Fischer	Infineon Corporation, Germany
Christophe Giraud	Oberthur Card Systems, France
Shay Gueron	University of Haifa and Intel Corporation, Israel
Louis Goubin	University of Versailles, France
Mohaned Kafi	Axalto Corporation, France
Ramesh Karri	Polytechnic University of Brooklyn, USA
Jong Rok Kim	Samsung Corporation, Korea
Vanessa Gratzer	University of Paris 2, France
Çetin Kaya Koç	Oregon State University, USA
Israel Koren	University of Massachusetts at Amherst, USA
Pierre-Yvan Liardet	STMicroelectronics Corporation, France
Wenbo Mao	HP Corporation, USA
Sandra Marcello	Thalès Corporation, France
David Naccache	École Normale Supérieure de Paris, France (PC Co-chair)
Elisabeth Oswald	Graz University of Technology, Austria
Jean-Pierre Seifert	University of Innsbruck, Austria and University of Haifa, Israel (PC Co-chair)
Elena Trichina	Spansion Corporation, USA
Michael Tunstall	Royal Holloway University of London, UK
Wen-Guey Tzeng	National Chiao Tung University, Taiwan
Claire Whelan	Dublin City University, Ireland
Kaiji Wu	University of Illinois at Chicago, USA
Moti Yung	Columbia University, USA

Program Committee of FDTC 2005

Luca Breveglieri	Politecnico di Milano, Italy
Joan Daemen	STMicroelectronics Corporation, Belgium
Christophe Giraud	Oberthur Card Systems, France
Shay Gueron	Intel Corporation, Israel
Marc Joye	Gemplus & CIM-PACA, France
Mark Karpovsky	University of Boston, USA
Çetin Kaya Koç	Oregon State University, USA
Israel Koren	University of Massachusetts at Amherst, USA
Régis Leveugle	TIMA Laboratory Grenoble, France
Ramesh Karri	Polytechnic University of Brooklyn, USA
David Naccache	Gemplus Card International, France, and Royal Holloway, UK
Christof Paar	University of Ruhr at Bochum, Germany
Jean-Pierre Seifert	Intel Corporation, USA

Program Committee of FDTC 2004

Luca Breveglieri	Politecnico di Milano, Italy
Joan Daemen	STMicroelectronics Corporation, Belgium
Çetin Kaya Koç	Oregon State University, USA
Israel Koren	University of Massachusetts at Amherst, USA
Régis Leveugle	TIMA Laboratory Grenoble, France
David Naccache	Gemplus Card International, France
Ramesh Karri	Polytechnic University of Brooklyn, USA
Christof Paar	University of Ruhr at Bochum, Germany

Table of Contents

Models for Fault Attacks on Cryptographic Devices

Fault-Resistant Arithmetic for Cryptography

Fault Attacks and Other Security Threats

Is It Wise to Publish Your Public RSA Keys?

Shay Gueron[1,3] and Jean-Pierre Seifert[1,2]

[1] Applied Security Research Group
The Center for Computational Mathematics and Scientific Computation,
University of Haifa, Haifa 31905, Israel
[2] Institute for Computer Science, University of Innsbruck
6020 Innsbruck, Austria
[3] Intel Corporation, IDC, Israel
shay@math.haifa.ac.il
jeanpierreseifert@yahoo.com

Abstract. Only very recently, the study of introducing faults into the public-key elements of the RSA signature scheme was initiated. Following the seminal work of Seifert on fault inductions during the RSA signature verification, Brier, Chevallier-Mames, Ciet, and Clavier considered in a recent paper the signature counterpart and showed how to recover the private exponent — even with absolutely no knowledge of the faults behavior. Consequently, this paper reconsiders the RSA signature verification and proposes two embassaring simple new fault attacks against the RSA verification process. Despite their trivial nature, both of our methods bear heavy practical consequences. While the first new attack of our methods simply eliminates the "somehow cumbersome" and subtle mathematical two-phase attack analysis of Seifert's attack, the second methodology removes the so called "one-shot success" of Seifert's attack and paves the way for a permanent and universal "mass-market" RSA signature forgery. Motivated by the obvious security threats through tampering attacks during the RSA verification process we will also consider some heuristic but practical countermeasures.

Keywords: Authenticated computing, Fault attacks, Hardware attacks, RSA, Secure/Trusted boot.

1 Introduction

In the context of tamper-resistant devices that implement the RSA algorithm, most of the concern and the efforts for countermeasures against "physical attacks" are directed towards protecting the signature procedures. These are perceived sensitive because they involve operations that use the device's secret exponent. The general perception here is that the RSA verification process is inherently secure because it only deals with public information.

But, continuing the recently introduced fault attacks against the public keys of an RSA system, cf. [Sei, Mui, BCCC], this paper casts new doubts on the above perception. We show that if the threat model includes tampering with the

L. Breveglieri et al. (Eds.): FDTC 2006, LNCS 4236, pp. 1–12, 2006.

device, fault attacks become a real practical threat to the trustworthiness of the authentication procedure.

To put a real practical perspective on the former attack scenario, consider a device which is a locked system that is supposed to execute some input code, but only this code is signed and the signature is validated. This is a standard situation with various DRM applications. Since the user is part of the threat model in such cases, hardware attacks that include tampering with the device are a plausible concern. The big threat to the device is a so called BORE *(Break Once Run Everywhere)* attack, similar to those that exist in the smartcard business, where a successful attack can be reproduced and then applied to many devices. In such real-world scenarios, it is conceivable that the attacker would invest even significant initial effort in hacking the device, would manage to build a cheap hardware device that circumvents this authentication, and then publicly sell (or distribute) this circumvention device. One known example for a BORE attack is the "unlooper" business, where fraudulent pay-TV users install a cheap device in order to circumvent the pay-TV protection mechanism. The unlooper device induces the right spikes, glitches, etc. in order to "unlock" an invalid smartcard, cf. [And, BCNT$^+$, Unl]. Another prominent example is the X-box, where despite the cryptographically strong RSA authentication procedure that it implemented, a trivial change in the public key value lead to a total security break, cf. [Hua], or [Har] for details about the commercial authentication-circumvention business.

Indeed, this paper discusses two very simple but practical types of fault based attacks against a device that performs RSA authentication, facilitating the signature forgery dramatically. Following the seminal work of Seifert [Sei] on fault inductions during the RSA signature verification, Brier, Chevallier-Mames, Ciet, and Clavier [BCCC] considered in a recent paper the signature counterpart and showed how to recover the private exponent — even with absolutely no knowledge of the faults behavior. Consequently, this paper reconsiders the RSA signature verification and proposes two embassaring simple new fault attacks aginst the RSA verification process. Despite their trivial nature, both of our methods bear heavy practical consequences. While the first new attack of our methods only eliminates the "somehow cumbersome" and subtle mathematical two-phase attack analysis of Seifert's attack, the second methodology removes the so called "one-shot success" of Seifert's attack and paves the way for a permanent and universal "mass-market" RSA signature forgery.

Our new attacks undermine again the underlying assumption upon which the authentication is based, namely that the device uses an authentic copy of the public data. Thus, the conclusion is that if a device cannot remotely verify the authenticity of the public data, and can be physically manipulated by an attacker, new types of countermeasures against faults induction, must be taken. In the context of Elliptic Curve Cryptography this fact was already known, cf. [BMM, CJ].

The present paper is organized as follows. The next section recalls some basic definitions, presents the used fault models, and as well the simple attack idea due to Seifert, cf. [Sei]. Herafter, we will show our two new very simple attack methodologies, called bypass attack and permanent fault attack. Then, we will investigate some simple but practical countermeasures to thwart the known fault attacks against the RSA signature verification process. The paper concludes with recommendations for further research directions.

2 Definitions and Preliminaries

An RSA system for bit-length k is defined as follows, see for e.g. [MvOV]. Uniformly pick from the set of all $k/2$-bit primes two secret primes p and q and let $N = p \cdot q$ be their respective product. Then, uniformly pick from the set Z_N^* a number e. Here, $\mathbb{Z}_N^*$ denotes the multiplicative group of all natural numbers which are smaller than N and are relatively prime to N. Using p and q compute now the e's multiplicative inverse d such that $e \cdot d \equiv 1 \bmod \varphi(N)$. Finally, one announces the public key e and N and keeps the key d secretly.

In order to actually sign with RSA in the standard way, one uses a hash function $\mathsf{hash}(\cdot)$ (for e.g. SHA-1) and a redundancy function $\mathsf{F}(\cdot)$ in the following way, cf. [MvOV]. First, one hashes the messages $m \in \mathbb{Z}_N$ to a fixed length hash value $h_m := \mathsf{hash}(m)$, hereafter one uses the redundacy function F to re-expand the hash value h_m into an k-bit value $f_m := \mathsf{F}(h_m)$, and finally one computes the RSA-signature of the message m as $S := (f_m)^d \bmod N$ using the private exponent d and the modulus N. For clarity, we will give a detailed standard RSA signature authentication flow below in Figure 1.

---

input: m, S, N
ROM (or fuse) storage: h_N

1. /* validate N
   a. $t := \mathsf{hash}(N)$;
   b. **if** $t \neq h_N$ **then** output "fail" and stop;

2. /* validate m
   a. $h_m := \mathsf{hash}(m)$;
   b. $a := S^e \bmod N$;
   c. extract the expected hash value e_m from a;
   d. **if** $h_m \neq e_m$ **then** output "fail" and stop;

   "accept" message m if and only if N and m were valid

Fig. 1. Standard RSA signature authentication flow

A standard RSA authentication flow. The inputs includes the message m to be authenticated, the RSA public modulus N, the public exponent e, and the signature S on the hash value (denoted by $\mathsf{hash}(m)$) of the authentic message m. This signature S is computed by the signer, using his private RSA exponent.

To avoid alleviate expensive ROM or fuse storage for the complete value of N, the device stores a trusted copy of its hash value hash(N). The input public modulus N is validated first, by computing its hash value and comparing it to hash(N). The validation of the message follows, and is carried out by performing the required modular exponentiation, and comparing the extracted hash to the hash value of m.

2.1   The Physical Fault Model or Recalling Seifert's Attack

Without an exhaustive elaboration on the concrete realization of fault attacks or on the various existing (mathematical) models we will briefly describe our simple model of transient fault attacks when applied to a computing device under attack. For a thorough treatment of their physical realization we refer to [ABFHS, BCNT$^+$] and for a proper mathematical treatment we refer to [BOS, LP]. As in [BDL] or many other related publications, we assume that the attacker is able to enforce random register faults, resulting in a uniformly chosen register content. The only preciseness on the induced fault is the precise timing on the register fault. Note that this is a weak assumption as the timing can be fully controlled or observed by the attacker at least in open computing devices with some equipment — which is our overall assumption. Given the strong practically demonstrated results on faults attacks, cf. [ABFHS, BCNT$^+$], our simple model seems fairly valid.

Seifert's attack, cf. [Sei] is based on a simple idea. Induced data faults can be used in order to change the value of the public modulus. If the attacker can change N to a new fake modulus, N', that he can factor, then he can easily derive a fake private exponent d', and use it to compute a signature S' of a message m. The question that arises is, therefore, how easy is it to transform N to a pre-computed value N' by means of random faults on N. This question was recently discussed in [Sei] and enhanced in [Mui], where it was shown that this is indeed easy. Given some 1024-bit RSA modulus, there is a probability of more than 50% that it could be transformed to an easy factorable fake modulus, by affecting only 4 bits, and for a 2048 bits modulus, this can be achieved by changing only 6 bits. Consequently, the attacker's strategy is the following. Using the public value of N, he goes (off-line) over all the new values that differ from N by only b least significant bits, for some small b, and finds (if possible) a derived value which is a prime number (or has otherwise an easy factorization). If manipulating only b bits does not yield a desirable fake modulus, the attacker simply increases the search space by using a larger value of b. To illustrate the above strategy, consider the following very simple example. For realistically large parameters, and small practical bound on the search space, we chose a random string T of 1012 bits, multiplied it by 2006 (standing for the current year), and constructed $N = pq$ where p and q were defined as the two next primes exceeding $2006 \cdot T$. To account for tampering with at most the 10 least significant bits of N, we screened (offline) the numbers $\hat{N} = i + N - (N \bmod 512)$, for $i = 1, 2, \ldots, 511$. Starting from the value

$N = $ 1B10FAB24763BD3C20A4DA2464B68ADB36A2A39FFEECF6A5453DA269CCE5
    870F3A309C1211131977AA9D523263222BAAA19E1B2318BD37B3967FDEF5
    B4D76F54543267162BFF9C9907A175271435D38EE7068D1CF020E2DC0D28
    087941F59B382D9EBAFACA46FD9433D9D6E2AC97BDC2C793FB744C1EB01D
    840B2F230E713431E93B4385354589DEA67C559FE6AF6550863446FA941B
    62EC6313ECC4B09A65A201FD61113DE425602DACCE8E32A2A75E2A6CD8A8
    0A5F42FCA7699AEA53D64BB43898C5E12509A72AE6AF60A9A9CC77AC7C53
    9EE8BEC9A4FD587CE7ED0148FFE25AA1F2A1ABF073CE84A0E11F2EEBDE48
    AFCEF1EAACED6F2ACE110DEEDD5

a prime N' was found for $i = 35$, namely,

$N' = $ 1B10FAB24763BD3C20A4DA2464B68ADB36A2A39FFEECF6A5453DA269CCE5
    870F3A309C1211131977AA9D523263222BAAA19E1B2318BD37B3967FDEF5
    B4D76F54543267162BFF9C9907A175271435D38EE7068D1CF020E2DC0D28
    087941F59B382D9EBAFACA46FD9433D9D6E2AC97BDC2C793FB744C1EB01D
    840B2F230E713431E93B4385354589DEA67C559FE6AF6550863446FA941B
    62EC6313ECC4B09A65A201FD61113DE425602DACCE8E32A2A75E2A6CD8A8
    0A5F42FCA7699AEA53D64BB43898C5E12509A72AE6AF60A9A9CC77AC7C53
    9EE8BEC9A4FD587CE7ED0148FFE25AA1F2A1ABF073CE84A0E11F2EEBDE48
    AFCEF1EAACED6F2ACE110DEEC23.

At this point the attacker can sign any message with modulus N', public exponent e and fake private exponent d' satisfying $e \cdot d' = 1 \bmod (N'-1)$, which is trivial to compute, assuming (with high probability) $\gcd(e, (N'-1)) = 1$. To make the device accept the message as authentic, the attacker simply induces random faults on the least significant chunk of N. He repeats this fault induction until N is converted to N'. These faults must be induced after the off-line phase and before the authentication flow, so as to pass the public key validation. Since theory indicates that a favorable fake modulus N' can be obtained by tampering with a small number of bits, the search space for the results that are obtained by the random faults is small enough to make the attack practical with a number of several such attempts.

Observe now, that verifying or creating an RSA signature on a standard CPU is due to the underlying long modular multiplication a quite complicated task. Especially, even modern high end CPUs cannot handle a full RSA modulus, say 2048 bits, in one single register (operation). Therefore a chain of successive operations is needed just when loading or preparing an RSA modulus from some memory into a set of CPU registers. Once the modulus is prepared across several CPU registers it will be used from there until the end of the full RSA operation. The long sequence of underlying squares and multiplies must frequently use the RSA modulus which is therefore permanently stored in some CPU registers.

Thus, during loading or preparing the long RSA modulus we are able — according to our above model — to draw an arbitrary but given small number of least significant bits of a RSA modulus from a uniform distribution. Simply enforce several fault attacks during several successive loads of multiple CPU registers which together represent the correct number of required bits beyond the smaller register length.

3 Novel Fault Attacks Against RSA Authentication

While the formerly described Seifert attack scenario looks like indeed feasible — given its liberal transient fault induction method — we will now describe two new attack scenarios, being much more practical. Compared to the Seifert attack scenario they offer the following attacker's advantages.

- Instead of transient data errors it assumes that the attacker can change by inducing faults the control flow, which is investigated for the prominent public exponent $e = 5$. This attack has the advantage that it eliminates the "somehow cumbersome" and subtle mathematical two-phase attack analysis of Seifert's attack.
- The second new attack assumes that the attacker is able to invest even a significant initial effort in inspecting the underlying piece of silicon upfront. I.e., we assume that he can do even a full reverse engineering of the chip under attack. This reverse engineering knowledge is then used to modify "customer devices" by simple permanent fault attacks through FIB (Focused Ion Beam), Eddy Currents or other methods, etc., cf. [FIB, QS, BCNT⁺]. This then enables to avoid the so called "one-shot success" of Seifert's attack and paves the way for a permanent and universal "mass-market" RSA signature forgery, without building a dedicated hardware device that circumvents the RSA authentication.

3.1 Bypass Fault Attacks

While the formerly described Seifert attack against RSA verification is targeted towards the general case for a randomly chosen $e \in \mathbb{Z}_N^*$, in practice most often a fixed low exponent e is used. So let us consider the more practical case, as shown in the following Figure 2.

Now, consider potential so called bypass attacks, as described for e.g. in [BCNT⁺]. Bypass attacks are based on purposely inducing some errors by the attacker, in a way that the authentication flow is changed. There are several potential vulnerabilities arising.

- Bypass the exponentiation loop. This implies that instead of computing $S^5 \bmod N$, the flow computes only $S \bmod N$. Therefore, the attacker can force the device to accept any signature.
- Bypass the "N validation step". In that case, the attacker can forge N. This would allow the attacker to eventually sign any message.

---

input: m, S, N
ROM (or fuse) storage: h_N

$t := \mathsf{hash}(N);$
if $t \neq h_N$ **then** output "fail" and stop;

$h_m := \mathsf{hash}(m);$
$a := S;$
repeat 2 times
    $a := a^2 \bmod N;$
$a := a \cdot S \bmod N;$
extract the expected hash value e_m from $a;$
if $h_m \neq e_m$ **then** output "fail" and stop;

"accept" message m if and only if N and m were valid

Fig. 2. RSA signature authentication flow for $e = 5$

– Bypass the final "hash value check".

To accomplish one of these attacks, the attacker needs only to find one sucessful error to be induced in one device. Since errors are typically repeatable, finding one "bypass" error could enable the construction of a dedicated hacker device that circumvents the RSA authentication procedure in all devices of the same type. See [BCNT$^+$] for practical implementations of such bypass attacks showing that they are relatively easy in practice.

3.2 Permanent Fault Attacks

In this strong fault model, we assume that the attacker is all powerful and even able to fully reverse-engineer the whole piece of silicon under attack. Knowing completely every single transistor of the chip the following is a possible fault attack threat scenario leading to a so called permanent fault attack. The Permanent Fault Attack (PFA) is a way to circumvent the authentication mechanism by completely undermining the anchor of trust — by faking N permanently. To do this, the steps for realizing a commercial PFA are as follows.

– The attacker computes from the public N some public key at will, say N', whose factorization is known to him.
– The attacker computes $\mathsf{hash}(N')$.
– The attacker compares the strings $\mathsf{hash}(N)$ and $\mathsf{hash}(N')$. Both values are h bits strings (e.g., $h = 160$ for SHA-1).
– The attacker marks the locations of the bits where $\mathsf{hash}(N)$ and $\mathsf{hash}(N')$ do not agree.
– Using the methods described in [FIB, QS, BCNT$^+$], the attacker induces permanent faults on sample devices (the authentication device) until he manages to transform $\mathsf{hash}(N)$ into $\mathsf{hash}(N')$.

- Once this is successfully done for one device, the attacker can start to sell his "unlocking-service" to the market which consists of:
  - Taking a customer device, changing its $\mathsf{hash}(N)$ to $\mathsf{hash}(N')$.
  - Giving the customer either the new private RSA exponent d' or giving him directly a new code enabling the device's new services.
  - Sending the customer's device back to the customer including the private exponent d' including new code.
- The attacker sells now his comprehensive web-service to customers who can load messages that are signed by the attacker (or the customer itself) (a degenerate case would be that N' is trivial, which allows anyone to forge any message).

To demonstrate that permanent fault attacks are no "fiction" at all and are very simple to achieve (say with a FIB machinery), we would like to show the following picture from [FIB]. It shows the precise disconnect of a certain metal connection and its corresponding reconnect at a different place.

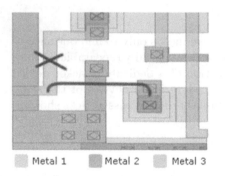 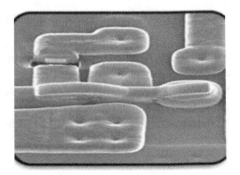

Metal 1   Metal 2   Metal 3

Fig. 3. Permanent fault attack via Focused Ion Beam

We would like to make the following comments on the above attack.

- For how to realize permanent fault attacks without opening the package, we refer especially to [QS, BCNT$^+$] and the above Figure 3 which shows why and how (simple it is) to mount such attacks in a cheap way.
- After one device is successfully modified, "mass market productization" of PFA's can be deployed.
- Reverse-engineering and "re-wiring" a complete piece of silicon is indeed a very powerful technique, especially given the recent result that there is no hope of any mathematical "obfuscation technique", i.e., to hide mathematically a secret inside a circuit, cf. [BGIR$^+$], assuming that the adversary is very powerful. Indeed, this cost-intensive method might be an interesting business for a "mass-market productization" of turning a cheap piece of silicon into a premium piece of silicon.

Finally, we would like to note that this permanent fault attack avoids the so called "one-shot success" of Seifert's attack and paves the way for a permanent and universal "mass-market" RSA signature forgery, without building a dedicated hardware device that circumvents the RSA authentication. Also, the "price" of this attack is directly linked with the number of bits to be changed to obtain a useful $\mathsf{hash}(N')$, which was recently improved by Muir [Mui].

4 Mitigating Fault Attacks Against RSA Authentication

Motivated by the different threats through the formerly described various fault attack models, we will now gradually and seperately develop for each of the individual different attack scenarios a heuristic countermeasure. In addition to our disclaimer about their perfect security we also expect them in practice to be somehow combined with each other and other best known countermeasures against fault attacks.

4.1 Mitigating Seifert-Like Attacks

To mitigate an RSA authentication process against Seifert-like attacks, we propose in Figure 4 the following so called *Interleaved Validation Scheme*, where an unpredictable multiple of N is computed before the modulus validation step (i.e., before N can be modified by the attacker to N'). This value is embedded into the modular exponentiation flow, and "blinds" the exponentiation base. The attacker cannot select N' in a way that the exponentiation result is still unchanged modulo N'. The additional computational cost of these countermeasures is relatively small.

Here, u is an unpredictable value that depends on the modulus N, and computed before N is validated (i.e., before it can be modified to the "attacker's selected" N'). This value is embedded into the modular exponentiation flow, which takes place during the signature validation phase. Since u is randomly chosen, the attacker cannot select N' in a way such that $u \ (\mathrm{mod}\ N') = 0$.

4.2 Mitigating Bypass Fault Attacks

To provide a more robust RSA authentication process against bypass attacks, we propose in Figure 5 the following scheme.

Let us make some comments on the above RSA signature authentication flow combating bypass attacks on $e = 5$.

- The function $s_a := \mathsf{stamp}(\cdot)$ generates one word out of some (randomly) selected bits from a. The test $s_a \neq s'_a$ checks that a has been changed during some previous modular multiplications steps, which implies that no loop bypass attack was launched.
- Protected branching ensures that an attacker introducing random faults needs to handle and manipulate multiple hard to fault-controllable computations simultaneously to be successful.

input: m, S, N
ROM (or fuse) storage: h_N, X, Y

1. /* validate N
   a. choose random number r;
   b. $u := r \cdot N$;
   c. $t := \mathsf{hash}(N)$;
   d. if $t \neq h_N$ then output "fail" and stop;

2. /* validate m with authentic N interleaved
   a. $h_m := \mathsf{hash}(m)$;
   b. $a := (S + u) \pmod{N}$;
   c. $b := a^e \bmod N$;
   d. extract the expected hash value e_m from b;
   e. if $h_m \neq e_m$ then output "fail" and stop;

"accept" message m if and only if N and m were valid

Fig. 4. RSA signature authentication flow combating Seifert-like attacks

input: m, S, N
ROM (or fuse) storage: h_N

generate secret 32-bit rnd number $0 < sec_{\mathrm{init}} < 2^{32} - 4$;
$t := \mathsf{hash}(N)$;
$h_m := \mathsf{hash}(m)$;
$a := S$;
$s_a := \mathsf{stamp}(a)$; /* generate one word from some selected bits of a

repeat 2 times
    $a := a^2 \bmod N$;
$a := a \cdot S \bmod N$;
$s_a' := \mathsf{stamp}(a)$;
extract the expected hash value e_m from a;
$sec := sec_{\mathrm{init}}$

/* validate all steps with protected branch
if $h_N = t$ && sec++ $\wedge$ $e_m = h_m$ && sec++ $\wedge$ $s_a \neq s_a'$ && sec++ then
    "accept" the signture iff $(sec\texttt{--})\texttt{--} = sec_{\mathrm{init}}\texttt{++}$
else
    output "fail" and stop;

Fig. 5. RSA signature authentication flow combating bypass attacks on $e = 5$

– The delay of decision whether or not to accept the signature, to the end of the procedure, increases the random space of the program counter. This makes it more difficult to find an error that would generate the right bypass.

4.3 Mitigating Permanent Fault — A Mission Impossible?

According to our above very strong attack through permanent fault attacks it is indeed very difficult to design some mitigation strategy against permanent faults. In order to do so, we have to make the following very strong assumption. *It is physically possible to safely embed a symmetric key* k *into the device which cannot be read out (even by reverse-engineering methods) "too" easily.* This key k can then be used to hide the exact N validation step from the attacker. Note that the attack is enabled because the attacker knows that the device compares hash(N) to its expected value. To counter this attack, we propose to have the device use the key in order to check for a different expected value, namely $h_{kN} :=$ hash(k$||N$), which depends on both k and N. Note that h_{kN} can be different from device to device (to resist the potential for BORE attacks). Figure 6 illustrates an authentication flow combating permanent fault attacks.

---

reverse-engineering protected embedded secret key k

ROM (or fuse) storage: h_{kN} /* $h_{kN} :=$ hash(k$||N$)
input: m, S, N

1. /* validate N
   a. $t :=$ hash(k$||N$);
   b. if $t \neq h_{kN}$ **then** output "fail" and stop;

2. /* validate m
   a. $h_m :=$ hash(m);
   b. $a := S^e \bmod N$;
   c. extract the expected hash value e_m from a;
   d. if $h_m \neq e_m$ **then** output "fail" and stop;

"accept" message m if and only if N and m were valid

Fig. 6. RSA signature authentication flow combating permanent fault attacks on N

Acknowledgments

The authors would like to thank Eric Brier, Benoit Chevallier-Mames, Mathieu Ciet, and Christophe Clavier for sharing an early version of their paper [BCCC].

References

[And]   R. Anderson, *Security Engineering*, John Wiley & Sons, Ltd., 2001.
[ABFHS]   C. Aumüller, P. Bier, W. Fischer, P. Hofreiter, J.-P. Seifert, "Fault attacks on RSA: Concrete results and practical countermeasures", Proc. of CHES '02, Springer LNCS, pp. 261-276, 2002.

[BGIR⁺]   B. Barak, O. Goldreich, R. Impagliazzo, S. Rudich, A. Sahay, S. Vadhan, and K. Yang, "On the (Im)possibility of Obfuscating Programs", Crypto '01, pp. 1-18, 2001, LNCS vol. 2139, 2001.

[BCNT⁺]   H. Bar-El, H. Choukri, D. Naccache, M. Tunstall, C. Whelan, "The Sorcerer's Apprentice Guide to Fault Attacks", *Proc. of IEEE* **94**(2):370-382, 2006.

[BCCC]   E. Brier, B. Chevallier-Mames, M. Ciet, and C. Clavier, "Why One Should Also Secure RSA Public Key Elements", Cryptographic Hardware and Embedded Systems CHES 2006, Lecture Notes in Computer Science, Springer-Verlag, 2006.

[BMM]   I. Biehl, B. Meyer, and V. Müller, "Differential fault analysis on elliptic curve cryptosystems", Advances in Cryptology CRYPTO 2000, vol. 1880 of LNCS, pp. 131146, Springer, 2000.

[BOS]   J. Blömer, M. Otto, J.-P. Seifert, "A new CRT-RSA algorithm secure against Bellcore attacks", Proc. of 10th ACM Conference on Computer and Communications Security, ACM Press, pp. 311-320, 2003.

[BDL]   D. Boneh, R. A. DeMillo, R. Lipton, "On the Importance of Eliminating Errors in Cryptographic Computations" *Journal of Cryptology* **14**(2):101-120, 2001.

[CJ]   M. Ciet, M. Joye, "Elliptic curve cryptosystem in presence of permanent and transient faults", *Designs Codes and Cryptography* **36**(1), 2005.

[FIB]   FIB (Focused Ion Beam), `http://www.ith.co.il/specs/fib.html`.

[Har]   J.S. Harbour, *The Black Art of Xbox Mods*, Sams, 2004.

[Hua]   A. "Bunnie" Huang, *Hacking the Xbox*, No Starch Press, Inc., San Francisco, 2003.

[LP]   K. Lemke, C. Paar, "An Adversarial Model for Fault Analysis against Low-Cost Cryptographic Devices", Workshop on Fault Diagnosis and Tolerance in Cryptography - FDTC 2006, Lecture Notes in Computer Science, Springer-Verlag, 2006.

[MvOV]   A. J. Menezes, P. van Oorschot, S. Vanstone, *Handbook of Applied Cryptography*, CRC Press, New York, 1997.

[Mui]   J.A. Muir, "Seiferts RSA fault attack: Simplified analysis and generalizations", IACR Eprint archive 2005.

[QS]   J.-J. Quisquater, D. Samyde, "Eddy current for Magnetic Analysis with Active Sensor", Esmart 2002, Nice, France, September 2002.

[Sei]   J.-P. Seifert, "On authenticated computing and RSA-based authentication", Proc. of ACM Conference on Computer and Communications Security 2005, pp. 122127, 2005.

[Unl]   HU-Cards, Unlooper devices, `http://www.hu-cards.org/products.html`.

Wagner's Attack on a Secure CRT-RSA Algorithm Reconsidered

Johannes Blömer[1,*] and Martin Otto[2,**]

[1] Paderborn University, Institute for Computer Science, 33095 Paderborn, Germany
bloemer@uni-paderborn.de
[2] Siemens AG, Corporate Technology CT IC3, Otto-Hahn-Ring 6, 81730 Munich,
Germany
m.otto@siemens.com

Abstract. At CCS 2003, a new CRT-RSA algorithm was presented in
[BOS03], which was claimed to be secure against fault attacks for various
fault models. At CCS 2004, David Wagner presented an attack on the
proposed scheme, claiming that the so-called BOS scheme was insecure
for all presented fault models [Wag04]. However, the attack itself contains a flaw which shows that although the BOS scheme is broken in
some fault models, it is not broken in the most realistic "random fault
model". This paper points out the flaw in the attack on the BOS scheme,
aiming to clarify this issue.

Keywords: CRT-RSA, fault attacks, smartcards, BOS-Scheme, Wagner's attack.

1   Introduction

At CCS 2003, Blömer, Otto, and Seifert presented a new CRT-RSA algorithm,
which was claimed to be secure against fault attacks [BOS03]. One year later, at
CCS 2004, Wagner published an acclaimed attack on the so-called *BOS scheme*
that he claimed to break the scheme [Wag04]. Wagner's results are correct for
most of the fault models defined in [BOS03], namely models, where an adversary
is assumed to be able to target individual bits and bytes in a selected variable.

However, the attack on the most often used fault model presented in [BOS03]
contains a flaw, which renders the attack invalid against the BOS scheme. This
flaw seems to be overlooked easily. Consequently, the attack is widely cited in
various publications, e.g., [CJ05], [Gir05], without realizing the implications of
the flaw.

In this paper, we point out the flaw in Wagner's attack in detail, aiming to
clarify this issue. Moreover, we present the correct attacks and suggest possible
countermeasures.

This paper is organized as follows. In Section 2, we briefly recall the fault
models used in both papers, [BOS03] and [Wag04]. In Section 3, we recall the

---

* Research partially supported by a research grant of Intel Cop., Portland, USA.
** This work was done during Ph.D. studies at the University of Paderborn, supported
by the DFG graduate school No. 693 and the PaSCo Institute, Paderborn.

L. Breveglieri et al. (Eds.): FDTC 2006, LNCS 4236, pp. 13–23, 2006.
© Springer-Verlag Berlin Heidelberg 2006

14   J. Blömer and M. Otto

original BOS scheme as proposed in [BOS03]. Section 4 is devoted to Wagner's
attack and its analysis. Here, Section 4.1 describes the correct attacks and points
out possible countermeasures. Section 4.2 analyzes the flawed attack on the BOS
scheme in the "random fault model" and points of the erroneous part. Section
5 concludes the paper.

2 Fault Models

In [BOS03], the following five fault models have been defined and used as a basis for the security claims. Note that we denote by $l(X)$ the binary length of a
variable X.

Fault Model #1: Precise Bit Errors
Parameter setting. For this strong fault model, we assume that the adversary
has precise control on both timing and location. This means that the adversary
knows the attacked bit as well as the attacked operation. Note that an attack
usually happens before the variable is used in a line of an algorithm. We assume
that only a single bit is affected. This resembles the "bit set or reset" (bsr)
fault type that is achieved by attacks described in [SA02] or [QS02] on RAM or
EEPROM of an unprotected smartcard.

Mathematical model. This attack can be modeled as an addition or subtraction
of a single bit, i.e., a variable X is changed to $X' = X \pm 2^k$ for $0 \le k \le l(X) - 1$.

Motivation from the real world. Although high-end smartcards implement
sophisticated hardware countermeasures, many smartcards currently used are
either too old or too cheap to do so. Hence, this fault model is a realistic one. It
assumes the strongest adversary and the weakest card. Since algorithms secure
in this fault model are secure in the weaker models as well, it is a particularly
interesting model.

Fault Model #2: Precise Byte Errors
Parameter setting. In this scenario, we assume that the timing is precise. Hence,
a specific operation can be targeted. However, control on location is loose, i.e.
the number of bits affected can only be bounded by a block of few bits (we
assume a byte). We allow any fault type in this model, e.g., stuck-at faults, bit
flip faults, or random faults (cf. [Ott05]).

Mathematical model. The attack can be modeled as an addition or subtraction
of an unknown error byte at a known position, i.e., a variable X is changed to
$X' = X \pm b \cdot 2^k$ for a *known* $0 \le k \le l(X) - 8$ and an unknown $b \in \mathbb{Z}_{2^8}$.

Motivation from the real world. This model is motivated by the fact that the
strong adversary's power defined in Fault Model #1 is reduced on smartcards if
encryption of the data is used. Usually, all data stored in EEPROM and RAM
is encrypted [RE00]. Hence, if an error is induced into memory, the CPU will
see a random block of data. The same model is derived if the bus lines are
attacked.

Fault Model #3: Unknown Byte Errors
Parameter setting. In this scenario, we assume loose control on both timing and location. The loose control on location means that a certain variable can be targeted but the number of bits affected can only be bounded by a block of few bits (usually a byte). In addition, loose control on timing means that the attacker can only affect the variable within a specific time frame that usually contains several instructions. The exact instruction affected by the attack is unknown. Hence, the attacker does not know for sure which byte of the variable is currently used by the algorithm. Again, we allow any fault type in this model.

Mathematical model. This attack can be modeled as an addition or subtraction of an error byte, i.e., a variable X is changed to $X' = X \pm b \cdot 2^k$ for an *unknown* $0 \leq k \leq l(X) - 8$ and an unknown $b \in \mathbb{Z}_{2^8}$.

Motivation from the real world. This model is motivated by the fact that attacks on EEPROM and RAM with address scrambling (cf. [RE00]) will not allow to specify when the attacked block is requested by the CPU. Encryption of the memory ensures that a faulty bit affects a whole block of data.

Fault Model #3': Unknown Byte Errors in Unknown Variables
Parameter setting. This model assumes loose control on location, once again a whole byte is affected, and no control on timing. Due to the latter it is unknown at which exact time within the program the attack is mounted. It is even unknown, which variable is faulty.

Mathematical model. We model this type of fault as a variable dependent error, i.e., a variable X is changed to $X' = X \pm b \cdot 2^k$ for an *unknown* $0 \leq k \leq l(X) - 8$ and an unknown $b \in \mathbb{Z}_{2^8}$. Note that due to the unprecise timing, the attacked variable X is also unknown (to some degree).

Motivation from the real world. The strong adversary's power defined in Fault Model #1 is effectively reduced to this model if the smardcard uses memory encryption in RAM and EEPROM. This causes any bit fault to affect a whole block of data. In addition, some smartcards use a randomized clock (cf. [CCD00]). In this case, the attacker knows that a successful attack will change a block of data. But he does not know the exact time of the change within the algorithm. Therefore the attacker does not know the position of the block as it is used in the CPU.

Fault Model #4: Random Errors
Parameter setting. In this fault model, we assume that the adversary has no control on the location of a fault and only a loose timing, i.e., he can target an interval of some operations. This interval may have been derived from other sources of information, for example from the power profile of the card (see [ABF+02]). The number of affected bits is unknown.

Mathematical model. We model this uncertainty on the number of affected bits by a random fault. We assume that for a given variable X, the uniformly distributed random value $f(X) \in [0, 2^{l(X)} - 1]$ is used by the algorithm. In this model, any fault may result in any faulty value.

Motivation from the real world. This scenario is motivated by strong high-end smartcards completely armed with countermeasures. Memory encryption, address scrambling and a randomized clock imply that any error induced into memory or the CPU at a vague point will leave the attacker at most with the information that a certain variable is faulty. It therefore enforces a very weak adversary.

3   The BOS Scheme

The BOS scheme as presented in [BOS03] extends an idea proposed by Shamir (see [Sha99]) and the idea of "infective computations" as introduced by Yen, Kim, Lim, and Moon in [YKLM01] and [YKLM03].

Infective computation means that any error introduced by a fault attack on the CRT-RSA algorithm propagates through the whole computation. In particular, if it can be ensured that in CRT-RSA a faulty signature will always be faulty modulo both prime factors, a Bellcore attack as presented in [BDL01] will be prevented.

The BOS scheme proposed in [BOS03] extends Shamir's idea to protect every single computation step of the signature algorithm, including the CRT combination. This is achieved by using two small integers t_1 and t_2 to compute $S_p = m^d \bmod pt_1$ and $S_q = m^d \bmod qt_2$. These values are combined to $S \bmod Nt_1t_2$ via the CRT. This combination with a larger modulus allows to use infective computation steps afterwards. These infective steps ensure that an error will cause the final signature to be false modulo both primes p and q. Infective computations not only avoid single points of failures. They also allow a device to continue its computation, even if a fault is detected.

Algorithm 1: Infective CRT-RSA

      Input: A message $m \in \mathbb{Z}_N$
      Output: Sig $:= m^d \bmod N$ or a random number in $\mathbb{Z}_N$
In Memory: $p \cdot t_1, q \cdot t_2, N, N \cdot t_1 \cdot t_2, d_p, d_q, t_1, t_2, e_{t_1}$, and e_{t_2}
1 Let $S_p := m^{d_p} \bmod p \cdot t_1$
2 Let $S_q := m^{d_q} \bmod q \cdot t_2$
3 Let $S := \mathrm{CRT}(S_p, S_q) \bmod N \cdot t_1 \cdot t_2$
4 Let $c_1 := (m - S^{e_{t_1}} + 1) \bmod t_1$
5 Let $c_2 := (m - S^{e_{t_2}} + 1) \bmod t_2$
6 Let Sig $:= S^{c_1 \cdot c_2} \bmod N$
7 **Output** Sig

Selecting the Parameters. As a precomputation step that can be performed for any smartcard at production time, generate a valid RSA key with (N, e), $N = p \cdot q$, as the public key and d as the corresponding private key satisfying $e \cdot d \equiv 1 \bmod \varphi(N)$.

Additionally, select two integers t_1 and t_2 of sufficiently large bitlength to withstand exhaustive search (recommended to comprise of at least $60 - 80$ bits) which must satisfy several conditions in order to allow a secure scheme:

> 1. t_1 and t_2 must be coprime
> 2. $\gcd(d, \varphi(t_1)) = 1$ and $\gcd(d, \varphi(t_2)) = 1$
> 3. t_1 and t_2 are squarefree
> 4. $t_i \equiv 3 \bmod 4$ for $i \in \{1, 2\}$
> 5. $t_2 \nmid X = pt_1 \cdot ((pt_1)^{-1} \bmod qt_2)$

Let $d_p := d \bmod \varphi(p \cdot t_1)$, $d_q := d \bmod \varphi(q \cdot t_2)$. Afterwards, compute two corresponding public keys e_{t_1} and e_{t_2} such that $d \cdot e_{t_i} = 1 \bmod \varphi(t_i)$. Store $p \cdot t_1$, $q \cdot t_2$, N, $N \cdot t_1 \cdot t_2$, d_p, d_q, t_1, t_2, e_{t_1} and e_{t_2} on the smartcard. It is easy to see that the algorithm computes the correct signature if no error occurs. In this case, the two infective variables c_1 and c_2 computed in Lines 4 and 5 are both equal to 1, hence, $\text{Sig} \equiv S \equiv m^d \bmod N$.

For details on the choice of the two primes, we refer to [BOS03] or [Ott05]. There, it is recommended to choose both t_i as strong primes.

3.1 Obvious Security Considerations

Disclosure of most intermediate variables can be used to break the system. Attacks on most intermediate variables, e.g., d_p or m, have a negligible success probability for almost all messages. However, there are messages, where an adversary can mount a successful Bellcore-like attack (as presented in [BDL01]) with extremely high probability. These messages depend on t_1 or t_2, e.g., $m \equiv \pm 1 \bmod t_1$ for an attack targeting d_p, or $m \equiv 0 \bmod t_1$ for an attack targeting m or the intermediate values of the exponentiation. Therefore, it is crucial to the security of Algorithm 1 that no intermediate variables are disclosed. This does not only hold for the secret randomization parameters t_1 and t_2. As an example, assume that our countermeasure prevents a Bellcore attack on a faulty S_p using $c_1 \neq 1$ and $c_2 = 1$. If c_1 is revealed, we have

$$\gcd\left(m^{c_1} - Sig^e, N\right) = p.$$

4 Wagner's Attacks Against the BOS Scheme

In [BOS03], it is claimed that the proposed countermeasure secures the CRT-RSA algorithm against faults based on the Random Fault Model #4. Unfortunately, it does not provide sufficient security against faults based on the stronger fault models, namely the Single Bit Fault Model #1 or the Byte Fault Models #2 and #3. This has been described in detail by Wagner in [Wag04]. Moreover, another attack has been described in [Wag04]. However, the latter contains a flaw that seems to be overlooked easily. Consequently, the attack is widely cited without honoring the implications of the flaw. We describe the correct attacks and the flawed attack in detail.

In the following, we denote by $\tilde{X}$ a faulty variable X and by $e(X)$ the absolute error induced into X as an additive term, i.e., $\tilde{X} = X + e(X)$. The possible values and distribution of the random variable $e(X)$ depend on the chosen fault model.

4.1   Bit and Byte Faults

For the BOS scheme, it has been described in Section 3.1 that if $c_1 \neq 1$ or $c_2 \neq 1$ and the infective value c_i is disclosed, an attacker can mount a Bellcore-like attack by computing $\gcd(m^{c_i} - Sig^e, N)$. This yields a factor of N. For bit faults and byte faults, the number of possible errors is rather small, hence, an adversary can guess a possible error value $e(X)$, resulting from a fault induced into some variable X and try to verify his assumption.

As a concrete example, consider a transient fault induced into m according to the Single Bit Fault Model #1 in Line 1 of Algorithm 1. In this case, S_p is faulty and S_q is correct, hence, the variable S is faulty. As usual, we denote a faulty S by $\tilde{S}$. Since $\tilde{S} \equiv S \bmod qt_2$, we have $c_2 = 1$. However, a faulty $\tilde{m} = m + e(m)$ yields the value $\tilde{S}_p = \tilde{m}^{d_p} \bmod pt_1$, hence, we have $c_1 = (m - \tilde{m} + 1) \bmod t_1 = 1 - e(m) \bmod t_1$. This is not equal to $1 \bmod t_1$, since $t_1 \nmid e(m) = \pm 2^k$ for any choice of $k > 0$.

Let $-t_1 + 1 < e(m) < 0$. In this case, the modular reduction in the computation of $c_1 = 1 - e(m) \bmod t_1$ does not take place. For bit faults, all values of $e(m) = -2^k$ for $0 \leq k \leq l(t_1) - 1$ satisfy this condition, and for byte faults, all values of $e(m) = b \cdot 2^k$ for $-2^8 + 1 \leq b \leq -1$ and $0 \leq k \leq l(t_1) - 8$. In these cases, c_1 can be recovered by testing all possible values for $e(m)$ according to the chosen fault model. The probability of inducing such a *usable* fault is approximately $1/2 \cdot l(t_1)/l(N)$ according to [Wag04], assuming a variant of the Byte Fault Models #2 and #3. The crucial fact exploited by this attack is that the set of usable errors is efficiently sampleable and highly probable, since they form a large fraction of all possible error values. Hence, an adversary can perform computations for all possible guesses in polynomial time and he can hope to induce a usable error after polynomial many tries. This is fundamentally different from random faults, where the number of possible faults is too large to be sampled in polynomial time.

Infective computations aim at randomizing the output, but they do not use an own source of randomness. Instead, they use the random source provided by the error. Consequently, their effectiveness depends on the quality of the random error source. If the error is truly random, i.e., uniformly distributed in a large set, a randomization of the final output is possible. Hence, an adversary using the Random Fault Model #4 faces a randomized faulty output, where the infective randomization strategy provides a good randomization. For all other attacks, which assume errors, that do not represent a good source of randomness, infective computations will always be insecure. This is what happens for the Bit Fault Model #1 and the Byte Fault Models #2 and #3, where most of the values $e(m) \in \mathbb{Z}_{pt_1}$ occur with probability 0 and only a small fraction occurs with non-zero probability. Any distribution of the error, which is strongly biased or asymmetric, can be susceptible to the attack described above.

Simple Solution for Attacks with Efficiently Sampleable Errors. A simple solution to this problem is straightforward. If the adversary can always recover $\tilde{S}$ if a strong fault model is used, the algorithm must not output a result. Hence, we present with Algorithm 2 a simple countermeasure suitable for bit and byte faults.

Algorithm 2: Secure CRT-RSA Algorithm with Explicit Checking Procedures

     Input: A message $m \in \mathbb{Z}_N$
     Output: Sig $:= m^d \bmod N$ or a random number in $\mathbb{Z}_N$
In Memory: $p \cdot t_1, q \cdot t_2, N, N \cdot t_1 \cdot t_2, d_p, d_q, t_1, t_2, e_{t_1}$, and e_{t_2}
1 Let $S_p := m^{d_p} \bmod p \cdot t_1$
2 Let $S_q := m^{d_q} \bmod q \cdot t_2$
3 Let $S := \text{CRT}(S_p, S_q) \bmod N \cdot t_1 \cdot t_2$
4 Let $c_1 := (m - S^{e_{t_1}} + 1) \bmod t_1$
5 Let $c_2 := (m - S^{e_{t_2}} + 1) \bmod t_2$
6 If $(c_1 \neq 1)$ or $(c_2 \neq 1)$ then **output** FAILURE
7 **Output** $S \bmod N$

Infective computations have the advantage to replace explicit checking procedures, which always pose a single point of failure. However, a weak source of randomness suggests to dispose of infective computations and return to the explicit checks. Explicit checking procedures are dangerous only if an adversary can induce two faults during one run of the algorithm. Moreover, modern high-end smartcards are equipped with a variety of countermeasures, which allow users to be confident that the strong power of an adversary is reduced to the Random Fault Model #4. Algorithm 1 is secure in this model.

More Sophisticated Solutions for Attacks with Efficiently Sampleable Errors. However, with a little additional work, it might also be possible to protect Algorithm 1 against bit or byte faults while still using infective computations. This is a new direction of research, hence, we will only briefly sketch the ideas here. Since the error does not provide enough randomness to sufficiently randomize the two infective values c_1 and c_2, the algorithm needs to acquire another source of randomness. To show how this can add security, assume that we have two random values R_1 and R_2.

The attack described above, using the Single Bit Fault Model #1 or the Byte Fault Models #2 and #2 to break Algorithm 1, exploits the fact that it can enumerate all possible values of the term $S^{e_{t_1}} \bmod t_1$ efficiently, if m has been attacked in Line 1. If c_1 is smaller than t_1, a reduction does not take place. The latter allows the adversary to recover c_1 by testing all possible error values as described above, since the chance to induce such errors is very high. The same considerations apply for a fault induced into m in Line 2, however, due to symmetry, we will only describe attacks targeting the first line.

If the resulting value $c_1 > 1$ is randomized by a sufficiently large random integer R_1, the value c_1 will be a random value as well. In this case, the advantage of the strong fault models #1, #2, and #3, which provide an efficiently sampleable set of error values, can no longer be used. We present the modified algorithm as Algorithm 3.

It is obvious from Algorithm 3, that $c_1 = c_2 = 1$ if no error occurs. In this case, we have $m - S^{e_{t_i}} \equiv 0 \bmod t_i$ for $i \in \{1,2\}$. If both R_1 and R_2 are random integers with $l(t_1) = l(t_2)$ bits, then there are $2^{(l(t_1)-1)}$ many possible values for R_1 and R_2. Consequently, there are $2^{(l(t_1)-1)}$ many values for c_1 and c_2 unless $m - S^{e_{t_i}} \equiv 0 \bmod t$. Hence, the values c_1 and c_2 are random integers in $\mathbb{Z}_{t_i}$ as well. Therefore, they cannot be recovered using only information about the induced error. In this case, c_1 and c_2 will not be disclosed unless an adversary has some knowledge about R_1 and R_2. Therefore, the attack described in [Wag04] cannot be applied any longer.

Algorithm 3: Secure CRT-RSA Algorithm with Additional Randomization

        Input: A message $m \in \mathbb{Z}_N$
        Output: Sig $:= m^d \bmod N$ or a random number in $\mathbb{Z}_N$
In Memory: $p \cdot t_1, q \cdot t_2, N, N \cdot t_1 \cdot t_2, d_p, d_q, t_1, t_2, e_{t_1}, e_{t_2}$
1 Let R_1 and R_2 be new random values
2 Let $S_p := m^{d_p} \bmod p \cdot t_1$
3 Let $S_q := m^{d_q} \bmod q \cdot t_2$
4 Let $S := CRT(S_p, S_q) \bmod N \cdot t_1 \cdot t_2$
5 Let $c_1 := (m - S^{e_{t_1}}) \cdot R_1 + 1 \bmod t_1$
6 Let $c_2 := (m - S^{e_{t_2}}) \cdot R_2 + 1 \bmod t_2$
7 Let Sig $:= S^{c_1 \cdot c_2} \bmod N$
8 **Output** S

However, randomness is expensive on smartcards. Hence, it is preferable to protect the CRT-RSA algorithm without requiring random values R_1 and R_2, generated freshly for each run of the algorithm. Consequently, a new idea is to replace the notion of randomness by the notion of unpredictability. The attack described above requires than an adversary is able to enumerate all possible values for c_1. However, if the two factors R_1 and R_2 are large unknown values, the adversary loses the information about the set of possible values for faulty c_1 and c_2. This might already be enough to defend against the attack described above. In this case, there are several possible choices for R_1 and R_2, e.g.,

- two different fixed random values computed and stored on the card at production time,
- $R_1 = R_2 = d$,
- $R_1 = R_2 = S$,
- $R_1 = p$, $R_2 = q$ (or any combination of p and q),
- $R_1 = S_p$, $R_2 = S_q$ (or any combination of S_p and S_q), or
- $R_1 = H(r_1)$, $R_2 = H(r_2)$, where H is a cryptographically strong hash function and r_1 and r_2 are any of the values d, S, S_p, or S_q.

Since the adversary has no better choice to recover c_1 and c_2 than to check all possible values from $\mathbb{Z}_{t_1}$ or $\mathbb{Z}_{t_2}$ (depending on which line has been attacked), it should be sufficient to choose $R_1 = R_2$. Of the above suggested choices for R_1 and R_2, it is preferable to have R_1 and R_2 depend on S, S_p, and/or S_q rather than on other values, because these ensure that the random factors depend on the chosen message and on the induced fault, for a lot of possible fault locations. However, the security of Algorithm 3 has not yet been proven, it is still an open problem.

4.2   Wagner's Attack

Another attack has been described in [Wag04] using a fault model close to Fault Model #4. If this attack was successful, it would render the use of Algorithm 1 useless as a countermeasure. The fault model proposed in [Wag04] uses an extremely asymmetric error distribution, where all faults only affect the lower $l(x) - 160$ bits of an affected variable x, whereas the highest 160 bits are unchanged. Therefore, it is somewhere between the Byte Fault Models #2 and #3 and the Random Fault Model #4. We will refer to this fault model as *Wagner's Fault Model*.

We consider Wagner's Fault Model to be leaving the defined models of BOS. It has never been considered before, and though it can be realized in practice, its practicability has not been demonstrated yet. Moreover, it cannot be achieved using the Random Fault Model #4, since an adversary can only hope to induce a random fault with an effect of the required kind with probability $1/2^{160}$, which is negligible. For bit faults and byte faults, however, this is possible with high probability. Moreover, if a smartcard only uses block-wise encryption of the data in memory, an attack can easily target the $l(x) - 160$ least significant bits of a variable x. Modern smartcards, however, implement a variety of countermeasures, which allows to put great confidence in the assumption that Wagner's Fault Model is unrealistic. Moreover, Wagner's attack requires several faulty results.

In the attack described in [Wag04], the modulus N in Line 6 of Algorithm 1 is targeted with Wagner's Fault Model. This attack aims at disclosing t_1 and t_2. Such a disclosure allows to break the system as explained in Section 3.1. A correct "large" signature S as computed in Line 3 can be written as $S = (S \bmod N) + k \cdot N$, for some $0 \leq k < 2^{161}$ (since $l(t_1 \cdot t_2) \leq 2^{160}$). A fault induced into N according to this new fault model yields the faulty value $\tilde{N}$. Given the correct result $Sig = S \bmod N$ and a faulty final result $\widetilde{Sig} = S \bmod \tilde{N}$, we have

$$\widetilde{Sig} - Sig \equiv S - Sig \equiv S - S + k \cdot N \equiv k \cdot (N - \tilde{N}) \bmod \tilde{N}.$$

Since we know that $|\tilde{N} - N| \leq 2^{l(N)-161}$, we have $|k \cdot (\tilde{N} - N)| < 2^{l(N)}$. With probability at least $1/2$, we have $l(N) = l(\tilde{N})$, hence, when computing $\widetilde{Sig} - Sig \bmod \tilde{N}$, there will be no overflow or modular reduction with sufficiently high probability. In this case, an integer multiple of k is known to the adversary and several attacks on N will allow him to compute k. This can be done by computing many pair-wise gcd's and taking the majority vote. Once an adversary has k, he can compute $S = Sig + k \cdot N$. Wagner erroneously assumes that $t_1 \cdot t_2 = (S - Sig)/N$.

A closer analysis shows the flaw. Let $t = t_1 \cdot t_2$, $S_t = S \bmod t$, and $S_N = S \bmod N$. This means that we have $S = S_N + k \cdot N$, and $Sig = S_N$. Consequently, the term $(S - Sig)/N = k$ yields $k \equiv (S_t - S_N)N^{-1} \bmod t$ (Garner's formula). If t ist fixed, then $N^{-1} \bmod t$ is also fixed. However, due to the term S_t, the value of $k = (S_t - S_N)N^{-1} \bmod t$ can take on *any value* in $\mathbb{Z}_t$. Moreover, since t and d are unknown, given a message m it should be hard for an attacker to predict the value S_t. Therefore, what the attacker will most probably see if he determines the value k for messages m are random looking elements in $\mathbb{Z}_t$. To determine t from this kind of information is not feasible. Hence, we consider this attack not to be a threat to our proposed algorithm.

5 Conclusion

We have shown that Wagner's attack on the BOS scheme does not completely break the security of the BOS scheme due to a flaw in the proof. Therefore, the BOS scheme should still be considered secure against fault attacks in the Random Fault Model.

References

[ABF+02]   C. Aumüller, P. Bier, W. Fischer, P. Hofreiter, and J.-P. Seifert, *Fault attacks on RSA with CRT: Concrete results and practical countermeasures*, Workshop on Cryptographic Hardware and Embedded Systems 2002 (CHES 2002) (Hotel Sofitel, San Francisco Bay (Redwood City), USA), August 13–15 2002.

[BDL01]   D. Boneh, R. A. DeMillo, and R. J. Lipton, *On the importance of eliminating errors in cryptographic computations*, J. Cryptology **14** (2001), no. 2, 101–119.

[BOS03]   J. Blömer, M. Otto, and J.-P. Seifert, *A new CRT-RSA algorithm secure against Bellcore attacks*, Conference on Computer and Communications Security — CCS 2003 (V. Atluri and P. Liu, eds.), ACM SIGSAC, ACM Press, 2003, pp. 311–320.

[CCD00]   C. Clavier, J.-S. Coron, and N. Dabbous, *Differential power analysis in the presence of hardware countermeasures*, Cryptographic Hardware and Embedded Systems – Proceedings of CHES 2000, Worcester, MA, USA, Lecture Notes in Computer Science, vol. 1965, Springer-Verlag, 2000, pp. 252–263.

[CJ05]   M. Ciet and M. Joye, *Practical fault countermeasures for chinese remaindering based RSA*, 2nd Workshop on Fault Diagnosis and Tolerance in Cryptography (FDTC 05) (Edinburgh, Scotland), September 2, 2005.

[Gir05]   C. Giraud, *Fault resistant RSA implementation*, Fault Diagnosis and Tolerance in Cryptography   FDTC 2005 (Edinburgh, Scotland) (L. Breveglieri and I. Koren, eds.), September 2, 2005.

[Ott05]   M. Otto, *Fault attacks and countermeasures*, Ph.D. thesis, University of Paderborn, 2005, http://wwwcs.uni-paderborn.de/cs/ag-bloemer/forschung/publikationen/DissertationMartinOtto.pdf .

[QS02]   J.-J. Quisquater and D. Samyde, *Eddy current for magnetic analysis with active sensor*, Proceedings of Esmart 2002, 2002.

[RE00]   W. Rankl and W. Effing, *Smart card handbook*, 2 ed., John Wiley & Sons, 2000.

[SA02]   S. Skorobogatov and R. Anderson, *Optical fault induction attacks*, Workshop on Cryptographic Hardware and Embedded Systems 2002 (CHES 2002) (Hotel Sofitel, San Francisco Bay (Redwood City), USA, August 13 - 15, 2002), 2002.

[Sha99]   A. Shamir, *Method and apparatus for protecting public key schemes from timing and fault attacks*, 1999, US Patent No. 5,991,415, Nov. 23, 1999.

[Wag04]   D. Wagner, *Cryptanalysis of a provably secure CRT-RSA algorithm*, Conference on Computer and Communications Security — CCS 2004 (V. Atluri, B. Pfitzmann, and P. D. McDaniel, eds.), ACM SIGSAC, ACM Press, 2004, pp. 92–97.

[YKLM01]   S.-M. Yen, S. Kim, S. Lim, and S. Moon, *RSA speedup with residue number system immune against hardware fault cryptanalysis*, Information Security and Cryptology - ICISC 2001 (4th International Conference Seoul, Korea, December 6-7, 2001. Proceedings) (K. Kim, ed.), LNCS, vol. 2288, Springer-Verlag, 2001, p. 397 ff.

[YKLM03]   S.-M. Yen, S. Kim, S. Lim, and S.-J. Moon, *RSA Speedup with Chinese Remainder Theorem Immune against Hardware Fault Cryptanalysis*, IEEE Transactions on Computers **52** (2003), no. 4, 461–472.

Attacking Right-to-Left Modular Exponentiation with Timely Random Faults*

Michele Boreale

Dipartimento di Sistemi e Informatica
Università di Firenze

Abstract. We show that timely induction of random failures can potentially be used to mount very cost effective attacks against smartcards deploying cryptographic schemes based on (right-to-left) modular exponentiation. We introduce a model where an external perturbation, or *glitch*, may cause a single modular multiplication to produce a truly random result. Based on this assumption, we present a probabilistic attack against the implemented cryptosystem. Under reasonable assumptions, we prove that using a single faulty signature the attack recovers a target bit of the secret exponent with an error probability bounded by $\frac{3}{7}$. We show the attack is effective even in the presence of message blinding.

Keywords: fault-based cryptanalysis, smartcards, public-key cryptosystems.

1   Introduction

In the past decade, a variety of potential attacks against supposedly tamper-proof devices have been put forward. Many of these attacks exploit side-channel information, such as that provided by timing analysis [11], differential power analysis [12], or computation faults [3,2,9,8,13].

In this paper, we focus on attacks against implementations of public-key cryptosystems based on modular exponentiation, such as RSA, El-Gamal and Diffie-Hellman. The Bellcore attack [9] revealed that induction of random faults in a device implementing RSA decryption with the Chinese Remainder Theorem (CRT) optimization could lead to disclosure of the key material.

Subsequent works have extended fault-analysis beyond CRT-based exponentiation. While revealing many potential weaknesses, these extensions have often been regarded as too idealized [1]. The original Bellcore attack just made use of one random computation fault. Subsequent models typically assumed the ability of the attacker to selectively alter the content of data registers, like flipping a few individual bits of the exponent [5], or modifying a segment of a register during the execution of a modular multiplication (e.g. the *safe errors* of [17]).

In the present paper we consider a model where truly random, hence "practical", computation faults are combined with a simple form of timing control. As pointed out

---

* Author's address: Dipartimento di Sistemi e Informatica, Viale Morgagni 65, I–50134 Firenze, Italy. Email: boreale@dsi.unifi.it. Work partially supported by the EU within the FET-GC2 initiative, project SENSORIA, and by University of Firenze, projects "ex-60%".

by several works [4,6,15], it is relatively simple to induce random computational errors in smartcards using *glitch*-based techniques. A glitch is an external perturbation, like a rapid variation in the clock frequency or power supply voltage, which causes a malfunction of the device. The effect of a glitch could be having a few instructions skipped or misinterpreted by the processor. The induced error is transient in the sense that the device will generally resume its correct functioning some μ-seconds after the glitch, with possibly the only observable effect of data corruption in some register. To quote Bar-El *et al.* [6], who have experimented using this technique: for a certain set of experiments, *"the outcome was that the value of the data could be corrupted, while the interpretation of instruction was left unchanged."*. According to [6], this method is widely researched and practiced behind closed doors by the smartcard industry. An alternative to this technique is optical fault induction, presented by Skorobogatov and Anderson in [15].

Given these premises, we can formulate our basic assumption as follows: a glitch applied during the execution of a modular multiplication $A \leftarrow B \cdot C \bmod n$ will result in a random value to be written into register A. This assumption seems reasonable, as execution of a modular multiplication provides a time window wide enough to allow a processor to resume its correct functioning after the glitch and before the next operation. Another relevant assumption we make is that the attacker has a control on the timing of the device that is fine enough to allow the choice of an appropriate instant in time for applying the glitch. This assumption (already present in other works on fault analysis) is justified by the circumstance that the clock signal is supplied to the device by an external card reader, which is presumably controlled by the attacker. In any case, we will show that precision in timing control can be traded off with success probability of the attack.

The basic idea is of the attack is easily explained. We focus on the right-to-left binary exponentiation algorithm (see e.g. [10]). For the purpose of illustration, suppose that the device implements the RSA signature scheme with secret exponent d and modulus n, and suppose for simplicity that the message to be signed is a quadratic residue mod n. Assuming the attacker has already determined the $i - 1$ least significant bits of d, he can determine the initial instant in time of the ith iteration (the one dealing with the ith bit of d), and apply a glitch during the squaring operation that immediately precedes this iteration. As a result, a random r will be written in a certain register in place of the squaring correct result. Then, if bit d_i is set, the attacker will observe a faulty signature of the form $r \cdot C^2$, otherwise the observed faulty signature will be of the form C^2, for some C. With high probability, the attacker can tell these two cases apart by computing the Jacobi symbol of the faulty signature, thus determining the ith bit of the exponent.

The rest of the paper is organized as follows. In Section 2 some preliminary notions are recalled. Section 3 introduce the basic model, where the attacker has a complete control on timing (the multiplication time is constant and known to the attacker, time due to control flow instructions is ignored). Section 4 presents the attack based on this model as a probabilistic algorithm. The attack is presented in detail for the case of a RSA modulus; the obvious modifications for a prime modulus are outlined. The results of some software simulations are also discussed. Section 5 extends the model and the attack to the case where time is randomized, possibly meaning partial control of the attacker on timing. A few software countermeasures are discussed in Section 6; the technique of message blinding is shown to be not effective against the attack. Some concluding remarks and lines for further research are discussed in Section 7. Details of proofs have been confined to Appendix A.

2   Preliminary Notions

Recall (see [16]) that for a given prime p, x is a *quadratic residue* mod p if $\gcd(x, p) = 1$ and $x = y^2$ mod p for some y. If $\gcd(x, p) = 1$ and x is not a quadratic residue mod p, then x is called *quadratic non-residue* mod p.

The *Jacobi symbol* $\left(\dfrac{m}{n}\right)$, for m and n integers, $n \geq 3$ odd, is defined as follows. If $n = p$ is prime (in this case one also speaks of *Legendre* symbol), then

$$\left(\frac{m}{p}\right) \stackrel{\text{def}}{=} \begin{cases} 1 & \text{if } m \text{ is a quadratic residue mod } p \\ -1 & \text{if } m \text{ is a quadratic non-residue mod } p \\ 0 & \text{otherwise.} \end{cases}$$

If $k = p_1 \cdots p_l$, with p_j's primes not necessarily distinct, then $\left(\dfrac{m}{n}\right)$ is the product $\left(\dfrac{m}{p_1}\right) \cdots \left(\dfrac{m}{p_l}\right)$. It can be shown that

$$\text{If } m = m_1 \cdots m_h \text{ mod } n \text{ then } \quad \left(\frac{m}{n}\right) = \left(\frac{m_1}{n}\right) \cdots \left(\frac{m_h}{n}\right). \tag{1}$$

It is well-known that $\left(\dfrac{m}{n}\right)$ can be efficiently computed without knowing the factorizations of m or n.

Suppose that $n = p \cdot q$, with p, q distinct primes. Since in $\mathbb{Z}_p$ there are exactly $(p-1)/2$ quadratic residues mod p and an equal number of quadratic non-residues mod p (similarly for q), using the Chinese Remainder Theorem and (1) above, it is immediate to check that

$$\left| \left\{ r \in \mathbb{Z}_n \mid \left(\frac{r}{n}\right) = -1 \right\} \right| = (p-1) \cdot (q-1)/2 = \phi(n)/2 .$$

where $\phi(\cdot)$ is Euler's totient function.

3   The Model

Throughout the rest of the paper, unless otherwise stated, we assume a fixed modulus $n = p \cdot q$ (with p, q distinct secret primes) and a fixed document $M \in \mathbb{Z}_n$. The secret exponent $d \leq n$ has been chosen according to some possibly unknown probability distribution; in particular, we need not assume that d is an RSA exponent. The *signature* of M is $S = M^d$ mod n. Both n and d are representable in l bits, in particular $d = (d_{l-1} \cdots d_1 d_0)_2$, where l need not to be known to the attacker.

In our scenario the attacker has got to know the device's PIN, or the device is not PIN operated. We also assume that the attacker controls the clock of the device, and can apply a glitch (e.g. through a rapid variation of clock frequency) during the computation at an instant of his choice, and read the resulting value S'. The device can be queried in this way repeatedly. The rest of the section is devoted to a detailed description of algorithmic, timing and failure assumptions, and of faulty computations that can be induced by exploiting these assumptions.

Assumptions. We assume the device implements the *right-to-left* exponentiation algorithm (Figure 1). The algorithm uses two variables w and z, viewed as (physical or logical) s-bit registers with $s \geq l$. The value returned by the algorithm is the final content of register w, that is the (correct) signature, $S = M^d \bmod n$ (see below).

Input: M
Output: $S = M^d \bmod n$

1   $w \leftarrow 1$
2   $z \leftarrow M$
3   **for** $j = 0 \ldots l - 1$ **do**
4   **if** $d_j = 1$ **then** $w \leftarrow w \cdot z \bmod n$
5      $z \leftarrow z \cdot z \bmod n$
6   **end**
7   **return** w

Fig. 1. The right-to-left exponentiation algorithm

Concerning timing and failures, we make the following assumptions:

1. each modular multiplication/squaring operation takes a constant time, say δ clock cycles, and δ is a constant known to the attacker;
2. time taken by control-flow instructions is ignored, in other words, we view the algorithm as a sequence of modular multiplications, grouped for ease of reference into the l iterations or *phases* depicted in Figure 2. Each phase i takes either δ or 2δ cycles, depending on the value of d_i, $0 \leq i \leq l - 1$;

$$\text{phase } 0 \begin{bmatrix} \textbf{if } d_0 = 1 \textbf{ then } w \leftarrow w \cdot z \bmod n \\ z \leftarrow z \cdot z \bmod n \end{bmatrix}$$

$$\text{phase } 1 \begin{bmatrix} \textbf{if } d_1 = 1 \textbf{ then } w \leftarrow w \cdot z \bmod n \\ z \leftarrow z \cdot z \bmod n \end{bmatrix}$$

$$\vdots$$

$$\text{phase } l - 1 \begin{bmatrix} \textbf{if } d_{l-1} = 1 \textbf{ then } w \leftarrow w \cdot z \bmod n \\ z \leftarrow z \cdot z \bmod n \end{bmatrix}$$

Fig. 2. The right-to-left exponentiation algorithm as a sequence of l phases

3. a glitch applied onto the device during the execution of a modular multiplication will result in a random value $r \in \mathbb{Z}_{2^s}$ to be written in the involved register (w or z), in place of the multiplication's correct result.

(We will discard conditions 1 and 2 in Section 5.) If we denote by T_i the first cycle of phase i in a correct computation (counting from $T_0 = 1$), then

$$T_i = \delta\left(i - 1 + \sum_{j=0}^{i-1} d_j\right) + 1 \quad 0 \le i \le l - 1. \tag{2}$$

Faulty computations. Let us first analyze the use of variables w and z in a correct execution of the algorithm. Variable z is used to store successive squaring of M; more precisely, when entering phase i, z contains c_i, where:

$$c_i \stackrel{\text{def}}{=} M^{2^i} \bmod n \quad 0 \le i \le l - 1.$$

Variable w is used to store intermediate products of the c_i's; more precisely, when leaving phase i, w contains S_i, where:

$$S_i = (c_0)^{d_0} \cdot (c_1)^{d_1} \cdot \ldots \cdot (c_{i-1})^{d_{i-1}} \cdot (c_i)^{d_i} \bmod n \tag{3}$$

in particular at, the end of phase $l - 1$, S will be obtained as the product:

$$S = (c_0)^{d_0} \cdot (c_1)^{d_1} \cdot \ldots \cdot (c_{l-2})^{d_{l-2}} \cdot (c_{l-1})^{d_{l-1}} = M^d \bmod n.$$

Suppose the bits of the exponent from d_0 to d_{i-1} have been determined, and that bit d_i must be determined, for some $0 < i \le l - 1$; note that d_0 can easily be guessed/determined by other means (and in case d is a RSA exponent, one already knows that $d_0 = 1$). The attacker computes the first instant T_i of phase i using (2), and applies a glitch at time T, for some $T_i > T > T_i - \delta$. This glitch will affect a single operation, i.e. the squaring $z \leftarrow z \cdot z$ of phase $i - 1$. As a consequence, a random value $r \in \mathbb{Z}_{2^s}$ will be written in register z at the end of phase $i - 1$. Let us see how this fault affects the final result of the computation, the *faulty signature* S'. It is easy to see, relying on (3) or on Figure 2, that S' will be computed as:

$$S' = (c_0)^{d_0}(c_1)^{d_1} \cdots (c_{i-1})^{d_{i-1}} \cdot r^{d_i} \cdot (r^2)^{d_{i+1}} \cdots (r^{2^{l-i-1}})^{d_{l-1}} \bmod n. \tag{4}$$

It is convenient to sum up the above considerations in the definition below. We code up the faulty behavior of a device where the ith bit is targeted as a random variable, assuming $d_0, ..., d_{i-1}$ have been determined and are fixed binary constants.

Definition 1. *Let $d_i, ..., d_{l-1}$ be binary random variables and r be a random variable uniformly distributed in $\mathbb{Z}_{2^s}$ and independent from $d_i, ..., d_{l-1}$. We denote by $S'(r, d_i, ..., d_{l-1})$ the random variable whose value is given by the RHS of (4).*

4   The Basic Attack

For the rest of the section, we fix i with $0 < i \le l - 1$. The target of the attack will be bit d_i, assuming that bits from d_0 to d_{i-1} have been determined. We assume without loss of generality that:

$$\left(\frac{M}{n}\right) = 1.$$

We shall indicate below how to modify the attack if $\left(\dfrac{M}{n}\right) \neq 1$ (see Remark 1 below).

Equation (4) allows an attacker to extract information about the d_i by computing the Jacobi symbol of S', i.e., by taking the result of the random variable J:

$$J \overset{\text{def}}{=} \left(\frac{S'}{n}\right).$$

All factors of S' different from r^{d_i} have Jacobi symbol $\neq -1$. Hence, if one gets $J = -1$, one can immediately conclude that $d_i = 1$ (by (1)). On the other hand, if one gets $J \neq -1$ then one concludes that d_i is *probably* 0 (in case $\left(\dfrac{M}{n}\right) = -1$, we should just reverse the role of '1' and '-1'). For ease of reference, we code the test just outlined as a random variable.

Definition 2 (a test for d_i). *The random variable* $\mathbf{A}$ *is defined as:*

$$\mathbf{A} \overset{\text{def}}{=} \begin{cases} 1 & \text{if } J = -1 \\ 0 & \text{if } J \neq -1. \end{cases}$$

Remark 1. Suppose that $\left(\dfrac{M}{n}\right) = -1$. A moment's thought shows that the test $\mathbf{A}$ still works if $d_0 = 0$. If $d_0 = 1$, then we can make $\mathbf{A}$ work by modifying it as follows:

$$\mathbf{A} \overset{\text{def}}{=} \begin{cases} 1 & \text{if } J = 1 \\ 0 & \text{if } J \neq 1. \end{cases}$$

That is, if $d_0 = 1$ and one gets $J \neq -1$ then from (4) one can immediately conclude that $d_i = 1$.

Of course, if $\left(\dfrac{M}{n}\right) = 0$ one can immediately factor n by computing $\gcd(M, n)$. From now onward, we shall assume without loss of generality that $\left(\dfrac{M}{n}\right) = 1$.

The analysis of the test $\mathbf{A}$ is straightforward. In the sequel, let $\alpha \overset{\text{def}}{=} \Pr[d_i = 1]$, and let the success probability of $\mathbf{A}$ be $\rho \overset{\text{def}}{=} \Pr[\mathbf{A} = 1 \mid d_i = 1]$, where we stipulate that $\rho \overset{\text{def}}{=} 1$ if $\alpha = 0$. Finally let the error probability of $\mathbf{A}$ be $\varepsilon \overset{\text{def}}{=} \Pr[d_i = 1 \mid \mathbf{A} = 0]$.

Lemma 1. *It holds that:*

(a) $\Pr[d_i = 1 \mid J = -1] = 1$;
(b) $\rho = \Pr[J = -1 \mid d_i = 1] \geq \phi(n)/2^{s+1}$.

PROOF: See Appendix. □

The following theorem says that $\mathbf{A}$ may be viewed as a Monte-Carlo type probabilistic algorithm.

Theorem 1. *The random variable* $\mathbf{A}$ *is a 1-biased probabilistic test for d_i, more precisely:*

(a) $\Pr[d_i = 1 | \mathbf{A} = 1] = 1$;

(b) $\varepsilon = \frac{(1-\rho)\alpha}{(1-\rho)\alpha+1-\alpha} \leq \frac{(1-\frac{\phi(n)}{2^{s+1}})\alpha}{(1-\frac{\phi(n)}{2^{s+1}})\alpha+(1-\alpha)}$.

PROOF: Part (a) follows from Lemma 1(a). For part (b), we may assume $\alpha \neq 0,1$, otherwise the wanted equality and inequality hold trivially. First observe that $\Pr[\mathbf{A} = 0 | d_i = 0] = 1 - \Pr[\mathbf{A} = 1 | d_i = 0] = 1$, by part (a). Then, observe that, by definition of $\mathbf{A}$, $\Pr[\mathbf{A} = 1 | d_i = 1] = \Pr[J = -1 | d_i = 1] = \rho$. Apply Bayes theorem to get:

$$\varepsilon = \Pr[d_i = 1 | \mathbf{A} = 0] = \frac{\Pr[\mathbf{A}=0|d_i=1] \cdot \Pr[d_i=1]}{\Pr[\mathbf{A}=0|d_i=1] \cdot \Pr[d_i=1] + \Pr[\mathbf{A}=0|d_i=0] \cdot \Pr[d_i=0]}$$

$$= \frac{(1-\rho)\alpha}{(1-\rho)\alpha+(1-\alpha)}.$$

The last expression is decreasing with respect to ρ in $[0,1]$. By Lemma 1(b) we know that $\rho \geq \phi(n)/2^{s+1}$, whence the thesis. $\qquad\square$

As usual, one can make the error probability arbitrarily small by repeating the test m times independently in succession, for a suitable m, for fixed values of $d_0, ..., d_{l-1}$. In this case, the error probability is bounded above by:

$$\frac{(1-\rho)^m \alpha}{(1-\rho)^m \alpha + 1 - \alpha}.$$

A more precise estimation of ε is obtained by making some further assumptions. In particular, it seems reasonable to assume $\alpha = 1/2$ (this is not exact if d is a RSA exponent, but seems a good approximation in practice). Let us say that $n = p \cdot q$ is *balanced* if p and q have the same size (an integer m has size t if $2^{t-1} \leq m < 2^t$). Finally, let us assume that size of n fits the size s of the registers.

Corollary 1. *If n is balanced and has size s and $\alpha = \frac{1}{2}$ then $\varepsilon \leq \frac{3}{7}$.*

PROOF: Since p and q have the same size, it must be $p, q > 2^{\frac{s-1}{2}}$. Easy calculations then yields $\phi(n)/2^{s+1} \geq 1/4$. When we substitute this value for $\phi(n)/2^{s+1}$ and $1/2$ for α in the upper bound for ε given in the previous theorem, we get the value $3/7$. $\qquad\square$

Here is a small example to illustrate.

i	7	6	5	4	3	2	1	0
S', J	44, 1	58, -1	11, 1	86, 1	120, 0	43, -1	34, 1	-
	44, 1		106, 1	113, 1	77, 1		100, 1	-
	44, 1		35, 1	79, 1	5, 1		29, 1	-
	44, 1		43, -1	59, -1	92, 1		53, -1	-
d_i	0	1	1	1	0	1	1	1

Fig. 3. An attack on the exponent $d = 119 = (01110111)_2$ with $n = 141$

Example 1. Suppose that $n = 141 = 3 \cdot 47$ and $M = 23$. The bits of the exponent d are determined in $l = 8$ successive stages, as in illustrated in Figure 3 (the value of l is not known in advance), starting from the least significant bit d_0 which is guessed to be 1. For each stage, the test is repeated at most $m = 4$ times independently. At each stage, the glitch time is given by $T = T_i - \varepsilon$ for some $0 < \varepsilon < \delta$. In conclusion, $d = (01110111)_2 = 119$. Of course, on $J = 0$ we could have factored the modulus right away. Also note that, in the last column, 44 is the correct value of $M^d \bmod n$: the squaring in the last but one iteration has no effect on the final result, as $d_{l-1} = 0$.

Remark 2 (software simulations). In the hypotheses of the corollary above, to obtain an error probability less say, than 2^{-10}, one may have to run the test up to $m = 25$ times independently. In practice, software simulations have shown that a bit less than 5000 queries (=faulty signatures) are sufficient to recover a RSA-768 key in about 70% of the cases. Considering a realistic time of 300 ms per query, and ignoring the time taken by a common PC to perform the test, this means that about 25 minutes are enough to recover such a key with a success probability of 0.7.

Remark 3 (Discrete log cryptosystems). The attack presented in this section can be repeated essentially unchanged when the modulus is a prime p. In this case, the success probability $\rho = \Pr[J = -1 \mid d_i = 1]$ can be lower-bounded by $|\phi(p)|/2^{s+1} = (p-1)/2^{s+1}$. If the size of p is $l = s$, then again $\rho \geq 1/4$ and $\varepsilon \leq 3/7$. Thus, in principle, in both El-Gamal decryption and Diffie-Hellman key-exchange an attacker might target and recover the secret exponent.

5 Randomized Time

We discard the assumption that all modular multiplications in the algorithm take the same known constant time δ. We represent multiplication times as random variables, possibly absorbing the time taken by control flow instructions. Times might change from an execution to the next, depending e.g. on instructions schedule, random delays or blinding of the argument. Or simply the randomness might represent the attacker's incomplete knowledge about the timing of the device (i.e. initial instant of each phase).

The first instant of phase i is given by the random variable

$$T_i = \sum_{j=0}^{i-1} (d_j \cdot \mu_j + v_j) + 1 \quad 0 \leq i \leq l-1$$

where for $0 \leq j \leq i-1$: d_j's are known values and μ_j's and v_j's are continuous random variables, which, following [11], we assume to be normally distributed, with known variance and mean. We also assume that all these random variables $(\mu_j, v_j$'s) are pairwise independent, and independent from d_i as a random variable. The model of the device (Definition 1) is modified as expected: S' yields the RHS of (4) whenever the glitch time T is such that $T_i > T > T_i - v_{i-1}$, for $0 < i \leq i-1$. Now, the midpoint in time of the squaring operation at phase $i-1$ is given by $\tau \overset{\text{def}}{=} T_{i-1} + d_{i-1}\mu_{i-1} + v_{i-1}/2$. We take the glitch time T to be the expectation:

$$T \overset{\text{def}}{=} \mathrm{E}[\tau] .$$

The definition of J and $\mathbf{A}$ remain unchanged. As we show below, with these definitions $\mathbf{A}$ yields a 2-sided probabilistic algorithm. Let $\gamma > 0$ be half the minimal duration of the squaring at phase $i-1$, i.e. take the supremum of all γ s.t. $\Pr[v_{i-1} < 2\gamma] = 0$, and let $\Gamma \stackrel{\text{def}}{=} \Pr[|T - \tau| < \gamma]$: this value can be computed exactly as τ is normally distributed with mean T and standard deviation $\sigma \stackrel{\text{def}}{=} \sum_{j=0}^{i-2}(d_j \text{var}(\mu_j) + \text{var}(v_j)) + d_{i-1}\text{var}(\mu_{i-1}) + \frac{1}{4}\text{var}(v_{i-1})$. Recall that $\alpha = \Pr[d_i = 1]$. The following result is proven by noting that if τ falls within γ of the glitch time T, then the glitch will be 'correct', i.e. it will affect the squaring in phase $i-1$.

Theorem 2. *The random variable $\mathbf{A}$ is a 2-sided probabilistic algorithm for bit d_i. In particular:*

a) *the success probability for 1 is:* $\rho \stackrel{\text{def}}{=} \Pr[\mathbf{A} = 1 | d_i = 1] \geq \frac{\phi(n)}{2^{s+1}} \cdot \Gamma$, *with* $\rho \stackrel{\text{def}}{=} 1$ *if* $\alpha = 0$;

b) *the error probability for 1 is:* $\varepsilon_1 \stackrel{\text{def}}{=} \Pr[d = 1 | \mathbf{A} = 0] \leq \frac{(1-\Gamma)(1-\alpha)}{(1-\Gamma)(1-\alpha)+\rho\alpha}$;

c) *the error probability for 0 is:* $\varepsilon_0 \stackrel{\text{def}}{=} \Pr[d = 0 | \mathbf{A} = 1] \leq \frac{(1-\rho)\alpha}{(1-\rho)\alpha+\Gamma(1-\alpha)}$.

The expressions for $\varepsilon_0, \varepsilon_1$ are monotonically decreasing w.r.t. $\rho \in [0,1]$.

PROOF: See Appendix   □

Given that $\mathbf{A}$ is a two-sided probabilistic test, one has to run the test m times independently with fixed values of the exponent bits and take the majority of the outcomes to have a reliable result. Note that for m independent iterations of $\mathbf{A}$, with fixed values of the exponent bits, the error probabilities for 1 and 0 can be lower-bounded respectively as:

$$\frac{(1-\Gamma)^m(1-\alpha)}{(1-\Gamma)^m(1-\alpha)+\rho^m\alpha} \quad \text{and} \quad \frac{(1-\rho)^m\alpha}{(1-\rho)^m\alpha+\Gamma^m(1-\alpha)} \ .$$

For the test to be useful, one has to make sure that the above values vanish as m grows. This is the case precisely when $\rho + \Gamma > 1$; by virtue of (a) above, this holds if $\Gamma > \frac{1}{1+\phi(n)/2^{s+1}}$.

As a general remark, the attack performs well in situations with a moderate variance of multiplication times, that is, when timing attacks are more difficult to mount. The following example provides some numerical evidence that for typical values of Γ the randomized version of the attack is feasible.

Example 2. For ease of reference, we use numerical data drawn from Kocher's original paper [11]. The following figures refer to time measurements (in μ-seconds) of actual modular multiplications executed during modular exponentiations. The random variables μ_j and v_j's are all normally distributed with standard deviation $\sigma_m = 12.01$ and mean $t = 1167.8$. The minimal duration of a modular multiplication can be taken 1130, hence we set $\gamma = 565$. Suppose we target the 512th bit of a secret exponent of size $l = 1024$ bit. Assuming, on average, that half of the bits from d_0 to d_{511} are set, we can compute the mean of τ as $T = t(511 + \frac{1}{2} + 256) = 896286.5$ and its variance as $\sigma^2 = \sigma_m^2(511 + \frac{1}{4} + 256) = 110668.2167$. These values gives (here

$\Phi(\cdot)$ denotes the cumulative distribution function of standard normal distribution): $\Gamma = \Phi(\gamma/\sigma) - \Phi(-\gamma/\sigma) \approx 0.9105$. Under the hypotheses of Corollary 1, we get

$$\rho \geq \frac{1}{4} \cdot \Gamma \approx 0.2275 \qquad \varepsilon_0 \leq 0.4590 \quad \text{and} \quad \varepsilon_1 \leq 0.2825 .$$

If we want both error probabilities to decrease under, say, 2^{-10}, we may have to run the test up to 43 times independently.

6 Countermeasures

We discuss a few software countermeasures.

Blinding Exponentiation with *blinding* (Figure 4) is a common and effective technique to thwart attacks based on timing [11].

1 choose at random $v \in \mathbb{Z}_n^*$
2 $X \leftarrow Mv^e \bmod n$
3 $Y \leftarrow X^d \bmod n$
4 $S \leftarrow Yv^{-1} \bmod n$

Fig. 4. RSA with message blinding

It is easy to see that message blinding has no effect on our attack. Suppose the attacker's target is bit d_i. Given that the values $v^e, v^{-1} \bmod n$ are usually precomputed, the attacker can easily target the ith bit during the exponentiation at step 3 and induce a faulty computation yielding Y' as a result (i.e. a faulty signature of Y, without blinding), hence getting from the device a faulty signature

$$S'' = Y'v^{-1} \bmod n .$$

Let S' be the faulty signature one would obtain by targeting the ith bit in the case with no blinding – but with the same choice of the random $r \in \mathbb{Z}_{2^s}$. Let $\bar{c}_i \overset{\text{def}}{=} (v^e)^{2^i}$, for $i = 0, ..., l-1$. It is easy to see, relying on equation (4), that:

$$S'' = S' \cdot C \cdot v^{-1} \bmod n$$

where $C = (\bar{c}_0)^{d_0} \cdots (\bar{c}_{l-1})^{d_{l-1}}$. Noting that that e is odd we have:

$$\left(\frac{v^e}{n}\right) = \left(\frac{v}{n}\right) = \left(\frac{v^{-1}}{n}\right)$$

and since $d_0 = 1$, hence $\bar{c}_0 = v^e$, we get

$$\left(\frac{S''}{n}\right) = \left(\frac{S'}{n}\right) .$$

Effective countermeasures Checking before output, i.e. checking that $S^e = M \bmod n$, with e a RSA public exponent (see [9]), before transmitting the signature has been proposed to contrast fault attacks. This is feasible in case the public exponent e is small. In the case of a prime modulus p, a strategy suggested by Shamir [14] involves doing exponentiation twice, once mod p and once mod $p \cdot r$, for r a 32-bit prime, and then comparing the results. *Random delays* (see [11]) have been proposed as a countermeasure against timing analysis. An alternative form of blinding, also proposed in [11], is blinding of the exponent, which consists in summing a quantity $k\phi(n)$, with k random, to the exponent d before performing modular exponentiation. Adoption of one of above listed methods appears to thwart our attacks.

7 Conclusions

We have demonstrated that fault analysis can be combined with timing control to potentially get effective cryptanalysis of cryptographic schemes implemented using the (right-to-left) modular exponentiation algorithm. Our model is based on random, transient computation faults, that appear to be easier to induce than faults based on modifying individual bits of data registers.

At the moment it is not clear how to extend the attack presented here to the left-to-right version of the exponentiation algorithm. Indeed, one can easily show that, in the case of a prime modulus p, a straightforward extension of this attacks based on detecting 2^i-th power mod p permits to recover the k least significant bits of the exponent, where k is the exponent of 2 in the factorization of $p-1$: however, these bits are already known to be "easy" to recover.

Also, one wonders whether an analog of the present attack might work against ECC schemes that rely on "double and add" algorithms, perhaps along the lines of the attacks presented in [7]. These extensions will be the subject of further study.

References

1. R.J. Anderson, M. Bond, J. Clulow, S. Skorobogatov. Cryptographic processors – a survey, Technical Report UCAM-CL-TR-641, University of Cambridge, Computer Laboratory, August 2005.
2. R.J. Anderson, M.J.Kuhn, Tamper resistance – a cautionary note. *The second USENIX Workshop on Electronic Commerce proceedings*, Nov. 1996.
3. R.J. Anderson, M.J. Kuhn, Low cost attacks on tamper-resistant devices, *Security protocols, 5th International Workshop*, Paris, 1997.
4. C. Aumüller, P. Bier, P. Hofreiter, W. Fischer and J.- P. Seifert. Fault attacks on RSA with CRT: Concrete Results and Practical Countermeasures, *Cryptology ePrint Archive: Report 2002/073*.
5. F.Bao, R.H.Deng, Y.Han, A.Jeng, A.D.Nirasimhalu, T.Ngair. Breaking Public Key Cryptosystems on Tamper Resistant Devices in the Presence of Transient Faults. In *Proc. of the 5th Workshop on Secure Protocols*, LNCS 1361, Springer, 1997.
6. H.Bar-El, H.Choukri, D.Naccache, M.Tunstall, C.Whelan. The Sorcerer's Apprentice Guide to Fault Attacks, In *Workshop on Fault Detection and Tolerance in Cryptography*, Florence, 2004. Also in *Cryptology ePrint Archive: Report 2004/100*, 2004.
7. I. Biehl, B. Meyer, V. Müller. Differential Fault Attacks on Elliptic Curve Cryptosystems, In *Advances in Cryptology - Crypto 2000*, LNCS 1880, Ed. Mihir Bellare, Springer, 2000.
8. E.Biham, A.Shamir. Differential fault analysis of secret key cryptosystem, In *Advances in Cryptology, CRYPTO '97*, LNCS 1294, Springer, 1997.
9. D.Boneh, R.A.DeMillo, R.J.Lipton. On the importance of checking cryptographic protocols for faults, *Journal of Cryptology*, 14(2), Springer, 2001.
10. D.E.Knuth. *The art of computer programming vol.2, Seminumerical algorithms*. Addison Wesley, third edition, 1997.
11. P.Kocher. Timing attacks on implementations of Diffie-Hellman, RSA, DSS, and other systems, *Advances in Cryptology-CRYPTO'96*, LNCS 1109, Springer, 1996.
12. P.Kocher, J.Jaffe, B.Jun. Differential Power Analysis, In *Advances in Cryptology, CRYPTO'99*, LNCS 1294, Springer, 1999.

13. J.J.Quisquater, G.Piret. A Differential Fault Attack Technique Against SPN Structures, with Application to the AES and KHAZAD, In *Fifth International Workshop on Cryptographic Hardware and Embedded Systems (CHES 2003)*, LNCS 2779, Springer, 2003.
14. A. Shamir. How to check modular exponentiation. Presented at *EUROCRYPT'97* rump session, Konstanz, May 1997.
15. S. Skorobogatov, R. Aderson. Optical Fault Induction Attacks. In *Workshop on Cryptographic Hardware and Embedded Systems (CHES 2002)*, LNCS 2523, Springer, 2002.
16. D.R.Stinson. *Cryptography: Theory and Practice*. CRC Press, second edition, 2002.
17. S-M. Yen, M.Joye. Checking before output may not be enough against fault-based cryptanalysis. In *IEEE Transactions on Computers*, 49(9), 2000.

A   Proofs

PROOF OF LEMMA 1: Part (a) follows from the discussion immediately preceding the statement of the lemma. For part (b), suppose that $d_i = 1$. Then, by definition of S' and J and by the property of the Jacobi symbol (1), $J = \left(\frac{r}{n}\right)$ with r chosen at random in $\mathbb{Z}_{2^s}$. Thus

$$\rho = |\{r \in \mathbb{Z}_{2^s} : \left(\frac{r}{n}\right) = -1\}|/2^s \geq |\{r \in \mathbb{Z}_{2^n} : \left(\frac{r}{n}\right) = -1\}|/2^s$$

since $n \leq 2^s$. But, as noted in Section 2, the set that appears at the numerator in the last expression has cardinality $\phi(n)/2$.   □

PROOF OF THEOREM 2: Concerning (a), one can lower bound the success probability $\rho = \Pr[J = -1|d_i = 1]$ by noting that if τ falls within γ of the glitch time T, then the glitch will be 'correct', i.e. it will affect the squaring in phase $i - 1$. Therefore

$$\Pr[J = -1|d_i = 1, |T - \tau| < \gamma] \geq \frac{\phi(n)}{2^{s+1}} .$$

By the independence of d_i and τ, we have:

$$\rho = \Pr[J = -1|d_i = 1, |T - \tau| < \gamma] \cdot \Gamma + \Pr[J = -1|d_i = 1, |T - \tau| \geq \gamma] \cdot (1 - \Gamma)$$
$$\geq \Pr[J = -1|d_i = 1, |T - \tau| < \gamma] \cdot \Gamma$$
$$\geq \frac{\phi(n)}{2^{s+1}} \cdot \Gamma .$$

The upper bounds for ε_0 and ε_1 follow using Bayes theorem. In particular, for ε_1 we use the lower-bound:

$$\Pr[A = 0|d_i = 0] = \Pr[J \neq -1|d_i = 0, |T - \tau| < \gamma] \cdot \Gamma +$$
$$\Pr[J \neq -1|d_i = 0, |T - \tau| \geq \gamma] \cdot (1 - \Gamma)$$
$$= 1 \cdot \Gamma + (\cdots)$$
$$\geq \Gamma .$$

It is immediate to check that the given bounds are monotonic decreasing in ρ.   □

Sign Change Fault Attacks on Elliptic Curve Cryptosystems

Johannes Blömer[1], Martin Otto[1,*], and Jean-Pierre Seifert[2]

[1] Paderborn University, Institute for Computer Science, 33095 Paderborn, Germany
bloemer@upb.de, martin@martin-otto.de
[2] Intel Corporation, Virtualization & Trust Lab — CTG, 2111 NE 25th Avenue,
M/S JF2-55, Hillsboro, OR 97124-5961, USA
jeanpierreseifert@yahoo.com

Abstract. We present a new type of fault attacks on elliptic curve scalar multiplications: Sign Change Attacks. These attacks exploit different number representations as they are often employed in modern cryptographic applications. Previously, fault attacks on elliptic curves aimed to force a device to output points which are on a cryptographically weak curve. Such attacks can easily be defended against. Our attack produces points which do not leave the curve and are not easily detected. The paper also presents a revised scalar multiplication algorithm that protects against Sign Change Attacks.

Keywords: elliptic curve cryptosystem, fault attacks, smartcards.

1 Introduction

Secure cryptographic applications require a secure platform, which is not offered by today's desktop computers. Consequently, sensitive applications, especially for digital signatures, are deployed on smartcards. Smartcards are tamper-resistant and not threatened by viruses and other malicious code. However, smartcards must adhere to the laws of physics, a fact that can be exploited by an adversary to collect additional information about their computations using side-channel information. The most prominent side-channels are given by timing measurements, power consumption measurements, and faulty outputs.

In 1997, Boneh, DeMillo and Lipton ([BDL01]) introduced fault attacks, which exploit faulty outputs. They showed how to use errors in the computation of an RSA signature to recover the secret key. Today, several different methods to purposely induce faults into devices and memory structures have been reported (e.g., [AK96], [SA02]). As it is a quite natural idea to extend the results to other group based cryptosystems, [BMM00] show how to exploit errors in elliptic curve scalar multiplications. This result has been refined in [CJ03].

All fault attacks on elliptic curve cryptosystems presented so far ([BMM00], [CJ03]) tried to induce faults into the computation of a scalar multiplication

---

* Supported by the DFG graduate school No. 693 and the PaSCo Institute, Paderborn.

L. Breveglieri et al. (Eds.): FDTC 2006, LNCS 4236, pp. 36–52, 2006.
© Springer-Verlag Berlin Heidelberg 2006

kP on the elliptic curve E such that the computation no longer takes place on the original curve E. By changing the base point P or an intermediate point randomly, by changing the curve parameters of E, or by changing the defining field, the operations leave the group defined by the elliptic curve E. Instead the scalar multiplication is done on a different curve $\tilde{E}$ and/or with a different base point $\tilde{P}$. Then the so-called pseudo-addition can be used to recover the secret key if the point $k \cdot \tilde{P}$ on the new curve $\tilde{E}$ allows to solve the discrete logarithm problem at least partially. The disadvantage (or advantage) of the proposed attacks is that there is an obvious and efficient countermeasure: simply check whether the result is a point on the original curve E or not.

In this paper, we present a new type of fault attacks on elliptic curve scalar multiplication, Sign Change Attacks. Our attack does not change the original curve E and works with points on the curve E. We show how sign changes of intermediate points can be used to recover the secret scalar factor. Our attack leads to a faulty output that is a valid point on the original elliptic curve. Then we can use an algorithm similar to the one presented for RSA in [BDL01] to recover the secret scalar factor in expected polynomial time. We present our attack for the NAF-based left-to-right repeated doubling algorithm, because here Sign Change Faults seem to be easier to realize than for other repeated doubling variants (see Section 5). However, we stress the fact that the attack can also be used against other scalar multiplication algorithms, e.g., the right-to-left version, binary expansion based repeated doubling, and the Montgomery ladder ([Mon87]) if the y-coordinate is used.

Our attacks show that the basic ideas of [BDL01] carry over to elliptic curve cryptosystems as well. Clearly, the standard countermeasures described above, namely checking whether the result lies on the original curve, fail to detect Sign Change Attacks. In fact, they even support Sign Change Attacks by holding back a great variety of faulty results if they have been caused by errors other than Sign Change Faults. This allows an adversary to use a less precise attack setting.

We also present a revised version of the basic scalar multiplication algorithm for elliptic curves that is secure against Sign Change Attacks in Section 4. Our countermeasure is motivated by a similar countermeasure by Shamir against attacks on CRT-RSA exponentiations ([Sha99]). We use the original elliptic curve together with a second small curve, which allows to define a larger "combined curve", where the desired scalar multiplication is performed. Using this combined curve, one can check the final result efficiently. We show that this technique secures all standard repeated doubling algorithms against Sign Change Attacks and previously reported attacks. Our analysis proves ad hoc security against these attacks only, it does not provide a general security proof or security reduction. Research on fault attacks has not yet established a mathematical framework to allow general security claims.

One can also use randomization schemes to counteract a differential fault attack with Sign Change Faults. However, smartcard certification authorities often require that algorithms are secure against fault attacks even without random-ization. Moreover, randomization schemes that only randomize the base point are not guaranteed to counteract an SCA, e.g., Coron's third countermeasure in [Cor99, §5.3] or the proposed elliptic curve isomorphism in [JT01, §4.1]. Al-ternatively, some scalar multiplication algorithms like the Montgomery ladder ([Mon87]) can be used without the y-coordinate. Therefore, these methods can-not be attacked by a Sign Change Attack. However, patent issues prevent the usage of the Montgomery ladder and endorse the widespread use of variants of the standard repeated doubling algorithm, mostly based on the NAF.

The paper is organized as follows: After briefly recalling the basics of elliptic curve arithmetic, we present the Sign Change Attack on Elliptic Curve Scalar Multiplication in Section 3. Section 4 is devoted to presentation and analysis of the proposed countermeasure. In Section 5, we discuss methods to carry out Sign Change Faults in practice. Section 6 concludes the paper. Since the main contribution of this paper is the presentation of the new Sign Change Faults and the countermeasure presented in Section 4, we concentrate in this extended abstract on Sections 4 and 5.

2   Elliptic Curve Cryptography

An elliptic curve over a field $\mathbb{F}_p$ with $p > 3$ is defined as the set of points $(x : y : z) \in \mathbb{F}_p^3$ that satisfy the projective Weierstraß equation

$$y^2 z \equiv x^3 + Axz^2 + Bz^3 \bmod p. \tag{1}$$

Moreover, $\mathcal{O}$ denotes the point at infinity $(0 : 1 : 0)$. The points of E form an additive group. The elliptic curve E as well as points on E can be expressed in a variety of coordinate representations, e.g., affine coordinates, projective coordi-nates, Jacobian coordinates, or Hessian coordinates. This paper concentrates on projective representations as defined above. As we do not need to consider the projective addition formula in detail, we refer the reader to standard literature for a description of the actual computation of the sum of two projective points. A nice overview of several addition formulas can be found in [CMO98].

In cryptosystems based on elliptic curves, e.g., the ElGamal cryptosystem and its variants, a crucial computation is the scalar multiplication of a public base point P with a secret scalar factor k. Attacks aim to recover the value k. Several implementations of fast scalar multiplication algorithms have been presented in the literature. In Algorithm 1, we present a left-to-right version of the well known repeated doubling algorithm to present our attack. Algorithm 1 already implements a standard countermeasure against random fault attacks in Line 5. It protects against previously proposed fault attacks on elliptic curve cryptosystems ([BMM00], [CJ03]). For all subsequent considerations, we will always assume that this standard countermeasure is applied.

Algorithm 1: NAF-based Repeated Doubling on Elliptic Curve E

Input: A point P on E, and a secret key $1 < k < ord(P)$ in non-adjacent form, where n denotes the binary length of k, i.e. the number of bits of k

Output: kP on E

1 Set $Q_n := \mathcal{O}$

2 For i from n − 1 downto 0 do

3   Set $Q'_i := 2Q_{i+1}$

4   If $k_i = 1$ then set $Q_i := Q'_i + P$

              else if $k_i = -1$ then set $Q_i := Q'_i - P$

                    else set $Q_i := Q'_i$

5 If Q_0 is not on E then set $Q_0 := \mathcal{O}$

6 **Output** Q_0

In Algorithm 1, we use the non-adjacent form (NAF) representation of the secret scalar k. The performance of most variants of the the classical repeated doubling algorithm will improve if the scalar k is recoded into non-adjacent form (NAF). The 2-NAF uses digits from $\{-1, 0, 1\}$ and ensures that no two adjacent digits are non-zero. It achieves a higher ratio of zeros to non-zeros. For details on the NAF, see [Boo51], or [JY00]. Using the NAF, subtractions are introduced. Since negating a point on an elliptic curve simply means to change the sign of the y-coordinate, subtractions are cheap operations on elliptic curves. The savings using repeated doubling based on the NAF are 11.11% on average (see [MO90]).

3   The Sign Change Attack on Elliptic Curve Repeated Doubling

Previous fault attacks on elliptic curve scalar multiplication used the fact that a pertubated point is not a valid point on the given curve with high probability. However, such a situation can be easily detected and defended against. In the following, we present a new type of faults, Sign Change Faults. They allow to recover the secret scalar factor of a scalar multiplication operation. Section 5 will investigate how such faults can be induced. It will be shown that these attacks are practical.

Our Fault Model. We assume that an adversary is able to induce a *Sign Change Fault* (SCF) on a specific elliptic curve point used in Algorithm 1. A Sign Change Fault changes the sign of the y-coordinate of an attacked point, e.g., Q'_i on E, such that $Q'_i \mapsto -Q'_i$. The adversary does not know in which iteration of the loop the error occurs. However, we assume that the loop iteration determined by i is chosen i.i.d. according to the uniform distribution. Throughout this paper, we denote the correct final result by Q and a faulty final result by $\tilde{Q}$.

Elliptic curves defined over prime fields, which are recommended by current standards such as ANSI, SEC, and IEEE, have prime order or use a subgroup of prime order. Therefore, we will assume this property for our curves as well. It implies that any point $P \neq \mathcal{O}$ on E must have the same (large) prime order. We will use this assumption frequently.

We state our attack using an algorithm similar to the attack presented by Boneh, DeMillo and Lipton in [BDL01] on RSA. Similar to [BDL01], we need a polynomial number of faulty outputs for the same inputs to achieve a sufficiently high success probability. We use the following result from [BDL01] to bound the number of necessary faulty outputs needed by our attack.

Fact 2 (Number of Necessary Attacks). *Let $x = (x_1, x_2, \ldots, x_n) \in \{0,1\}^n$ and let M be the set of all contiguous intervals of length $m < n$ in x. If $c = (n/m) \cdot \log(2n)$ bits of x are chosen uniformly independently at random, then the probability that each interval in M contains at least one chosen bit is at least $1/2$.*

3.1 Sign Change Attack on Q_i' in Line 4

All of the variables in Lines 3 and 4 can be successfully attacked with a Sign Change Attack (SCA). In the following, we present the attack on the variable Q_i' in Line 4 during some loop iteration $0 \leq i \leq n - 1$.

The basic idea of our attack algorithm is to recover the bits of k in pieces of $1 \leq r \leq m$ bits. Here, m is chosen to reflect a trade-off between the number of necessary faulty results derived from Fact 2 and the approximate amount 2^m of offline work. Throughout this paper, we assume that $2^m \ll \#E$. To motivate the algorithm, assume that a faulty value $\tilde{Q}$ is given that resulted from an SCF in Q_i'. We have

$$\tilde{Q} = -2^i Q_i' + \sum_{j=0}^{i} k_j \cdot 2^j \cdot P = -Q + 2L_i(k) \quad \text{with } L_i(k) := \sum_{j=0}^{i} k_j 2^j P \quad (2)$$

On the right hand side of Equation (2), the only unknown part is $L_i(k)$, which defines a multiple of P. If only a small number of the signed bits $k_0, k_1, \ldots, k_i$ used in that sum is unknown, these bits can be guessed and verified using Equation (2). This allows to recover the signed bits of k starting from the LSBs. Moreover, due to the fact that $Q = L_i(k) + H_{i+1}(k)$, where $H_{i+1}(k) := \sum_{j=i+1}^{n-1} k_j 2^j P$, it is also possible to recover the signed bits of k starting from the MSBs. As we assume that errors are induced uniformly at random, an adversary may choose freely between these two recovery strategies. In the following, we will use the LSB version based on Equation (2). We assume that both Q and $\tilde{Q}$ are known. The complete attack is stated as the following algorithm.

Comment. Algorithm 3 has been abbreviated for clarity in two minor details. On the one hand, the highest iteration that suffered a SCF in Line 2 of Algorithm 3 does not need to be the last iteration $n-1$. However, since we assume the "lucky case" of Fact 2, this special case can be handled efficiently by an exhaustive search for at most m bits.

Algorithm 3: The Sign Change Attack on Q'_i

Input: Access to Algorithm 1, n the length of the secret key $k > 0$ in non-adjacent form, $Q = kP$ the correct result, m a parameter for acceptable amount of offline work.

Output: k with probability at least $1/2$.

  # Phase 1: Collect Faulty Outputs

  1 Set $c := (n/m) \cdot \log(2n)$

  2 Create c faulty outputs of Alg. 1 by inducing a SCF in Q'_i for random values i.

  3 Collect the set $S = \{\tilde{Q} \mid \tilde{Q} \neq Q$ is a faulty output of Algorithm 1 on input $P\}$.

  # Phase 2: Inductive Retrieval of Secret Key Bits

  4 Set $s := -1$ indicating the number $s + 1$ of known bits of k.

  5 While $(s < n - 1)$ do

  # Compute the known LSB part.

  6   Set $L := 2\sum_{j=0}^{s} k_j 2^j P$

  # Try all possible bit patterns with length $r \leq m$.

  7   For all lengths $r = 1, 2, \ldots m$ do

  8   For all valid NAF-patterns $x = (x_{s+1}, x_{s+2}, \ldots, x_{s+r})$ with $x_{s+r} \neq 0$ do

  # Compute and verify the test candidate T_x

  9   Set $T_x := L + 2\sum_{j=s+1}^{s+r} x_j 2^j P$

  10   for all $\tilde{Q} \in S$ do

  11   if $\left(T_x - \tilde{Q}\right) = Q$ then

  12   conclude that $k_{s+1} = x_{s+1}, k_{s+2} = x_{s+2}, \ldots, k_{s+r} = x_{s+r}$,

  13   set $s := s + r$, and continue at Line 5

  # Handle a Zero Block Failure

  14   If no test candidate satisfies the verification step, then

  15   assume that $k_{s+1} = 0$ and set $s := s + 1$.

  16 Verify $Q = kP$. If this fails then output "failure".

  17 **Output k**

Furthermore, it is clear that given n as the length of the NAF of k, Algorithm 3 does not need to test patterns whenever $s + r \geq n$. Note that s indicates that the $s + 1$ least significant bits $k_0, k_1, \ldots, k_s$ are known. In fact, we may assume that the most significant bit of k is $k_{n-1} = 1$, otherwise n cannot be uniquely defined. Therefore, we may assume w.l.o.g. that $s + r < n - 1$. Note that we assume $k > 0$. We also assume that $(k_0, k_1, \ldots, k_s, x_{s+1}, \ldots, x_{s+r})$ is always in valid NAF.

We will prove the success of Algorithm 3 in two lemmas. First, we will show that only a correct guess for the pattern of k can satisfy the verification step in Line 11. Then, we will show that Algorithm 3 will always correctly recover at least the next unknown bit of k. The analysis of these two cases is very similar to the analysis of a similar attack on RSA, presented in [BDL01]. Therefore, we omit the proofs of the two lemmas and the summarizing theorem. They can be found in the appendix. Before stating the results, we introduce Zero Block Failures.

Definition 4 (Zero Block Failure). *Assume that Algorithm 3 already recovered the $s+1$ least significant signed bits $k_0, k_1, \ldots, k_s$ of k. If the signed bits k_{s+1}, $k_{s+2}, \ldots, k_{s+r}$ are all zero and all Sign Change Faults that happened in iterations $s+1, \ldots, s+m$ really occurred in the first r iterations $s+1, s+2, \ldots, s+r$, the situation is called a* Zero Block Failure.

A Zero Block Failure is named after the fact that errors in a block of zeros will not be detected as errors within that block. Equation (2) shows that for any s, $L_s(k)$ $= L_{s+1}(k) = \ldots = L_{s+r}(k)$ for all sequences $k_{s+1} = 0, k_{s+2} = 0, \ldots, k_{s+r} = 0$. In this case, the values $\tilde{Q}_1 = -Q + 2L_s(k)$ and $\tilde{Q}_2 = -Q + 2L_{s+r}(k)$ are equal. Therefore, given $\tilde{Q} = -Q + 2L_s(k)$, Algorithm 3 cannot determine how many zero bits — if any — follow k_s. Hence, tailing zeros must be neglected, because their number cannot be determined correctly. This is the reason why Algorithm 3 only tests patterns x which end in ± 1 in Line 8.

In Algorithm 3, we may have one of two cases in each iteration of the loop of Lines 5–15. First, we may encounter a test pattern, which satisfies the verification step in Line 11. Second, no test pattern may satisfy the verification step. The following two lemmas show that Algorithm 3 recovers at least one bit of k correctly in either case.

Lemma 5 (No False Positives). *We assume that the bits $k_0, k_1, \ldots, k_s$ of k have already been computed by Algorithm 3. If Algorithm 3 computes a test bit pattern $x = (x_{s+1}, x_{s+2}, \ldots, x_{s+r})$, $r \leq m$, such that T_x satisfies the verification step in Line 11 for some $\tilde{Q} \in S$, then x is the correct bit pattern, i.e., $x_j = k_j$ for all $s+1 \leq j \leq s+r$.*

Lemma 6 (Correct Recovery). *We assume that the bits $k_0, k_1, \ldots, k_s$ of k have already been computed by Algorithm 3. Furthermore, we assume that a Sign Change Fault was induced into the intermediate value Q_i' in Line 4 of Algorithm 1 for some $i \in \{s+1, s+2, \ldots, s+m\}$.*

Then, in order to recover the next signed bit k_{s+1}, Algorithm 3 will be in one of two cases: In the first case, it finds a test bit pattern $x = (x_{s+1}, x_{s+2}, \ldots, x_{s+r})$, $r \leq m$, that satisfies the verification step in Line 11 and concludes that $k_j = x_j$ for all $s+1 \leq j \leq s+r$ in Line 12. In the second case, it detects a Zero Block Failure and concludes that $k_{s+1} = 0$ in Line 15. In both cases, the conclusion is correct and between 1 and r bits of k are recovered correctly.

The results of the previous lemmas are summarized in the following theorem. It is a straightforward result from the two previous lemmas, combined with a simple count of operations performed by Algorithm 3.

Theorem 7 (Success of the Proposed Sign Change Attack). *Algorithm 3 succeeds to recover the secret scalar multiple k of bit length n in time $O(n \cdot 3^m \cdot c \cdot M)$ with probability at least $1/2$. Here, $c = (n/m) \cdot \log(2n)$ and M is the maximal cost of a full scalar multiplication or a scalar multiplication including the induction of a Sign Change Fault.*

The results of Theorem 7 carry over similarly to Sign Change Attacks on all other variables used inside the loop in Algorithm 1. The ideas presented in the attack also apply to the NAF-based right-to-left repeated squaring version and to the binary expansion based versions (cf. [Ott05]). Sign Change Attacks can also be used against the Montgomery ladder [Mon87] if the y-coordinate is used.

4   Countermeasures

As explained in the introduction, previously proposed countermeasures cannot be used to defend against Sign Change Faults. Therefore, we propose a modified scalar multiplication algorithm presented as Algorithm 8 as an alternative countermeasure against Sign Change Attacks (SCA). It adds little overhead at the benefit of checking the correctness of the final result. Moreover, it can be based on any scalar multiplication algorithm which does not need field divisions. We will present our countermeasure in the remainder of this section and analyze it using the NAF-based version presented as Algorithm 1. The countermeasure has been motivated by Shamir's countermeasure against attacks on CRT-RSA exponentiations [Sha99].

We first explain the basic idea of the countermeasure. For the modified algorithm, we assume that the curve $E = E_p$ is defined over a prime field $\mathbb{F}_p$, i.e., we have $E_p := E(\mathbb{F}_p)$. Furthermore, we choose a small prime t of about 60 – 80 bits to form the "small" curve $E_t := E(\mathbb{F}_t)$. E_t does not depend on E_p. Given both curves, we define a "combined" elliptic curve E_{pt} over the ring $\mathbb{Z}_{pt}$. This curve E_{pt} is defined with parameters A_{pt} and B_{pt} such that $A_{pt} \equiv A_p \bmod p$, $A_{pt} \equiv A_t \bmod t$ and $B_{pt} \equiv B_p \bmod p$, $B_{pt} \equiv B_t \bmod t$. Here, A_p and A_t denote the A-parameters and B_p and B_t denote the B-parameters in Equation (1) of E_p and E_t respectively. Both A_{pt} and B_{pt} can be easily computed using the Chinese Remainder Theorem (CRT). We also choose a base point P_t on E_t and use the combined point P_{pt} as the base point for the scalar multiplication in E_{pt}. Here, P_{pt} is computed using the CRT in the same manner as A_{pt} and B_{pt} above. Computing $Q = kP_{pt}$ on E_{pt} allows to verify the result on the small curve E_t.

Algorithm 8: Sign Change Attack Secure Scalar Multiplication
***
Input: A point P on E_p, and a secret key $1 < k < ord(P)$, where n denotes the binary length of k, i.e., the number of bits of k
Output: kP on E_p
\# offline initialization (i.e., at production time)
1 Choose a prime t and an elliptic curve E_t
2 Determine the combined curve E_{pt}
\# main part
3 Set $Q := kP_{pt}$ on E_{pt} (e.g., using Algorithm 1)
4 Set $R := kP_t$ on E_t (e.g., using Algorithm 1)
5 If $R \neq Q \bmod t$ then **output** "failure".
6 Else **output** Q on E_p

Scalar Multiplication is used twice, once in Line 3 and once in Line 4. For the algorithm used, we assume that it features a check of the final result that returns $\mathcal{O}$ if the result is not a valid point on the curve (e.g., Line 5 of Algorithm 1). In the case where E_{pt} is used, we assume for simplicity that this check is performed both modulo p and modulo t, i.e., both on E_p and on E_t.

On the Choice of $\boldsymbol{E_p}$ and $\boldsymbol{E_t}$. For the security of our countermeasure against Sign Change Attacks, we assume that both E_p and E_t have prime order. Both curves are chosen independently, which allows to use recommended curves (e.g., by [SEC00]) for E_p. The security analysis will show that the security depends on the order of P_t on E_t. This does not require E_t to be secret. Moreover, it also does not require $\#E_t$ to be prime. It is sufficient to choose a curve E_t and a point P_t such that the order of P_t on E_t is large. We will specify a minimal size for the order of P_t on E_t later. Finding such a curve E_t is feasible as shown in [BSS99, §VI.5].

4.1   Analysis of the Countermeasure

It is easily shown that Algorithm 8 computes the correct result if no error occurs. This is evident from modular arithmetic.

It remains to show that the proposed algorithm is secure against Fault Attacks. We only consider ad-hoc security for our proofs, i.e., we only prove security against known Fault Attacks. Research on fault attacks has not yet established a mathematical framework to allow general security claims. For our analysis, we assume that Algorithm 1 has been chosen as the scalar multiplication algorithm, although the result holds for other scalar multiplication algorithms as well. To defend against previously proposed fault attacks, the standard countermeasure introduced in Section 2 has been included as an integral part of Algorithm 1. Therefore, we concentrate on security against Sign Change Attacks on Line 3 of Algorithm 8 only.

We use the same fault model as in Section 3, i.e., a Sign Change Fault can be induced in any intermediate variable used by the scalar multiplication $Q = kP$ on E_{pt}. Sign Change Faults can only be induced in points of elliptic curves, the scalar k cannot be attacked. Furthermore, we assume that only a single SCF can be induced during each computation of kP. We do not consider multiple correlated attacks, since such attacks are not a realistic scenario. The adversary can target a specific variable, e.g., Q_i', but he cannot target a specific iteration i. As we are interested to show that a faulty value is returned with negligible probability, we only need to investigate Sign Change Attacks on the computation in Line 3 of Algorithm 8. Attacks in Line 4 cannot yield a faulty output as Q is not changed by Line 4. We first investigate the basic requirement for an error to be undetected by the countermeasure in Line 5.

Lemma 9 (Undetectable Sign Change Faults). *Let $Q = kP_{pt}$ be the correct result of the scalar multiplication in Line 3 of Algorithm 8 and let $\tilde{Q} = Q + \kappa_i \cdot P \neq Q$ be a faulty result from an attack on Line 3. Let $r_t := \#E_t$ be the group order of*

E_t, assumed to be prime. The faulty result $\tilde{Q}$ passes by the detection mechanism in Line 5, iff $r_t \mid \kappa_i$.

Proof. Let R and Q denote the variables used in Algorithm 8. If $r_t \mid \kappa_i$, we have $\kappa_i P = \mathcal{O}$ on E_t. Therefore, the test "R $\neq$ Q" in Line 5 of Algorithm 8 yields $kP_t = Q + \mathcal{O}$ on E_t. As the correct result Q satisfies $Q = kP_t$ on E_t, this would not trigger a "failure" output and the faulty value $\tilde{Q}$ would be returned. As $\tilde{Q} \neq Q$ on E_{pt} is assumed, we also have $\tilde{Q} \neq Q$ on E_p. This case results in a faulty output.

If $r_t \nmid \kappa_i$, we must show that $kP_t \neq \tilde{Q}$ on E_t. We know that for the correct value Q, it holds that R = Q on E_t. If $r_t \nmid \kappa_i$, we have $\kappa_i P \neq \mathcal{O}$ on E_t because r_t is the prime group order. Therefore, the order of P is r_t as well. Consequently, we have R $\neq$ Q $= \tilde{Q}$ on E_t and the security alert in Line 5 is triggered. $\square$

Lemma 10 (Number of Undetectable Sign Change Faults). *Let r_t be the group order of E_t, assumed to be prime. Let m be the blocksize used in Algorithm 3. Then a Sign Change Attack on Algorithm 8 needs a blocksize $m \geq \lfloor \log(r_t) \rfloor$ to be successful. Moreover, at most $(n-1)/\lfloor \log(r_t) \rfloor$ many undetectable faulty outputs exist.*

Proof. Assume that a Sign Change Fault was induced into Q_i' for some i, resulting in a faulty output $\tilde{Q}_1$. By Equation (2), we have

$$\tilde{Q}_1 = -Q + 2L_i(k) = Q + \kappa_i P \qquad \text{where} \qquad \kappa_i := -2^{i+2} \sum_{j=i+1}^{n-1} k_j 2^{j-i-1}.$$

We further assume that $r_t \mid \kappa_i$, i.e., $\tilde{Q}_1$ has not been detected as a faulty value according to Lemma 9. We now consider another faulty output $\tilde{Q}_2 \neq \tilde{Q}_1$ collected by Algorithm 3. Let $u \neq i$ denote the fault position, i.e., $\tilde{Q}_2 = Q + \kappa_u P$.

We claim that for all u with $|u - i| \leq \lfloor \log(r_t) \rfloor$, $u - i \neq 0$, it holds that $r_t \nmid \kappa_u$. We consider the two cases $u < i$ and $u > i$. For $u < i$, we have

$$\kappa_u = -2^{u+2} \sum_{j=u+1}^{n-1} k_j 2^{j-u-1} = \kappa_i - 2^{u+2} \cdot \sigma_u, \quad \text{where } \sigma_u := \sum_{j=u+1}^{i} k_j 2^{j-u-1},$$

$$(3)$$

and for $u > i$, we have

$$\kappa_u = -2^{u+2} \sum_{j=u+1}^{n-1} k_j 2^{j-u-1} = \kappa_i + 2^{i+2} \cdot \rho_u, \text{ where } \rho_u := \sum_{j=i+1}^{u} k_j 2^{j-i-1}. \quad (4)$$

The value $\tilde{Q}_2$ is only output if it is an undetectable fault that bypassed Line 5 of Algorithm 8. According to Lemma 9, this requires that $r_t \mid \kappa_u$. As we assume that $r_t \mid \kappa_i$, we need to analyze the case that $r_t \mid \sigma_u$ and $r_t \mid \rho_u$ respectively. We first investigate σ_u. Here, we have two cases: Either $\sigma_u = 0$ or $\sigma_u > 0$ over the integers. If $\sigma_u = 0$ over the integers, we have $\kappa_u = \kappa_i$ and $\tilde{Q}_1 = \tilde{Q}_2$. As this contradicts our assumption that $\tilde{Q}_1 \neq \tilde{Q}_2$, we may assume that σ_u is not equal to 0 over the integers. If the sum in Equation (3) is not equal to 0 over the integers, its absolute value must be at least as large as r_t in order to be a multiple of r_t. The same considerations hold for $u > i$.

Algorithm 3 recovers bits in blocks of at most m bits. If it has found a valid test pattern, it starts at the position immediately following that test pattern and tries to recover the next block of length m starting at this position. If $m < \lfloor \log(r_t) \rfloor$, the arguments above shows that in this block there cannot be a faulty output $\tilde{Q}$ in the list of collected faulty outputs that satisfies the verification step. Therefore, Algorithm 3 needs a minimal blocksize of $m = \lfloor \log(r_t) \rfloor$ in order to be able to reconstruct another faulty output $\tilde{Q}$.

As the fault positions of two undetected faulty outputs $\tilde{Q}_1$ and $\tilde{Q}_2$ are at least $\lfloor \log(r_t) \rfloor$ bits away from each other, we have a maximum of $(n - 1)/\lfloor \log(r_t) \rfloor$ many different faulty outputs in the set collected by Algorithm 3.   □

Lemma 10 shows that the proposed algorithm secures the scalar multiplication algorithm against the new Sign Change Faults if the group order of $\#E_t$ is large enough. A group order of $\#E_t > 2^{80}$ guarantees that the required block size of $m > 80$ exceeds the acceptable amount of offline work significantly. For many practical applications, $\#E_t > 2^{60}$ should already be enough.

The computational overhead is acceptable. Line 3 requires computations with 30 – 40 % larger moduli (for $l(p) = 192$ and $l(t) = 60 - 80$), Line 4 requires a scalar multiplication on a considerably smaller curve with the scalar factor $k \bmod \#E_t$, which is considerably smaller than k.

As the computations in Line 3 prohibit the use of inversions, projective coordinates must be used. We have stated our results for the basic version of projective coordinates but other weighted projective representations such as Jacobian or Hessian representations will do just as well.

5 Realization of Sign Change Attacks

At first sight, a Sign Change Attack does not seem to be easily performed in a general setting. A random change of the y-coordinate cannot hope to yield $-y$ with non-negligible probability. However, there exist several special yet common settings, where Sign Change Faults can be realized. We will give examples for attacks on NAF-based variants of the scalar multiplication algorithm as well as examples for attacks on certain properties of the crypto co-processor. The latter attacks can be applied to any variant of repeated doubling.

One special way to attack the NAF is offered by the fact that any NAF-based algorithm has to incorporate a conditional branch, where for secret key bit $k_i = 1$ an addition is performed and for secret key bit $k_i = -1$, a subtraction is performed. Currently, a whole zoo of physical attacks is available that targets such conditional decisions, e.g., power spikes or clock glitches ([BCN+04], [ABF+02]). These attacks aim at forcing the conditional statement to choose the wrong branch. In our case, choosing the wrong branch means to add $-P$ instead of P or vice versa. Although this attack cannot be applied to mount a Sign Change Attack on other intermediate variables, such as Q_i' as analyzed in Section 3, it is an instructive example. Moreover, a Sign Change Attack on P can also be used to recover the secret key, similar to the attack described in Section 3. This attack is also valid for more sophisticated NAF-based repeated doubling variants, which aim to secure the basic scheme against power and timing attacks, e.g., by using dummy operations.

To achieve sign changes of any intermediate variable, consider the following scenario. Many real-world embedded crypto co-processors supporting modular arithmetic most often also rely on the non-adjacent form to speed up the time-critical modular *multiplication* operation, cf. [HP98], [Kor93]. Here, the factors used during the computation of $P_1 + P_2$ for two elliptic curve points P_1 and P_2 are attacked. Any efficient implementation of the NAF must provide special hardware to handle negative numbers, i.e., being able to compute the two's complement of any register used as a multiplicand without time delay, cf. [Sed87], [WQ90], or [Mon85]. This task is trivial to solve by simply inverting every bit sent to the long integer arithmetic unit (ALU) and additionally adding $+1$. Given this functionality, it can be used for an attack.

As a concrete example, we consider such a crypto co-processor, cf. [Sed87], adding simultaneously at least three different operands with a possible sign change in one single instruction. Changing the value of an operand to its negative, i.e., to its two's complement, one usually needs to change only one single bit among the control signals of the corresponding ALU. This is due to the fact that the ALU of most crypto co-processors is, as already explained above, designed to handle automatically the two's complement of any operand. Here, a fault attack can be mounted that results in an SCF.

For concreteness, let us consider the following projective addition formula, cf. [IEE98], for points $P_0 = (X_0 : Y_0 : Z_0)$, $P_1 = (X_1 : Y_1 : Z_1)$:

$$U_0 := X_0 Z_1^2, \qquad S_0 := Y_0 Z_1^3, \qquad U_1 := X_1 Z_0^2, \qquad S_1 := Y_1 Z_0^3,$$
$$W := U_0 - U_1, \qquad R := S_0 - S_1, \qquad T := U_0 + U_1, \qquad M := S_0 + S_1,$$
$$Z_2 := W Z_0 Z_1, \qquad X_2 := R^2 - T W^2, \qquad V := T W^2 - 2 X_2, \qquad 2 Y_2 := V R - M W^3.$$

Here it becomes clear, that lots of load/store or exchange instructions are needed to realize this formulas involving the original points P_0 and P_1. For example, an implementation could use Y_0 or Y_1 via previous load/store or exchange instructions as a multiplicand in the modular multiplications to compute S_0, or S_1. The attack on Q_i' described in Section 3 can be realized by attacking Y_0 during the computation of S_0. During this preparing load/store or exchange instruction, the corresponding value must go through the ALU. While executing this operation, the handled value is susceptible to an SCF as only a single bit among the control signals must be changed to load/store or exchange the value in its target multiplicand register to $-Y_0$ or $-Y_1$. This yields an SCF by changing one single control signal. Note that [BCN+04] actually describes how to implement such attacks in practice. A similar consideration also applies to the projective doubling formula.

6   Conclusions and Open Problems

Fault attacks are a significant threat to secure communication based on mobile devices. We have introduced a new type of fault attacks on elliptic curve cryptosystems, Sign Change Attacks, which allow attacks with a high success probability, especially for NAF-based repeated doubling algorithms. Current and future cryptosystems based on elliptic curves must be guarded against this type of attacks carefully. As a first step in this direction, a new secure algorithm is presented that withstands Sign Change Attacks with acceptable computational overhead. Attack and countermeasure have been presented in the context of projective coordinates and elliptic curves defined over prime fields. However, both attack and countermeasure also apply to other commonly used representations and defining fields.

Interestingly, the Sign Change Attack presented in this paper does not apply to elliptic curves of characteristic 2. It is an open problem to extend our attack to elliptic curves of characteristic 2.

The results from Section 5 show that the most efficient solutions often pay their performance advantage with security, just like in the case of CRT-RSA [BDL01]. Since Montgomery's version is secure, our attack strengthens the claim from [JY03], that the "Montgomery ladder may be a first-class substitute of the celebrated square-and-multiply algorithm". It is an open problem whether it is possible to successfully attack the Montgomery method where the y-coordinate is not used in a way such that faulty results are created which are valid points on the curve.

References

[ABF+02]   C. Aumüller, P. Bier, W. Fischer, P. Hofreiter, and J.-P. Seifert, *Fault attacks on RSA with CRT: Concrete results and practical countermeasures*, CHES 2002, LNCS, vol. 2523, Springer-Verlag, 2002, pp. 260–275.

[AK96]   R. J. Anderson and M. G. Kuhn, *Tamper resistance — a cautionary note*, Proceedings of the Second USENIX Workshop on Electronic Commerce, USENIX Association, 1996, pp. 1 – 11.

[BCN+04]   H. Bar-El, H. Choukri, D. Naccache, M. Tunstall, and C. Whelan, *The sorcerer's apprentice guide to fault attacks*, Cryptology ePrint Archive, 2004/100, 2004, http://eprint.iacr.org/2004/100.pdf

[BDL01]   D. Boneh, R. A. DeMillo, and R. J. Lipton, *On the importance of eliminating errors in cryptographic computations*, J. Cryptology **14** (2001), no. 2, 101–119.

[BMM00]   I. Biehl, B. Meyer, and V. Müller, *Differential fault attacks on elliptic curve cryptosystems*, CRYPTO 2000, LNCS, vol. 1880, Springer-Verlag, 2000, pp. 131–146.

[Boo51]   A. D. Booth, *A signed binary multiplication technique*, Quart. Journ. Mech. and Applied Math. **IV** (1951), no. 2, 236–240.

[BSS99]   I. Blake, G. Seroussi, and N. Smart, *Elliptic curves in cryptography*, London Mathematical Society Lecture Note Series, vol. 265, Cambridge University Press, 1999.

[CJ03]   M. Ciet and M. Joye, *Elliptic curve cryptosystems in the presence of permanent and transient faults*, Cryptology ePrint Archive, 2003/028, 2003, http://eprint.iacr.org/2003/028.pdf

[CMO98]   H. Cohen, A. Miyaji, and T. Ono, *Efficient elliptic curve exponentiation using mixed coordinates*, ASIACRYPT'98, LNCS, vol. 1514, Springer-Verlag, 1998, pp. 51–65.

[Cor99]   J.-S. Coron, *Resistance against differential power analysis for elliptic curve cryptosystems*, CHES'99, LNCS, vol. 1717, Springer-Verlag, 1999, pp. 292–302.

[EK90]   Ö. Eğecioğlu and Ç. K. Koç, *Fast modular exponentiation*, Communication, Control, and Signal Processing (1990), pp. 188–194.

[HP98]   H. Handschuh and P. Pailler, *Smart card crypto-coprocessors for public-key cryptography*, Proc. of CARDIS '98, LNCS, vol. 1820, Springer-Verlag, 1998, pp. 372–379.

[IEE98]   IEEE P1363/D3 (Draft Version 3), *Standard specifications for public key cryptography*, May 1998.

[JT01]   M. Joye and C. Tymen, *Protections against differential analysis for elliptic curve cryptography — an algebraic approach*, CRYPTO 2001, LNCS, vol. 2162, Springer-Verlag, 2001, pp. 377–390.

[JY00]   M. Joye and S. M. Yen, *Optimal left-to-right binary signed-digit recoding*, IEEE Trans. on Computers **49** (2000), no. 7, 740–748.

[JY03]   M. Joye and S.-M. Yen, *The montgomery powering ladder*, CHES 2002, LNCS, vol. 2523, Springer-Verlag, 2003, pp. 291–302.

[Kor93]   I. Koren, *Computer arithmetic algorithms*, Prentice-Hall, 1993.

[MO90]   F. Morain and J. Olivos, *Speeding up the computations on an elliptic curve using addition-subtractions chains*, Theoretical Informatics and Applications (1990), no. 24, 531–543.

[Mon85]   P. L. Montgomery, *Modular multiplication without trial division*, Math. Comp. (1985), no. 44, 519–521.

[Mon87]   P. L. Montgomery, *Speeding the Pollard and elliptic curve methods of factorization*, Mathematics of Computation **48** (1987), no. 177, 243–264.

[Ott05]   M. Otto, *Fault attacks and countermeasures*, Ph.D. thesis, University of Paderborn, 2005, http://wwwcs.uni-paderborn.de/cs/ag-bloemer/forschung/publikationen/Dis sertationMartinOtto.pdf.

[SA02]   S. Skorobogatov and R. Anderson, *Optical fault induction attacks*, CHES 2002, LNCS, vol. 2523, Springer-Verlag, 2002, pp. 2–12.

[SEC00]   Standards for Efficient Cryptography Group (SECG), *SEC 2: Recommended elliptic curve domain parameters*, 2000, http://www.secg.org/collateral/sec2_final.pdf

[Sed87]   H. Sedlak, *The RSA cryptography processor*, EUROCRYPT'87, LNCS, vol. 304, Springer-Verlag, 1987, pp. 95–108.

[Sha99]   A. Shamir, *Method and apparatus for protecting public key schemes from timing and fault attacks*, 1999, US Patent No. 5,991,415, Nov. 23, 1999.

[WQ90]   D. de Waleffe and J.-J. Quisquater, *CORSAIR, a smart card for public-key cryptosystems*, CRYPTO '90, LNCS, vol. 537, Springer-Verlag, 1990, pp. 503–513.

A   Proofs of Lemma 5, Lemma 6, and Theorem 7

Lemma 5 (No False Positives). *We assume that the bits $k_0, k_1, \ldots, k_s$ of k have already been computed by Algorithm 3. If Algorithm 3 computes a test bit pattern $x = (x_{s+1}, x_{s+2}, \ldots, x_{s+r})$, $r \leq m$, such that T_x satisfies the verification step in Line 11 for some $\tilde{Q} \in S$, then x is the correct bit pattern, i.e., $x_j = k_j$ for all $s + 1 \leq j \leq s + r$.*

Proof. Assume that the verification step is satisfied for a given test bit pattern $x = (x_{s+1}, \ldots, x_{s+r})$ with $1 \leq r \leq m$ and $x_{s+r} \neq 0$, x in non-adjacent form. We assume that we have a false positive, i.e., the pattern x is different from the corresponding pattern of k, namely $k_{s+1}, k_{s+2}, \ldots, k_{s+r}$. Hence, there must be a faulty result $\tilde{Q} \in S$ that satisfies the verification step in Line 11 together with this x. The verification step in Line 11 yields $\mathcal{O} = T_x - \tilde{Q} - Q$. We use Line 9 of Algorithm 3 to express T_x and Equation (2) to express $\tilde{Q}$ in detail.

We know that $\tilde{Q} = -Q + 2L_s(k)$ for some value s. The considerations about Zero Block Failures have shown that tailing zeros in $L_i(k)$ do not change the value of $\tilde{Q}$. Hence, we may write $\tilde{Q} = -Q + 2L_i(k)$ with $k_i \neq 0$ for some unknown i if $\tilde{Q} \neq -Q$. Moreover, if it is known that $\tilde{Q} = -Q + 2L_s(k)$, we may specify i in greater detail. In fact, we have $\tilde{Q} = -Q + 2L_i(k)$ with $i := \max\{j \mid k_j \neq 0 \wedge j \leq s\}$. The case where $\tilde{Q} = -Q$, i.e., when the maximum does not exist, can be represented by choosing $i = -1$.

We have

$$
\mathcal{O} = \left(2 \cdot \sum_{j=0}^{s} k_j 2^j P + 2 \cdot \sum_{j=s+1}^{s+r} x_j 2^j P \right) - \left(-Q + 2 \cdot \sum_{j=0}^{i} k_j 2^j P \right) - Q
$$

$$
= 2 \cdot \left(\underbrace{\sum_{j=0}^{s} k_j 2^j + \sum_{j=s+1}^{s+r} x_j 2^j}_{R_+} - \underbrace{\sum_{j=0}^{i} k_j 2^j}_{R_-} \right) \cdot P \quad = \quad R_x \cdot P \tag{5}
$$

where $\quad R_x = 2 \cdot \displaystyle\sum_{j=0}^{\max(i, s+r)} y_j 2^j \quad$ and $\quad y_j = \begin{cases} 0 & \text{if } j \leq \min(i, s) \\ k_j & \text{if } i < j \leq s \\ (x_j - k_j) & \text{if } s < j \leq \min(i, s+r) \\ x_j & \text{if } \max(i, s) < j \leq s + r \\ -k_j & \text{if } s + r < j \leq i. \end{cases}$

Equation (5) implies that either $R_x = 0$ or R_x is a multiple of the order of P.

Case 1. Assume that $R_x = 0$. This is easily shown to be impossible. It implies that $R_+ = R_-$, i.e., both sums are valid NAF representations of the same number. As the NAF is unique, this implies that both representations are equal. Hence, all digits are equal in contradiction to the assumption that there is as least one $x_j \neq k_j$ with $s + 1 \leq j \leq s + r$.

Case 2. Assume that $R_x \neq 0$ is a multiple of the order of P on E. We know that $\text{ord}(P) = \#E \gg 2^m$ as $\#E$ is prime. Therefore, $\#E$ divides R_x. If $i = -1$, i.e., $\tilde{Q} = -Q$, we have $R_x \cdot P = T_x$. As we may assume that $s + r < n - 1$ as explained above, we have $R_x < \#E$. This contradicts our assumption that $\#E$ divides R_x. If $0 \leq i \leq s$, we have $R_x = 2^{i+2} \cdot R'_x$ with $|R'_x| < 2^{s+r-i} < 2^{n-1-i} \leq k < \#E$. Therefore, $\#E$ cannot divide R_x. If $s + 1 \leq i \leq s + r$, we have $R_x = 2^{s+2} \cdot R'_x$ with $|R'_x| < 2^{m+1}$. Again, $\#E$ cannot divide R_x. For $s + r < i < n - 1$, we have $R_x = 2^{s+2} \cdot R'_x$ with $|R'_x| < 2^{i-s+1} \leq 2^{n-2-s+1} \leq 2^{n-1} \leq k < \#E$. Therefore, $\#E$ cannot divide R_x. The last case, $i = n - 1$, is impossible. It would imply that $Q'_i = \mathcal{O}$ has been attacked, where no Sign Change Fault can be induced, i.e., $\tilde{Q} = Q$. However, we explicitly prevent values $\tilde{Q} = Q$ from being members of the set S in Line 3 of Algorithm 3. Therefore, Case 2 is impossible. □

Lemma 6 (Correct Recovery). *We assume that the bits $k_0, k_1, \ldots, k_s$ of k have already been computed by Algorithm 3. Furthermore, we assume that a Sign Change Fault was induced into the intermediate value Q'_i in Line 4 of Algorithm 1 for some $i \in \{s + 1, s + 2, \ldots, s + m\}$.*

Then, in order to recover the next signed bit k_{s+1}, Algorithm 3 will be in one of two cases: In the first case, it finds a test bit pattern $x = (x_{s+1}, x_{s+2}, \ldots, x_{s+r})$, $r \leq m$, that satisfies the verification step in Line 11 and concludes that $k_j = x_j$ for all $s + 1 \leq j \leq s + r$ in Line 12. In the second case, it detects a Zero Block Failure and concludes that $k_{s+1} = 0$ in Line 15. In both cases, the conclusion is correct and between 1 and r bits of k are recovered correctly.

Proof. We will investigate the two cases of the lemma separately.
Case 1. Assume that Algorithm 3 finds a test bit pattern $x = (x_{s+1}, x_{s+2}, \ldots, x_{s+r})$ that satisfies the verification step in Line 11. According to Lemma 5, there cannot be a false positive and x correctly represents the bit pattern of k. Therefore, the conclusion $k_j = x_j$ for all $s + 1 \leq j \leq s + r$ is correct.
Case 2. Assume that Algorithm 3 does not find a test bit pattern x that satisfies the verification step. In this case, a Zero Block Failure is conjectured by Algorithm 3 and it sets $k_{s+1} = 0$.

We assume that this conjecture is wrong. We know by the assumption in the lemma that at least one of the iterations $s + 1, s + 2, \ldots, s + m$ was targeted by a Sign Change Fault. Let $\tilde{Q} \in S$ be the faulty output of such an attack, i.e., $\tilde{Q} = -Q + 2L_i(k)$ with $s + 1 \leq i \leq s + m$ according to Equation (2). If the conjecture that we have a Zero Block Failure is wrong, we know by Definition 4 that we may choose $\tilde{Q}$ such that at least one of the bits $k_{s+1}, k_{s+2}, \ldots, k_i$ is not zero. This implies that we may write $\tilde{Q} = -Q + 2L_w(k)$ with $w := \max\{j \mid k_j \neq 0 \wedge s + 1 \leq j \leq i\}$ as explained above. Now it is easy to see that the test bit pattern $0 \neq x = (k_{s+1}, k_{s+2}, \ldots, k_{w-1}, k_w)$ of length $1 \leq r \leq m$ satisfies the verification step. This means that the value T_x defined in Line 9 of Algorithm 3 correctly represents $2L_w(k)$. Therefore, a valid test pattern x exists and Algorithm 3 will find a value for k_{s+1} in Line 12. Therefore, the assumption that a Zero Block Failure is detected incorrectly must be wrong. □

Theorem 7 (Success of the Proposed Sign Change Attack). *Algorithm 3 succeeds to recover the secret scalar multiple k of bit length n in time $O(n \cdot 3^m \cdot c \cdot M)$ with probability at least $1/2$. Here, $c = (n/m) \cdot \log(2n)$ and M is the* *maximal cost of a full scalar multiplication or a scalar multiplication including the induction of a Sign Change Fault.*

Proof. The result of Lemma 6 relies on the assumption that every contiguous interval of length m was targeted by at least one Sign Change Fault in Line 2 of Algorithm 3. According to Fact 2, this assumption holds with probability $1/2$ if $c = (n/m) \cdot \log(2n)$ faulty results are collected. This requires c scalar multiplications with the ability to induce a SCF.

According to Lemma 6, every iteration of the while loop of Algorithm 3 recovers either a zero bit or a test bit pattern x. It shows that this recovery is always correct if the "lucky case" of Fact 2 is assumed. Therefore, Algorithm 3 recovers between 1 and m bits in each while iteration. Therefore, at most n iterations are needed. The worst case occurs when $k = 2^{n-1}$ and no SCF was induced into Q_n while Algorithm 3 created the set of faulty outputs in Line 2. As all bits but the most significant are zero, only Zero Block Failures would occur, allowing to recover only a single bit in each iteration of Algorithm 3.

In a single iteration, Algorithm 3 tests at most 3^m test bit patterns (a more careful analysis due to [EK90] even yields at most 2^m non-adjacent test bit patterns). Every test bit pattern x yields a test candidate T_x using one scalar multiplication in Line 9. Obviously, some speedups could be applied, e.g., storing T_x allows to compute a new T_x using a single addition. Note that the precomputation of L in Line 6 already represents a speed up. For each test candidate T_x, at most c point additions and comparisons need to be done in Line 11. To present a short result, we simply treat the addition and comparison cost of Line 11 as a full scalar multiplication. If all possible bits of k have been recovered, a last full scalar multiplication must be applied to differentiate between Zero Block Failures and a real failure.

Altogether, the worst case running time of Algorithm 3 is $O((c + n3^m c + 1) \cdot M)$ where $c = (n/m) \cdot \log(2n)$ and M is the maximal cost of a full scalar multiplication or a scalar multiplication including the induction of a Sign Change Fault. $\qquad\square$

Cryptanalysis of Two Protocols for RSA with CRT Based on Fault Infection*

Sung-Ming Yen[1], Dongryeol Kim[2], and SangJae Moon[3]

[1] Laboratory of Cryptography and Information Security (LCIS)
Department of Computer Science and Information Engineering
National Central University
Chung-Li, Taiwan 320, R.O.C.
yensm@csie.ncu.edu.tw
http://www.csie.ncu.edu.tw/~yensm/
[2] Strategy Development Team
Information Security Policy Division
Korea Information Security Agency
Seoul, Korea 138-803
drkim@kisa.or.kr
[3] School of Electronic and Electrical Engineering
Kyungpook National University
Taegu, Korea 702-701
sjmoon@knu.ac.kr

Abstract. The technique of RSA private computation speedup by using Chinese Remainder Theorem (CRT) is well known and has already been widely employed in almost all RSA implementations. A recent CRT-based factorization attack exploiting hardware fault has received growing attention because of its potential vulnerability on most existing implementations. In this attack any single erroneous computation will make the RSA system be vulnerable to factorizing the public modulus. Recently, two hardware fault immune protocols for CRT speedup on RSA private computation were reported based on the concept of fault infective computation. A special property of these two protocols is that they do not assume the existence of totally fault free and tamper free comparison operation within the machine in order to enhance the reliability. However, it will be shown in this paper that these two protocols are still vulnerable to a potential computational fault attack on an auxiliary process that was not considered in the usual CRT-based factorization attack.

Keywords: Chinese remainder theorem (CRT), Cryptography, Factorization attack, Fault infective CRT, Hardware fault cryptanalysis, Residue number system.

---

* The research of S.M. Yen was supported by University IT Research Center Project. The research of D. Kim was supported by KISA, Korea. S. Moon was supported by University IT Research Center Project.

L. Breveglieri et al. (Eds.): FDTC 2006, LNCS 4236, pp. 53–61, 2006.

1   Introduction

Many implementations of public key cryptosystems based on tamper-proof devices (e.g., smart IC cards) were proposed. Much attention has been paid recently to consider the security issues of cryptosystem implementation on tamper-proof devices [1,2,3,4,5,6,7,8,9,10] from the view point of presence of hardware faults. This category of cryptanalysis is called the *fault-based cryptanalysis* in which it is assumed that when an adversary has physical access to a tamper-proof device she may purposely induce a certain type of fault into the device. Based on a set of incorrect responses or outputs from the device, due to the presence of faults, the adversary can extract the secrets embedded within the tamper-proof device.

In this paper, we focus our attention on public key cryptosystems in which their private computation can be sped up using the Chinese remainder theorem (CRT) [11,12], e.g., the RSA signature or decryption computation [13]. These cryptosystems may be vulnerable to the hardware fault cryptanalysis to reveal the secret key if the following three conditions are met: (1) the message m to sign (or the cipher to decrypt) is known or the correct signature on message m is available; (2) a random fault occurs during the computation of a residue number system (RNS); (3) the device outputs the faulty signature on message m. This kind of fault-based attacks was called the CRT-based factorization cryptanalysis [1,6,7]. Our main objective is to emphasize the importance of a careful implementation of cryptosystems with CRT-based speedup. Suppose you are in a context involving trusted third parties (e.g., bank or certificate authority) where hundreds of thousands of signatures being produced each day. If, for some reasons, a single signature is faulty and is available to an attacker, then the security of the whole system may be compromised.

Shamir developed a countermeasure [8,9] trying to disable the CRT-based factorization attack and this countermeasure becomes well known. However, one important thing to notice is that a countermeasure will become less reliable and less secure if more *checking procedures* will be employed like what existed in Shamir's countermeasure. It is likely that the countermeasure may fail if two spikes attacks can be conducted such that the first spikes attack will be used to introduce a computational fault for the CRT speedup computation (in order to perform a CRT-based factorization attack) and the second spikes attack will be used to tamper (or just to skip) the checking procedure (which is controversially assumed to be always fault free and tamper free in Shamir's countermeasure). Notice that in any processor a checking procedure (often as a conditional JUMP machine instruction) always relies on a single flag bit and it is usually the ZERO flag. Therefore, tampering on this checking procedure can fail the countermeasure easily. So, it will be necessary to develop a countermeasure without depending its security on any checking procedure within it.

Some related work can be found in [14] on attacking countermeasures assuming error free checking procedures, e.g., Shamir's method. These attacks also employ hardware fault to mount a CRT-based factorization attack, but on different scenarios. In [14], it was pointed out that both Shamir's countermeasure and an enhanced countermeasure [15] (trying to improve Shamir's method) are vulnerable to some fault induced (by a computational fault or a memory access fault) into some important modulo reduction operation within their countermeasures. One special property of the above two countermeasures is that they were designed highly depended on one or more checking operations, but provides only with heuristic reason to their design.

Recently, two hardware fault immune protocols for CRT speedup on RSA private computation were proposed in [16] which were developed based on a novel concept of *fault infective* computation in order to overcome the above mentioned disadvantage of relying on checking procedure. In these two protocols, in case of computational fault, the CRT-based factorization attack can be avoided without any unreasonable assumption. Notice that all prior solutions assumed that all the comparison operations should be totally fault free and tamper free.

The main contribution of this paper is that a potential computational fault on an *auxiliary* process which accomplishes the fault infection property in the protocols of [16] in order to protect the RSA private computation against the CRT-based factorization attack will be pointed out. This computational fault (or memory access fault) will enable the CRT-based factorization attack. Our research result shows that the fault infective process itself can still be vulnerable to the hardware fault attack if it is not carefully developed. Since the CRT speedup technique has already been widely employed in almost all popular implementations, any potential physical cryptanalysis on the original RSA with CRT or any countermeasure trying to enhance it becomes nontrivial.

2   Preliminary Background of CRT-Based Cryptanalysis

2.1   Chinese Remainder Theorem

Chinese remainder theorem [12] (CRT) for speeding up RSA [13] private computation is briefly reviewed in the following. Let p and q be two distinct primes and $n = p \cdot q$. In the RSA cryptosystem, a message m is signed with a secret key d as $s = m^d \bmod n$. Using the CRT-based approach, the value of s can be evaluated more efficiently by computing both $s_p = m^{d \bmod (p-1)} \bmod p$ and $s_q = m^{d \bmod (q-1)} \bmod q$, then by using the following two well known CRT recombination algorithms to reconstruct s. Given s_p and s_q, the Gauss's CRT recombination algorithm [12, p.68] computes $s = (s_p \cdot q \cdot (q^{-1} \bmod p) + s_q \cdot p \cdot (p^{-1} \bmod q)) \bmod n$. There is a well known improved CRT recombination, called Garner's algorithm [12, pp.612–613], which computes $s = s_p + ((s_q - s_p) \cdot (p^{-1} \bmod q) \bmod q) \cdot p$. In this paper, $CRT(s_p, s_q)$ denotes the above CRT recombination computation.

2.2   The CRT-Based Cryptanalysis

Suppose that an error (any random error) occurs during the computation of s_p (s'_p denotes the erroneous result), but the computation of s_q is error free. Applying the CRT on both s'_p and s_q will produce a faulty signature s'. The CRT-based factorization cryptanalysis [1,6,7] enables the factorization of n by computing

$$q = \gcd((s' - s) \bmod n, n) = \gcd(s' - s, n) \tag{1}$$

or

$$q = \gcd((s'^e - m) \bmod n, n) = \gcd(s'^e - m, n). \tag{2}$$

2.3 Shamir's Countermeasure

In Shamir's countermeasure [8,9], for each RSA private computation a random prime r is chosen, then $\widehat{p} = p \cdot r$ and $\widehat{d_p} = d \bmod (p-1) \cdot (r-1)$ are computed. The intermediate value $\widehat{s_p} = (m \bmod \widehat{p})^{\widehat{d_p}} \bmod \widehat{p}$ is computed, then $s_p = \widehat{s_p} \bmod p$ is computed. A value of $s_q = \widehat{s_q} \bmod q$ is also computed in a similar approach where $\widehat{s_q} = (m \bmod \widehat{q})^{\widehat{d_q}} \bmod \widehat{q}$. The IC card checks whether $\widehat{s_p} \equiv \widehat{s_q} \pmod{r}$. If the above checking is correct, then both s_p and s_q are assumed to be error free.

3 Review of Two Protocols for RSA with CRT Based on Fault Infection

In order to develop a *highly reliable* CRT-based speedup, no error free *checking procedure* (e.g., if statement in high level language or conditional JUMP in assembly instruction) could be assumed. Because in that situation and design, the checking procedure itself will become extremely vulnerable to the CRT-based hardware fault cryptanalysis and all other parts of the countermeasure will be in vain.

A key point of developing a secure CRT-based computation protocol without using a checking procedure is to influence the computation of s_q or the overall computation of s when an error occurred in the computation of s_p or vice versa. In [16], the above concept is called the *fault infective CRT* computation. This design makes the Eq. 1 and Eq. 2 be invalid and the CRT-based factorization cryptanalysis no longer applicable. Two fault infective CRT protocols in [16] will be reviewed in the following with small modification (simplification) indicated in the following.

3.1 The First Protocol – CRT-1 Protocol

Let $n = p \cdot q$ as usual RSA system. The smart card also prepares another set of key pair such that $d_r = d - r$ where r is a small integer (with the property of $\gcd(r, \phi(n)) = 1$ to guarantee security, refer to [16] for the details) selected in order to let $e_r \equiv d_r^{-1} \pmod{\phi(n)}$ be a small integer.

Step-1 Compute both $k_p = \lfloor m/p \rfloor$ and $k_q = \lfloor m/q \rfloor$.
Step-2 Compute $m^{d_r} \bmod n$ via a conventional CRT speedup as

$$\begin{cases} s_p = m^{d_r \bmod (p-1)} \bmod p \\ s_q = \widehat{m}^{d_r \bmod (q-1)} \bmod q \end{cases} \tag{3}$$

where

$$\widehat{m} = ((s_p^{e_r} \bmod p) + k_p \cdot p) \bmod q. \tag{4}$$

Step-3 A CRT recombination operation and some additional manipulation are employed to compute the required signature as

$$s = CRT(s_p, s_q) \cdot (\widetilde{m}^r) \bmod n$$

where

$$\widetilde{m} = (s_q^{er} \bmod q) + k_q \cdot q. \tag{5}$$

Notice that in the original work [16], a parameter $\delta = p - q$ is selected and the Eq. 4 in the above brief review is slightly different from its original one. But, the simplified version (without δ) is sufficient to achieve the same functionality.

3.2   The Second Protocol – CRT-2 Protocol

All the parameters are the same as in the CRT-1 protocol.

Step-1 Compute both $k_p = \lfloor m/p \rfloor$ and $k_q = \lfloor m/q \rfloor$.
Step-2 Compute $m^{dr} \bmod n$ via a conventional CRT speedup as

$$\begin{cases} s_p = m^{dr \bmod (p-1)} \bmod p \\ s_q = m^{dr \bmod (q-1)} \bmod q. \end{cases} \tag{6}$$

Step-3 A CRT recombination operation and some additional manipulation are employed to compute the required signature as

$$s = CRT(s_p, s_q) \cdot (\widehat{m}^r) \bmod n$$

where

$$\widehat{m} = \lfloor \frac{((s_p^{er} \bmod p) + k_p \cdot p) + ((s_q^{er} \bmod q) + k_q \cdot q)}{2} \rfloor. \tag{7}$$

Notice that in the above CRT-2 protocol when given any faulty s_p' or s_q' (or both) with random faults, a random faulty $\widehat{m}'$ in Eq. 7 will be generated.

4   Hardware Fault Cryptanalysis on Fault Infective RSA with CRT

Security of the CRT-1 and CRT-2 protocols in [16] has been proven such that a random fault occurred in one of the two CRT speedup computation modules[1] (in order to obtain s_p and s_q) will not reveal the factorization of n. However, other possible computational fault or memory access fault on some temporary parameters of the above CRT-1 and CRT-2 protocols has been overlooked previously. In this section, hardware fault cryptanalysis on CRT-1 and CRT-2 will be given.

---

[1] This is the usual approach to mount a CRT-based factorization attack.

4.1   Hardware Fault Cryptanalysis on CRT-1 Protocol

Suppose the computation of $k_q = \lfloor m/q \rfloor$ is not error free or memory access fault has occurred when retrieving a correct value of k_q, then the erroneous k_q' can be represented as $k_q' = k_q + t$ where t is a random integer.

It is supposed that both s_p and s_q are error free. So, in the Step-3, the erroneous $\tilde{m}'$ becomes

$$
\begin{aligned}
\tilde{m}' &= (s_q^{e_r} \bmod q) + (k_q + t) \cdot q \\
&= \tilde{m} + t \cdot q = m + t \cdot q.
\end{aligned}
\tag{8}
$$

Notice that $\tilde{m} = m$ if the computation of $\tilde{m}$ is error free.

Therefore, the recombined erroneous signature s' is

$$
\begin{aligned}
s' &= CRT(s_p, s_q) \cdot \tilde{m}'^r \bmod n \\
&= CRT(s_p, s_q) \cdot (m + t \cdot q)^r \bmod n \\
&= CRT(s_p, s_q) \cdot (m^r + R_1 \cdot q) \bmod n \\
&= CRT(s_p, s_q) \cdot m^r + CRT(s_p, s_q) \cdot R_1 \cdot q \bmod n \\
&= m^d + R_2 \cdot q \bmod n
\end{aligned}
\tag{9}
$$

where both R_1 and R_2 are random integers.

Based on the above observation, it can be derived that

$$
\begin{aligned}
\gcd(s'^e - m, n) &= \gcd((m^d + R_2 \cdot q)^e - m, n) \\
&= \gcd((m + R_3 \cdot q) - m, n) \\
&= q
\end{aligned}
$$

where R_3 is also a random integer. Similarly, it also leads to $\gcd(s' - s, n) = q$.

In the above hardware fault cryptanalysis on CRT-1 protocol, suppose that both s_p and s_q are correct, given the faulty k_q' (notice that k_p is error free) with random computational fault or random access fault (accordingly producing an erroneous $\tilde{m}'$ and an erroneous final signature s'), $\gcd(s'^e - m, n)$ gives q.

On the other hand, given the faulty $k_p' = k_p + t$ and the correct k_q, it can be shown that the CRT-based factorization attack is not applicable because of the intrinsic fault infection property of the CRT-1 protocol. The erroneous $\hat{m}'$ in Eq. 4 becomes $\hat{m}' = ((s_p^{e_r} \bmod p) + (k_p + t) \cdot p) \bmod q = \hat{m} + R_1$ and the erroneous s_q' in Eq. 3 becomes $s_q' = \hat{m}'^{d_r} \bmod q = (\hat{m}^{d_r} + R_2) \bmod q = s_q + R_3$ where all R_i are random integers. Accordingly, the erroneous $\tilde{m}'$ in Eq. 5 becomes $\tilde{m}' = ((s_q + R_3)^{e_r} \bmod q) + k_q \cdot q = \tilde{m} + R_4$ and the final erroneous signature becomes $s' = CRT(s_p, s_q') \cdot (\tilde{m} + R_4)^r \bmod n = CRT(s_p, s_q') \cdot (\tilde{m}^r) + R_5 \bmod n$ where both R_4 and R_5 are random integers. It is obvious that the incorrect signature s' is not useful for the CRT-based factorization attack because of the random integer R_5.

4.2   Hardware Fault Cryptanalysis on CRT-2 Protocol

Suppose the computation of $k_q = \lfloor m/q \rfloor$ is not error free or memory access fault has occurred when retrieving a correct value of k_q, then the erroneous k'_q can be represented as $k'_q = k_q + t$ where t is a random integer.

It is supposed that both s_p and s_q are error free. So, in the Step-3, the erroneous $\widehat{m}'$ becomes

$$\widehat{m}' = \lfloor \frac{((s_p^{er} \bmod p)+k_p \cdot p)+((s_q^{er} \bmod q)+(k_q+t)\cdot q)}{2} \rfloor$$
$$= \lfloor \frac{m+(m+t\cdot q)}{2} \rfloor$$
$$= m + \lfloor \frac{t\cdot q}{2} \rfloor$$
$$= m + T \cdot q \tag{10}$$

if $2 \mid t$ and T is therefore an integer.

Therefore, the recombined erroneous signature s' is

$$s' = CRT(s_p, s_q) \cdot \widehat{m}'^r \bmod n$$
$$= CRT(s_p, s_q) \cdot (m + T \cdot q)^r \bmod n$$
$$= CRT(s_p, s_q) \cdot (m^r + R_1 \cdot q) \bmod n$$
$$= CRT(s_p, s_q) \cdot m^r + CRT(s_p, s_q) \cdot R_1 \cdot q \bmod n$$
$$= m^d + R_2 \cdot q \bmod n \tag{11}$$

where both R_1 and R_2 are random integers.

Based on the above observation, it can be derived that

$$\gcd(s'^e - m, n) = \gcd((m^d + R_2 \cdot q)^e - m, n)$$
$$= \gcd((m + R_3 \cdot q) - m, n)$$
$$= q$$

where R_3 is also a random integer. Similarly, it also leads to $\gcd(s' - s, n) = q$.

In the above hardware fault cryptanalysis on CRT-2 protocol, suppose that both s_p and s_q are correct, given the faulty k'_q or k'_p with random computational fault or random access fault (accordingly producing an erroneous $\widehat{m}'$ and an erroneous final signature s'), $\gcd(s'^e - m, n)$ gives q or p, respectively.

5   Concluding Remarks

In this paper, we consider attacks on countermeasures by employing fault infective CRT computation. Note that the two fault infective CRT computation protocols were previously developed in order to be more reliable as countermeasures against the CRT-based factorization attack without assuming the existence of any fault free or tamper free checking (or comparison) procedure. After further careful re-examination, a potential attack is pointed out which was not considered in the usual CRT-based factorization attack scenario. These two fault infective CRT computation protocols can be modified and enhanced to be immune from the proposed attack pointed out in this paper. However, this may require the usage of reliable checking (or comparison) procedures.

We notice that two recent papers [17,18] presented at FDTC 2005 also consider RSA with CRT against factorization attack. However, the countermeasure proposed in [17] still assumes the usage of fault free checking computation. On the other hand, the countermeasure proposed in [18] has not yet been carefully analyzed since a factorization attack might still be possible due to the *linearity* of the CRC checking employed in their countermeasure. Take the usual 32-bit CRC as an example, the complexity to mount a successful attack will be only 2^{32}. If we consider a one-byte error on d_p, the complexity to factorize the RSA modulus will be only about 2500. So, to conclude this paper, an open problem is pointed out in the following. According to the above observation, it is still unknown whether it is possible to develop highly reliable algorithmic countermeasures against CRT-based factorization attack without employing any fault free or tamper free checking procedure.

References

1. D. Boneh, R.A. DeMillo, and R.J. Lipton, "On the importance of checking cryptographic protocols for faults," *Advances in Cryptology – EUROCRYPT '97*, LNCS 1233, pp. 37–51, Springer-Verlag, 1997.
2. F. Bao, R.H. Deng, Y. Han, A. Jeng, A.D. Narasimbalu, and T. Ngair, "Breaking public key cryptosystems on tamper resistant devices in the presence of transient faults," *Pre-proceedings of the 1997 Security Protocols Workshop*, Paris, France, 1997.
3. M. Joye, J.-J. Quisquater, F. Bao, and R.H. Deng, "RSA-type signatures in the presence of transient faults," *Proceedings of Cryptography and Coding*, LNCS 1355, pp. 155–160, Springer-Verlag, 1997.
4. D.P. Maher, "Fault induction attacks, tamper resistance, and hostile reverse engineering in perspective," *Proceedings of Financial Cryptography*, LNCS 1318, pp. 109–121, Springer-Verlag, 1997.
5. E. Biham and A. Shamir, "Differential fault analysis of secret key cryptosystems," *Advances in Cryptology – CRYPTO '97*, LNCS 1294, pp. 513–525, Springer-Verlag, 1997.
6. A.K. Lenstra, "Memo on RSA signature generation in the presence of faults," September 1996.
7. M. Joye, A.K. Lenstra, and J.-J. Quisquater, "Chinese remaindering based cryptosystems in the presence of faults," *Journal of Cryptology*, Vol. 12, No. 4, pp. 241–245, 1999.
8. A. Shamir, "How to check modular exponentiation," presented at the rump session of *EUROCRYPT '97*, Konstanz, Germany, 11–15th May 1997.
9. A. Shamir, "Method and apparatus for protecting public key schemes from timing and fault attacks," United States Patent 5991415, November 23, 1999.
10. S.M. Yen and M. Joye, "Checking before output may not be enough against fault-based cryptanalysis," *IEEE Trans. on Computers*, Vol. 49, No. 9, pp. 967–970, Sept. 2000.

11. J.-J. Quisquater and C. Couvreur, "Fast decipherment algorithm for RSA public-key cryptosystem," *Electronics Letters*, Vol. 18, No. 21, pp. 905–907, 1982.
12. A.J. Menezes, P.C. van Oorschot, and S.A. Vanstone. *Handbook of applied cryptography*. CRC Press, 1997.
13. R.L. Rivest, A. Shamir, and L. Adleman, "A method for obtaining digital signatures and public-key cryptosystem," *Commun. of ACM*, Vol. 21, No. 2, pp. 120–126, 1978.
14. S.M. Yen, S.J. Moon, and J.C. Ha, "Hardware fault attack on RSA with CRT revisited," *Proceedings of Information Security and Cryptology – ICISC 2002*, LNCS 2587, pp. 374–388, Springer-Verlag, 2003.
15. C. Aumüller, P. Bier, W. Fischer, P. Hofreiter, and J.-P. Seifert, "Fault attacks on RSA with CRT: Concrete results and practical countermeasures," *Proceedings of Cryptographic Hardware and Embedded Systems – CHES 2002*, LNCS 2523, pp. 260–275, Springer-Verlag, 2003.
16. S.M. Yen, S.J. Kim, S.G. Lim, and S.J. Moon, "RSA speedup with Chinese remainder theorem immune against hardware fault cryptanalysis," *IEEE Trans. on Computers – Special issue on CHES*, Vol. 52, No. 4, pp. 461–472, April 2003.
17. C. Giraud, "Fault-resistant RSA implementation," Proc. of the 2nd Workshop on Fault Diagnosis and Tolerance in Cryptography–FDTC 2005, Sept. 2, 2005.
18. M. Ciet and M. Joye, "Practical fault countermeasures for Chinese remaindering based RSA," Proc. of the 2nd Workshop on Fault Diagnosis and Tolerance in Cryptography–FDTC 2005, Sept. 2, 2005.

Blinded Fault Resistant Exponentiation*

Guillaume Fumaroli[1] and David Vigilant[2]

[1] Thales Communications
160 bd. de Valmy, F-92704 Colombes, France
guillaume.fumaroli@fr.thalesgroup.com
[2] Gemalto
6 rue de la Verrerie, F-92190 Meudon, France
david.vigilant@gemalto.com

Abstract. As the core operation of many public key cryptosystems, group exponentiation is central to cryptography. Attacks on its implementation in embedded device setting is hence of great concern. Recently, implementations resisting both simple side-channel analysis and fault attacks were proposed. In this paper, we go further and present an algorithm that also inherently thwarts differential side-channel attacks in finite abelian groups with only limited time and storage overhead.

1 Introduction

In traditional cryptanalysis, only inputs and outputs of cryptographic algorithms are available to the attacker. Unfortunately, this assumption is inaccurate when the hardware implementation is in the hands of the attacker. A new range of attacks known as implementation attacks is then applicable. Embedded devices such as smartcards are especially targeted by these implementation attacks, that may be either passive or active.

Passive attacks are based on side-channel analysis introduced in [1], whose principle consists in monitoring the device to find correlations between some physical information leakage and the secret key manipulated by the device. While simple side-channel analysis refers to a correlation involving a single acquisition, differential side-channel analysis recovers the secret in several attempts by using the correlation between different acquisitions and a part of the secret.

Active attacks or fault attacks consist in carefully forcing the cryptographic device to perform erroneous operations such that the result leaks information about the secret data involved in the computation.

Group exponentiation is at the basis of many public key cryptosystems such as RSA, ECC or the Diffie-Hellman key exchange in some group. Cryptosystems based on exponentiation are particularly sensitive to implementation attacks both active [2] and passive [3].

In this paper, we present an exponentiation algorithm that resists all forementionned implementation attacks in finite abelian groups.

---

* This work was performed when the first author was with Gemalto.

L. Breveglieri et al. (Eds.): FDTC 2006, LNCS 4236, pp. 62–70, 2006.

Our countermeasure features a novel base point blinding technique, based on the so-called Montgomery ladder introduced in [4], that requires fewer group operations than other techniques achieving the same level of protection.

In any finite abelian group whose order is unknown, our technique becomes the most efficient one requiring no pre-computations. In particular, this is the case for RSA as the factorization of the modulus and the public exponent are rarely available to the device. Note that our countermeasure also fully applies to the ECC setting since the randomization of projective coordinates, introduced by Coron in [5], was later proven insufficiant by Goubin in [6]. As pointed out recently by Dupuy and Kuntz-Jacques [7], when the attacker can tamper with the base element, scalar point multiplications also require randomization of the computation flow to provide DPA resistance.

In section 2, the history of exponentiation algorithms targetting constrained embedded devices is reviewed. Section 3 presents our algorithm and analyses its security and efficiency. Section 4 concludes.

2   A Review of Previous Work

In the sequel, $\mathbb{G}$ denotes a multiplicatively-written finite abelian group.

Though more refined algorithms for computing group exponentiations exist in the litterature, only those based on binary ladders are relevant in constrained environments such as smartcards.

Square-and-multiply algorithms (Fig. 1) have first been considered for implementation, but they are easily broken by simple side-channel attacks.

Input: $x \in \mathbb{G}$, $k = \sum_{i=0}^{t-1} k_i 2^i \in \mathbb{N}$
Output: $x^k \in \mathbb{G}$

$R_0 \leftarrow 1$; $R_1 \leftarrow x$
for $j = t - 1$ **down to** 0 **do**
    $R_0 \leftarrow R_0{}^2$
    if $k_j = 1$ **then** $R_0 \leftarrow R_0 R_1$
end for
return R_0

Fig. 1. Square-and-multiply

Further, square-and-multiply-always algorithms (Fig. 2) introduced by Coron [5] were designed to prevent simple side-channel attacks by performing dummy operations. However, such algorithms bring specific weaknesses with respect to so-called safe-error attacks [8].

Montgomery ladder [4] was initially developped for elliptic curve scalar multiplication. Later, Joye et al. [8] extended it to exponentiation in any abelian group and pointed out its intrinsic resistance to simple side-channel attacks and

---

Input: $x \in \mathbb{G}$, $k = \sum_{i=0}^{t-1} k_i 2^i \in \mathbb{N}$
Output: $x^k \in \mathbb{G}$

$R_0 \leftarrow 1$; $R_2 \leftarrow x$
for $j = t - 1$ **down to** 0 **do**
$\quad R_0 \leftarrow R_0{}^2$
$\quad R_{\bar{k_j}} \leftarrow R_{\bar{k_j}} R_2$
end for
return R_0

Fig. 2. Square-and-multiply-always

safe-error attacks leveraging a slight modification. Let $L_j = \sum_{i=j}^{t-1} k_i 2^{i-j}$ and $H_j = L_j + 1$. As pointed out in [8], the principle of Montgomery ladder is based on the following observation:

$$
(x^{L_j}, x^{H_j}) = \begin{cases} \left(\left(x^{L_{j+1}} \right)^2, x^{L_{j+1}} x^{H_{j+1}} \right) & \text{if } k_j = 0 \\ \left(x^{L_{j+1}} x^{H_{j+1}}, \left(x^{H_{j+1}} \right)^2 \right) & \text{if } k_j = 1 \end{cases}.
$$

This formula leads to Fig. 3 algorithm. The registers R_0 and R_1 contain the values of x^{L_j} and x^{H_j} respectively. (R_0, R_1) is initialized with $(x^{L_t}, x^{H_t}) = (1, x)$. After t iterations, (R_0, R_1) contains $(x^{L_0}, x^{H_0}) = (x^k, x^{k+1})$.

Input: $x \in \mathbb{G}$, $k = \sum_{i=0}^{t-1} k_i 2^i \in \mathbb{N}$
Output: $x^k \in \mathbb{G}$

$R_0 \leftarrow 1$; $R_1 \leftarrow x$
for $j = t - 1$ **down to** 0 **do**
$\quad R_{\bar{k_j}} \leftarrow R_{\bar{k_j}} R_{k_j}$
$\quad R_{k_j} \leftarrow R_{k_j}^2$
end for
return R_0

Fig. 3. Joye *et al.* Montgomery ladder

However, Montgomery ladder remains sensitive to differential side-channel analysis. As for group exponentiations, differential side-channel analysis may be prevented by randomizing either the group, the exponent or the base element. Randomization of the group structure was not explored in this paper. Known techniques targeting the exponent and the base element are presented in more details in [5,9]. Blinding the exponent is not well suited for exponentiations in finite abelian groups. Indeed, the group order is generally unknown and its computation may be difficult. So blinding the base seems to be the most appropriate countermeasure. Usually, blinding the base element consists in multiplying the input $x \in \mathbb{G}$ with a random element r picked at random from $\mathbb{G}$; the value of $x^d \in \mathbb{G}$ is then obtained as $(xr)^d \times (r^{-1})^d$. This countermeasure introduced in [5] requires two balanced group exponentiations, or a subtle but unpractical pre-computation trick that may be difficult to handle by the personalization process.

3   Our Algorithm

As in the previous section, $L_j = \sum_{i=j}^{t-1} k_i 2^{i-j}$ and $H_j = L_j + 1$. Let us consider Fig. 3 algorithm and suppose (R_0, R_1) contains $\rho(x^{L_{j+1}}, x^{H_{j+1}})$ at the beginning of some iteration for some $\rho \in \mathbb{G}$. Then, (R_0, R_1) will contain $\rho^2(x^{L_j}, x^{H_j})$ at the beginning of the next iteration. This remark leads to Fig. 4 algorithm.

Input: $x \in \mathbb{G}$, $k = \sum_{i=0}^{t-1} k_i 2^i \in \mathbb{N}$
Output: $x^k \in \mathbb{G}$

Pick a random $r \in \mathbb{G}$
$R_0 \leftarrow r$; $R_1 \leftarrow rx$; $R_2 \leftarrow r^{-1}$
for $j = t - 1$ **down to** 0 **do**
$\quad R_{\bar{k}_j} \leftarrow R_{\bar{k}_j} R_{k_j}$
$\quad R_{k_j} \leftarrow R_{k_j}^2$
$\quad R_2 \leftarrow R_2^2$
end for
return $R_2 R_0$

Fig. 4. Side-channel analysis resistant Montgomery ladder

As will be shown in the sequel, the more refined Fig. 5 algorithm will have to be considered as Fig. 4 algorithm fails to detect some fault attacks.

At initialization, the couple of registers (R_0, R_1) is multiplicatively blinded by a secret random element $r \in \mathbb{G}$. Throughout the computation, (R_0, R_1) is then instrinsically multiplicatively masked by the element $r^{2^{t-j}} \in \mathbb{G}$. The register R_2 is initialized with $r^{-1} \in \mathbb{G}$ and holds the compensative factor $r^{-2^{t-j}} \in \mathbb{G}$ such that $R_2(R_0, R_1)$ equals $(x^{L_j}, x^{H_j}) \in \mathbb{G}^2$. At the end of the computation, the actual multiplication $R_2 R_0$ hence evaluates to $x^k \in \mathbb{G}$.

3.1   Security Analysis

Some masking elements $r \in \mathbb{G}$ exhibit the undesirable property that $r^{2^j} = 1$ for some $j \in \mathbb{N}$. For such elements, (R_0, R_1) is permanently unmasked after j iterations.

Input: $x \in \mathbb{G}$, $k = \sum_{i=0}^{t-1} k_i 2^i \in \mathbb{N}$,
$\quad$ CKS$_{\text{ref}}$ the checksum of k.
Output: $x^k \in \mathbb{G}$

Pick a random $r \in \mathbb{G}$
$R_0 \leftarrow r$; $R_1 \leftarrow rx$; $R_2 \leftarrow r^{-1}$
init(CKS)
for $j = t - 1$ **down to** 0 **do**
$\quad R_{\bar{k}_j} \leftarrow R_{\bar{k}_j} R_{k_j}$
$\quad R_{k_j} \leftarrow R_{k_j}^2$
$\quad R_2 \leftarrow R_2^2$
$\quad$ update(CKS, k_j)
end for
$R_2 \leftarrow R_2 \oplus \text{CKS} \oplus \text{CKS}_{\text{ref}}$
return $R_2 R_0$

Fig. 5. Side-channel analysis and fault attacks resistant Montgomery ladder

Definition 1 (Weak mask). *Let* $\mathcal{W}_{\mathbb{G}} = \bigcup_{i \in \mathbb{N}} \left\{ x \in \mathbb{G} \mid x^{2^i} = 1 \right\}$. *Any element* $x \in \mathcal{W}_{\mathbb{G}}$ *is called a weak mask.*

Theorem 1 (Weak mask probability in finite abelian groups). *Let* $\mathbb{G}$ *be a finite abelian group with* $|\mathbb{G}| = \alpha 2^{\beta}$ *for some odd* α. *Let* $\Pr_{r \leftarrow \mathbb{G}} \{ r \in \mathcal{W}_{\mathbb{G}} \}$ *denote the probability that* r *be a weak mask when* r *is picked randomly uniformly from* $\mathbb{G}$. *We have*

$$\Pr_{r \leftarrow \mathbb{G}} \{ r \in \mathcal{W}_{\mathbb{G}} \} = \frac{1}{\alpha} .$$

Proof. See Appendix A.

In our context, the fraction $1/\alpha$ where α denotes the greatest odd factor of $|\mathbb{G}|$ is necessarily negligible. Otherwise, $|\mathbb{G}|$ would be smooth and the discrete logarithm in $\mathbb{G}$ would be efficiently solved by the Pohlig–Hellman algorithm [10].

Suppose $\beta = 100$ and $|\mathbb{G}| \simeq 2^{1024}$. Then, the probability of picking a weak mask is about $1/2^{924} < 10^{-278}$. This shows that weak masks never happen in practice.

Simple Side-Channel Analysis and Safe-Error Attacks. The square-and-multiply algorithm (Fig. 1) is sensitive to simple side-channel analysis. Indeed, it contains a conditional branching on the multiplication that directly depends on the secret exponent. Then, since the physical leakage of a square can be distinguished from that of a multiplication, the secret data can be easily retrieved from just one acquisition.

The square-and-multiply-always algorithm (Fig. 2) perfectly balances the former conditional branching by adding dummy multiplications. However, it introduces a specific weakness toward safe-error attacks that consist in carefully injecting a fault during the execution and checking whether it impacts on the result. In particular, the so-called M-safe-error attack consist in disturbing the multiplication. The value of the secret exponent can then be retrieved by distinguishing between required and dummy multiplications, corresponding to an exponent bit equal to 1 and 0, respectively.

Because of its high regularity, the Montgomery ladder algorithm (Fig. 3) is intrinsically resistant to simple side-channel attacks. It is also insensitive to safe-error attacks [8]. If a fault is injected at any time during the computation, the result is necessarily faulty. As it keeps the same structure, our algorithm (Fig. 4) clearly remains equivalent to Montgomery ladder in terms of simple side-channel analysis and fault attack resistance.

Differential Side-Channel Analysis. The intermediate variables are masked by r^{2^i} at each step i of the computation, and are hence statistically independant from the input and the output throughout the computation, so they cannot be exploited by the attacker.

Only those acquisitions for which r is a weak mask may be relevant to an attacker. In this case, the intermediate variables are unmasked after some steps of our algorithm. Clearly, the expected number of acquisitions to mount a differential side-channel attack against our algorithm grows inversely proportional with the probability that r be a weak mask. Since the probability of picking a weak mask is negligible, differential side-channel attacks are infeasible in practice.

Fault Attacks. The resistance of our algorithm against fault attacks is based on the relationship $R_2(R_0, R_1) = (x^\kappa, x^{\kappa+1})$ for some $\kappa \in \mathbb{N}$. If an error occurs on a temporary result or during one of the group operations at any time during the computation, the mutual coherence of R_0, R_1, and R_2 is definitively lost. As a consequence, the result of the last multiplication $R_2 R_0$ is just some perfect random number to an attacker that cannot be exploited as such, at least if we assume the input was not blinded with a weak mask. Again, as weak masks are extremely unlikely in practice, any such error will be caught by our countermeasure.

However, as in [11], Fig. 4 algorithm fails to thwart exponent or loop counter disturbance as it does preserve the former relationship. Such faults hence have to be handled by other techniques. As pointed out in [12], avoiding conditional branching is safer since modifying the result of a comparison or the value of a loop counter by tampering with the associated register is easy. On the contrary, in order to by-pass an instruction, the attacker would have to increment the program counter. Such a precise modification is hardly feasible in practice. For that reason, we propose combining the on-the-fly checksum computation of [11] with the infective computation technique of [12] (Fig. 5). Let $\gamma = \mathrm{CKS} \oplus \mathrm{CKS_{ref}}$ be the difference between the re-computed checksum CKS and the reference checksum value $\mathrm{CKS_{ref}}$. The most significant bits of R_2 are xored with γ before the last multiplication. Hence, the final result will be spoiled whenever $\gamma \neq 0$ i.e. whenever the exponent or the loop counter has been tampered with.

3.2   Efficiency Analysis

Time. Montgomery ladder (Fig. 3) requires t multiplications and t squarings. Our algorithm (Fig. 4) requires t more squarings for computing the compensative factor. The inversion and the two multiplications involved in the masking and unmasking process can be neglected with respect to the cost of the overall computation. Let M denote the cost of a multiplication. The cost of a squaring can be approximated to $0.8M$. Each step of our algorithm costs $2.6M$ compared to $1.8M$ for Montgomery ladder, that is a 44.44% time complexity increase.

Storage. Compared to Montgomery ladder, our algorithm requires one more register R_2 for the compensative factor, that is a 50% storage increase.

Note however that many cryptographic co-processors cannot store the result of some operations – as the modular multiplication or squaring – at the address of the operands. With such architectures, three registers for the standard Montgomery ladder and four registers for our algorithm are needed, corresponding to a 33% storage increase.

4   Conclusion

This paper presents an algorithm for computing exponentiations in finite abelian groups, especially relevant in the RSA and ECC setting, that is intrinsically resistant to all known simple and differential side-channel analysis and fault attacks, while requiring roughly at most 50% more time and storage compared to traditional balanced implementations.

Our countermeasure is especially suited when only the parameters needed for the computation itself are known, which is extremely valuable as additional parameters are rarely available to the cryptographic device. In particular, neither the group order nor the public exponent are required.

Acknowledgment

The authors would like to thank Jean Creignou and Hervé Chabanne for many helpful remarks on the preliminary version of this paper.

References

1. Kocher, P.C.: Timing Attacks on Implementations of Diffie-Hellman, RSA, DSS, and Other Systems. In: CRYPTO. Volume 1109 of Lecture Notes in Computer Science. (1996) 104–113
2. Boneh, D., DeMillo, R.A., Lipton, R.J.: On the Importance of Checking Cryptographic Protocols for Faults. Lecture Notes in Computer Science **1233** (1997) 37–51
3. Kocher, P., Jaffe, J., Jun, B.: Differential Power Analysis. Lecture Notes in Computer Science **1666** (1999) 388–397

4. Montgomery, P.L.: Speeding the Pollard and elliptic curve methods of factorization. Mathematics of Computation **48(177)** (January 1987) 243264

5. Coron, J.S.: Resistance Against Differential Power Analysis for Elliptic Curve Cryptosystems. In Ç.K. Koç, Paar, C., eds.: Cryptographic Hardware and Embedded Systems — CHES 2002. Volume 1717 of Lecture Notes in Computer Science. (1999) 292–302

6. Goubin, L.: A refined power analysis attack on elliptic curve cryptosystems. In Springer-Verlag, ed.: Public Key Cryptography PKC 2003. Volume 2567 of Lecture Notes in Computer Science. (2003) 199211

7. Dupuy, W., Kunz-Jacques, S.: Resistance of Randomized Projective Coordinates Against Power Analysis. In B.S. Kaliski Jr., c.K., Paar, C., eds.: Cryptographic Hardware and Embedded Systems — CHES 2005. Volume 3659 of Lecture Notes in Computer Science. (2005) 1–12

8. Joye, M., Yen, S.M.: The Montgomery Powering Ladder. In B.S. Kaliski Jr., c.K., Paar, C., eds.: Cryptographic Hardware and Embedded Systems — CHES 2002. Volume 2523 of Lecture Notes in Computer Science. (2002) 291–302

9. Trichina, E., Bellezza, A.: Implementation of elliptic curve cryptography with built-in counter measures against side channel attacks. In B.S. Kaliski Jr., c.K., Paar, C., eds.: Cryptographic Hardware and Embedded Systems — CHES 2002. Volume 2523 of Lecture Notes in Computer Science. (2002) 98–113

10. Pohlig, S.C., Hellman, M.E.: An improved algorithm for computing logarithms over $GF(p)$ and its cryptographic significance. IEEE Transactions on Information Theory **24** (1978) 106–110

11. Giraud, C.: Fault Resistant RSA Implementation. In Breveglieri, L., Koren, I., eds.: 2nd Workshop on Fault Diagnosis and Tolerance in Cryptography — FDTC 2005. (2005) 142–151

12. Ciet, M., Joye, M.: Practical Fault Countermeasures for Chinese Remaindering Based RSA. In Breveglieri, L., Koren, I., eds.: 2nd Workshop on Fault Diagnosis and Tolerance in Cryptography — FDTC 2005. (2005) 124–131

A   Proof of Theorem 1

Lemma 1 (Cauchy's Lemma). *Any finite group whose order is divisible by a prime number p contains an element of order p.*

Definition 2. *Let $\mathbb{G}$ be a finite abelian group and p be a prime number. Let $\mathbb{G}_p$ denote the subgroup of all elements of $\mathbb{G}$ whose order is a power of p. Any element $x \in \mathbb{G}_p$ is called a p-torsion element of $\mathbb{G}$.*

Lemma 2. *Let $\mathbb{G}$ be a finite abelian group. We have*

$$\mathbb{G} \cong \prod_{p \mid |\mathbb{G}|} \mathbb{G}_p \ .$$

Proof. Let $|\mathbb{G}| = \prod_{i=1}^{n} p_i^{\beta_i}$ where $p_{i,i \in \{1,\dots,n\}}$ are prime numbers.

Let us show that the homomorphism ψ defined as

$$\prod_{i=1}^{n} \mathbb{G}_{p_i} \xrightarrow{\psi} \mathbb{G}$$

$$(x_1, \ldots, x_n) \longmapsto \prod_{i=1}^{n} x_i$$

is an isomorphism. First, we show that ψ is a monomorphism.

Let x and y be in the abelian group $\mathbb{G}$. Let $|\langle x \rangle| = a$ be the order of x and $|\langle y \rangle| = b$ the order of y in $\mathbb{G}$. First, observe that if a and b are coprime, then $xy = 1 \Rightarrow x = y = 1$. This is a consequence of Bézout's identity. Since a and b are coprime, there exists integers u and v such that $au + bv = 1$. We have

$$xy = 1 \Rightarrow (xy)^{au} = 1 \tag{1}$$

and as $x^a = 1$, we have $(xy)^{au} = x^{au} y^{au} = y^{au}$. Then, since $y^b = 1$, we get

$$(xy)^{au} = y^{au} = y^{au} y^{bv} = y^{au+bv} = y . \tag{2}$$

From (1) and (2), we have $y = 1$. In the same way, we show $xy = 1 \Rightarrow x = 1$.

Now let us suppose that $\psi(x_1, \ldots, x_n) = \prod_{i=1}^{n} x_i = 1$. Clearly the order of x_1 and the order of $\prod_{i=2}^{n} x_i$ are coprime, and as we have shown above, $x_1 \times \prod_{i=2}^{n} x_i = 1 \Rightarrow x_1 = 1$ and $\prod_{i=2}^{n} x_i = 1$. In particular $x_1 = 1$. Then, by induction on the relation $\prod_{i=2}^{n} x_i = 1$, we get the expected result

$$\psi(x_1, \ldots, x_n) = \prod_{i=1}^{n} x_i = 1 \Rightarrow x_1 = \ldots = x_n = 1 .$$

Now let us show that ψ is an epimorphism.

For all $y \in \mathbb{G}$, $|\langle y \rangle|$ divides $|\mathbb{G}|$. Hence, $|\langle y \rangle| = \prod_{i=1}^{n} p_i^{\gamma_i}$ where $\gamma_i \leq \beta_i$ for all $i \in \{1, \ldots, n\}$. Let $u_i = \prod_{j \neq i} p_j^{\gamma_j}$ for $i \in \{1, \ldots, n\}$. Then, $y^{u_i} \in \mathbb{G}_{p_i}$ since $|\langle y^{u_i} \rangle| = p_i^{\gamma_i}$. Moreover, the $u_{i, i \in \{1, \ldots, n\}}$ are coprime as there exists no integer dividing all u_i. According to Bézout's identity, there exists $a_1, \ldots, a_n$ such that $\sum_{i=1}^{n} a_i u_i = 1$. Hence, for all $y \in \mathbb{G}$, $y = \prod_{i=1}^{n} x_i$ with $x_i = y^{u_i a_i} \in \mathbb{G}_{p_i}$. □

Lemma 3. *Let $\mathbb{G}$ be a group with $|\mathbb{G}| = \prod_{i=1}^{n} p_i^{\beta_i}$ where $p_{i, i=1 \ldots n}$ are prime numbers. Then, $|\mathbb{G}_{p_i}| = p_i^{\beta_i}$.*

Proof. Necessarily, $|\mathbb{G}_{p_i}|$ is a power of p_i, say $p_i^{\gamma_i}$. Indeed, from Cauchy's Lemma, if $|\mathbb{G}_{p_i}|$ were divisible by some prime number $p \neq p_i$, it would contain an element of order p, which is contradictory with the definition of $\mathbb{G}_{p_i}$. Then, since $\mathbb{G} \cong \prod_{p \mid |\mathbb{G}|} \mathbb{G}_p$, we have $\prod_i p_i^{\beta_i} = \prod_i p_i^{\gamma_i}$, so $\gamma_i = \beta_i$ for all i. □

We have $\mathcal{W}_{\mathbb{G}} = \mathbb{G}_2$ and, from lemma 3, $|\mathbb{G}_2| = 2^{\beta}$. Finally,

$$\Pr_{r \leftarrow \mathbb{G}} \{r \in \mathcal{W}_{\mathbb{G}}\} = \frac{|\mathcal{W}_{\mathbb{G}}|}{|\mathbb{G}|} = \frac{1}{\alpha} .$$

Incorporating Error Detection in an RSA Architecture

L. Breveglieri[1], I. Koren[2], P. Maistri[1], and M. Ravasio[3]

[1] Department of Electronics and Information Technology, Politecnico di Milano,
Milano, Italy
{brevegli, maistri}@elet.polimi.it
[2] Department of Electrical and Computer Engineering, University of Massachusetts,
Amherst, MA, USA
koren@ecs.umass.edu
[3] STMicroelectronics, Agrate Brianza, Milano, Italy
moris.ravasio@st.com

Abstract. Most successful attacks against hardware implementations of cryptographic systems make use of side-channel information leakage. Recently, some attacks have been proposed against various cryptosystems, which exploit deliberate error injection during the computation process. Several error detection schemes have been proposed in order to counteract these attacks. In this paper, we add a residue-based error detection scheme to an RSA architecture and evaluate the area and latency overheads with respect to the basic architecture.

1 Introduction

Hardware implementations of cryptographic systems have become very popular, in order to satisfy the latest demands in terms of performance and tamper resistance. The most widely adopted public-key algorithm is currently the RSA cryptosystem (proposed by Rivest, Shamir and Adleman) that relies on the difficulty in factorizing large integers.

In the past, most attacks were aimed at solving the factorization problem. However, RSA uses currently 1024-bit operands and factorization of such large integers is unaffordable with current computational power. An alternative way to attack a cipher is through attempts to break a specific implementation by finding a correlation between physical information leakage and the secret keys (e.g., simple and differential power analysis, timing attacks). Recently, new side channel attacks have been proposed. In [4], the authors showed how deliberate hardware faults can be exploited to break a cryptographic algorithm and retrieve the key. They have addressed public-key schemes in general and provided examples, including a description of an attack against RSA. Attacks against RSA were later refined in [1] where the authors showed how a single faulty ciphertext can be used to easily factor the RSA modulus, thus breaking the cryptosystem. It should be pointed out that RSA implementations based on the Chinese Remainder Theorem (CRT) can be broken more easily than a basic implementation [2,4]. Other attacks against CRT-RSA appear in [13] and [14].

L. Breveglieri et al. (Eds.): FDTC 2006, LNCS 4236, pp. 71–79, 2006.

Fault-based attacks are highly effective, since few carefully localized errors can break the cipher. While attacking regular RSA requires the ability to inject single-bit errors, it must be noted that the only requirement to successfully break CRT-RSA is that *only one* of the two sub-signatures is corrupted. Hence, if the attacker can inject any error into one sub-exponentiation and have a result back, he can break the cryptosystem. This implies that the error model could be as general as possible.

Although they may have been considered to be of only theoretical value, some initial experiments have shown that such attacks are possible in practice. Therefore, several countermeasures were proposed to foil the attacks. In 1999, Shamir registered a patent [10] where a multiplicative masking is used against timing and fault attacks. In 2000, Walter [12] has suggested to use residue codes to protect modular arithmetic operations. The residue code can help detect both transient and permanent faults. The error coverage depends on the value of the base modulus that is chosen: higher values of the base modulus allow higher detection rates. The overhead of the residue code is approximately the cost of an extra digit in the operands. In general, this overhead can be in terms of area if an extra element is included in each functional unit or in terms of time when the same functional unit is reused. In 2004, Gueron [5] described an extended version of the modular exponentiation and Montgomery multiplication algorithms by using a residue code in multi-digit algorithms. If the base modulus is chosen to be the maximum value of a digit (i.e., $2^d - 1$, where d is the digit size in bits), generation is very simple [8,12].

In this paper, we present a reasonably simple architecture for computing the RSA with protection against injected faults using residue codes. Residue codes were chosen since they can protect arithmetic operations quite efficiently. Moreover, if a specific fault pattern is likely to occur, a sufficiently large base modulus can be chosen in order to provide good coverage. We adapt the suggestion made by Walter [12] to a specific architecture and evaluate the benefits and overheads. We also show how to further improve this specific solution.

In Section 2 we briefly describe the RSA cryptosystem and our reference architecture. In Section 3 we present the detection mechanism by means of residue codes. Section 4 provides the details of our implementation of a circuit with error detection capabilities, detailing the implementation choices. Finally, Section 5 concludes the paper.

2   The RSA Cryptosystem

The RSA cryptosystem [9] is based on few essential parameters, namely, the public moduli $N = p \cdot q$, where p and q are two large primes, each $n/2$ bits long; d, the private exponent key; and e, the public exponent key, selected such that $e \cdot d = 1 \mod (p-1)(q-1)$. Encryption of a message m is done by computing $m^e \mod N$. Decryption is computed by another exponentiation, namely $(m^e)^d \mod N$. The most critical operation is therefore the modular exponentiation. A large number of multiplications is needed to perform exponentiation and quite often, a simple Square-and-Multiply algorithm is used. Various exponentiation algorithms are described in [7]. Most implementations of exponentiation use the modified Montgomery multiplication algorithm (depicted in Figure 1), since it avoids the use of expensive trial divisions and avoids conditional branches which might benefit side channel attacks at the cost of few additional iterations, while maintaining the correctness of the algorithm [11]. Many different architec-

---

Input: $X = (0\ 0\ X_n \cdots X_1 X_0)$
$Y = (Y_n \cdots Y_1 Y_0)$
$M = (M_{n-1} \cdots M_1 M_0)$
Output: $X \cdot Y \cdot 2^{-(n+2)} \bmod M$

---

1. $U \leftarrow 0$
2. for i from 0 to $(n+2)$ do
    a   if $(U_0 = 1)$ then $U = U + M$
    b $U = (U/2) + X_i Y$
3. return U

Fig. 1. The modified Montgomery Multiplication, radix-2 [6]

tures have been proposed, differing mostly in some minor modifications to the Montgomery algorithm and in the digit size. The designer can thus obtain the desired trade-off between area and latency.

Our selected architecture was inspired by the design presented in [6]. Our solution differs from the original design mainly in the absence of the Z-processor, i.e., the squaring functional unit; this modification has also been suggested by the authors of [6]. The basic implementation includes a core (consisting of a *control unit* and a *Processing Element* (PE)), an internal memory and a bridge. The architecture is highly parameterized and it can therefore support future operand sizes. A small area is achieved by using a serial-digit approach. The exponentiation is computed by using the Square-and-Multiply algorithm; each multiplication scans the multiplier one bit at a time, and computes the result by using the Double-and-Add algorithm. Finally, each addition is performed by computing the result one digit at a time.

The PE is able to perform the basic required operations (addition, subtraction and addition with extra shifting) on the n-bit operands by repeated steps. The word size of the computational core is only 25% of the memory word size, which is in turn considerably smaller than the size of the modulus N. This allows to reduce the PE critical path and achieve higher frequencies. Accessing the memory implies a certain latency, due to the signal setup time and the register layers required to obtain stable values at the PE inputs. However, since the PE word size is 25% of the memory word size, producing a single result requires 4 clock cycles to fetch the next memory read. This is done at each iteration except the last one, when the PE is processing the last word.

3   Online Detection

In this section, we describe our detection scheme for errors injected during an RSA operation. The underlying principle is associating check bits to the data we are processing. If we are able to maintain the relationship between the data and the corresponding check bits throughout the entire process, the final result and the associated check bits should still satisfy the same relationship. This can be accomplished by propagating the check bits according to a specified set of prediction rules. When the data is processed by a specific functional unit, the corresponding check bits are processed in parallel using the associated prediction rule in order to preserve the relationship. As an example, consider a parity bit associated with a data word. When computing the exclusive OR of two different words, we can predict the parity bit of the result by XOR'ing the parity bits of the operands.

The code chosen for error detection must be simple. First of all, its generation and propagation overheads should be negligible relative to the computation of the main algorithm. Moreover, the need for prediction does not allow the use of complex codes, which may be very efficient in detecting faults but will be very expensive when implementing the various prediction circuits. The overhead of the error detection code should always be compared to brute force duplication which is the simplest way to detect errors. If detecting errors using codes is cheaper than duplication, then it is a viable solution.

To make the prediction rules as simple as possible, the code must be compatible with the operations performed on the data. Since RSA is based on modular integer arithmetic, residue codes are a natural choice. From the theory on modular arithmetic we know that the residue of the sum is the sum of the residues, possibly reduced once more:

$$(X + Y) \bmod R = ((X \bmod R) + (Y \bmod R)) \bmod R \qquad (1)$$

where X and Y are two operands and R is the base modulus. For instance, take $X = 8$, $Y = 13$ and $R = 3$: $8 \bmod 3 = 2$, $13 \bmod 3 = 1$, $8 + 13 = 21$ and $21 \bmod 3 = 0$, and finally $(2) + 1 \bmod 3 = 3 \bmod 3 = 0$. A similar rule holds for subtraction and multiplication. However, since all the high-level operations are implemented in terms of simple additions, this is the only prediction rule employed in our system.

The main issue is that we have to deal with two different moduli at the same time: the modulus of the residue code, usually smaller than the word size, and the modulus used by the RSA, which in contrast, is very large. When performing a reduction of the result, the check bits have to also be modified accordingly. Extending the algorithm with residue codes is straightforward, thanks to the properties of modular arithmetic, but there are several issues that must be considered: the residue code may require an additional reduction as shown in Equation (1), and the required division by 2. The former issue is addressed by correcting the residue if it overflows the boundaries of its domain. No information is lost, since the residue is stored in a larger data register. Regarding the latter issue, the right shift is computed in the Montgomery multiplication only after we are sure that the operand is even, by adding the modulus only to odd inputs (see algorithm in Figure 1, instruction 2.a). However, nothing can be said about the value of the residue. The residue of an even (odd) value can be either odd or even; therefore, when an odd residue must be right shifted, the (odd) residue base must be added to provide a congruent even residue value before dividing by 2.

4   Implementation

In this section we present our implementation of an RSA architecture with error detection capabilities, discuss the differences from the basic architecture and estimate the resulting overheads in terms of area and latency.

When incorporating an error detection code in the architecture, there are three new components to be considered:

1. A code generator: the check bits must be first generated from the initial raw data, possibly using a dedicated unit;
2. A set of prediction rules, needed to propagate the check bits through any operation performed in the encryption process;
3. A code validator: at the end of the encryption, the check bits must be verified against the computed data.

The code generation is obtained by using a dedicated functional unit, which is situated between the input interface and the memory. While operands are loaded into memory one word at a time, the residue generator computes and accumulates the residue into an internal register. When an additional word is loaded into memory, the partial residue value is updated. Upon deactivation of the memory write signal, the final residue value is written into the next memory word.

The check bits generated from a single word depend on the base modulus: choosing a modulus of the form $2^h - 1$ allows to compute the check bits by splitting each word into h-bit-long nibbles and adding them together. In our implementation, the size of the residue base modulus is chosen as 1/8 of the memory word size, i.e., half the PE word size. A tree of Carry-Save Adders (CSAs) is used to reduce the 9 input nibbles (8 coming from the data word, and the current value stored in the internal register) down to a single pair (Carry, Sum). However, any other size can be chosen: smaller values will give deeper trees, while larger values will require fewer steps. The size of the processing element should be considered as the upper bound, since the residue base must fit within the adder. Our choice was the largest divisor that fits the PE size, allowing a simpler design.

Although the carry output of each CSA is shifted with respect to the sum output by one bit position, the values are implicitly reduced by routing the most significant bit into the least significant position. For instance, if the size of the residue code is r, the sum output is $(s_{r-1} \ldots s_0)$, while the carry output is

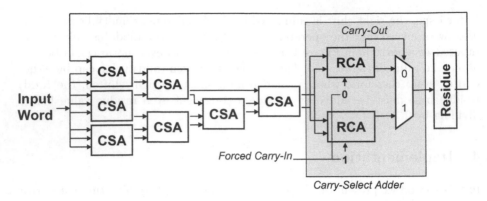

Fig. 2. Residue generation unit, with residue size being 1/8 of memory word size

$(c_r c_{r-1} \ldots c_1 0)$. The residue of the carry output can be computed in the same way (one more time) by splitting the carry into a least significant word and a single most significant bit and adding them together. Since the least significant bit of the carry vector is null, adding the most significant bit is just a simple rerouting.

The final residue generation, i.e., the summation of the carry and sum vectors is computed by using a Carry-Select Adder. In principle, the final addition might result in an $r + 1$-bit-long vector. Hence, two additions are computed in parallel, forcing the carry-in to 0 or 1, respectively. Finally, the carry out of the adder with null carry-in is used to select the proper result to be stored in the internal register. Figure 2 illustrates the overall architecture of the residue generation unit. The CSA layer allows to shrink the sum of 9 operands down to only 2 addends with a delay of only a few gates. On the other hand, the twin ripple-carry adders allow to obtain a value in the residue domain within the PE delay.

The code prediction is performed within each single operation, since the rule often matches the operation itself: the residue of an addition, for instance, is the sum of the input residues. Therefore, the PE can also be used for residue calculation after the main operation is completed. This is a straightforward application of Equation (1). This simple rule is integrated into the existing architecture exploiting the pipelining in order to minimize the latency overhead. When all the words are fetched into the PE, prefetching continues to load both residue codes. Control signals are set up so that the residue prediction is an atomic operation, with no impact on or from other operations (carries, overflows, etc.). Input residues are ready as soon as the PE finishes processing the last word. In addition, the residue fits the PE size since it is smaller (in our implementation, it is half the PE word size), therefore the operation can be completed in a single clock cycle. Using only few additional controls, the residue prediction can be achieved with almost no increase in the circuit area and with a single added clock cycle to the overall latency of each operation. If we consider that each operation requires 4 clock cycles per word and any operand is made of several words, the overhead for residue prediction becomes negligible. For example, in our reference implementation we have a 128-bit-word memory module, a 32-bit PE and an operand size that starts from 768 bits. In this case, the overhead is only 3.7%. With longer operands, the overheads become significantly smaller.

Finally, the resulting residue must be validated against the computed data. This validation does not have to be scheduled immediately. It is possible to delay the validation to a later time, for instance before reading the result from the memory. This is possible since any occurring error in the data does not affect the check bits during computation; on the other hand, local generation of the check bits (i.e., just before any operation) would force to schedule a code validation checkpoint after each operation, in order to avoid residue generation from corrupted data. Our solution follows the former approach. In particular, an error would not be detected at an immediate checkpoint only if the corrupted value had the same check bits as the correct data. This implies that the detection coverage is inversely proportional to the size of the check modulus which can be chosen accordingly. It should be clear that such a fault will not be detected even afterward.

In our implementation, the memory read policy is changed. In the basic architecture, each memory word had to be individually read, by setting up the read address properly and issuing the read command. In the error detecting version, only the initial address must be submitted. Subsequent memory reads are automatically fetched, while an additional buffer intercepts the data coming from the memory and computes the final residue on-the-fly. Finally, the actual check bits are compared with the predicted check bits, which are stored in the last position. If the two match and no errors are detected, then the read process is repeated and the output is enabled, allowing for external reads. Reissuing the read command may seem a waste of time, but the architecture was developed with area constrained implementation as a goal. Using a buffer to store the data when it

Table 1. Synthesis results – Area does *not* include any memory module

Version	Area (GE)	Latency (ns)
Basic	11, 400	4.7
Error Detecting	13, 400	4.7

Table 2. Area and latency overheads

Key Length (bits)	Global Overheads		
	Area	Memory	Latency
768	+17.8%	+14.3%	+3.7%
1024	+17.8%	+11.1%	+2.9%
1536	+17.8%	+7.7%	+2.0%
2048	+17.8%	+5.9%	+1.5%

is read from memory would have resulted in a large area overhead, while the few additional clock cycles are negligible with respect to the complete process.

The check bits validation unit makes reuse of the residue generation unit described above. In principle, a new residue generator could be implemented. However, the area overhead (an additional increase of 10.3%) would not be compensated by a significant reduction in the delay. Both architectures, in fact, were able to run at the target frequency of 200 MHz. The latency overheads were obtained by running several simulations in ModelSim with realistic data, while the area figures were obtained by synthesizing both designs with Design Compiler by Synopsys with STM $0.18\mu m$ High-Speed libraries.

5 Conclusions

One of the most effective techniques for attacking a cryptosystem is through deliberate error injection during computation. The faulty results can be used by attackers to retrieve the secret keys after a few attempts. In this paper, we extend an RSA architecture to include error detection capabilities based on the residue code. Our design incurs a 17.8% overhead in circuit area and only small latency and memory overheads, which become even smaller with longer keys.

The expected fault coverage, based on our previous experience with error detecting codes and on some simulations, depends on the level of redundancy, i.e., the size of the residue base modulus. After injecting an error, the data and the corresponding check bits become uncorrelated: the error is not detected if and only if the check bits match the data by chance. The probability of this event occurring, when $2^h - 1$ is the residue base modulus, is $(2^h - 1)^{-1} \approx 2^{-h}$.

References

1. R. Anderson and M. Kuhn, "Low Cost Attacks on Tamper Resistant Devices," *Proc. of the International Workshop on Security Protocols*, Lecture Notes in Computer Science, Springer-Verlag, 1997.
2. C. Aumüller, P. Bier, W. Fischer, P. Hofreiter, J.-P. Seifert, "Fault Attacks on RSA with CRT: Concrete Results and Practical Countermeasures," Cryptographic Hardware and Embedded Systems - CHES 2002, *Lecture Notes in Computer Science*, Vol. 2523, pp. 260-275, Springer-Verlag, 2003.
3. E. Biham, A. Shamir, "Differential Fault Analysis of Secret Key Cryptosystems," Technical Report, Technion - Computer Science Department, 1997.
4. D. Boneh, R. DeMillo, R. Lipton, "On the Importance of Eliminating Errors in Cryptographic Computations," *Journal of Cryptology*, vol. 14, pp. 101-119, 2001.
5. S. Gueron, "Fault Detection Mechanism for Smartcards Performing Modular Exponentiation," *Workshop on Fault Diagnosis and Tolerance in Cryptography 2004*, Supplemental Volume of the 2004 Intern. Conf. on Dependable Systems and Networks, pp. 368-372, 2004.
6. A. Mazzeo, L. Romano, G.P. Saggese, N. Mazzocca, "FPGA-based implementation of a serial RSA processor," *Design, Automation and Test in Europe Conference and Exhibition '03*, pp. 582 - 587, 2003.
7. A. Menezes, P. van Oorschot, S. Vanstone, *Handbook of Applied Cryptography*, CRC Press, 1996.
8. B. Parhami and A. Avizienis, "Design of Fault-Tolerant Associative Processors," ISCA, pp. 141-145, 1973.
9. R. L. Rivest, A. Shamir and L. Adleman, "A method for obtaining digital signatures and public-key cryptosystems," *Communications of the ACM*, Vol. 21, Issue 2, pp. 120–126, ACM Press, 1978.
10. A. Shamir, "Method and Apparatus for Protecting Public Key Schemes from Timing and Fault Attacks," US Patent 5991415, 1999.

11. C. Walter, "Montgomery's Multiplication Technique: How to Make It Smaller and Faster", Cryptographic Hardware and Embedded Systems, First International Workshop, CHES'99, Proceedings. Lecture Notes in Computer Science, Vol. 1717, pp. 80-93, 1999.
12. C. Walter, "Data Integrity in Hardware for Modular Arithmetic," Workshop on Cryptographic Hardware and Embedded Systems (CHES), Lecture Notes in Computer Science, Vol. 1965, pp. 204-215, 2000.
13. S.-M. Yen, S. Moon, J.-C. Ha, "Hardware Fault Attack on RSA with CRT Revisited," *Information Security and Cryptology - ICISC '02*, Lecture Notes in Computer Science, Vol. 2587, pp. 374-388, 2002.
14. S.-M. Yen, S. Moon, J.-C. Ha, "Permanent Fault Attack on the Parameters of RSA with CRT," Lecture Notes in Computer Science, Vol. 2727, pp. 285-296, 2003.

Data and Computational Fault Detection Mechanism for Devices That Perform Modular Exponentiation

Shay Gueron[1,2]

[1] Applied Security Research Group
The Center for Computational Mathematics and Scientific Computation,
University of Haifa, Haifa 31905, Israel
[2] Intel Corporation, IDC, Israel
shay@math.haifa.ac.il

Abstract. Fault attacks have become an efficient methodology for extracting secrets stored in embedded devices, and proper countermeasures against such attacks are nowadays considered necessary. This paper describes a simple method for foiling transient fault attacks on devices that perform modular exponentiation with a secret exponent. In the considered scenario, acknowledging an error only at the end of the computations leaks out secret information, and should be avoided. To tackle this difficulty, we propose a scheme that checks, independently, each step (i.e., multiplication/squaring) of the exponentiation algorithm, and aborts the procedure as soon as an error is detected, without completing the computation.

Keywords: Fault attacks, safe errors, countermeasures, RSA, embedded devices, smartcards.

1 Introduction

Intentional faults induction on embedded devices (e.g., smartcards) in order to extract their secrets is an effective type of active attack that has already become a serious threat on such devices. In this paper, we concentrate on fault attacks on devices that implement RSA signature schemes and perform modular exponentiation with a secret exponent. Modular exponentiation algorithms are known to be vulnerable to fault attacks and various countermeasures have been considered in this context (see e.g., [1, 3, 4, 8, 9] and the references therein). Protection against permanent damage can be achieved by running test vectors before the actually computations commence, but this is obviously insufficient if the attacker can induce transient faults on the device at selected time points during the exponentiation process. A common method for countering transient faults is to perform the verification step internally, and release the signature only if it is successfully verified. This solution is adequate in many situations, carries relatively low performance penalty, but there are some scenarios where it is insufficient Safe-error attacks are a recent fault attack strategy [10] that

L. Breveglieri et al. (Eds.): FDTC 2006, LNCS 4236, pp. 80–87, 2006.
© Springer-Verlag Berlin Heidelberg 2006

exploits the fact that some algorithms use differently (or do not use) intermediate results according to the bits of the secret key that is under attack. For
modular exponentiation, this leads to the following attack strategy: inject faults
to induce an error during some modular multiplication step, and check if the
resulting signature is validated. This test can reveal the value of the particular
bit of the secret exponent. An attacker who can induce faults during separate
modular multiplication steps (which is conceivable because these are lengthy
operations), can repeat the experiment and extract a sufficient number of bits
from the secret exponent that allows factorization of the modulus. An example
for an algorithm where such strategy works is the square-and-always-multiply
exponentiation, where dummy modular multiplications are added to the inner
loop of the exponentiation algorithm, in order to resist timing attacks. Here, for
each bit of the secret exponent D, the device computes one modular square and
one modular multiplication, but the result is used only if that bit equals 1. The
attacker tracks the time points where separate modular multiplications/squares
steps begin (without necessarily being able to distinguish between them), and
induces errors. Faults that do not lead to a false/rejected signature must have
occurred during a dummy operation (i.e., when the exponent bit was 0). Another safe-error attack scenario occurs when the attacker induces some glitch
that forces a particular bit of the secret exponent to be 0. In this case, a valid
signature implies that the results remains correct even with the forced-to-0 bit,
and indicates that the original value of affected bit was 0. An erroneous signature implies that the bit was 1. The conclusion is that checking the signature
before releasing it is insufficient against some fault attacks scenarios because the
unavoidable acknowledgement of an error leaks information that the attacker
can use. We describe here a simple method to detect computational errors as
they occur, which can be used to mitigate safe-error and other types of fault
attacks.

2   Data-and-Compute Error Detection Method

In general, we assume here that the attacker can induce faults that cause either
a) "data errors" - modifying the value(s) of some operand(s) stored in memory,
or b) "computational error" - damaging the computed result of some operation.
If the operands are "stationary" for sufficiently long time, and the operations
are sufficient long, it is reasonable to assume that the attacker can damage them
without extremely precise timing. Further, inducing random faults is sufficient,
as long as they produce some errors. Safe-error attacks are possible whenever
the correctness of the signature (i.e., the final result) can be related to a particular bit of the secret exponent. To avoid such situations, we propose a "Data-
and-Compute" error detection approach: a simple mechanism that allows for
independent checks of each step of the exponentiation algorithm, and for abort-
ing the procedure as soon as an error is detected. The Data-and-Compute error

82   S. Gueron

detection relies on enhancing the data structure that is used for all operands
in the system: each operand K includes some additional structure, denoted K'
= Stamp (K), and this enhanced data structure is denoted K ‖ K'. Stamp (K)
should have the following properties: a) Stamp (K) is short, compared with
the bit-length of K b) Stamp (K) can be easily computed c) There is a small
probability that a random change in K results in a value that has the same
Stamp, d) If C = (A op B) for any operation (op) that is used in the procedure, it
is possible (and easy) to predict the value of Stamp (C) from the values of Stamp
(A) and Stamp (B). The enhanced data structure K‖K' is used for validating the
integrity of the operands and the correctness of the operation, therefore providing
a Data-and-Compute error detection mechanism that handles both data errors
and computational errors. An schematic illustration is given in Fig. 1.

Data-and-Compute Error Detection Method
input: A ‖ A', B ‖ B'
output: C ‖ C' (where C = A op B and op is the operation that is carried out

1. Detect data errors
    b. T = Stamp (A) If T ≠ A' error is detected;
    b. T = Stamp (B) If T ≠ B' error is detected;

2. Detect computational operation errors
    a. Compute T = Predicted Stamp (C);
    b. Compute C = A op B;
    c. Compute C' = Stamp (C);
    d. if If T ≠ R error is detected;

If errors were detected - abort; Return C ‖ C';

Fig. 1. Checking the operation (A op B), using the enhanced data structure. The
integrity of the inputs is verified by computing Stamp (A) and comparing it to A' (the
same is performed for B). The correctness of the computation is verified by predicting
Stamp (C) and comparing it to the computed C' after C = (A op B) is computed. If
the process is successful, the output is C ‖ C', which completes the Data-and-Compute
loop.

Example 1. Consider a system that performs a circular shift operation, and define the Stamp to be the parity bit of the operands. The enhanced data structure
includes one additional parity bit, which detects any single bit data error. Further, single bit computational errors can be detected because Stamp prediction
is possible: the parity bit of the circular shift of A equals to the parity bit of
A. Consequently, this structure supports a Data-and-Compute single bit error
detection.

3   The Arithmetic Stamp

The practical question in our context is how to find a suitable Stamp that can be used in a system that performs modular exponentiation. To this end we define the Arithmetic Stamp as follows:

Definition 1. *The Arithmetic Stamp of a positive integer X is $X' = Stamp\ (X)$ $= ((X-1)\ mod\ F) + 1$, where F is some chosen positive integer. Hereafter, we use $F = 2^t - 1$ for some integer value t.*

For example, $t=32$ is the natural choice for a system that use 32 bits words. The probability that a random fault induced on the operand A would leave Stamp (A) unchanged, is small enough to make fault attacks that rely on such occurrence impractical. The following property shows why the arithmetic stamp is practical.

Remark 1. Computing $X' = Stamp\ (X)$: Let $X = [X(L-1), .., X1, X0]$ be a positive integer written in base F. X consists of L $(L < F)$ "digits" which are words having of t bits (altogether X has $L.t$ bits). These digits are denoted by Xi, $i = 0$ to $L-1$ where $X0$ is the least significant word of X. Stamp (X) can be computed by adding Xi into a two-words long accumulator, and applying two final reduction steps in the end. The algorithm is illustrated in Figure 2.

---

input: $X = [X(L-1), .., X1, X0]$
output: $X' = Stamp\ (X) = ((X-1)\ mod\ F) + 1$

Computation:
   1. S=X0;
   2. for i from 1 to L-1 do
   3.   S = S+Xi;
   4. end;
   5. S = lsw(S)+ msw(S);
   6. S = lsw(S)+ msw(S);
   7. Return S;

Fig. 2. An algorithm for computing the Arithmetic Stamp of an L words positive integer X. A two words accumulator (S) is initialized to S=X0. The subsequent L-1 words (Xi) are added to S, successively. Assuming L ¡ F (reasonable in any practical context), the cumulative sum is bounded by F2 and can therefore be stored in the two words accumulator. At the end of the L steps, the result stored in S needs to be reduced to in order to produce X'. This is done by adding, twice, the most significant word to the least significant word of S (steps 3 and 4). In general, one reduction step is insufficient: lsw(S)+ msw(S) can exceed F in Step 3. The final (reduced) output S satisfies S ? F. The computations are accomplished within L+2 steps.

Example 2. Computing X' for X = 7922815967346575001034476747I, where F = $2^{32} - 1$. In binary representation X has L=3 words of length t=32 bits (separated by a "//" notation) X= [X2 X1 X0]= 11111111111111111111111101100101 // 11111111111111111111111111001001 // 11111111111111111111111111101111.
Computing X'=Stamp (X) within L+2 = 4 cycles is carried out as follows:
S= X0=11111111111111111111111111101111 (S has 32 bits)
S = X1+X0 = 111111111111111111111111110111000 (S has 33 bits)
S = X2+S = 1011111111111111111111111100011101 (S has 34 bits)
S = lsw(S) + msw(S) = 11111111111111111111111100011111 (S has 32 bits)
S = lsw(S) + msw(S) = 11111111111111111111111100011111 (S has 32 bits)
Stamp (X) = X' = S.
S = 4294967071 (decimal representation);
it can be verified that S = ((X-1)) mod F + 1 (=X').

Remark 2. Computing the Arithmetic Stamp of an L words value requires L+2 successive additions of t bits words. These can be performed by L+2 instructions using a processor that operates on t-bit words, which is a relatively low cost compared with that of (modular) multiplication.

Remark 3. Dedicated circuitry computing the Arithmetic Stamp can perform the reduction steps (3 & 4 above) after each addition, use a one-word accumulator, and obtain reduced results at the end of the loop.

Remark 4. In general, Stamp (A) $\neq$ A mod F. These quantities differ for values of A which are divisible by F, where Stamp (A) = F and A mod F = 0.

4   Computing the Arithmetic Step of a Non-reduced Montgomery Multiplications

Here we show how to predict the Arithmetic Stamp of a Non-reduced Montgomery multiplication (NRMM) as a function of the Arithmetic Stamps of its inputs. NRMM is defined for two s-bits positive integers A and B, n-bits odd modulus N, where s $\geq$ n, and equals

$$NRMM (A, B, N, s) = (AB + Y N) / 2^s, \text{ where } Y = \text{-}ABN^{-1} \bmod 2^s.$$

The NRMM operation is very helpful for modular exponentiation. We refer the reader to the Appendix where, it is shown that NRMM is the only operation required for computing the modular exponents AX mod N where A is an n-bits positive integer, N is an n-bits odd modulus, X is a positive integer, and s = n+2.

The Arithmetic Stamp of NRMM (A, B, N, s) can be computed by the following identity:

$$((A \ B + Y \ N) / 2^s)' = (\ (A' \ B' + Y' \ N')' \ (2^{-s})')' \qquad (*)$$

Example 3. N = 8000082D80216E1B, A = 80002407, B = 8000082D8020EE1B
(in hexadecimal representation) n = 64 (the bit length of N), s= n+2 = 66.
The enhanced data structure includes N' = 217649, Z = $(2^{-s})'$ = 40000000, A'
= 80002407, B' = 20F649. The task: Check the correctness of the result T =
NRMM (A, B, N, s) = 1D8921075EC05D7A, and Y = EC48F921E8425BF9.
Computations: T' = 7C497E81, Y' = D48B551B, Q1 = (A' B')' = 23997B28,
Q2 = (Y' N')' = CD8C7EDD, Q3 = (Q1 + Q2)' = F125FA05, Q4 = (Q3 Z)'
= 7C497E81. Compare Q4 to T'. (as Q4=T'= 7C497E81, the result is verified.)

5   Protecting the Full Modular Exponentiation Procedure

This section extends the method that is already described in [5]. Algorithm 1
provided in the Appendix illustrates a modular exponentiation procedure that
uses only NRMM operations. This procedure can be protected against fault attacks by using the Data-and-Compute error detection principle with an enhanced
data structure that includes the Arithmetic Stamp, and by using identity (*) for
verifying each one of the intermediate NRMM results. Since Algorithm 1 uses
a fixed multiplicand (B) in all multiplication steps, B' is computed only once
at the beginning of the exponentiation. Note also that in a typical application,
N, F and s are fixed. Therefore, N', F' and Z = $(2^{-s})'$ = 2^{-s} mod F can be
pre-computed.

6   Conclusion

We have described a simple method that provides protection against different
types of fault attacks, including attacks based on safe-errors, where merely acknowledging a detected error at the end of the computations leaks out secret
information. Of course, this method is only one of several available countermeasures that can provide such protection, and the appropriate choice should be
made according to the actual implementation that is at hand. The underlying
idea is a variation of a classical method for checking arithmetic computations
(probabilistically): repeat the computations modulo some U, and compare with
the result modulo U to the predicted value. As a method for correcting computational error in computer systems it is described, for example, in [2]. This method
is also described in [7] (for +,-,* in base 10, using the modulus 9), and reported
to be a much earlier common practice; I personally learned this method (in base
10) in my childhood, from my late father, to whom I dedicate this paper).
   In this paper, we considered the inputs as if they are written in base 2^t and
take the modulus F= 2^t-1, where a practical choice for a real implementation
would be t=32. Note that the Arithmetic Stamp is not identical to the residue
modulo F. Different exponentiation algorithms can be protected in a similar
way. One example is the case where the classical Montgomery multiplication
algorithm is used .Here, s=n and a final reduction step (if S > N then S = S
-N) is required. In such case, the Arithmetic Stamp prediction (*) can be easily
changed to account for the conditional subtraction.

References

1. C. Aumüller, P. Bier, W. Fischer, P. Hofreiter, and J.P. Seifert, "Fault attacks on RSA with CRT: Concrete Results and Practical Countermeasures", CHES 2002, Lecture Notes in Computer Science, 2523, Springer-Verlag, 260-275 (2002).
2. A. Avizienis, "Arithmetic Algorithms for Error-Coded Operands," IEEE Trans. Comp. Vol. C-22, 567-572 (1973).
3. D. Boneh, R. A. De Millo, and R. J. Lipton, "On the Importance of Eliminating Errors in Cryptographic Computations," Journal of Cryptology, vol. 14, 101-119 (2001).
4. C. Giraud and H. Thiebeauld, "A Survey on Fault Attacks," Smart Card Research and Advanced Applications VI -CARDIS 2004, in J.-J.Quisquater, P. Paradinas, Y. Deswarte, and A. E. Kalam, Eds. Kluwer Academic Publishers, 159-176 (2004).
5. S. Gueron, Fault Detection Mechanism for Smartcards Performing Modular Exponentiation, Workshop on Fault Diagnosis and Tolerance in Cryptography 2004, Supplemental Volume of the 2004 Intern. Conf. on Dependable Systems and Networks, 368-372 (2004).
6. S. Gueron, "Enhanced Montgomery Multiplication", CHES 2002 Lecture Notes in Computer Science 2523, Springer-Verlag, 46-56 (2002).
7. Jhunjhunwala, "Indian Mathematics - an Introduction", Wiley Eastern Ltd., New Delhi, 1993.
8. M. Joye, A. Lenstra, and J. J. Quisquater, "Chinese Remaindering Based Cryptosystems in the Presence of Faults," Journal of Cryptology, 12: 241-246 (1999).
9. S. M. Yen, S. Moon, and J. C. Ha, "Hardware Fault Attack on RSA with CRT Revisited," ICISC 2002, Lecture Notes in Computer Science, 2587, Springer-Verlag, 374-388 (2002).
10. S. M. Yen and M. Joye, "Checking Before Output May Not Be Enough Against Fault-Based Cryptanalysis", IEEE Trans. on Comp., 49:967-970 (2000).

Appendix: Modular Exponentiation Algorithm Using NRMM

The following algorithm shows how modular exponentiation can be computed by using only the NRMM operation (details, and can be found in [6]).

---

input: X (x bits long integer) A (n bits long integer), A ($<$ N)
N (n bits long odd integer), s = n+2
output: A^X mod N
pre-computation: H = 2^{2n} mod N

Computation:
   1. B = NRMM (A, H, N, s);   /* convert to the Montgomery domain
   2. For i from x-2 to 0 do
   3.   T = NRMM (T, T, N, s);   /* squaring
   4.   if X_i=1 then T = NRMM (T, B, N, s);   /* multiplication
   5. end;
   6. T = NRMM (T, 1, N, s);   /* convert back to the integer domain
   7. Return T;

Fig. 3. A modular exponentiation algorithm that uses only one type of operation, namely NRMM. With the choice s =n+2, no final reduction is required at the end of each NRMM. Step 1 transforms the input into the Montgomery domain, and Step 4 converts the result (T) back to the integer domain, and (due to the choice s =n+2) provides a reduced result. Note that all multiplications are performed with a fixed multiplicand (B).

Case Study of a Fault Attack on Asynchronous DES Crypto-Processors

Yannick Monnet[1], Marc Renaudin[1], Régis Leveugle[1],
Christophe Clavier[2], and Pascal Moitrel[2]

[1] TIMA Laboratory
46, Avenue Felix Viallet
38031 Grenoble cedex-France
{yannick.monnet, marc.renaudin, regis.leveugle}@imag.fr
[2] Gemalto
La Vigie, Avenue du Jujubier, ZI athelia IV
13705 La Ciotat Cedex, France
{christophe.clavier, pascal.moitrel}@gemalto.com

Abstract. This paper proposes a practical fault attack on two asynchronous DES crypto-processors, a reference version and a hardened version, using round reduction. Because of their specific architecture, asynchronous circuits have a very specific behavior in the presence of faults. Previous works show that they are an interesting alternative to design robust systems. However, this paper demonstrates that there are weaknesses left, and that we are able both to identify and exploit them. The effect of the fault is to reduce the number of rounds by corrupting the multi-rail round counter protected by alarm cells. The fault injection mean is a laser. A description of the fault injection process is presented, followed by how the results can be used to retrieve the key. Weaknesses are theoretically identified and analyzed. Finally, possible counter-measures are described.

1 Introduction

Fault attacks are considered as a serious threat by designers of secure embedded systems. The security level of secret cryptographic algorithms such as DES and AES relies on the number of iterations (rounds) that are computed. One of the most efficient ways to break such algorithms is to implement a fault attack that reduces the number of rounds [1]. A practical fault attack using round reduction was presented in [2] and applied to attack a synchronous AES implementation, showing the potential of this class of attack.

Asynchronous circuits represent a class of circuits which are not controlled by a global clock but by the data themselves. Because of their specific architecture, asynchronous circuits have a very different behavior than synchronous circuits in the presence of faults. Quasi Delay Insensitive (QDI) circuits are asynchronous circuits that operate correctly regardless of gate delays. This class of circuits has well recognized potentials in terms of power, speed, noise and robustness against process, voltage and temperature variations [5]. Their delay-insensitive property makes them inherently

L. Breveglieri et al. (Eds.): FDTC 2006, LNCS 4236, pp. 88–97, 2006.
© Springer-Verlag Berlin Heidelberg 2006

robust against some categories of faults such as delay faults [6]. Moreover, this class of circuit uses multi-rail encoding, which is often considered as a native counter-measure against faults. Thus, QDI circuits are attractive to design fault tolerant/resistant systems. However, only theoretical studies have been done, and to our knowledge no practical results were reported yet.

In [3], we presented two asynchronous DES implementations, a reference one and a hardened one. Counter-measures were implemented to protect S-Boxes against differential cryptanalysis. These counter-measures were validated in [4]. In practice, the reference version didn't leak valuable information to retrieve the secret key, and the hardened version didn't leak any information at all.

In this paper, we propose a practical fault attack on the asynchronous DES using round reduction, thus revealing weaknesses in the circuits. Faults are injected by means of a laser beam. Weaknesses are analyzed and counter-measures are proposed to inhibit this attack.

The counter of the reference version is an asynchronous state machine that uses a 1-out-of-17 code: each round number is coded using 1 wire. Sixteen wires are used to encode the 16 rounds. The hardened version implements the same counter but protected with alarm cells. These cells are able to detect any wrong code generated in the counter module, i.e. any state using 2 wires or more is detected. Alarms inform the environment when a wrong code is detected.

Our work presents a practical fault attack on both the reference and the hardened version of the circuits. In Section 2, we briefly present the quasi delay insensitive logic. Section 3 presents the DES crypto-processors that were designed and fabricated, and details the counter module architecture. Section 4 describes the laser setup that was used to perform the fault injection. Section 5 presents how the results are interpreted to retrieve the secret key. We present the results of the attacks both on the reference and hardened DES, showing a successful attack that is not detected by alarm cells in the hardened version. In Section 6, we analyze the weaknesses that were exploited. Section 7 proposes counter-measures and Section 8 concludes the paper.

2 Quasi Delay Insensitive Logic

An asynchronous circuit is composed of individual modules which communicate to each other by means of point-to-point communication channels [5]. Therefore, a given module becomes active when it senses the presence of incoming data. It then computes and sends the result to the output channels. Communications through channels are governed by a protocol which requires a bi-directional signalling between senders and receivers (request and acknowledgment). They are called handshaking protocols. In Section 6, we present a theoretical fault injection that exploits the properties of a handshaking protocol. A 1-out-of-n data encoding scheme is commonly used to ensure delay insensitive handshake protocol implementations. The dual-rail code [5] is the most often used because it is a good compromise between speed and area cost. This scheme can be extended to 1-out-of-n codes, where one bit is coded with n wires. The DES crypto-processor described in the next section uses a dual-rail encoding scheme for the data path, and a 1-out-of-17 encoding scheme for the counter module.

3 The Asynchronous DES Architecture

The asynchronous DES crypto-processor is basically an iterative structure, based on three self-timed loops synchronized through communicating channels (Figure 1a). Channel Sub-Key synchronizes the ciphering data-path. More details about the designed architecture can be found in [4].

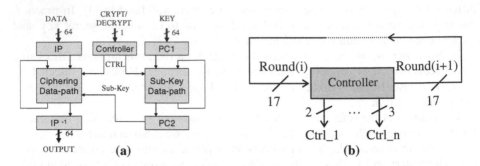

Fig. 1. (a) The DES architecture. (b) The controller state machine

CTRL is a set of channels generated by the Controller block (a finite state machine shown in Figure 1b) that controls the data-path along sixteen iterations as specified by the DES algorithm. This module takes as an input the 1-out-of-17 code of the current round, computes the control channels according to this round, and computes the 1-out-of-17 code of the next round. Sixteen wires are used to encode the sixteen rounds, and the last wire outputs the final result.

Figure 2 shows how such control signals are used in the data-path. The dual-rail channel ctrl_1 controls the demultiplexer structure as shown in the table. When ctrl_1 is "01" the output O1 is selected, when ctrl_1 is "10" then O2 is selected. In practice, O1 is used along the sixteen iterations of the algorithm, and O2 is finally used to output the final result. The state"11" is unused in the normal execution process. However, in the case of a fault injection that generates "11" on the ctrl_1 signal, both O1 and O2 are activated. This is how a standard implantation of a DMUX structure behaves in the presence of faults (Figure 2).

Several counter-measures were implemented in the hardened DES to prevent fault attacks. As stated in [3], S-Boxes were protected using the rail synchronization technique that provides a good protection with a very low area overhead and low performance penalty. This countermeasure was validated in [4]. However, it was not possible to apply this technique on the counter block because this module has no concurrent block to synchronize with.

The counter was protected using alarm cells [7]. These alarms are implemented to detect any wrong code generated on the 1-out-of-17 counter, and any wrong code generated on the control channels, such as ctrl_1. The alarm output signal is stored in a register, thus enabling the environment to read the alarm status and to know which module of the circuit triggered the alarm. In a real product, the environment should apply a security strategy such as resetting the circuit or providing random outputs to prevent the attack. In our case study, we collect the alarm signal as status information. Both circuits were fabricated using the 130 nm STmicroelectronics CMOS process, with constrained floor plan to ease fault injection in particular blocks of the design. More details are presented in [3].

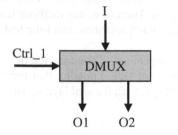

Ctrl_1	Activated output
"01"	O1
"10"	O2
"11 "(faulty)	O1 and O2

Fig. 2. Demultiplexer behavior

4 Fault Injection Process

To perform fault injection, we had the choices of various types of injection means [8]. Since we want to be efficient both in the fault exploitation and in the fault injection, we have discarded VCC glitches, Clock glitches and white light, since all of them just allow to make rough variations on time location and on the perturbation duration, with no possibility to specify accurate locations of the fault on some dedicated parts of the circuit. Glitches are applied to all the circuit logic, and white light illuminate the whole surface of the circuit since the minimum spot we can obtain is 1mm². On the contrary, a laser can reproduce a wide variety of faults. The effect produced is similar to white light but the advantage of a laser is its directionality that allows the precise targeting of a small circuit area (for example 5 μm²).

The Laser platform is composed of a computer to organize both the fault injection and the driving of the device under tests, an XY table to perform fine localization of the targeted area of the device, and an optional oscilloscope to control that the device under test receives commands and sends results. The laser itself is a pulsed Yag laser with a green output at 532 nm, an energy tunable from 0 to 100%, with a possibility to control the spot size.

Time scan, spatial scan and energy set-up
The first step of a fault injection campaign consists in determining the right time to force a faulty behavior of the device. The objective is to inject a fault while the process is running. In our case, we know that the DES module is running its 16 rounds in about 200 ns for its hardened version. Knowing that our sampling clock is 100 MHz, the only possible delays between two shots is 10 ns. We have then 20 times positions during the DES computation. Moreover, if we want to measure the reproducibility of the fault, when a fault or an alarm is detected then we can decide to replay the test with same location in space and time N times. We have to notice that with such a granularity we have at least one chance to have a fault induced during each round of the DES.

The second step consists in choosing the right scan area. In the context of our case study, we chose to target the counter in a "white box" approach, knowing the coordinates of this block. Since the floor plan was constrained, the block is spatially identified. After trying several configurations, we choose a spot size of 220 μm² to scan the counter block.

In a real product context, a complete scan of the device under test should be performed in order to identify the most interesting areas. Therefore, this methods leads to a very huge amount of fault injections and log files interpretations, and long test campaign durations.

The adequate laser parameters are completely dependant of the targeted device. In this work, the DES modules were illuminated in front side, knowing that they were designed in a 0,13 μm STMicroelectronics technology, with 6 metal layers. An energy density of 0.8 pJ/μm² was adequate to reveal errors.

5   Results Interpretation

The fault injection campaign consisted in both a spatial and a time scan of the counter block, which represent over 5000 shoots for each circuit during a simple encryption computation. About 40% of the shoots revealed errors. Among the revealed errors, some of them were identified as a modification of the sequence of rounds. The next sub-section presents this analysis and sub-section 5.2 shows how the results can be interpreted to retrieve the key. Then the results obtained for the reference DES and the hardened DES are presented in sub-sections 5.3 and 5.4.

5.1   Rounds Sequences Modification

Several faulty results correspond to the computation of a faulty sequence of rounds. The correct execution process is noted as follows:

$$T_C \; = \; (1,2,3,4,5,6,7,8,9,10,11,12,13,14,15,16,17)$$

T_c represent the computation of the sixteen rounds plus the output of the final result, noted "17". In the state machine previously described, the output operation (which includes the final permutation IP_1) is actually coded 17.

The expression [i → j] represents a fault that was injected in the round i and corrupted the counter to the value j. As a consequence, round i is not computed and the execution jumps to the round j. For example, [7 → 10] represent the following sequence:

$$T_1 \; = \; (1,2,3,4,5,6,10,11,12,13,14,15,16,17)$$

Round 7 is not computed. The execution jumps to round 10 and follows the normal sequence to the end. Both forward (i < j) and backward (i > j) jumps were observed for both circuits.

As specified by the DES algorithm, a sub-key is computed for each round. Since the counter controls both the data-path and the sub-key path, [i → j] corrupts the shift key sequence as well:

$$S_c = (1,1,2,2,2,2,2,2,1,2,2,2,2,2,2,1)$$
$$S_1 = (1,1,2,2,2,2,2,2,2,2,2,2,1)$$

S_c represents the correct shift key sequence, and S_1 is the sequence that is computed in the faulty case described above. We note that different sequences of rounds may map to the same sequence of shifts.

From a sequence S_i of shifts, we derive a sequence σ_i of accumulated shifts computed since the beginning of the encryption:

$$\sigma_C = (1,2,4,6,8,10,12,14,15,17,19,21,23,25,27,29,31,32)$$
$$\sigma_1 = (1,2,4,6,8,10,12,14,16,18,20,22,23)$$

The next sub-section shows how to exploit these sequences, which are cryptographically meaningful as they correspond to sequences of sub-keys actually used in the encryption process.

5.2 Exploitation

In the following analysis we suppose that the attacker knows both the plain text and the correct cipher text. We suppose also that the plain text remains constant during the attack campaign. For this fixed plain text, we obtain a set $\{\sigma_1 \dots \sigma_I\}$ corresponding to I different faulty sequences obtained from the laser shoots. We define Σ as the set of sub-key sequences that the attacker can exploit. For each of these sequences, the attacker knows the corresponding cipher text.

$$\Sigma = \{\sigma_1, \dots, \sigma_I\} \cup \{\sigma_C\} \cup \{\sigma_P\}$$

σ_c stands for the sub-key sequence of the correct result, while σ_P is the empty set that represents the sub-key sequence of the plain text.

In order to exploit Σ, we propose to analyze pairs $\sigma, \sigma' \in \Sigma$ of sub-key sequences. We are particularly interested in pairs where the common prefix represents the major part of the sequences. For such a pair, we define π the shared prefix, $\{\alpha_1, \dots, \alpha_t\}$ the suffix of σ, and $\{\alpha'_1, \dots, \alpha'_{t'}\}$ the suffix of σ'. Without loss of generality, we assume that $t' \le t$.

We give the following example for the sequences σ_2 and σ_3 corresponding to the sequences of rounds [9 → 12] and [9 → 13] respectively.

$$\sigma_2 = (1,2,4,6,8,10,12,14,16,18,20,22,23) = \pi \mid \alpha_1 \mid \alpha_2$$
$$\sigma_3 = (1,2,4,6,8,10,12,14,16,18,20,21) \quad = \pi \mid \alpha'_1$$

with:

$$\pi = (1,2,4,6,8,10,12,14,16,18,20)$$
$$\alpha_1 = 22, \ \alpha_2 = 23 \ (t = 2)$$
$$\alpha'_1 = 21 \ (t'=1)$$

As will be shown in the following example, short suffixes (both t and t' being small) provide easy cryptanalysis, leading to successful key recovery.

We denote L_i (resp. L'_i) and R_i (resp. R'_i) the left and right 32-bit parts of the intermediate value at the beginning of round i for sequence σ (resp. σ'). We note k the number of the round immediately following the common prefix for sub-key sequence. With these notations, we have:

- $L_k = L'_k$ and $R_k = R'_k$
- L_{k+t}, R_{k+t}, $L'_{k+t'}$ and $R'_{k+t'}$ known

Case t=2 and t'=1

In this case:

- $L_{k+1} \oplus R_{k+2}$ is known. This is because R_{k+2} is known as t=2, and L_{k+1} is also known as $L_{k+1} = R_k$, and $R_k = R'_k$, and $R'_k = L'_{k+1}$ which is known as t'=1.
- R_{k+1} is known because $R_{k+1} = L_{k+2}$ which is known as t=2.

We so know both input and output of the round function for the round number k+2 of the sequence σ. Knowing inputs and outputs of the 8 s-boxes, it is possible to derive 32 bits of information about the sub-key K_{k+2} involved in this round. The key K may then be easily recovered by exhausting a remaining key space of size 2^{24}.

Other Cases

For small values of (t,t'), we found that the key may be easily recovered in the following cases: (1,0), (2,0), (1,1), (2,1) and (2,2).

This corresponds to an important number of faulty pairs obtained in our experiments.

In the other cases (t>2), the cryptanalysis difficulty increases with t.

Note that the case where t'=0 corresponds to an attacker knowing the input and output of a DES with only t rounds. For a fixed small t (typically t=3 or t=4), and if the attacker makes the input varying, it is possible to apply classical linear cryptanalysis techniques. Note that differential cryptanalysis is not possible in this case as the input is known but not chosen.

5.3   Reference DES Results

Half of revealed errors lead the circuit to deadlock. In this case, the attack is detected and no exploitable information is given to the attacker to retrieve the key. Among the remaining errors, 50 results have been identified as faulty sequences, which give us a large Σ to perform a cryptanalysis. 8 of them offer a situation where t=1 and t'=0.

Moreover, some of the sequences correspond to a round reduced DES computation, such as 2-round DES (a DES reduced to 2 rounds), up to 10-round DES. These samples are reproducible and could be used to perform a classical Differential-Linear cryptanalysis [9].

In most of the cases, the fault injection probably generated a wrong code on the counter. Then it generates faulty control channels. As shown in Section 3, a wrong control code generated in a structure that is similar to a DMUX is able to output a result very early. Since no alarms are implemented, it is not detected.

5.4 Hardened DES Results

The hardened DES counter provides the same behavior as the reference version but the wrong codes trigger alarms. As expected, most errors induced in the circuit lead to a wrong code. However, a few errors are not detected. The fault injection has corrupted the counter but generated a valid code. We discriminate two types of errors:

- The errors that we can reproduce: Figure 3 shows a [16 → 17] fault injection. The End_DES signal indicates that the DES ended the computation. As shown on the figure, the faulty computation is shortened with respect to the correct one of about 12 ns, which corresponds to 1 round execution time. In this example, a 15-round DES was computed and no alarm signal was triggered. This error is reproducible: 10 shoots with the same time/location parameters produced 10 times the same failure.

- The errors that seem not or hardly reproducible: several faulty sequences that correspond to a round-reduction were obtained. For example, a sample showed a 9-round DES that could help finding the key if combined with another close (in terms of short specific suffixes) sequence. However, this result appeared difficult to reproduce.

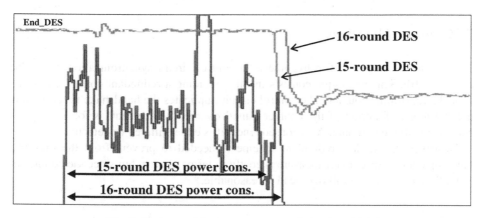

Fig. 3. Undetected faulty sequence on the hardened DES

6 Theoretical Analysis of the Weaknesses

We propose two behavior models to understand the undetected results on the hardened DES. The first hypothesis is a multiple bit-flip: 2 bit-flips are injected. The first bit-flip disables the active wire in the 1-out-of-17 counter, while the second bit flip enables another wire. These two bit-flips have to occur nearly at the same time so that a transient faulty code has not enough time to propagate to the alarm cell. Moreover, since the attack is localized, the gates have to be close to each other in the floor plan.

The second hypothesis is a single bit-flip that occurs at the right time in the communication protocol. Figure 4 describes the four-phase protocol, which requires a return to zero phase for both data requests and acknowledgments. In phase 1, a valid data is detected. This data is acknowledged in phase 2. Then the data is re-initialized in phase 3 (return to zero phase) and the acknowledgment signal is reset in phase 4. If a fault occurs during phase 3 or phase 4 (when all the wires are reset), then a single bit flip is able to generate a valid 1-out-of-n code. With respect to some timing conditions between the events that sequence the handshake, the fault is able to be inserted without being detected.

These two hypotheses have been verified and characterized in a simulation environment with the help of the floor plan database.

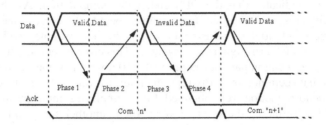

Fig. 4. Four-phase handshaking protocol

7 Counter-Measures

To prevent the single bit-flip hypothesis, a control circuit synchronization would be efficient [10]. This technique consists in implementing a redundant control circuit to handshake with the counter. The control circuit duplicates the handshake function, but not the logical function of the counter (small overhead). The fault is forced to synchronize with the real data. As a consequence, it is either filtered or detected.

However, a complete redundant scheme is needed to prevent from the multiple fault injection. This counter-measure is costly in terms of area, but since the counter is a small module, the overall overhead is reasonable.

8 Conclusion

We presented a practical fault attack on two asynchronous DES crypto-processors. The hardened version of the DES showed a higher security level than the reference version, since most of the attacks were detected. However, we proved that the proposed protection do not provide a full security level. Weaknesses were reported and clearly identified. Further hardening techniques can be implemented in specific parts of the circuit to guaranty a very high security level for a low cost (area, speed, power), in addition to those already implemented and characterized.

This work showed that even complex systems using redundant coding scheme and detection systems are sensitive to fault attacks. However, this attack was realized in study conditions with a constrained floor plan and a good knowledge of the design under test. Although a real-case attack would be much more difficult to implement, this work showed the feasibility.

Acknowledgments

This work is partially supported by the French Ministry of Research through the RNRT Duracell project. The authors wish to thank Félie M'Buwa N'Zenguet, Jean-Baptiste Rigaud and Assia Tria from the Gardanne Laboratory of Ecole Nationale Supérieur des Mines de Saint-Etienne for the development of the communication tool between the Device Under Test and the Setup. The authors are grateful to Christophe Mourtel and Nathalie Feyt from Gemalto Security SmartCard Laboratory for discussion and support.

References

[1] R. Anderson and M. Khun, Low cost attacks on tamper resistant devices. Security Protocols, pp. 125-136, 1998. Lectures Notes in Computer Science No. 1361.

[2] H. Choukri, M. Tunstall, Round Reduction Using Faults. 2nd Workshop on Fault Diagnosis and Tolerance in Cryptography (FDTC 05), pp. 13-24, Edinburgh, Scotland, September 2, 2005.

[3] Y. Monnet, M. Renaudin, R. Leveugle, S. Dumont, F. Bouesse, An Asynchronous DES Crypto-Processor Secured against Fault Attacks, International Conference on Very Large Scale Integration (VLSI-SOC), 2005, pp. 21-26.

[4] Y. Monnet, M. Renaudin, R. Leveugle, N. Feyt, P. Moitrel, Practical Evaluation of Fault Countermeasures on an Asynchronous DES Crypto Processor, 12th IEEE International On-Line Testing Symposium (IOLTS), Lake of Como, Italy, July 10th-12th, 2006.

[5] M. Renaudin, Asynchronous Circuits and Systems: a promising design alternative, Microelectronics-Engineering Journal, Elsevier Science, Guest Editors: P.Senn, M. Renaudin, J. Boussey, Vol54, N°1-2, December 2000, pp.133-149.

[6] C. LaFrieda, R.Manohar, Fault Detection and Isolation Techniques for Quasi Delay-Insensitive Circuits, International Conference on Dependable Systems and Networks (DSN'04), Florence Italy, June 28 - July 01, 2004, pp.41-50.

[7] S. Moore, R. Anderson, R. Mullins, G. Taylor, J. J. A. Fournier, Balanced self-checking asynchronous logic for smart card applications, Microprocessors and Microsystems, Elsevier Science Publishers, vol. 27, 2003, pp. 421-430.

[8] H. Bar-El, H. Choukri, D. Naccache, M. Tunstall, C. Whelan, The sorcerers apprentice guide to fault attacks, Proceedings of the IEEE, Vol. 94, N°2, February 2006, pp. 370-382.

[9] M. Hellman and S. Langford, Differential-Linear Cryptanalysis, Advances in Cryptology - CRYPTO '94 (Lecture Notes in Computer Science no. 839), Springer-Verlag, pp. 26-39, 1994.

[10] Y. Monnet, M. Renaudin, R. Leveugle, Hardening Techniques against Transient Faults for Asynchronous Circuits, 11th IEEE International On-Line Testing Symposium (IOLTS), Saint Raphael, French Riviera, France, July 6th-8th, 2005, pp. 129-134.

A Fault Attack Against the FOX Cipher Family

L. Breveglieri[1], I. Koren[2], and P. Maistri[1]

[1] Department of Electronics and Information Technology, Politecnico di Milano,
Milano, Italy
{brevegli, maistri}@elet.polimi.it
[2] Department of Electrical and Computer Engineering, University of Massachusetts,
Amherst, MA, USA
koren@ecs.umass.edu

Abstract. Since its first introduction, differential fault analysis has proved to be one of the most effective techniques to break a cipher implementation. In this paper, we apply a fault attack to a generic implementation of the recently introduced FOX family of symmetric block ciphers (also known as Idea Nxt). We show the steps needed to mount an effective attack against FOX-64. Although the basic characteristics of this cipher are similar to those of AES, FOX uses a non-invertible key schedule which makes it necessary to use a different attack plan. We also estimate the number of faulty ciphertexts required to reveal the secret key. Our results can be easily extended to other variations of the cipher that use longer inputs and keys.

1 Introduction

Most recent cryptosystems are now designed to be secure against common attack techniques, such as linear or differential cryptanalysis. To this end, encryption algorithms are often made public, allowing the research community to analyze them and find possible weaknesses. As a result, the attackers' attention has been shifted to the actual implementations of cryptosystems, which can leak useful information about the secret key (e.g., simple and differential power analysis).

Recently, a technique exploiting errors injected during the encryption (or decryption) process proved to be a very effective attack. In [4], the authors showed how a single faulty encryption is enough to break a CRT-RSA cryptosystem; in [2], faults injected into a DES architecture were successfully used to recover the secret key. Since then, fault-based attacks have been applied to a variety of cryptosystems: public-key based ones (ECC, XTR), stream ciphers (RC4) and block ciphers.

Initially, there was skepticism about the feasibility of these fault-based attacks, until in [10] the authors showed that even with very cheap equipment (a microscope and a camera flash) they were able to change the stored values in static RAM cells. Nowadays, smart cards are tested by manufacturers to study their vulnerabilities to fault attacks using specialized laser equipment. Obviously, laser beams increase the chance of a successful fault attack compared to

L. Breveglieri et al. (Eds.): FDTC 2006, LNCS 4236, pp. 98–105, 2006.

a simple camera flash, since the attacker can control more precisely parameters like wavelength, energy, duration and location.

Most research efforts in the area of fault-based attacks have focused on AES, due to its adoption as an NIST standard. In the first proposed attacks, the attacker was assumed to be able to flip single bits within the chip with very precise timing [3]. Such an assumption is getting harder to justify due to technological restrictions. As die size shrinks, the precision required to affect a single flip-flop requires expensive equipment (e.g., laser). Moreover, designers are beginning to consider fault attacks as a serious security risk and are introducing countermeasures that can overcome single bit errors.

Later, new types of attacks were proposed, were the fault model was relaxed and random byte errors were considered. In this scenario, the attacker is able to alter the value of a whole byte, possibly being able to either decide or know its location, but without having knowledge of its previous value. On the other hand, timing is still important, since imprecise injections are useless. One of the most impressive results is the attack published in [9], where only two precisely injected faults can break the AES-128 cipher.

Several countermeasures have already been proposed, mostly based on some form of redundancy. In [7], it is suggested to compute the inverse operation at the encryption, round or operation level. In [1,6,8] an error detecting code is used to protect the internal data path. In [11], a pipeline architecture is used to detect any transient fault. In addition to these techniques, the chip may also be protected by means of sensors or shielding.

So far, to the best of our knowledge, there is no published fault attack against the Idea Nxt cipher which has some unique characteristics. In this paper, we describe how to mount a successful fault-based attack against this cipher. In particular, we show the number of required faults that have to be injected, on average, to mount a successful attack and recover the key.

The paper is organized as follows. Section 2 describes the Fox family of ciphers, focusing on the details needed to understand the basics of the attack, which is described, step-by-step, in Section 3. Section 4 concludes the paper, summarizing the results and suggesting possible countermeasures.

2   The FOX Cipher Family

FOX is a family of symmetric block ciphers recently presented as Idea Nxt [5] and aimed at multimedia streaming and secure data storage. The cipher can be customized in terms of the block length (see Table 1), key size and number of iterations.

The algorithm contains repetition of the round function *lmor*, followed by a single instance of the function *lmid*. The latter differs in the absence of an additional automorphism applied to the leftmost part of the input block, which constitutes a single Feistel iteration (see Figure 1). Moreover, these two functions have a fixed high-level structure, but are customized in width and in the internal parameters to suit both Nxt64 and Nxt128.

Table 1. The FOX cipher family

Name	Input size	Key size	Iterations
NXT64	64 bits	128 bits	16
NXT128	128 bits	256 bits	16

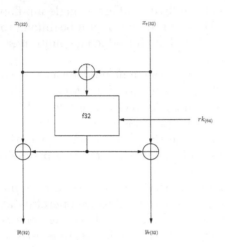

Fig. 1. *lmid* function

Fig. 2. The *f32* function used in Idea Nxt 64

The core part of every round iteration is the *f32* (*f64* in Idea Nxt128) function, which includes linear and non-linear operations (see Figure 2). In this function, the key is split into two parts: the left one is added at the beginning and at the end, while the right one is added in the central body, right after the diffusion step. There are two non-linear steps implemented by means of substitution boxes (Sboxes): the Sbox can be implemented either as a byte lookup table, or as a combination of three different smaller tables operating on 4-bit nibbles. This is similar to the AES Sboxes, which can be defined by using composite fields. However, unlike AES, an algebraic definition does not seem to exist here. The diffusion step is defined as a linear transformation over the Galois Field $GF(2^8)$. The irreducible polynomial is $x^8 + x^7 + x^6 + x^5 + x^4 + x^3 + 1$ which is different from the one used by AES.

The key schedule routine uses the same operations employed in the encryption datapath. The master secret key is updated in every iteration by using some precomputed constant. Each updated key is then used to generate a single round key for the encryption datapath, through a sequence of non-linear and linear operations. In addition, a compression stage exists, where bit pairs are exclusive ORed. This process is shown in Figure 3: the *sigma* block shown in the figure is the non-linear stage made of substitution boxes.

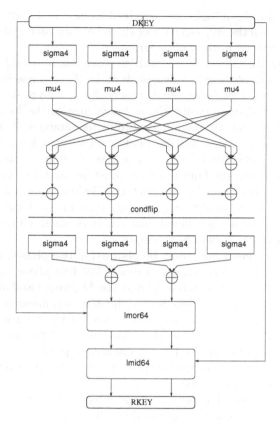

Fig. 3. Round key generation from secret key

3   The Attack

A Differential Fault Analysis (DFA) attack allows to apply differential and linear analysis to only a few rounds of the cipher, possibly only one. This allows to mount a very effective attack at an almost negligible cost. A conventional differential attack would consider the whole cipher (in terms of the number of iterations and size of the data block), which often leads to the ability to only attack reduced versions of the cryptosystems.

By collecting a few differential pairs relative to the last non-linear step, the attacker can reduce and finally guess the values computed in the last rounds, thus being able to infer the last round key. Once the key has been recovered, the key schedule can be inverted to obtain the initial secret key; if this is not possible, then the attack can be reiterated on each round, starting from the last, until the whole key material is exposed.

The key schedule for the FOX ciphers is non-invertible: hence, once the last round key is revealed, the attack will be repeated either on the preceding round or on the key schedule directly to recover the master secret key. In this extended abstract we describe the initial steps required to mount the attack and recover the last round key. All the steps to recover the whole key material and the related results will be described in the full paper.

In the following, we will consider a fault as a random byte addition in $GF(2^8)$, i.e., a XOR with a random byte value, such as in [9]. A single bit fault, in fact, would lead to a simpler problem, but is less realistic. A byte fault, on the other hand, can be injected more easily. Exact knowledge of the location of the affected byte is not crucial, although it simplifies the analysis. If this information is not available, then a guess can be made and verified later with additional experiments (i.e., faults) until a unique guess is possible. Timing, on the other hand, is very important: the fault injection must be carefully synchronized with the encryption process, in order to affect the desired operations. This can be achieved, for instance, by analyzing the power trace of the device while computing and identifying the desired round. The exact location within the round can be determined after few (random) attempts.

The attack on the last round must be planned in two phases, since the round key is actually used in two separate instances. The first phase allows to retrieve the leftmost part of the key, which is used at the beginning and at the end of the round. The fault must be injected before the last non-linear operation, which means between the first and the last Sbox stages of the final round. Any time instance in this interval is fine, but the effectiveness of the attack is increased if the injection occurs before the linear diffusion step, i.e., the $mu4$ operation. In this case, the linear transformation spreads the fault through the whole word and more information is provided.

For instance, suppose that an error ϵ is injected into the leftmost byte of the word, right before the $mu4$ operation, resulting in the error word $(\epsilon, 0, 0, 0)$. Then, the error is spread by the diffusion step and the error word becomes $(\epsilon, \epsilon, c\epsilon, \alpha\epsilon)$, where c and α are coefficients of $mu4$. This is the differential input to the last substitution operation, and although unknown, we can still identify some regularity, and prune for instance all those values which are not admissible for each byte of the word (i.e., error values that would give an empty set of candidates for the Sbox inputs). The output differential, on the other hand, is known and this information can be used to narrow the search.

The first fault injection is used to build the set of all possible candidates, considering any admissible fault value. For each additional fault, a new candidate set is built and intersected with the current solution set, thus narrowing the number of possible candidates. The process continues until a unique candidate is identified for each possible byte. The value found in this way is the input to the last Sbox step. Thus, it is easy to recover the key value used in the last key addition, i.e., the left part of the last round key.

In this phase, knowing where the fault has been injected simplifies the analysis, because we know how the error spreads after the $mu4$ operation. If this is not the case, however, the actual location may be guessed and the analysis performed as described above; for each additional fault, a new guess is made. If the guesses are all correct, then the procedure will give the unique desired solution. If an empty candidate set is found, then at least one of the guesses was incorrect and we have to backtrack and try another possible solution. Although this procedure increases the complexity of the search tree, we found that the correct key value could be often identified after only 2 or 3 attempts when the location was known. The whole search tree, with a new branch for each location guess and for each injected fault, gives 4^f leaves where f is the number of faults. This number is an upper bound, since many branches can be pruned after each fault injection, thus reducing the complexity of the attack.

The second phase aims at recovering the rightmost part of the round key. The approach is the same and is based on injecting a fault before the first non-linear step of the last round. In this case, however, the structure of the last round (see Figure 1) gives us both the input and the output differentials, making the analysis much easier. On the other hand, the diffusion step does not provide any additional information, which means that each byte must be targeted individually.

Based on our simulations, the last round key was completely revealed after 11.45 injected faults on average. Further analysis of the distribution of the faults required to recover the key reveals that the first phase requires from 2 to 8 faults, while the second phase uses from 8 to 28 faults: the worst case is however rare, and the average values are about 2.94 and 8.51 for the first and second phase, respectively. The complete attack requires from 8 to 31 faults. The distribution curves are shown in Figure 4 where the worst cases (when more than 20 faults are required) are not shown for clarity, but they constitute a negligible percentage of the overall test space (less than 0.02%).

If the fault location is unknown, we are confident that a few fault injections may be still enough to identify the leftmost part of the key. This issue does not arise when performing the second phase of the attack on the round, since the injected error can be inferred from the output result (see Figure 1). This phase, however, requires more faults since we cannot exploit the diffusion properties of the linear stage. In fact, each byte of the key must be attacked separately. In the full paper, we will provide the number of faults required to reveal the whole key material in the two main scenarios.

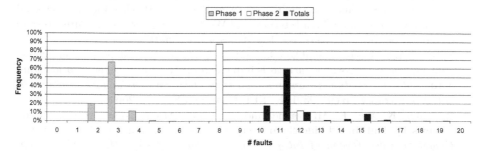

Fig. 4. Number of fault injections required to mount the attack and recover the key: left half (phase 1), right half (phase 2) and whole key (totals)

4   Conclusions

In this paper, we present a fault injection attack against the newly introduced
FOX family of ciphers. The attack resembles currently known attacks against
AES, but unlike AES the key schedule of Idea Nxt is not invertible. This forces
the attacker to iterate the fault injection on every round of the encryption algorithm to recover the whole key material, or to attack the key schedule directly,
as will be shown in the full paper.

The last round key can be found, on average, after 11.45 faulty encryptions. If
we assume that attacking any single round or the key schedule has the same complexity, then the whole cipher can be broken after 183 or 23 faults, respectively.
These results will be confirmed in the full paper.

Differential fault analysis proves to be one of the most effective attack techniques and can be used when the attacker has the ciphering device even for a
short time. Generic countermeasures such as those presented in [7,11] or shielding and sensors are possible. Moreover, the cipher is based on GF arithmetic and
can therefore be protected by means of a parity code, such as in [1]. We plan to
implement the cipher in hardware and evaluate the effectiveness and overhead
of these countermeasures.

References

1. G. Bertoni, L. Breveglieri, I. Koren, P. Maistri, and V. Piuri. "Error analysis and
   detection procedures for a hardware implementation of the advanced encryption
   standard," *IEEE Trans. Computers*, 52(4):492–505, 2003.
2. E. Biham, A. Shamir, "Differential Fault Analysis of Secret Key Cryptosystems,"
   Technical Report, Technion - Computer Science Department, 1997.
3. J. Blömer, J.-P. Seifert, "Fault Based Cryptanalysis of the Advanced Encryption
   Standard (AES)," Financial Cryptography, *Lecture Notes in Computer Science*,
   vol. 2742, pp. 162-181, 2003.
4. D. Boneh, R. DeMillo, R. Lipton, "On the Importance of Eliminating Errors in
   Cryptographic Computations," *Journal of Cryptology*, vol. 14, pp. 101-119, 2001.
5. P Junod and S. Vaudenay. "FOX : A New Family of Block Ciphers," Selected
   Areas in Cryptography, 11th International Workshop, SAC 2004, Lecture Notes in
   Computer Science, vol. 3357, pp. 114-129, Springer, 2004.
6. M. G. Karpovsky, K. J. Kulikowski, and A. Taubin, "Robust protection against
   fault-injection attacks on smart cards implementing the advanced encryption standard," *2004 International Conference on Dependable Systems and Networks (DSN
   2004), Proceedings*, pages 93–101. IEEE Computer Society, 2004.
7. R. Karri, K. Wu, P. Mishraand and Y. Kim.   "Concurrent error detection
   schemes for fault-based side-channel cryptanalysis of symmetric block ciphers,"
   *Computer-Aided Design of Integrated Circuits and Systems, IEEE Transactions
   on*, 21(12):1509–1517, Dec 2002.
8. R. Karri, G. Kuznetsov, and M. Gössel. "Parity-based concurrent error detection
   in symmetric block ciphers," *Proceedings 2003 International Test Conference (ITC
   2003)*, pages 919–926. IEEE Computer Society, 2003.

9. G. Piret, J.-J. Quisquater, "A Differential Fault Attack Technique against SPN Structures, with Application to the AES and Khazad," Cryptographic Hardware and Embedded Systems - CHES 2003, *Lecture Notes in Computer Science*, vol. 2779, Springer-Verlag, pp. 77-88, 2003.
10. S. P. Skorobogatov and R. J. Anderson, "Optical Fault Induction Attacks," Cryptographic Hardware and Embedded Systems - CHES 2002, Lecture Notes in Computer Science, vol. 2523, pp. 2-12, Springer, 2003.
11. K. Wu and R. Karri. "Idle cycles based concurrent error detection of RC6 encryption," *16th IEEE International Symposium on Defect and Fault-Tolerance in VLSI Systems (DFT 2001), Proceedings*, pages 200–205. IEEE Computer Society, 2001.

Fault Based Collision Attacks on AES

Johannes Blömer and Volker Krummel*

Faculty of Computer Science, Electrical Engineering and Mathematics
University of Paderborn, Germany
{bloemer, krummel}@uni-paderborn.de

Abstract. In this paper we present a new class of collision attacks that
are based on inducing faults into the encryption process. We combine the
classical fault attack of Biham and Shamir with the concept of collision attacks of Schramm et al. Unlike previous fault attacks by Blömer and Seifert
our new attacks only need bit flips not bit resets. Furthermore, the new attacks do not need the faulty ciphertext to derive the secret key. We only
need the weaker information whether a collision has occurred or not. This
is an improvement over previous attacks presented for example by Dusart,
Letourneux and Vivolo, Giraud, Chen and Yen or Piret and Quisquater.
As it turns out the new attacks are very powerful even against sophisticated countermeasures like error detection and memory encryption.

1 Introduction

A smartcard is a general purpose computer embedded in a plastic cover of a credit
card's size. The main building blocks of a smartcard are a CPU, a ROM that
contains for example the operating system, an EEPROM containing among other
things the secret key, and a RAM to store intermediate results of computations.
To communicate with the outside world the smartcard has to be inserted into
a so called smartcard reader that also provides the energy the smartcard needs
for operating.

Smartcards are perfectly suited for storing private information such as cryptographic keys because the corresponding cryptographic operations such as encryption or digital signature are computed directly on the smartcard. Therefore the
key never has to leave the smartcard and hence seems to be protected very well
even in hostile environments. However, it is well known that physical instances
of algorithms (in hardware or software) may leak information about the computation through so called side channels. Researchers identified several of those
side channels and managed to use information obtained through side channels
to determine secret keys of cryptographic applications. Kocher [13] was the first
who presented an attack based on timing measurements that successfully computed the secret key of RSA in 1996. This result was improved by Dhem et al.
[8]. Koeune and Quisquater [15] adapted timing attacks to the symmetric cipher
AES. In 1999 Kocher, Jaffe and Jun [14] presented a successful side channel
attack based on the power consumption of a smartcard.

---

* This work was partially supported by a grant from Intel Corporation, Portland.

L. Breveglieri et al. (Eds.): FDTC 2006, LNCS 4236, pp. 106–120, 2006.
© Springer-Verlag Berlin Heidelberg 2006

In this paper we focus on so called fault attacks on the advanced encryption standard AES [7]. Boneh, DeMillo and Lipton [4] showed that faults induced into the encryption process of asymmetric ciphers can reveal the secret key. Biham and Shamir [1] combined fault attacks with the concept of differentials and mounted a differential fault attack (DFA) on DES. Skorobogatov and Anderson showed in [20] that fault attacks are realizable with sufficient precision in practice. See Blömer and Seifert [3] for an overview of the physics of inducing faults.

There are several fault attacks on AES reported in the literature. The first attacks were due to Blömer and Seifert [3] followed by improved attacks of Dusart, Letourneux and Vivolo [9], Giraud [10], Chen and Yen [6] and Piret and Quisquater [17]. All these publications demonstrate the power of fault attacks. However, these attacks either use the fault model of bit resets [3] in which case they do not need the faulty ciphertexts. Or the attacks only require the fault model of bit flips, in which case, however, the attacks need the faulty ciphertexts [9],[10],[6],[17]. The attacks presented in this paper use bit flips and, instead of faulty ciphertexts, the attacks only use so called collision information. This turns out to be a much weaker requirement than the requirement that an attacker gets complete faulty ciphertexts. To obtain our new attacks, we show how to combine fault attacks with so called collision attacks. In a collision attack the adversary tries to detect identical intermediate results during the encryption of different plaintexts, e.g., by using side channel information, and use this information to derive the secret key. Basically this idea was due to Dobbertin. Schramm et al. developed collision attacks against DES [19] and AES [18] and showed how to detect collisions using power traces.

We combine the concepts of fault and collision attacks by inducing faults to generate collisions. This approach allows to relax the requirement of getting faulty ciphertexts to the requirement of detecting collisions in the encryption process. First we explain the basic idea underlying our attacks by presenting an attack based on some rather strong assumptions. Then we present an attack utilizing the same basic ideas that successfully attacks a smartcard that is protected by a memory encryption mechanism. To the best of our knowledge, this is the first fault attack on smartcards protected by memory encryption.

To defend against side channel attacks the manufacturer invented several countermeasures. One type of countermeasure is intended to protect the card, e.g., shields, sensors or error detection. Another type is designed to render side channel attacks useless using techniques to obfuscate the side channel information, e.g. by random masking [16],[11],[2]. Yet another more efficient approach is to use a so called memory encryption mechanism (MEMO). Memory encryption mechanisms encrypt an intermediate result directly after it leaves the processor and decrypts data right before it enters the processor (see Figure 1). This guarantees that all data stored in the RAM is encrypted. The intention is that memory encryption makes it harder for an adversary to derive information about intermediate states of the encryption process by using side channels of the smartcard. In general, it is assumed that unlike the RAM the highly integrated processor is much to complicated to induce faults with some reasonable precision. Hence, memory encryption is widely believed to be a useful countermeasure against side channel attacks.

Due to the limited computational power of smartcards the MEM has to be very fast. So the manufacturers of smartcards use some light encryption algorithms that are very fast but may not be secure against serious cryptanalysis. To increase the impact of the MEM the manufacturer like to keep their algorithms secret. However, many manufacturers do not analyze the impact of MEMs on security but simply present it as an improvement of security. The strategy is to implement as many good looking countermeasures as possible by not exceeding a certain cost threshold. Even a weak countermeasure should increase security.

Our attack that works even in the presence of a MEM shows that the security improvement of the MEM as generally used is rather limited. In particular, we present an attack on an AES implementation protected by MEM that determines the full AES-Key by inducing only 285 faults and detecting collisions.

The paper is organized as follows. In Section 2 we present our model for analyzing fault based collision attacks. In Section 3 we describe some fault based collision attacks and analyze their complexity. Unlike the classical fault attacks using bit flips in [9],[10],[6] and [17] obtaining faulty ciphertexts is not essential for our attacks. Therefore our attacks are applicable in scenarios where classical fault attacks do not work. On the other hand, our new attacks need more faults than the classical fault attacks. We explain the basic idea in our first attack. This attack is our basic attack and is based on rather strong assumptions. However, in the sequel we show how to strengthen it and how to adapt it to several other scenarios. The second attack we present is is our strongest attack. This attack shows how to successfully attack a smartcard that is protected by a MEM. To the best of our knowledge this is the first successful attack against a smartcard protected by a MEM.

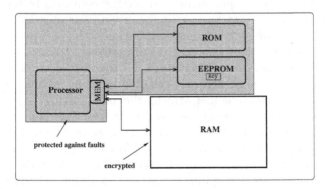

Fig. 1. Model of an enhanced smartcard with memory encryption mechanism (MEM)

2   Model

In our scenario we have a smartcard with an implementation of AES and a secret AES key K stored on it. We simplify the real world by assuming that only the RAM may leak some information and all other parts are well protected. An adversary

$\mathcal{A}$ is able to input chosen plaintexts and induce faults in terms of bit flips into the RAM in order to derive some information about the secret key K. To be more precise, $\mathcal{A}$ can flip a single bit of some specified byte in the memory and derive so called collision information about an internal state of the encryption process.

We regard the AES encryption as a bijective function AES_K that maps a plaintext p on a ciphertext depending on the secret key $K = (k_0, \ldots, k_{15})$ [1]. To model faults mathematically we extend that function with a second variable b that specifies a bit position during the computation of AES_K.

The set of all realizable functions via AES is extended by flipping bit b during the computation of AES_K. However, the extended function $\text{FAES}_K(p, b)$ is not bijective. So there exist collisions such that two intermediate states of computations of $\text{FAES}_K(p, b)$ and $\text{FAES}_K(p', b')$ with different inputs $(p, b) \neq (p', b')$ are equal. An attacker wants to detect those collisions and then use them to derive the secret key K.

We state three assumptions. First, $\mathcal{A}$ is able to feed chosen[2] plaintexts into the encryption algorithm. Second, $\mathcal{A}$ is able to induce faults in terms of bit flips into a specific bit of the RAM. Our third assumption is that $\mathcal{A}$ is able to derive some information about an intermediate state of the encryption process. However, we do not assume that this information lets $\mathcal{A}$ determine (parts of) the secret key directly. Nevertheless it enables $\mathcal{A}$ to detect if a collision occurred or not. We call any kind of information that lets $\mathcal{A}$ detect collisions *collision information* of some intermediate state of $\text{FAES}_K(p, b)$. Later we will show examples how to derive collision information.

We model collision information as the evaluation of an injective function f_K that depends on the concrete implementation of AES_K and the secret key K. It gets as input a plaintext p, the time t when a bit flip occurs, the byte position x and the bit position b inside that byte. The output is some information $f_K(p, t, x, b)$ about an intermediate state of the encryption. Certainly it is also possible to derive the collision information without inducing a fault.

Depending on the purpose of the smartcard f_K can have different realizations. Given the ciphertexts the detection of collisions is easy because the equality of ciphertexts implies equality of intermediate states. However, in many cases the output of an encryption is not available to the attacker. For example, if the smartcard computes a CBC-MAC or a hash value using AES as a building block $f_K(p, b)$ can simply be the MAC / hash value. Remember that the MAC is the final result of a number of interlinked AES encryptions and not the result of a single AES encryption. The final ciphertext could also be used as collision information if the smartcard computes multiple encryption with different encryption algorithms. Finally, if the smartcard computes a single encryption but does not output faulty ciphertexts, f_K could be the measurement of some side channel information, e.g., power consumption profile, that allows to detect collisions.

---

[1] For simplicity we only consider AES-128. However, all the attacks in this paper can easily be adapted to AES with larger key sizes.

[2] The attacks presented in this paper can also be transformed to known plaintext attacks.

To analyze the cost of an attack we simply count the number of faults we have to induce. The evaluation of f_K without inducing a fault is for free. We also neglect the complexity of additional computations that can be performed offline since in our cases they are obviously easy.

3   New Fault Attacks

3.1   Notation

For simplicity and clarity we define $p_i^{(r),(o)}$ to be the ith byte of the encryption state of plaintext p after the operation o of round r. The operation o is one of the following:

B   SubBytes
R   ShiftRows
C   MixColumns
K   AddRoundkey

For example, $p_5^{(3),(R)}$ is the 5th byte of the encryption state of plaintext p after the ShiftRows operation of round 3. The ith byte of the round key of round r is called $k_i^{(r)}$. We denote the transformation of SubBytes applied on a single byte x of the state simply as the application of the *sbox* on x and write it as $\mathbf{S}[x]$. To simplify notation we define $\Delta(p_i, q_i) = p_i + q_i$ to be the difference of two plaintext bytes p_i and q_i. Then $\Delta_{in}(p_i, q_i) = (p_i + k_i^{(0)}) + (q_i + k_i^{(0)}) = p_i + q_i$ is the input difference of (p_i, q_i) before the first application of the sbox and $\Delta_{out}(p_i, q_i) = (\mathbf{S}[p_i + k_i^{(0)}] + \mathbf{S}[p_i + k_i^{(0)}])$ is the output difference of (p_i, q_i) after the first application of the sbox. To simplify notation further we denote the collision information of encrypting plaintext p and inducing a bit flip into bit e of byte 0 of the state after the application of SubBytes in round 1 by $f_K(p_0^{(1),(B)}, e)$. We denote the evaluation of f_K without inducing a fault in the encryption process by $f_K(p_0^{(1),(B)}, -)$. From the context it will always be clear which plaintext is meant.

3.2   Scenarios

Below we describe some attacks that are based on the detection of collisions. For simplicity, we only show how to compute byte 0 of the secret key. Similar approaches can be used to compute the other key bytes.

We describe how to mount and analyze each attack in different scenarios. Each scenario is characterized by abilities of the adversary and/or the environment. The first characteristic defines the precision of the fault induction. We look at the two cases that the adversary is able to flip a specific bit of an intermediate state and that each possible bit flip occurs with probability $1/8$.

The second characteristic specifies whether the smart card is protected by a MEM (memory encryption mechanism) or not. The MEM encrypts every intermediate result that leaves the processor and decrypts a value right before it enters the processor (see Figure 1). Since a smart card has only restricted computational power and memory most manufacturers choose a byte oriented encryption function with a fixed key that is used for encryption and decryption. In our approach we simply model the memory encryption as an unknown but fixed function $h : \{0,1\}^8 \rightarrow \{0,1\}^8$. That means that we do not rely on a weakness in the memory encryption itself. In particular, we do not assume to have any information of how bit flips effect further processing of that byte.

The last characteristic defines whether collision information remains valid for a long period of time or not. If collision information does not remain valid there is no reason for $\mathcal{A}$ to store collision information since he cannot use it later in the attack. $\mathcal{A}$ is only able to compare collision information of two recently taken measurements and store the result. This effect could be caused by environments that are frequently changed such that collision information taken at different times is hardly comparable, e.g., due to some countermeasure that induces noise into the collision information. If, however, collision information remains valid over the time segment used for the attack it maybe useful for $\mathcal{A}$ to store this information in a preprocessing step to have it available once and for all. As we will see later stored information is useful as it helps to reduce the number of faults.

3.3   First Attack

First, we describe the scenario in which the attack takes place. We assume that $\mathcal{A}$ can flip a specific bit e of the intermediate state $p^{(1),(B)}$. We also assume that collision information remains valid over the time span of the attack. Finally, we assume that the smartcard is not protected by a MEM.

In a preprocessing step the adversary computes an array T_e of length 256. In position $T_e[y], y \in \{0, \ldots, 255\}$ the array stores the following information:

$$T_e[y] := \{\{s,t\} \mid s+t = y, \mathbf{S}[s] + \mathbf{S}[t] = 2^e\},$$

i.e., $T_e[y]$ stores all (unordered) pairs of bytes with $\Delta_{in}(s,t) = y$ and $\Delta_{out}(s,t) = \mathbf{S}[s] + \mathbf{S}[t] = 2^e$. Furthermore, by $C_e[y]$ denote the union of sets in $T_e[y]$. The sets $C_e[y]$ are pairwise disjoint. As it turns out, for every $e \in \{0,1,\ldots,7\}$ we have that 129 sets $C_e[y]$ are empty, 126 sets $C_e[y]$ contain exactly two elements, and one set $C_e[y]$ contains exactly four elements.

Next, $\mathcal{A}$ collects a set T of collision information $f_K(p_0^{(1)(B)}, -)$ for all 256 different values of p_0 and arbitrary but fixed $p_1, \ldots, p_{15}$. Then $\mathcal{A}$ chooses an arbitrary value q_0 and encrypts the corresponding plaintext flipping an arbitrary bit e of $q_0^{(1),(B)}$. If f_K has the property that $f_K(p_0^{(1),(B)}, -) = f_K(q_0^{(1),(B)}, e)$ $\mathcal{A}$ is able to find the corresponding plaintext p_0 satisfying $\mathbf{S}[p_0 + k_0] = \mathbf{S}[q_0 + k_0] + 2^e$ by comparing the collision information with the elements of T. Given the pair p_0, q_0 the adversary knows the difference $p_0 + k_0 + q_0 + k_0 = p_0 + q_0$. Using array T_e the adversary $\mathcal{A}$ now concludes $\{p_0 + k_0, q_0 + k_0\} \in T_e[p_0 + q_0]$. Hence, $\mathcal{A}$ knows that the correct key byte k_0 satisfies

$$k_0 \in \{p_0 + s \mid s \in C_e[p_0 + q_0]\}. \tag{1}$$

As mentioned above, $|C_e[y]| \leq 4$ for all y, and $|C_e[y]| = 2$ for all but one y. Hence, at this point $\mathcal{A}$ has reduced the number of possible values for key byte k_0 to at most 4.

Next, the adversary repeats the experiment described above with some value q_0', such that $q_0' + s \notin C_e[p_0 + q_0]$ for all $s \in \{p_0 + \bar{s} \mid \bar{s} \in C_e[p_0 + q_0]\}$. Using the collision information in set T, the adversary determines p_0' such that $\mathbf{S}[p_0' + k_0] = \mathbf{S}[q_0' + k_0] + 2^e$. As before $\mathcal{A}$ concludes that the key byte k_0 satisfies

$$k_0 \in \{p_0' + s \mid s \in C_e[p_0' + q_0']\}. \tag{2}$$

By choice of q_0', the adversary $\mathcal{A}$ is guaranteed that $p_0 + q_0 \neq p_0' + q_0'$. By elementary arithmetic it follows that if $|C_e[p_0' + q_0']| = |C_e[p_0 + q_0]| = 2$, then (1) and (2) uniquely determine the key byte k_0. As it turns out, the same is true if one of the sets has size four. However, to verify this, one has to perform a tedious case analysis based on the exact structure of the arrays T_e. We omit this in this extended abstract.

Cost Analysis To determine a single AES key byte $\mathcal{A}$ has to induce two faults. Thus 32 faults are enough to determine the full 128-bit AES key.

3.4   Second Attack

The scenario for this attack is as follows. We assume that $\mathcal{A}$ can flip a specific bit e of the intermediate state $p^{(0),(K)}$. We also assume that collision information remains valid over the time span of the attack. Finally, we assume that the smartcard is protected by a MEM modelled as a function $h : \{0,1\}^8 \to \{0,1\}^8$. This implies that after a flip of bit e the encryption continues using the value $h^{-1}(h(p_i + k_i) + 2^e)$ instead of $p_i + k_i$. Therefore, we assume that we have no information about the impact of bit flips on the encryption process.

The attack is divided into two steps. In the first step $\mathcal{A}$ collects the necessary information to compute a function g_0 that is equal to h up to some constant coefficient. To do so $\mathcal{A}$ selects a set S of 256 plaintexts p that take on all different values in byte p_0 and that are equal in each other byte. $\mathcal{A}$ uses the smartcard to derive the collision information for each of these plaintexts by evaluating $f_K(h(p_0^{(0)(K)}), -)$ and stores it in the table T. Then $\mathcal{A}$ encrypts plaintexts p of the set S and induces a bit fault into bit $0 \leq e \leq 7$ of $h(p_0^{(0),(K)})$ and compares the collision information $f_K(h(p_0^{(0),(K)}), e)$ with the entries of table T to find the corresponding plaintext p_0'. So $\mathcal{A}$ knows the difference

$$h(p_0 + k_0) + h(p_0' + k_0) = 2^e$$

and stores the triple (p_0, p_0', e) in a difference table DT. This step is repeated for different plaintexts p and for different faulty bit positions until $\mathcal{A}$ has enough information to compute the differences

$$h(p_0 + k_0) + h(p_0' + k_0)$$

of one byte p_0 with all other bytes p_0'. The details are given in the following lemma.

Lemma 1. *Let* $m : \{0,1\}^q \rightarrow \{0,1\}^q$ *be an unknown function defined over* $\mathbb{F}_{2^q}$. *There exists a set* D *of* $2^q - 1$ *pairs* $(u, v) \in \mathbb{F}_{2^q} \times \mathbb{F}_{2^q}$ *with the following property: If for all* $(u, v) \in D$ *we have that* $m(u) + m(v) = 2^e$ *for some known* $e \in \{0, \ldots, q - 1\}$, *then one can determine a function* g *such that* $g + c = m$ *for some constant* $c \in \mathbb{F}_{2^q}$.

Proof. Given some set $D \subseteq \mathbb{F}_{2^q} \times \mathbb{F}_{2^q}$ we construct a graph G whose set of vertices is $\mathbb{F}_{2^q}$ as follows. We connect two vertices u, v with an edge of weight e if $(u, v) \in D$.

If in G there exists a path between two vertices x, y then the difference $m(x) + m(y)$ is determined by the differences of pairs in D. Furthermore, if the graph G is connected we can compute the difference $m(x) + m(y)$ for all $(x, y) \in \mathbb{F}_{2^q} \times \mathbb{F}_{2^q}$. In particular, we can determine all differences of the form $m(u) + m(u_0)$ for an arbitrary but fixed input u_0. Then using Lagrange interpolation we can now compute the function $g(u) = m(u) + m(u_0)$. Setting $c := m(u_0)$ proves the lemma.

Next we describe a set D of pairs (u, v) with known differences $m(u) + m(v) = 2^e$, such that the graph G as defined above is in fact connected. First we fix an arbitrary $e_1 \in \{0, \ldots, q - 1\}$. Then there exists a set D_1 of 2^{q-1} distinct pairs $(u, v) \in \mathbb{F}_{2^q} \times \mathbb{F}_{2^q}$ such that $m(u) + m(v) = 2^{e_1}$. All pairs in D_1 will be elements of D. If we consider the graph whose edges are defined by pairs in D_1 we get a graph G_1 on the vertex set $\mathbb{F}_{2^q}$ that consists of 2^{q-1} connected components each consisting of exactly 2 vertices.

Next we choose $e_2 \neq e_1$. Then there exists a set D_2 of 2^{q-2} pairs of vertices (u, v) with $m(u) + m(v) = 2^{e_2}$ such that each pair in D_2 connects different connected components of G_1. We call the resulting graph G_2. The set D will also contain all elements from D_2.

Continuing in this way with all possible $e_i \in \{0, \ldots, q - 1\}$ we get sets of pairs $D_1, D_2 \ldots, D_q$ and graphs $G_1, G_2, \ldots, G_q$ such that G_i has 2^{q-i} connected components. In particular, G_q is connected. Moreover, the edges of G_q are given by the pairs in $D := \bigcup_{i=1}^{q} D_i$. The size of D is $2^q - 1$. This proves the lemma.

We want to apply Lemma 1 to the function $h(x + k_0)$. It is easy to see that $\mathcal{A}$ can compute exactly the set of differences D described in the proof of Lemma 1 since he is able to flip a specific bit. Hence, knowing D the adversary $\mathcal{A}$ can compute a function $g_0 : \{0,1\}^8 \rightarrow \{0,1\}^8$ such that for all $x \in \mathbb{F}_{256}$ the difference $g_0(x) + h(x + k_0)$ is some constant $c_0 \in \mathbb{F}_{256}$. Since $\mathcal{A}$ does not know the constant c_0 he does not get any information about the key byte k_0 at this point.

$\mathcal{A}$ continues by computing for all other byte positions i a function $g_1, \ldots, g_{15}$ such that for all $x \in \mathbb{F}_{256}$ the function $g_i : \{0,1\}^8 \rightarrow \{0,1\}^8$ has the property that $g_i(x) + h(x + k_i) = c_i$ for some unknown constant $c_i \in \mathbb{F}_{256}$. Each of the g_i's does not reveal any information about the involved key byte k_i because the constant c_i can take on all possible values and is unknown to $\mathcal{A}$.

To derive information about the key $\mathcal{A}$ proceeds as follows. He guesses two candidates $\widehat{k_0}, \widehat{k_i}$ for the keybytes k_0, k_i, respectively. To test this hypothesis on the key $\mathcal{A}$ selects several bytes x uniformly at random and computes

$$g_0(x + \widehat{k}_0) = h(x + \widehat{k}_0 + k_0) + c_0$$

and

$$g_i(x + \widehat{k}_i) = h(x + \widehat{k}_i + k_i) + c_i.$$

Depending on the hypothesis $(\widehat{k}_0, \widehat{k}_i)$ the difference $t_{0,i} := g_0(x + \widehat{k}_0) + g_i(x + \widehat{k}_i)$ computes to

$$h(x) + c_0 + h(x) + c_i = c_0 + c_i \text{ ,if } \widehat{k}_0 + k_0 = \widehat{k}_i + k_i \tag{3}$$

$$h(x + \widehat{k}_0 + k_0) + c_0 + h(x + \widehat{k}_i + k_i) + c_i \text{ ,if } \widehat{k}_0 \neq k_0 \text{ and } \widehat{k}_i \neq k_i \tag{4}$$

$$h(x) + c_0 + h(x + \widehat{k}_i + k_i) + c_i \text{ ,if } \widehat{k}_0 = k_0 \text{ and } \widehat{k}_i \neq k_i \tag{5}$$

$$h(x + \widehat{k}_0 + k_0) + c_0 + h(x) + c_i \text{ ,if } \widehat{k}_0 \neq k_0 \text{ and } \widehat{k}_i = k_i \tag{6}$$

Now we assume that the function h has the following property. There do not exist constants $a, c \in \mathbb{F}_{256}$ such that $h(x) + a = h(x + c)$ for all x. Note that this assumption does not restrict the choice of h for two reasons. First, a function used for memory encryption that does not have this property contains too much structure and is probably easier to attack. Secondly, most functions have this property. In fact, a random function has the property with probability at least $1 - 2^{-127}$.

This assumption implies that unlike in case (3) in cases (4),(5),(6) the difference $t_{0,i}$ is not constant. Moreover, if the guess $\widehat{k}_0, \widehat{k}_i$ was correct that is $\widehat{k}_0 = k_0$ and $\widehat{k}_i = k_i$ then $\mathcal{A}$ will always be in case (3). Now $\mathcal{A}$ can easily test the hypothesis $(\widehat{k}_0, \widehat{k}_1)$ by computing $t_{0,i}$ for several bytes x. If $t_{0,i}$ varies for several different x then $\mathcal{A}$ knows that he is not in case (3). It follows that the pair $(\widehat{k}_0, \widehat{k}_1)$ cannot be correct. On the other hand if $t_{0,i}$ remains constant $\mathcal{A}$ concludes to be in case (3) and keeps the pair $(\widehat{k}_0, \widehat{k}_1)$ as a potentially correct candidate.

This implies that for every possible key byte $\widehat{k}_0$ the adversary $\mathcal{A}$ obtains a single candidate $\widehat{k}_i$ for $1 \leq i \leq 15$ that fulfills condition (3). Guessing $\widehat{k}_0$ the adversary $\mathcal{A}$ can compute a vector $(\widehat{k}_1, \ldots, \widehat{k}_{15})$ composed of unique candidates $\widehat{k}_i$ that only depend on $\widehat{k}_0$. To uniquely determine the correct key $\mathcal{A}$ simply mounts an exhaustive search attack on the 256 possible values of $\widehat{k}_0$.

Cost Analysis. $\mathcal{A}$ has to induce 255 faults to compute a function g_i according to Lemma 1. To test a hypothesis of the key $\mathcal{A}$ does not need to induce faults. So the overall number of faults is $16 \cdot 255 = 4080$.

Improvement. The previous attack can be improved with respect to the number of induced faults as shown below. In the first step $\mathcal{A}$ computes the function g_0 such that $g_0(x) = h(x + k_0) + c_0$, where $c_0 \in \mathbb{F}_{256}$ is unknown, as above. To determine the other functions $g_1, \ldots, g_{15}$ $\mathcal{A}$ uses the fact that each g_i is related to g_0 by the following equation

$$g_i(x) = h(x + k_i) + c_i = g_0(x + \underbrace{k_i + k_0}_{s_i}) + c_i + c_0.$$

So knowing g_0 (determined as above) $\mathcal{A}$ computes a list of all 256 functions $g_{0,s} := g_0(x+s)$, $s \in \mathbb{F}_{256}$. To determine which of these functions equals g_i the adversary $\mathcal{A}$ chooses arbitrary p_i, q_i and evaluates $f_K(h(p_i^{(0),(K)}), -)$ and $f_K(h(q_i^{(0),(K)}), e)$ at byte position i. Using this information $\mathcal{A}$ computes some differences $g_i(p_i) + g_i(q_i)$ as described in the computation of g_0 above.

To determine the correct function $g_i = g_{0,s_i}$ $\mathcal{A}$ simply checks which of the function $g_{0,s}$ fulfills these differences simultaneously until only one function remains. See below for the required number of experiments. Then $\mathcal{A}$ knows the sum $s_i = k_0 + k_i$ of two AES key bytes. $\mathcal{A}$ repeats this procedure for all other byte positions $0 \leq i \leq 15$. As before guessing $\widehat{k_0}$ the adversary $\mathcal{A}$ can determine a unique candidate $\widehat{k_i}$. That means that $\mathcal{A}$ has a vector $(\widehat{k_1}, \ldots, \widehat{k_{15}})$ with fixed candidates $\widehat{k_i}$ for each of the 256 candidates $\widehat{k_0}$. Like in the original version of this attack this reduces the set of possible AES keys to only 256 candidates. An exhaustive search reveals the full AES key.

Cost Analysis. To compute g_0 the adversary $\mathcal{A}$ has to induce 255 faults like in the original version. To determine further g_i's $\mathcal{A}$ has to collect a set of differences $g_i(p) + g_i(q)$ that is fullfilled by only one of the 256 functions $g_{0,s}$ simultaneously. Notice that if the function $g_{0,s}$ fulfills a difference, i.e., $g_0(p+s) + g_0(q+s) = g_i(p) + g_i(q)$ then because of symmetry the function $g_{0,s'}$ given by $s' := p+q+s$ also fulfills this difference since

$$g_0(p+(p+q+s)) + g_0(q+(p+q+s)) = g_0(q+s) + g_0(p+s) = g_i(q) + g_i(p).$$

Assuming that the 256 functions $g_{0,s}$ behave like random permutations (except for the symmetry) we expect that $\mathcal{A}$ needs 2 differences to uniquely identify the correct one with high probability. We tested this assumption by various experiments and in our experiments it proved to be correct. Hence, we expect that $\mathcal{A}$ needs $255 + 15 \cdot 2 = 285$ faults to determine the full AES key.

As mentioned before we do not consider the complexity of the offline calculations like Lagrange interpolation etc. since all these calculations are easy to perform.

3.5   Third Attack

First, we describe the scenario in which the attack takes place. We assume that $\mathcal{A}$ can flip a specific bit e of the intermediate state $p^{(1),(B)}$. We do not assume that collision information remains valid over the time span of the attack. Hence, $\mathcal{A}$ is only able to compare collision information of two recently obtained measurements. Finally, we assume that the smartcard is not protected by a MEM. Because it is always clear from the context we simplify notation by identifying elements of $\mathbb{F}_{256}$ with their canonical representation as elements of the set $\{0, \ldots, 255\}$.

As a basis for his attack $\mathcal{A}$ fixes some input difference Δ_{in} and output difference Δ_{out} of the application of the sbox in round 1. To be able to detect collisions with a single bit flip we restrict Δ_{out} to be a power of 2.

The analysis of the sbox shows that there are a lot of suitable values for Δ_{in} and Δ_{out} (see technical analysis in the full version of the paper). E.g. $\mathcal{A}$ chooses $\Delta_{in} = 10$ and $\Delta_{out} = 4$. Only the two pairs

$$Z_1 := (p_0 + k_0 = 0, q_0 + k_0 = 10)$$

and

$$Z_2 := (p_0 + k_0 = 244, q_0 + k_0 = 254)$$

together with their commuted counterparts fulfill the chosen requirements. A fault that is induced into bit 2 of $q_0^{(1),(B)}$ after the application of the sbox results in a collision for one of these pairs. In order to detect such a collision the collision information f_K should have the property that

$$f_K(p_0^{(1),(B)}, -) = f_K(q_0^{(1),(B)}, 2).$$

If $\mathcal{A}$ finds such a collision he can conclude that the key byte k_0 is an element of the set

$$\mathcal{K} = \{p_0 + 0, p_0 + 10, p_0 + 244, p_0 + 254\}$$

More precisely, the attack using f_K with the property defined above works as follows. First, the adversary $\mathcal{A}$ generates all 128 pairs of plaintexts (p, q) (without symmetry) that have difference 10 in byte 0 ($p_0 = q_0 + 10$) and are equal in the other bytes, i.e.,

$$\Delta(p_i, q_i) = \begin{cases} 10, \text{ if } i=0 \\ 0, \text{ otherwise} \end{cases}$$

$\mathcal{A}$ knows that exactly two of these pairs have output difference 4 in byte 0. The input difference of the sbox is the same as the difference of p_0 and q_0 since AddRoundKey does not change it. $\mathcal{A}$ checks all 128 pairs (p, q) until

$$f_K(p_0^{(1),(B)}, -) = f_K(q_0^{(1),(B)}, 2).$$

Taking the symmetry into account it follows that either $p_0 + k_0 = 0$, $p_0 + k_0 = 10$, $p_0 + k_0 = 244$ or $p_0 + k_0 = 254$. So there are only 4 candidates for k_0 left. $\mathcal{A}$ can repeat this attack for all byte positions of the state. This leaves $2^{2 \cdot 16} = 2^{32}$ possible keys. To determine the complete 128-bit AES key $\mathcal{A}$ mounts an exhaustive search attack.

Cost Analysis In the first step $\mathcal{A}$ examines 128 pairs of plaintexts with difference 10. Two of these pairs result in a collision so the expected number of faults $\mathcal{A}$ has to induce is $(2/128)^{-1} = 64$. To compute a 128 bit AES key $\mathcal{A}$ expects to induce $16 * 64 = 1024$ faults and a brute force attack of size 2^{32}.

Alternative To determine the correct candidate of the key byte $\mathcal{A}$ could also repeat the same procedure as above with another difference. We assume that f_K lets $\mathcal{A}$ detect collisions when flipping bit 3, i.e.

$$f_K(p'_0^{(1),(B)}, -) = f_K(q'_0^{(1),(B)}, 3).$$

If we look at all pairs at all pairs (p', q') such that

$$\Delta(p'_i, q'_i) = \begin{cases} 5, \text{ if } i=0 \\ 0, \text{ otherwise} \end{cases}$$

an analysis of the sbox shows that $Z_3 := (p_0' + k_0 = 0, q_0' + k_0 = 5)$ and $Z_4 := (p_0' + k_0 = 122, q_0' + k_0 = 127)$ are the only pairs with $\Delta_{in} = 5$ and $\Delta_{out} = 8$. Detecting one of these pairs using f_K yields again a set of 4 candidates for k_0.

Next, $\mathcal{A}$ computes the difference of plaintexts p_0 and p_0'. The difference must be one of the differences listed in Table 1. Since all possible differences are distinct $\mathcal{A}$ can determine $p_0 + k_0$ and hence k_0.

Table 1. All possible differences of p_0, p_0'

	$p_0 + k_0$			
$p_0' + k_0$	0	10	244	254
0	0	10	244	254
5	5	15	241	251
122	122	112	142	132
127	127	117	139	129

Cost Analysis. Following the cost analysis as above this method determines the correct candidate of each key byte with 1024 faults as in the previous method plus additional 1024 faults.

3.6 Fourth Attack

First, we describe the scenario in which the attack takes place. We assume that $\mathcal{A}$ can flip a bit of a specific byte of the intermediate state $p^{(1),(B)}$. However, he has no control over the bit position. Instead, we assume that all of the 8 possible bit flips occur with the same probability $1/8$. We also assume that collision information remains valid over the time span of the attack. Finally, we assume that the smartcard is not protected by a MEM.

The attack works as follows. In a first step $\mathcal{A}$ selects a set S of 256 plaintexts p that take on all different values in byte p_0 and are equal in each other byte. $\mathcal{A}$ collects the collision information $f_K(p_0^{(1),(B)}, -)$ for all elements of S. Then he chooses an arbitrary q_0 and encrypts the corresponding plaintext inducing a fault into bit e of $q_0^{(1),(B)}$. By comparing the collision information $f_K(q_0^{(1),(B)}, e)$ with the collision information collected in the first step $\mathcal{A}$ can determine the corresponding plaintext p_0 such that $\mathbf{S}[p_0 + k_0] = \mathbf{S}[q_0 + k_0] + 2^e$. Note that e is unknown to $\mathcal{A}$ since he does not have any influence on the bit position. $\mathcal{A}$ can test all candidates $\widehat{k_0}$ of k_0 by simply checking if $\mathbf{S}[p_0 + \widehat{k_0}] + \mathbf{S}[q_0 + \widehat{k_0}]$ is a power of 2. If this condition is true $\mathcal{A}$ stores $\widehat{k_0}$ as a possible key value and discard it otherwise. Analysis of the AES sbox shows that after checking all candidates a set of at most 16 candidates will remain. $\mathcal{A}$ repeats this procedure with different q_0 until only one candidate is left. Using a refined method similar to the attack in Section 3.3 using several different q_0 we can determine the correct key.

3.7 Fifth Attack

First, we describe the scenario in which the attack takes place. We assume that $\mathcal{A}$ can flip a bit of a specific byte of the intermediate state $p^{(1),(B)}$. However, he has no control over the bit position. Instead, we assume that all of the 8 possible bit flips occur with the same probability $1/8$. We do not assume that collision information remains valid over the time span of the attack. Hence, $\mathcal{A}$ is only able to compare collision information of two recently obtained measurements. Finally, we assume that the smartcard is not protected by a MEM.

$\mathcal{A}$ chooses Δ_{in} of the sbox in round 1 in such a way that the number of pairs that have difference Δ_{in} and output difference with Hamming weight 1 is maximal. This choice reduces the number of faults $\mathcal{A}$ has to induce as we will see later. Analysis of the sbox shows that $\Delta_{in} = 216$ is the best choice since 8 is the maximum number of pairs that fulfill the requirements.

A single bit flip induced into $q_0^{(1)(B)}$ may produce a collision if and only if $p_0 + k_0$ is one of the following values:

$$0, 2, 8, 28, 29, 41, 111, 117, 173, 183, 196, 197, 208, 216, 218, 241.$$

To detect the collision f_K should have the property that

$$f_K(p_0^{(1)(B)}, -) = f_K(q_0^{(1)(B)}, b) \tag{7}$$

A collision implies that k_0 is an element of the set of 16 candidates

$$\mathcal{K} = \{ \, p_0, p_0 + 2, p_0 + 8, p_0 + 28, p_0 + 29, p_0 + 41, p_0 + 111, p_0 + 117, p_0 + 173, \\ p_0 + 183, p_0 + 196, p_0 + 197, p_0 + 208, p_0 + 216, p_0 + 218, p_0 + 241\}.$$

To determine p_0 the adversary $\mathcal{A}$ first builds a list of all 128 pairs (p_0, q_0) of plaintexts with difference 216 in byte 0 and difference 0 in all other bytes. Then $\mathcal{A}$ selects an arbitrary q_0, derives $f_K(q_0^{(1)(B)}, b)$ of the corresponding plaintext and compares it with the collision information $f_K(p_0^{(1)(B)}, -)$ of the corresponding plaintext of p_0. $\mathcal{A}$ repeats this procedure until he detects a collision. At his point $\mathcal{A}$ knows that k_0 is an element of the set $\mathcal{K}$.

To identify the correct candidate $\mathcal{A}$ could start an exhaustive search or repeat the procedure with a different combination of input and output differences. For example $\mathcal{A}$ chooses input difference 4 and output difference 32. Since $(88, 92)$ is the only such pair $\mathcal{A}$ can use f_K as a special case of (7) having the property

$$f_K(p_0^{(1)(B)}, -) = f_K(q_0^{(1)(B)}, 5)$$

to test each candidate $\widehat{k_0} \in \mathcal{K}$ of k_0.

To check whether a candidate $\widehat{k_0} \in \mathcal{K}$ is equal to k_0, $\mathcal{A}$ derives the collision information $f_K(p_0^{(1)(B)}, -)$ and $f_K(q_0^{(1)(B)}, b)$ for $p_0 = \widehat{k_0} + 92$ and $q_0 = \widehat{k_0} + 88$. Since $(92, 88)$ is the only pair with input difference 4 and Hamming weight of the output difference 1 $\mathcal{A}$ can check his hypothesis $\widehat{k_0}$. More precisely if $\widehat{k_0} \neq k_0$ the Hamming weight of the output difference will always be greater than 1 except for the case that $p_0^{(0)(K)} = 88$ and $q_0^{(0)(K)} = 92$. But this case implies that $\widehat{k_0}+4 = k_0$ which is impossible since every difference of two of the sixteen candidates is different from 4. So a wrong hypothesis cannot create a collision. On the other hand if $\widehat{k_0} = k_0$ then $p + k_0 = 92 + \widehat{k_0} + k_0 = 92$ and $q + k_0 = 88 + \widehat{k_0} + k_0 = 88$ is the demanded pair and $\mathcal{A}$ will detect a collision using f_K.

Cost Analysis. The success probability of finding one of the 8 pairs in part one of the attack choosing p_0 uniformly at random is $\frac{8}{128} \cdot \frac{1}{8} = \frac{1}{128}$. Hence 128 is the expected number of faults $\mathcal{A}$ has to induce.

The success probability in the second step is $(1/8) \cdot (1/16) = 1/128$. So we expect that $\mathcal{A}$ needs additional 128 faults. Hence the total number of faults to determine a key byte is $2 \cdot 128 = 256$.

To compute a complete 128 bit AES key we expect that $\mathcal{A}$ needs $16 \cdot 256 = 4096$ faults.

4   Concluding Remarks

In this paper we introduced the concept of fault based collision attacks that is a combination of collision attacks with fault attacks. We also showed how to mount fault based collision attacks on AES. Thereby we considered so called memory encryption mechanisms (MEM), a widely used countermeasure to protect against side channel attacks. We showed that using MEM in a straightforward manner does not increase security as much as one would expect. E.g., we presented a fault based collision attack that breaks an implementation protected by a MEM by inducing only about 285 faults.

To thwart our attack one has to be more careful. For example using different MEM functions for different bytes of a state obviously renders our attack useless. An alternative and more general approach is to use a general randomization strategy such as [2] based on [5].

References

1. Eli Biham and Adi Shamir. Differential fault analysis of secret key cryptosystems. In Burton S. Kaliski Jr., editor, *CRYPTO*, volume 1294 of *Lecture Notes in Computer Science*, pages 513–525. Springer, 1997.
2. Johannes Blömer, Jorge Guajardo, and Volker Krummel. Provably secure masking of AES. In H. Handschuh and M. Anwar Hasan, editors, *Proceedings Selected Areas in Cryptography (SAC), Lecture Notes in Computer Science Volume 3357*, pages 69–83. Springer-Verlag, 2004.
3. Johannes Blömer and Jean-Pierre Seifert. Fault based cryptanalysis of the advanced encryption standard (AES). In *Financial Cryptography'03, Lecture Notes in Computer Science Volume 2742*, pages 162–181. Springer-Verlag, 2003.
4. Dan Boneh, Richard A. DeMillo, and Richard J. Lipton. On the importance of checking cryptographic protocols for faults (extended abstract). In *EUROCRYPT*, pages 37–51, 1997.
5. Suresh Chari, Charanjit S. Jutla, Josyula R. Rao, and Pankaj Rohatgi. Towards sound approaches to counteract power-analysis attacks. In Wiener [21], pages 398–412.
6. Chien-Ning Chen and Sung-Ming Yen. Differential fault analysis on AES key schedule and some countermeasures. In Reihaneh Safavi-Naini and Jennifer Seberry, editors, *ACISP*, volume 2727 of *Lecture Notes in Computer Science*, pages 118–129. Springer, 2003.

7. Joan Daemen and Vincent Rijmen. *The Design of Rijndael.* Information Security and Cryptography. Springer Verlag, 2002.
8. Jean-François Dhem, François Koeune, Philippe-Alexandre Leroux, Patrick Mestré, Jean-Jacques Quisquater, and Jean-Louis Willems. A practical implementation of the timing attack. In Jean-Jacques Quisquater and Bruce Schneier, editors, *CARDIS*, volume 1820 of *Lecture Notes in Computer Science*, pages 167–182. Springer, 1998.
9. Pierre Dusart, Gilles Letourneux, and Olivier Vivolo. Differential fault analysis on A.E.S. In Jianying Zhou, Moti Yung, and Yongfei Han, editors, *ACNS*, volume 2846 of *Lecture Notes in Computer Science*, pages 293–306. Springer, 2003.
10. Christophe Giraud. DFA on AES. In Hans Dobbertin, Vincent Rijmen, and Aleksandra Sowa, editors, *AES Conference*, volume 3373 of *Lecture Notes in Computer Science*, pages 27–41. Springer, 2004.
11. Jovan Dj. Golic and Christophe Tymen. Multiplicative masking and power analysis of AES. In Kaliski Jr. et al. [12], pages 198–212.
12. Burton S. Kaliski Jr., Çetin Kaya Koç, and Christof Paar, editors. *Cryptographic Hardware and Embedded Systems - CHES 2002, 4th International Workshop, Redwood Shores, CA, USA, August 13-15, 2002, Revised Papers*, volume 2523 of *Lecture Notes in Computer Science*. Springer, 2003.
13. Paul C. Kocher. Timing attacks on implementations of Diffie-Hellman, RSA, DSS, and other systems. In Neal Koblitz, editor, *CRYPTO*, volume 1109 of *Lecture Notes in Computer Science*, pages 104–113. Springer, 1996.
14. Paul C. Kocher, Joshua Jaffe, and Benjamin Jun. Differential power analysis. In Wiener [21], pages 388–397.
15. François Koeune and Jean-Jacques Quisquater and. A timing attack against Rijndael. Technical Report CG-1999/1, Université Catholique de Louvain, 1999.
16. Thomas S. Messerges. Securing the AES finalists against power analysis attacks. In Bruce Schneier, editor, *FSE*, volume 1978 of *Lecture Notes in Computer Science*, pages 150–164. Springer, 2000.
17. Gilles Piret and Jean-Jacques Quisquater. A differential fault attack technique against SPN structures, with application to the AES and KHAZAD. In Colin D. Walter, Çetin Kaya Koç, and Christof Paar, editors, *CHES*, volume 2779 of *Lecture Notes in Computer Science*, pages 77–88. Springer, 2003.
18. Kai Schramm, Gregor Leander, Patrick Felke, and Christof Paar. A collision-attack on AES: Combining side channel- and differential-attack. In Marc Joye and Jean-Jacques Quisquater, editors, *CHES*, volume 3156 of *Lecture Notes in Computer Science*, pages 163–175. Springer, 2004.
19. Kai Schramm, Thomas J. Wollinger, and Christof Paar. A new class of collision attacks and its application to DES. In Thomas Johansson, editor, *FSE*, volume 2887 of *Lecture Notes in Computer Science*, pages 206–222. Springer, 2003.
20. Sergei P. Skorobogatov and Ross J. Anderson. Optical fault induction attacks. In Kaliski Jr. et al. [12], pages 2–12.
21. Michael J. Wiener, editor. *Advances in Cryptology - CRYPTO '99, 19th Annual International Cryptology Conference, Santa Barbara, California, USA, August 15-19, 1999, Proceedings*, volume 1666 of *Lecture Notes in Computer Science*. Springer, 1999.

An Easily Testable and Reconfigurable Pipeline for Symmetric Block Ciphers

Myeong-Hyeon Lee and Yoon-Hwa Choi

Computer Engineering Department
Hongik University, Seoul, Korea
yhchoi@cs.hongik.ac.kr

Abstract. In this paper, we present an easily-testable and reconfigurable pipeline for symmetric block ciphers. Bypass links with some extra pipeline stages are employed to detect errors, locate the corresponding faults, and reconfigure during normal operation. Duplicate computation, realized by using bypass links, is used to check the functionality of the modules for encryption. Test cycle insertion is controlled by activating bypass links either periodically or selectively, depending on the needs. Hardware overhead can be minimized by utilizing existing pipeline with one extra stage. Recovery from errors is achieved with negligible time overhead using the same bypass links employed for error detection.

1   Introduction

Securing data in wired/wireless transmission is the most common real-life cryptographic problem. It requires encryption of data to be transmitted and decryption to obtain the original data. Implementing encryption algorithms in hardware is desirable for various applications to meet the speed requirements under the power constraints. Secret-key block ciphers, such as DES, IDEA, and Rijndael [5][6], have similar internal structure, although their encryption functions may differ. Encryption is done with rounds of function, realizable with repeated use of a single functional module. Due to this feature the encryption algorithms can easily be implemented in hardware. Faults in the systems, however, may render the entire systems useless unless some effective fault tolerance techniques are provided.

Fault tolerance is generally achieved through redundancy in space or in time. It requires error detection, fault location, and subsequent reconfiguration to resume normal operation. In fault tolerance of symmetric block ciphers, most research has focused on concurrent error detection (CED) using time or space redundancy [1][3]. Without proper encoding of data, time redundancy based CED can only detect transient faults, although hardware overhead can be minimized. In space redundancy, some extra hardware, typically a copy, is used to perform the same function, and the results are compared. In [2] coding techniques have been applied to detect errors in block ciphers. The overhead required for encoding/decoding is relatively small compared to the traditional hardware redundancy technique.

L. Breveglieri et al. (Eds.): FDTC 2006, LNCS 4236, pp. 121–130, 2006.

Karri et al. [4] have proposed a concurrent error detection technique for symmetric encryption algorithms, exploiting the inverse relationship between encryption and decryption. It has been applied to three different levels of encryption: algorithm-level, round-level, and operation-level. A novel parity based error detection technique where the parity of cipher text is compared with the parity of plaintext to detect error has also been proposed in [7]. Since encryption process does not preserve the parity between input and output, a carefully calculated correction term is XORed to the parity of input to ensure that the resulting parity equals the parity of ciphertext in a fault-free operation.

The proposed techniques so far, however, are insufficient to tolerate faults since no mechanisms for fault location or recovery are provided. Although error detection is necessary to guarantee security, it would be desirable for the system to function correctly even with some faults. Fault tolerance requires a technique for locating faults and some facilities to isolate them from the rest of the system.

In this paper, we present an easily-testable and reconfigurable pipeline for achieving fault tolerance in symmetric block ciphers. Errors are detected during normal operation by time-space redundancy with bypass links. One or more extra stages with bypass links are employed to achieve fault tolerance. Duplicate computation in the next stage is used for error detection by comparison. A faulty stage identified is isolated by the same bypass link to resume normal operation. The time overhead due to the CED can be controlled by applying test cycles periodically or selectively depending on the needs.

2   Testable and Reconfigurable Pipeline for Block Ciphers

In order to provide dependable services while maintaining high throughput, we propose an easily-testable and reconfigurable pipeline for block ciphers. The idea is two-fold: 1) Exploit parallelism in encryption/decryption by pipelining to compensate for the time overhead inherent in a time redundancy based CED; 2) Implement CED and reconfiguration in a simple and unified structure to minimize the hardware overhead. Due to the similarity between encryption and decryption, without loss of generality, we focus on encryption of plaintexts. We begin with a virtual n-stage linear pipeline, realizing the n rounds of encryption. A slight variation should be allowed depending on preprocessing and postprocessing, if necessary. Since those special processing can be treated as partial utilization of the encryption block, our concern here is to detect faults in a pipeline of identical encryption blocks and to reconfigure during normal operation to achieve fault tolerance.

As a fault model, we assume that there is a single faulty encryption block in the n-stage virtual pipeline. More specifically, an error due to a faulty encryption block can be detected by duplicated computation using its neighboring block(s). A mismatch in comparison does not tell which of the two blocks is faulty. Hence, an additional computation/comparison is necessary to locate the faulty block and isolate it from the rest of the pipeline.

Let E_1, E_2,..., and E_n represent n encryption blocks in the n-stage virtual pipeline. Then the encryption will be completed when a plaintext passes through the chain of n blocks from left to right. In order to make the design easily testable and reconfigurable, we modify the design as shown in Fig. 1, where the n-rounds are realized using k pipeline stages, B_1,B_2,...,B_k. If $k < n$, circulation through the pipeline more than once may be necessary by controlling the two multiplexers M_a and M_b. The k-stage pipeline is extended to $k + r$ stages with $r(\geq 1)$ spare stages to detect faults using time-space redundancy and reconfigure with spares during normal operation. In addition, bypass links are added to each stage as shown in Fig. 2 to allow data duplication for error detection. The links will also be used for reconfiguration once a faulty block is identified. The architecture has a round-key generator and a diagnostic unit. The round key generator provides round-keys to the pipeline stages. It redistributes the keys whenever a new configuration is needed due to faults in the pipeline. The diagnostic unit is used to dynamically control the pipeline stages to operate in one of the normal, test, and bypass modes, to be addressed shortly, and to detect a fault, locate it, and reconfigure during normal operation. Comparators and one extra encryption block E_s are also included in the diagnostic unit for fault location.

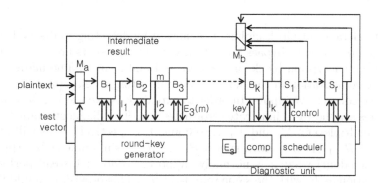

Fig. 1. An easily testable and reconfigurable pipeline for block ciphers

The multiplexer in front of B_1 is to select one of the three possible inputs: plaintext, intermediate result, and test vector. Each stage B_i receives a round key and bypass control signal, and generates $E_i(m)$ and I_i, where $E_i(m)$ is the encrypted output and I_i is the input to the next stage B_{i+1}. I_i will be used only when an error is detected. With this input, a third computation can be performed to locate the faulty encryption block.

In corporation of our concurrent error detection into symmetric block ciphers is straightforward. In Fig. 2, the first three blocks are redrawn with a more detailed internal structure for error detection and reconfiguration. Since all the blocks are identical, we only need to explain the structure of a single stage B_1, enclosed by dotted lines to highlight a stage of the pipeline. It consists of an encryption block E_1, a register R_1, and a 2-to-1 multiplexer M_1. E_1 takes an input and encrypts it with the key K_1, provided by the round-key generator. The result is stored in the intermediate pipeline register R_1 for the next round of operation. The multiplexer M_1 is employed for error detection and reconfiguration. For normal encryption, the lower input line will be selected. If the upper input line is selected, however, E_1 and R_1 will be bypassed. This configuration can be used to isolate a faulty stage from the rest of the pipeline. It may also be used for sending an input data to the next stage B_2. In other words, if the upper input line of M_1 is selected, the input to E_2 is the same as the input to E_1.

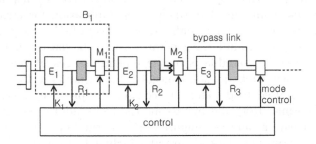

Fig. 2. Internal structure of each stage of the pipeline for block ciphers

Fault tolerance of block ciphers is achieved by detecting faults and reconfiguring the pipeline with bypass links. Hence we first presents how an error due to faults in an encryption block can be detected and located. The main idea is to duplicate computation in the next stage by inserting a delay (an idle cycle) between two consecutive inputs. In order to explain this, we use Fig. 3, where only two stages are shown to illustrate error detection. The diagnostic unit has to set the two multiplexers, M_i and M_{i+1}, to 0 and 1, respectively. This will allow the content of R_{i-1} to enter both stages B_i and B_{i+1} simultaneously. Apparently, B_{i+1} is not doing what it is normally supposed to do. It instead performs the same function as B_i with the same round-key K_i. This provision should be made under the control of the round-key generator and diagnostic unit. The results are compared to see if they match. A mismatch in the comparison will imply that there is a fault in one of the two encryption blocks, although we do not know which one is faulty.

In order to identify the faulty block by a majority voting, we need to perform one more computation and comparison. This additional computation is realized with a spare encryption block E_s. One multiplexer, under a single fault assumption, is used to select the input that has caused a mismatch in comparison. The selected data, I_i, is then encrypted with the same key K_i. A single comparison after the recomputation in E_s will be sufficient to determine which encryption block is faulty.

In the proposed design, the pipeline has been modified by adding $r \geq 1$ extra stages and bypass links to provide uninterrupted service even in the event of failure. Since the bypass links can be pretested or easily checked when the pipeline is idle, we assume that they are reliable for CED of the encryption

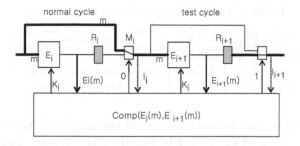

Fig. 3. Error detection using duplicate computation

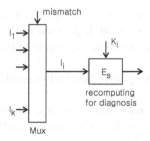

Fig. 4. Fault location with recomputing and comparison

blocks. Initially, all the stages except the spare stages participate in the normal operation.

Reconfiguration of the pipeline upon detection of a fault in stage i is straightforward with the bypass links. The newly formed pipeline may also perform the proposed CED along with encryption. In practice, we suggest to use one or two spare stages. This results in a low overhead design with fault tolerance capability. In fact, error detection has been done without hardware overhead since one extra stage for duplicate computation can be treated as a temporary utilization of the existing stage(s) for reconfiguration.

3   Scheduling for Error Detection and Reconfiguration

In this section, we will discuss how to schedule the pipeline stages to set them to operate momentarily in the test mode and how to isolate a pipeline stage in the event of failure. In order to realize the dynamic test scheduling, each stage in the pipeline is made to operate in one of three different modes: normal, bypass, and test modes as shown in Table 1, depending on values of the control signals to the multiplexers C_{i-1} and C_i and the round key to each stage K_{in}. A stage in the normal mode performs encryption. A stage in the bypass mode simply bypasses the input to the output and will be removed from the pipeline. A stage in the test mode will perform the same function as its previous stage for error detection.

Table 1. Three different modes of each stage B_i

mode	C_{i-1}	C_i	K_{in}	explanation
normal	1	×	K_i	
test	0	×	K_{i-1}	key of the previous stage
bypass	×	0	×	isolated all the time

Since the CED is done by stealing some of the normal cycles for testing purposes, the time overhead for error detection depends on how often we insert an idle cycle (for testing) in the pipeline. We consider the following four possible strategies, although they can be combined in practice.

(1) Complete checking: Every encryption operation is duplicated and compared to guarantee error-free operation. Inputs enter the pipeline every other cycles to provide a test cycle in between. Apparently this strategy requires a 100% time overhead.
(2) Periodic checking: A test cycle is inserted periodically depending on the load of the pipeline.
(3) Selective checking: Test rate may change depending on the pipeline status. If it is heavily loaded, we reduce the number of test cycles accordingly. If it is lightly loaded, we insert more test cycles, not necessarily periodically.
(4) Checking with test vectors: This can be used when there are some cycles without normal inputs (i.e., idle). The diagnostic unit generates test vectors to be applied to the pipeline for cleaning it up.

Regardless of the strategies chosen, the proposed CED involves one idle cycle for duplicate computation along the pipeline, equivalent to inserting a delay (test cycle) into the pipeline. This can be realized by applying a zero control signal to multiplexers, $M_1, M_2,...,M_k$, in the given order. Assuming that a test cycle starts at time $t=1$, the required control signals for the k multiplexers are shown in Table 2. A zero on a control line means a duplicated data for testing purposes is given to the next stage as opposed to the normal data. Since a zero needs to move along the pipeline, a shift register may be used.

As an illustration, assume that the pipeline consists of four stages B_{1-4} for normal operations and one extra stage S_1 for replacement in the event of failure.

Table 2. Controlling multiplexers for error detection

time	M_1	M_2	M_3	M_4	–	–	M_k	M_{s1}	–
$t=1$	0	1	1	1	1	1	1	1	1
$t=2$	1	0	1	1	1	1	1	1	1
$t=3$	1	1	0	1	1	1	1	1	1
$t=4$	1	1	1	0	1	1	1	1	1
$t=-$	1	1	1	1	0	1	1	1	1
$t=-$	1	1	1	1	1	0	1	1	1
$t=k$	1	1	1	1	1	1	0	1	1

Case 1 requires a 100% time overhead as shown in Table 3, where inputs are applied to the pipeline every other cycle with a test cycle between them (e.g, $\tilde{3}$ between 2 and 3). S_1 is used for duplicate computation of B_4. The entire operation is controlled by the diagnostic unit.

Table 3. Test scheduling for complete checking

stage	t_1	t_2	t_3	t_4	t_5	t_6	t_7	t_8	t_9	—		
B_1	1	-	2	-	3	-	4	-				
B_2	$\tilde{1}$	1	$\tilde{2}$	2	$\tilde{3}$	3	$\tilde{4}$	4				
B_3			$\tilde{1}$	1	$\tilde{2}$	2	$\tilde{3}$	3	$\tilde{4}$	4		
B_4					$\tilde{1}$	1	$\tilde{2}$	2	$\tilde{3}$	3	$\tilde{4}$	4
S_1						$\tilde{1}$		$\tilde{2}$		$\tilde{3}$		$\tilde{4}$

In case 3, test cycles are inserted selectively, as illustrated in Table 4, where at time t_5 the diagnostic unit inserts a delay for error detection. Only the result of the fifth input is checked as it moves along the pipeline. It may take longer to detect a fault due to selective checking.

Table 4. Test scheduling for selective checking

stage	t_1	t_2	t_3	t_4	t_5	t_6	t_7	t_8	t_9	—
B_1	1	2	3	4	-	5	6	7		
B_2		1	2	3	4	$\tilde{5}$	5	6	7	
B_3			1	2	3	4	$\tilde{5}$	5	6	7
B_4				1	2	3	4	$\tilde{5}$	5	6
S_1								$\tilde{5}$		

In case 4, the pipeline is idle and hence test vectors are applied instead of plaintext to check the functionality of the pipeline. Pipeline advances similar to case 1 until it receives a normal input. This testing will clean up the pipeline without affecting throughput. In practice, a combination of the above four strategies may be used to enhance system reliability with minimum degradation in throughput.

Although fault detection is necessary for reliable encryption of plaintext, the pipeline cannot resume normal operation unless fault location and reconfiguration techniques are provided. To locate a faulty encryption block, we use a majority voting, as discussed in the previous section, with one extra encryption block. Once the faulty block is identified, the diagnostic unit sets the faulty stage to operate in the bypass mode from that time on to isolate it from the rest of the pipeline. One of the spare stages has to participate in forming a new pipeline with k stages. As illustrated in Fig. 5, B_3 through B_k will take the role of B_2 through B_{k-1}, respectively, and S_1 will replace B_k. S_2, which has been unused so far, will now participate in error detection. B_2, which is faulty, is then isolated by setting the control input of its associated multiplexer, M_2, to 0. The bypass link highlighted in the figure is a logical view of the bypassing. It is actually realized by the internal bypass link in Fig. 2. Now the k-stage pipeline ends at stage S_1, control signal to the multiplexer which connects the last stage to the first stage has to be changed. Once the faulty stage is bypassed, keys have to be redistributed to resume normal operation.

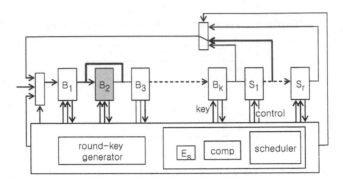

Fig. 5. Reconfigured pipeline after locating a faulty stage

4   Performance

In realizing symmetric block ciphers with a function of n rounds, we have employed a pipelined architecture to enhance throughput as well as fault tolerance capability. A fully pipelined implementation, i.e., an n-stage pipeline, would achieve the maximum throughput. If the cost or area is a concern, a compromised design with k stages, where $k < n$, may be a desirable alternative. For simplicity, we assume that n is a multiple of k (i.e., $n = c \cdot k$). In case $c \geq 2$, the k-stage pipeline has to be used repeatedly (c times).

We evaluate the performance in terms of throughput, hardware overhead, time overhead required for error detection, fault location, and reconfiguration. Suppose we insert a test cycle for every q normal cycles on average. Then every q normal inputs accompany one test input (i.e., a delay cycle) along the pipeline. For m inputs, we insert at most $\lceil \frac{m}{q} \rceil$ test cycles, equivalent to $m + \lceil \frac{m}{q} \rceil$ inputs along the pipeline. The resulting time overhead, is approximately $\frac{1}{q}$, regardless of the value of k. This overhead is incurred only when we duplicate a normal input for comparison. If test vectors are used for testing the pipeline when it is idle, the required time does not have to be treated as an overhead. The time overhead due to periodic or selective checking can be adjusted by properly choosing the value of q. Apparently, the time to identify a fault becomes longer as q increases.

Once an error is detected, however, the corresponding faulty encryption block can immediately be identified. The pipeline will then be reconfigured by using bypass links and resume normal operation. Keys for the pipeline stages have to be redistributed due to the reconfiguration. This extra time for recovery is negligibly small since setting the proper control signals will suffice.

In the design of block ciphers, pipelining is used to compensate for the loss of throughput due to the implementation of our CED technique. Overall the throughput can be improved even with a complete checking, compared to the non-pipelined design. Table 5 shows a comparison of our technique to a non-pipelined (with time redundancy for error detection) technique.

Table 5. Comparison of the proposed technique with a simple time redundancy technique (non-pipelined)

	non-pipelined	time-redundancy	proposed
Error detection	no	transient	transient/permanent
Fault tolerance	no	no	yes
No. of encryption blocks	1	1	$k+1$
Error detection time	n/a	1 cycle delayed	immediately
Time overhead	n/a	100%	$\frac{1}{q} \times 100\%$
Throughput	$\frac{1}{n}$	$\frac{1}{2n}$	$\frac{k}{n}\left(\frac{q}{1+q}\right)$

The proposed technique can detect both permanent and transient faults in an encryption block as long as the errors generated in the block are checked by duplicate computation. It can locate the corresponding faulty block right away. More importantly, it can tolerate faults through reconfiguration immediately after locating the faulty stage. Although the throughput goes down due to the delay insertion for error detection, the k-stage pipeline will bring it up to $\frac{k}{n}(\frac{q}{q+1})$. If $q=1$ (complete checking) and $k=2$ (two-stage pipeline), for example, the throughput is $\frac{1}{n}$, which is the same as the nonpipelined design. If k changes to 4, the throughput is doubled to $\frac{2}{n}$, while making a complete checking of the entire encryption operation. The throughput for various values of k and q is shown in Fig. 6.

The proposed pipelined architecture can tolerate multiple faulty blocks if there is more than one extra stage. Moreover, its performance degrades gracefully since the pipeline with bypass links can reconfigure itself into a pipeline with fewer stages.

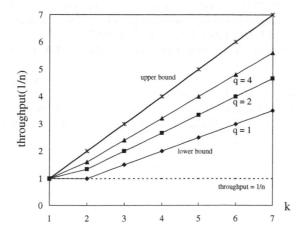

Fig. 6. Throughput for various values of k and q

5   Conclusions

In this paper, we have presented an easily-testable and reconfigurable pipeline for symmetric block ciphers. Errors are detected by duplicate computations using bypass links. A faulty encryption block has been isolated by activating the same bypass links for duplication. The time overhead for error detection can be controlled by dynamically inserting test cycles into the pipeline. The reduction in throughput due to the CED has been compensated by the increased performance through pipelining. A two-stage pipeline will achieve the same throughput as the original non-pipelined design. After that, throughput increases linearly in the number of stages. Moreover, the performance degrades gracefully since it can reconfigure itself to form a pipeline with fewer stages. The technique can best be used for block ciphers, where throughput and availability are of the utmost importance.

Acknowledgement

This work was supported by 2006 Hongik University Research Fund.

References

1. S. Wolter, H. Matz, A. Schubert, and R. Laur, "On the VLSI implementation of the International data encryption algorithm IDEA," IEEE Int. Symp. Circuits and Systems, vol.1, pp. 397-400, 1995.
2. S. Fernandez-Gomez, J.J. Rodriguez-Andina, and E. Mandado, "Concurrent error detection in block ciphers," IEEE International Test Conference, 2000, pp. 979-984.
3. H. Bonnenberg, A. Curiger, N. Felber, H. Kaeslin, R. Zimmermann, and W. Fichtner, "Vinci: Secure test of a VLSI high-speed encryption system," IEEE International Test Conference, 1993, pp. 782-790.
4. R. Karri, K. Wu, P. Mishra, and Y. Kim, "Concurrent error detection schemes for fault-based side-channel cryptanalysis of symmetric block ciphers," IEEE Trans. CAD, Vol. 21, No. 12, December 2002, pp. 1509-1517.
5. A. Menezes, P. van Oorschot, and S. Vanstone, Handbook of Applied Cryptography, CRC press, 1996.
6. J. Daemen, V. Rijmen, "AES proposal: Rijndael," http://www.esat.kuleuven.ac.be/ rijmen/rijndael/rijndaeldocV2.zip
7. R. Karri, G. Kuznetsov, and M. Goessel, "Parity-based concurrent error detection in symmetric block ciphers," IEEE Int. Test Conf., 2003, pp. 919-926.

An Adversarial Model for Fault Analysis Against Low-Cost Cryptographic Devices*

Kerstin Lemke-Rust and Christof Paar

Horst Görtz Institute for IT Security
Ruhr University Bochum
44780 Bochum, Germany
{lemke, cpaar}@crypto.rub.de

Abstract. This contribution presents a unified adversarial model for fault analysis which considers various natures of faults and attack scenarios with a focus on pervasive low-cost cryptographic devices. According to their fault induction techniques we distinguish the non-invasive adversary, the semi-invasive adversary, and the invasive adversary. We introduce an implementation based concept of achievable spatial and time resolution that results from the physical fault induction technique. Generic defense strategies are reviewed.

Keywords: Adversarial Model, Fault Analysis, Tampering, Physical Security, Implementation Attack, Tamper-Proof Hardware.

1 Introduction

Small low-cost cryptographic devices such as smartcards and RFID transponders have gained a high penetration in certain high-volume markets in the last decade. These devices are deployed for various security services like authentication purposes, ticketing and electronic payment. As cryptographic tokens become pervasive it is worth to reconsider the adversarial models of implementation attacks as the adversary might be the legitimate owner of the cryptographic device.

We focus on active implementation attacks which can be classified as fault analysis, physical manipulations and modifications. *Fault analysis* aims to cause an interference with the physical implementation and to enforce an erroneous behavior which can result in a vulnerability of a security service or even a total break. The terms manipulation and modification stem from definitions of physical security, e.g., from ISO-13491-1 [1] and address similar attacks. *Physical manipulation* aims to obtain a service in an unintended manner. *Physical modification* is an active invasive attack targeting the internal construction of the cryptographic device.

---

* This is a revised version of [15]. Follow-up work to this contribution can be found in [16]. The work described in this paper has been supported in part by the European Commission through the IST Programme under Contract IST-2002-507932 ECRYPT, the European Network of Excellence in Cryptology.

L. Breveglieri et al. (Eds.): FDTC 2006, LNCS 4236, pp. 131–143, 2006.
© Springer-Verlag Berlin Heidelberg 2006

If a cryptographic device is used in an hostile environment special properties for the device are required to ensure a certain level of physical security for the storage and processing of cryptographic keys. For the theoretical perspective on algorithmic tamper-proof security we refer to the concepts on *Read-Proof Hardware* and *Tamper-Proof Hardware* as given in [11]. *Read-Proof Hardware* prevents that an adversary is able to read internal data stored and *Tamper-Proof Hardware* prevents the adversary from changing internal data.

In a tamper-proof implementation, fault injections are not feasible per definitionem. However, in real life, practical experiences have shown that approaches towards tamper resistance are hard. Many contributions (e.g., [14,22,6,7,21]) have reported that semiconductor circuits are vulnerable against fault injections. Such findings are related to the development of devices for the use in space exploration and high-energy physics which have to tolerate particle radiation impact during operation [17,18]. In contrast to applications developed for safety and reliability reasons, security applications have to withstand an active malicious attacker. The importance of checking for errors in a cryptographic algorithm was also probably known before the first scientific contribution [10] appeared as the FIPS-140 standard already requires a cryptographic algorithm test ("known-answer test") [12] to be implemented in cryptographic modules during start-up. Moreover, in an error state, according to [12], the use of cryptographic algorithms shall be inhibited.

A variety of theoretical fault based attack scenarios has been published for different cryptographic algorithms in the past years. In the context of implementation attacks, however, the concrete assumptions on the adversarial capabilities remain vague in many theoretical contributions. This contribution aims to recapitulate and to present more graduated models that can be used as underlying assumptions to measure success probability of adversaries at real implementations.

We recollect previous fault induction techniques as well as concrete fault scenarios aiming at a unified adversarial model that may bridge the gap between the theoretical framework of algorithmic tamper-proof security and experiences from fault induction techniques. In our model we cover fault analysis against low-cost cryptographic devices. These devices are memory constrained and are not equipped with a self-destruct capability as required in the model of [11] and by the FIPS 140 security requirements for cryptographic modules [12]. We extend the concept of *Tamper-Proof Hardware* to computations, i.e., the adversary is not limited to induce the fault at data contents *prior to the computation*, as it is the case in [11]. In our model the fault can be induced also *during the computation* of a cryptographic service. By doing so, we are able to model the manifold nature of faults as well as to include Differential Fault Analysis [9,20] in a more adequate manner in case of constrained devices. Further, we also cover fault analysis at the use of non-cryptographic security services.

We have already learnt from [11] that tamper-proofness is not realizable against a powerful adversary applying a polynomial-time computable function to the actual memory contents without a self-destruct capability of the device.

We put forward the question whether experimental restrictions of the adversary exist that limit the full power of the adversary or whether the assessment of tamper-proofness is necessarily related to the efforts needed to break the cryptographic device. This contribution aims at providing an adversarial model for fault analysis that also captures implementation based properties.

1.1   Related Work

Reference [11] introduced algorithmic tamper-proof security. It defines a powerful tampering adversary who is able to perform (i) the cryptographic operation (the command Run($\cdot$)[1]), (ii) a probabilistic modification of secret data contents (the command Apply($\cdot$)), i.e., the fault injection, and (iii) a setup algorithm (the command Setup($\cdot$)) which loads key data. The adversary knows all construction details: especially, the adversary knows each bit-position in the device's memory. It is concluded in [11] that a component is needed which is both read-proof and tamper-proof to achieve general Algorithmic Tamper-Proof (ATP) Security. Reference [11] also discusses restrictions of the model assuming that the adversary is limited, for instance, it is only feasible for the adversary to perform a probabilistic flipping of bits in the device's memory. In this case [11] argues that checking for faults can be sufficient for ATP security, even if the device is not equipped with a self-destruct capability.

A recent survey on hardware security analysis with a strong focus on semi-invasive attacks is presented in [23]. It is stated that any individual bit of SRAM memory could be changed to a definitive state by optical fault induction. Both the targeting state '0' and '1' could be set, just by a lateral adjustment of the light spot.

Regarding the capabilities of adversaries other more practical approaches are done in [2] and [4]. These assessments cover implementation attacks in general and are not specialized to fault analysis.

The framework of Common Criteria [2] assesses the resistance of an implementation against attacks by rating the efforts that are needed for concrete attack scenarios. The highest grade achievable is resistance against high attack potential for all feasible attack paths. The rating takes into account the efforts needed for the identification and exploitation phase. Ratings are given for the categories "Elapsed Time", "Expertise", "Knowledge of TOE[2]", "Access to TOE" and "Equipment". To give an example for resistance against high attack potential we consider an attack known in the public domain: the TOE is assessed to be resistant against high potential if, e.g., an expert, who does not have detailed knowledge about the concrete TOE, needs bespoke[3] equipment and an attacking time (including access time to the TOE) of more than one month.

---

[1] Note that the command Run($\cdot$) itself is not subject to fault induction.

[2] Target of Evaluation.

[3] Extract of [2]: Bespoke equipment is not readily available to the public as it may need to be specially produced ..., or because the equipment is so specialised that its distribution is controlled, possibly even restricted. Alternatively, the equipment may be very expensive.

R. Anderson and M. Kuhn [4] referred to three different classes of attackers. They distinguish between "Class I (clever outsiders)", "Class II (knowledge-able insiders)", and "Class III (funded organisations)". Class I adversaries are bounded by moderately equipment and may have insufficient knowledge on the construction. The capabilities of Class II adversaries are manifold: they "have varying degrees of understanding of parts of the system but potential access to most of it. They often have highly sophisticated tools and instruments for analysis." Class III adversaries have access to great funding resources and can assemble teams of specialists.

2   Model of Low-Cost Cryptographic Devices

We consider low-cost cryptographic devices used in high-volume markets. Low-cost cryptographic devices may be based on hardware (circuitry) only such as, e.g., some RFID tags. Moreover, other devices additionally include software components such as, e.g., microcontroller based smart cards. In the latter case a reliable hardware-software co-design is also of interest. For example, error detection for hardware components might be (partially) implemented in software. In our discussions we aim to include both hardware and software aspects for fault induction. As memory building blocks are expensive, low-cost implementations iterate processing steps at the cost of an enlarged execution time. We assume that the implementation is deterministic to a certain extent.[4]

Physical security measures that aim to prevent the disclosure and modification of internals (software, cryptographic keys, application data and sub-components of the circuit) can be either *tamper resistant* or *tamper responsive*. Tamper resistance implies that the cryptographic module is able to avert all attacks even without any active reaction. Tamper response measures are active responses of the device once an attack is detected. Tamper responsiveness requires an internal non-interruptible surveillance of the device and mechanisms to zeroize cryptographic keys once an intrusion attempt is detected.

Typically, low-cost devices do not contain an internal battery and are supplied with energy and clock by a reader device. This has an implication towards tamper responsiveness: as these modules are not permanently powered up, an internal detection of active attacks is only possible if the device is powered up. The external interfaces of the cryptographic device include the channels used for communication and external supply of voltage and clocking. They are under complete control of the adversary. Computations are only feasible if the device is powered on and the computation can always be interrupted by removing the power supply. It is assumed that the power-on sequence carries out a test on the integrity of the internal construction. If the test fails, the device shall enter a non-responsive mode[5]. Also in case of a recognized error during operation, the device shall enter a non-responsive mode.

---

[4] The implementation may include internal timing jitter as caused by random process interrupts or asynchronous clocking.

[5] Not necessarily a permanent non-responsive mode.

We assume that the adversary has access to a security service, but it shall not be feasible for the adversary to load a key into the device[6] nor to modify the implementation and internal data without any active, physical interaction.

The security service may include a cryptographic algorithm, but also security enforcing services are feasible that work without any cryptographic means. An example for a non-cryptographic mechanism is a human authentication based on a Personal Identification Number (PIN) using an authentication failure counter.

3 Adversarial Models

The set-up for fault analysis based attacks consists of i) the physical device under test, ii) a reader device for the communication interface, and iii) a fault injection set-up. Optionally, iv) an analysis set-up can be additionally used to monitor the fault induction process and its effects, e.g, by measuring side channel leakage. The set-up as well as the information flow is illustrated in Fig. 1 and described in more detail below.

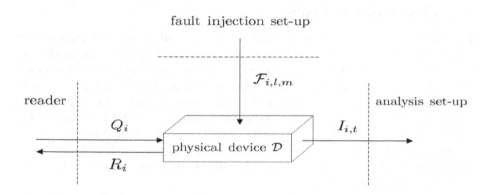

Fig. 1. Fault Analysis Set-Up

We denote the adversary by $\mathcal{A}$. By assumption $\mathcal{A}$ has physical access to the physical device $\mathcal{D}$ under attack and can run a high number of instances of a security service $\mathcal{S}$. Each instance is initiated by a query Q_i of $\mathcal{A}$ and $\mathcal{D}$ finishes after some computational time at time T_i returning a response R_i with $i \in \{1, \ldots, N\}$. $\mathcal{A}$ applies a probabilistic physical interaction process aiming at disturbing the intended computation of $\mathcal{S}$. $\mathcal{A}$ may be able to monitor the effects caused by physical interaction using auxiliary means, e.g., by observing the instantaneous leakage $I_{i,t}$ of the implementation at an analysis set-up at time t. If necessary, $\mathcal{A}$ applies cryptanalytical methods for a final analysis step.

Moreover, we assume that $\mathcal{A}$ is able to perform multiple fault injections that are bounded by M, wherein M is a small number. Let L be a small number of

---

[6] This is different to [11] that assumes that a setup command can be invoked by the adversary.

spatial separated fault injection set-ups that can be operated in parallel. The distinct fault injections during one invocation of S are numbered as $\mathcal{F}_{i,l,m}$ with $l \in \{1, \dots, L\}$ and $m \in \{1, \dots, M\}$. These fault injections occur at the times $\{t_{i,1,1}, \dots, t_{i,L,M}\}$ with $t_{i,1,1} \leq \dots \leq t_{i,L,M} \leq T_i$.

$\mathcal{A}$ acts in an active, adaptive way, i.e., both the queries Q_i as well as the parameters of $\mathcal{F}_{i,l,m}$ can be chosen adaptively. We point out that the leakage $I_{i,t}$ is typically not yet available for the configuration of $\mathcal{F}_{i,l,m}$ at the same instance of S unless a more demanding real-time analysis is applied.

Fault induction is a probabilistic process with success rate p. Complementary events with probability $1 - p$ are attempts that do not lead to any fault and attempts causing an unintended fault.

Informally speaking, an adversary $\mathcal{A}$ is *successful* if the insertion of faults either i) yields access to a security service S without knowledge of the required secret or ii) yields partial information about the secret.

The objectives of $\mathcal{A}$ are detailed in Section 3.2. We differentiate according to the means of $\mathcal{A}$ in Section 3.3.

3.1   Classification of Faults

For modeling, assumptions on the kind of faults as well as their consequences are needed. The first publication [10] considered a random transient fault model, i.e., 'from time to time the hardware performing the computation may induce errors'. The origin of the error is seen as a deficiency of the hardware that occurs by chance without any active enforcement of an adversary. Reference [9] introduces an asymmetric type of memory faults, so that changing one bit from zero to one (or the other way around) is much more likely. Further, Non-Differential Fault Analysis based on a permanent destruction of a memory cell is found in [9]. Reference [4] gives an example of a processing fault which leads to a bypass of a check of parameter bounds.

In this contribution we consider an active adversary physically enforcing the activation of faults. A fault is said to be *transient* if the device $\mathcal{D}$ remains full functional after fault injection. A fault is *permanent* if the device $\mathcal{D}$ stucks at the fault caused afterwards, i.e., the fault persists during life time of the device. If the fault affects data, we call it a *data fault*. If the fault affects the processing of the device $\mathcal{D}$, we call it a *processing fault*[7]. It is said that a data fault has a *preferred direction* if the probability to cause a bit transition from '0' to '1' is significantly different from the probability to cause a bit transition from '1' to '0'.

3.2   Objectives of the Adversary

Due to the variety of objectives of an adversary at a concrete implementation we aim to categorize them into main categories. $\mathcal{A}$ either aims to disclose the cryptographic secret by fault induction, or, alternatively, aims to disturb the intended operation of the security service that not necessarily need to be a cryptographic

---

[7] Note that processing faults may jeopardize any security service.

service. We distinguish Simple Fault Analysis (SFA), Successive Simple Fault Analysis (SSFA), and Differential Fault Analysis (DFA). SSFA and DFA apply to cryptographic implementations only, whereas SFA has a wider scope.

Definition 1 (Simple Fault Analysis). *Let S be a security service initiated by the query Q_i. Simple Fault Analysis (SFA) aims at the induction of faults (either transient or permanent, either data fault or processing fault) at an invocation of S and consists of the following steps:*

- *Choose the query Q_i and the parameterization of $\mathcal{F}_{i,l,m}$.*
  1. *Invocation: Send the query Q_i to the device $\mathcal{D}$.*
  2. *Fault Induction[8]: Apply physical interaction processes $\mathcal{F}_{i,l,m}$.*
  3. *Check (optional): Observe the processing of the device $\mathcal{D}$ by measuring $I_{i,t}$.*
  4. *Receipt (optional): Receipt and analysis of the response R_i.*
- *Exploitation: Exploit of the fault due to the concrete scenario.*

Example 1. i) An example of SFA is a transient or permanent processing fault like the physical deactivation of a hardware component, e.g., of an internal random number generator. Preparation work for physical destruction is conveniently done at power-down mode of the device. ii) Another example is the transient or permanent modification of a security enforcing data item aiming at a more privileged state. iii) Further, a modification of the security service itsself may occur, e.g., by causing a computational fault during fetching and decoding of program code in case of software implementations. iv) In the context of cryptographic security services, Fault Analysis at an RSA-CRT implementation [10] is a prominent example.

Definition 2 (Successive Simple Fault Analysis). *Let S be a cryptographic service using the secret key k and initiated by the query Q_i. Successive Simple Fault Analysis (SSFA) aims at the induction of multiple similar faults (either a transient or permanent data fault) and consists of the following steps:*

- *Choose the query Q_i and the parameterization of $\mathcal{F}_{i,l,m}$.*
  1. *Invocation: Send the query Q_i to the device $\mathcal{D}$.*
  2. *Fault Induction[8]: Apply physical interaction processes $\mathcal{F}_{i,l,m}$.*
  3. *Check (optional): Observe the processing of the device $\mathcal{D}$ by measuring $I_{i,t}$.*
  4. *Receipt: Receipt and analysis of the response R_i. Store R_i.*
- *Cryptanalysis: Apply mathematical cryptanalysis in order to determine the key k based on the responses R_i received.*

Example 2. i) Permanent fault induction can also be applied iteratively to compromise a cryptographic key successively by exploiting a preferred direction of data faults [8]. ii) In the presence of side channel countermeasures the probabilistic information 'error detected' and 'no error detected' is an oracle that can leak information on the secret key successively [13].

---

[8] Alternatively, this step can be (partially) scheduled before the invocation of S.

Definition 3 (Differential Fault Analysis). *Let* S *be a cryptographic service using the secret key* k *and initiated by a query* Q_i. *Differential Fault Analysis (DFA) consists of the following steps:*

- *Acquisition: Choose the query* Q_i *and the parameterization of* $\mathcal{F}_{i,l,m}$.
  1. *Invocation: Send the query* Q_i *to the device* $\mathcal{D}$.
  2. *Fault Induction[9]: Apply physical interaction processes* $\mathcal{F}_{i,l,m}$ *during computation of the cryptographic device.*
  3. *Check (optional): Observe the processing of the device* $\mathcal{D}$ *by measuring* $I_{i,t}$.
  4. *Receipt: Receipt and analysis of the response* R_i. *Store* R_i *if it is erroneous and appropriate for subsequent analysis.*
- *Cryptanalysis: Apply mathematical cryptanalysis in order to determine the key* k *based on the erroneous cryptograms* R_i *revealed.*

Example 3. DFA based on DES [9] and AES [20].

3.3 Means of the Adversary

According to FIPS 140-2 [3] we introduce the concept of the *cryptographic boundary* that encloses all security relevant and security enforcing parts of an implementation. Additionally, we define a second boundary that we call the *interaction boundary* that is specific for each physical interaction process. If the adversary does not pass the interaction boundary, the physical interaction is not effective at the cryptographic device. The interaction boundary can be an outer boundary of the cryptographic boundary, as, e.g., in case of temperature which affects the entire cryptographic module. Interaction with light is only feasible if a non-transparent encapsulation is partially removed, e.g., the chip is depackaged. Because of the limited range of the interaction, interaction processes using particles with non-zero mass may require to breach the cryptographic boundary.

The means of $\mathcal{A}$ can be manifold. In our view the main limitations are caused by the technical equipment available. The attacking time might not be that important and the knowledge about the implementation can be improved by reverse engineering. Because of this, we distinguish the non-invasive adversary $\mathcal{A}_{non-inv}$, the semi-invasive adversary $\mathcal{A}_{semi-inv}$, and the invasive adversary $\mathcal{A}_{inv}$ that are defined according to earlier work (e.g., [22]) on fault induction.

Definition 4 (Interaction Range). *Let* $\mathcal{A}$ *choose a physical interaction process.*
i) $\mathcal{A}$ *uses non-invasive means if the interaction boundary is an outer boundary of the cryptographic boundary. We denote the non-invasive adversary by* $\mathcal{A}_{non-inv}$.
ii) $\mathcal{A}$ *uses invasive means if the interaction boundary is an inner boundary of the cryptographic boundary. Accordingly, we denote the invasive adversary by* $\mathcal{A}_{inv}$.
iii) A semi-invasive adversary $\mathcal{A}_{semi-inv}$ *uses light or electromagnetic fields as the interaction process and is a special case of* $\mathcal{A}_{non-inv}$.

---

[9] Alternatively, this step can be partially scheduled before the invocation of S.

We outline that the interaction rate of physical interaction processes with matter is another important aspect that is not further detailed here.

If precision is needed for the fault injection, e.g., a specific SRAM cell of the cryptographic device is targeted, the fault has to be injected with sufficient resolution in space and time. The following two definitions yield a first estimation on the success rates for a given implementation.

Definition 5 (Spatial Resolution). *Let dA be the target area at depth z with depth dz so that $dA \cdot dz$ is the target volume of the device $\mathcal{D}$ for the fault induction. Let ΔA be the area and Δz be the depth of $\mathcal{D}$ that is affected by the fault induction process. Let $\mathcal{D}$ be consisting of homogeneous material and let the physical interaction depend only on the penetration depth z in $\mathcal{D}$.*

i) The probability to hit the target area is $p_{Area} = \begin{cases} 1 & : \quad \Delta A \leq dA \\ \frac{dA}{\Delta A} & : \quad \Delta A > dA \end{cases}$

ii) The probability to hit the target depth is $p_{Depth}(z) = \frac{\int_z^{z+dz} \eta(z')dz'}{\int_0^{\Delta z} \eta(z')dz'}$, *wherein* $0 \leq \eta(z) \leq 1$ *is the transmission of the physical interaction process in dependency on the penetration depth z.*

iii) The probability for the spatial resolution is $p_{Space} = p_{Area} \cdot p_{Depth}$.

If local precision is not needed for the concrete fault attack scenario it is $p_{Area} = p_{Depth} = 1$. Note that we assume a uniform distribution of the interaction rate which is the simplest possible approach. Due to the specific characteristics of the interaction process as well as the concrete layout of the device, deviations of the uniformity occur in practice. Consider an example for an optical interaction: the power distribution of the light beam might be spatially approximated by a Gaussian function and $\eta(z)$ is locally reduced beneath metal layers of the device. A derivation for spatial resolution considering the general case of both the physical interaction process and the concrete layout of $\mathcal{D}$ can be found in [16].

Definition 6 (Time Resolution). *Let dt be the targeted time interval for the fault induction. Given a timing resolution of ΔT for the fault induction process, we define* $p_{Time} = \begin{cases} 1 & : \quad \Delta T \leq dt \\ \frac{dt}{\Delta T} & : \quad \Delta T > dt \end{cases}$

In case of a precised fault $\mathcal{F}_{i,l,m}$ in space and time p is reduced by a factor of $p_{Area} \cdot p_{Depth} \cdot p_{Time}$.

3.4   Applications

The Non-invasive Adversary $\mathcal{A}_{non-inv}$: $\mathcal{A}_{non-inv}$ attacks the cryptographic device by using its external interfaces or by changing the environmental conditions. Faults that are injected are random and they are not precise, i.e., the affected area ΔA and the depth Δz are given by the dimensions of the physical device in our rough approximation. Changes in the environmental condition as overheating are long-lasting yielding a high value for ΔT which in turn gives a very small value for p_{Time}. ΔT for glitches in the external lines can be small so that glitches can yield high values for p_{Time}, however, the product of p_{Area} and p_{Depth} is nearly negligible resulting in a very low probability to induce specific errors.

The Semi-invasive Adversary $\mathcal{A}_{semi-inv}$: $\mathcal{A}_{semi-inv}$ penetrates the interaction boundary of light (by depackaging the chip), but not the cryptographic boundary. Note, that we allow photons, i.e., EM radiation, emitted by $\mathcal{A}_{semi-inv}$ to pass the cryptographic boundary. $\mathcal{A}_{semi-inv}$ applies optical fault induction [22] or electromagnetic induction [21]. $\mathcal{A}_{semi-inv}$ is able to target specific parts of the implementation that are most promising. The local area resolution achievable, i.e., p_{Area}, is of medium quality. Considering an optical interaction: if the area covered by the beam of photons exceeds the target area, the probability p_{Area} is roughly given by the ratio of the target area to the beam area. $\eta(z)$ is reduced exponentially with increasing target depth due to the interaction which is dominated by the photo effect. Accordingly p_{Depth} decreases exponentially in case of optical interactions. Failures in inner chip layers are hard to achieve for $\mathcal{A}_{semi-inv}$. However, $\mathcal{A}_{semi-inv}$ can achieve high values for p_{Time}.

The Invasive Adversary $\mathcal{A}_{inv}$: $\mathcal{A}_{inv}$ penetrates the cryptographic boundary. Matter can be inserted or removed from the cryptographic boundary. It is typically required that the chip passivation is removed at invasive attacks. Moreover, $\mathcal{A}_{inv}$ is able to probe within the overall internal construction, i.e., the analysis set-up used to observe the leakage of the implementation may consist of internal passive probes. By doing so, $\mathcal{A}_{inv}$ is bounded by L different locations that can be mounted in parallel. Fault injections are caused by particles with non-zero mass (as ions) or directly at active probes. $\mathcal{A}_{inv}$ adaptively acts within the cryptographic implementation. Therefore, $\mathcal{A}_{inv}$ is able to target and possibly deactivate the most critical parts of the implementation. $\mathcal{A}_{inv}$ is able to gain privileged insights by physical reverse engineering. The probabilities p_{Time}, p_{Area} and p_{Depth} are high resulting in a high overall probability to induce specific faults. Note, that also for $\mathcal{A}_{inv}$ p_{Depth} decreases with increasing depth z though the dependency is more complex and strongly depends on the concrete interaction process.

Defense Strategies: For the development of defense strategies, assumptions on the induced errors are required. Whereas data faults are assumed to lead to computational errors, such assumptions may be hard to capture in the case of processing faults. Defense strategies may be developed both for error detection as well as fault prevention.

Detection of computational errors can be classified in software and hardware measures. Software measures include well known error detection codes at data items and internal verifications of the correctness of cryptographic computations. Hardware measures comprise physical sensors and more advanced techniques as dual-rail logic [22] including an alarm mechanism. Typically, these measures are designed to detect *one* enforced error. The decision whether or not the device shall enter a permanent non-responsive mode in case of alarms depends on the concrete impact probability as well as the concrete security service. It is a matter of risk evaluation. Note that defenses are part of the implementation under attack and are therefore subject to fault induction, too. Especially for software based error detection, the time of the check is a parameter that can be used to shorten the potential time frame dt for fault analysis if the check is performed at a late point in time during computation of $\mathcal{S}$. Additional checks at the end of the computation of $\mathcal{S}$ are another choice of software implementations: by doing so the adversary may be enforced to succeed in applying additional precised faults. However, this measure is limited against $\mathcal{A}_{semi-inv}$ and $\mathcal{A}_{inv}$ as long as the physical target area remains unchanged.

Prevention of precise faults may be enhanced by shrinking of semiconductor devices. Shrinking decreases dA, but it may also enhance the sensitivity of the circuit towards fault inductions. Randomness of the timing in the implementation of $\mathcal{S}$ can be further used as fault prevention technique to reduce p, as $p \sim p_{Time}$ for all adversarial models. For $\mathcal{A}_{semi-inv}$ and $\mathcal{A}_{inv}$ it should be aimed to reduce $\eta(z)$ at the locations of security relevant and enforcing parts of the device, e.g. by shielding with metal layers. Another hardware based alternative is Random Register Renaming [19] which decouples the logical naming of registers from the physical location of the registers and was originally designed to counteract power analysis. The mapping between the virtual memory and the physical memory is renewed for each execution of the security service. However, $\mathcal{A}_{inv}$ may be able to analyze the memory management and to adaptively act immediately.

The question arises whether a low-cost implementation can ever achieve a reasonable security level against multiple precise fault injections, especially by $\mathcal{A}_{inv}$. An increase in the number of defenses generally requires a corresponding increase in the number of fault injections resulting in a decrease of the overall success rate p. By assumption, it is feasible for $\mathcal{A}_{inv}$ to monitor L locations in parallel, whereat at each location M successive fault injections can be done at different points in time. From the theoretical point of view the redundancy of an implementation shall therefore exceed L in space to counteract $\mathcal{A}_{inv}$ (implicitly assuming that L is considerably smaller than M). Such a redundancy of the circuit may be acceptable at specialized developments but surely not for high-volume products. Perfect protection against multiple fault injections of an invasive adversary may not be achievable, especially for low-cost cryptographic devices. Reliable protection against multiple fault injections of $\mathcal{A}_{non-inv}$ and $\mathcal{A}_{semi-inv}$ is, however, much more reasonable, as the reduction of success probability is much more rigorous – if compared with $\mathcal{A}_{inv}$ – because of limitations in spatial and time resolution.

4   Conclusion

In this contribution we presented an adversarial model that unifies various characteristic fault attacks. According to their fault induction techniques we distinguish three classes of adversaries as there are the non-invasive adversary, the semi-invasive adversary, and the invasive adversary. In this work we give more precise definitions of spatial and time resolution at fault injection and we review the effectiveness of generic countermeasures according to the classes of adversaries.

We hope that our considerations are valuable at practical implementations to categorize the efforts needed for concrete attacks. In our view, due to the manifold flavours of attack strategies in this research area further efforts at the graduation of adversarial capabilities are needed. It is concluded that reliable defenses are reasonable against adversaries who are restricted in terms of experimental equipment, but they are hard to achieve against an invasive adversary applying multiple fault injections.

Acknowledgments. We wish to thank Ahmad-Reza Sadeghi for fruitful discussions and comments which helped to improve this paper.

References

1. ISO 13491-1:1998 Banking – Secure cryptographic devices (retail)– Part 1: Concepts, requirements and evaluation methods.
2. Common Methodology for Information Technology Security Evaluation, CEM-99/045, Part 2: Evaluation Methodology, 1999.
3. FIPS PUB 140-2, Security Requirements for Cryptographic Modules, 2001.
4. Ross Anderson and Markus Kuhn. Tamper Resistance — A Cautionary Note. In *The Second USENIX Workshop on Electronic Commerce Proocedings*, pages 1–11, 1996.
5. Gildas Avoine. Adversarial Model for Radio Frequency Identification, available at http://eprint.iacr.org/2005/049. Technical report, 2005.
6. Hagai Bar-El, Hamid Choukri, David Naccache, Michael Tunstall, and Claire Whelan. The Sorcerer's Apprenctice's Guide to Fault Attacks. In *Workshop on Fault Detection and Tolerance in Cryptography*, 2004.
7. Hagai Bar-El, Hamid Choukri, David Naccache, Michael Tunstall, and Claire Whelan. The Sorcerer's Apprenctice's Guide to Fault Attacks, available at http://eprint.iacr.org/2004/100. Technical report, 2004.
8. Eli Biham and Adi Shamir. The Next Stage of Differential Fault Analysis: How to break completely unknown cryptosystems, available at http://jya.com/dfa.htm, 1996.
9. Eli Biham and Adi Shamir. Differential fault analysis of secret key cryptosystems. In Burton S. Kaliski Jr., editor, *CRYPTO*, volume 1294 of *Lecture Notes in Computer Science*, pages 513–525. Springer, 1997.
10. Dan Boneh, Richard A. DeMillo, and Richard J. Lipton. On the Importance of Checking Cryptographic Protocols for Faults (Extended Abstract). In Walter Fumy, editor, *Advances in Cryptology - EUROCRYPT '97*, volume 1233 of *Lecture Notes in Computer Science*, pages 37–51. Springer, 1997.
11. Rosario Gennaro, Anna Lysyanskaya, Tal Malkin, Silvio Micali, and Tal Rabin. Algorithmic Tamper-Proof (ATP) Security: Theoretical Foundations for Security against Hardware Tampering. In Moni Naor, editor, *Theory of Cryptography*, volume 2951 of *Lecture Notes in Computer Science*, pages 258–277. Springer, 2004.

12. William N. Havener, Roberta J. Medlock, Lisa D. Mitchell, and Robert J. Walcott. Derived Test Requirements for FIPS PUB 140-1, Security Requirements for Cryptographic Modules, 1995.
13. Marc Joye, Jean-Jacques Quisquater, Sung-Ming Yen, and Moti Yung. Observability analysis - detecting when improved cryptosystems fail. In Bart Preneel, editor, *CT-RSA*, volume 2271 of *Lecture Notes in Computer Science*, pages 17–29. Springer, 2002.
14. Oliver Kömmerling and Markus G. Kuhn. Design Principles for Tamper-Resistant Smartcard Processors. In *Proceedings of the USENIX Workshop on Smartcard Technology (Smartcard '99)*, pages 9–20, 1999.
15. Kerstin Lemke and Christof Paar. An Adversarial Model for Fault Analysis against Low-Cost Cryptographic Devices. In *Workshop on Fault Detection and Tolerance in Cryptography*, pages 82–94, 2005.
16. Kerstin Lemke, Christof Paar, and Ahmad-Reza Sadeghi. Physical Security Bounds Against Tampering. In *Applied Cryptography and Network Security*, volume 3989 of *Lecture Notes in Computer Science*, pages 253–267. Springer, 2006.
17. Regís Leveugle. Early Analysis of Fault Attack Effects for Cryptographic Hardware. In *Workshop on Fault Detection and Tolerance in Cryptography*, 2004.
18. P.-Y. Liardet and Y. Teglia. From Reliability to Safety. In *Workshop on Fault Detection and Tolerance in Cryptography*, 2004.
19. David May, Henk L. Muller, and Nigel P. Smart. Random Register Renaming to Foil DPA. In Çetin Kaya Koç, David Naccache, and Christof Paar, editors, *Cryptographic Hardware and Embedded Systems - CHES 2001*, volume 2162 of *Lecture Notes in Computer Science*, pages 28–38. Springer, 2001.
20. Gilles Piret and Jean-Jacques Quisquater. A Differential Fault Attack Technique against SPN Structures, with Application to the AES and KHAZAD. In Colin D. Walter, Çetin Kaya Koç, and Christof Paar, editors, *Cryptographic Hardware and Embedded Systems - CHES 2003*, volume 2779 of *Lecture Notes in Computer Science*, pages 77–88. Springer, 2003.
21. David Samyde and Jean-Jacques Quisquater. Eddy Current for Magnetic Analysis with Active Sensor. In *Proceedings of ESmart 2002*, pages 185–194, 2002.
22. Sergei P. Skorobogatov and Ross J. Anderson. Optical Fault Induction Attacks. In Burton S. Kaliski Jr., Çetin Kaya Koç, and Christof Paar, editors, *Cryptographic Hardware and Embedded Systems - CHES 2002*, volume 2523 of *Lecture Notes in Computer Science*, pages 2–12. Springer, 2002.
23. Sergei S. Skorobogatov. Semi-invasive attacks — A new approach to hardware security analysis, available at http://www.cl.cam.ac.uk/techreports/ucam-cl-tr-630.pdf. Technical report, 2005.

Cryptographic Key Reliable Lifetimes: Bounding the Risk of Key Exposure in the Presence of Faults*

Alfonso De Gregorio[†]

Andxor S.r.l.
via F.lli Gracchi, 27
Cinisello Balsamo (MI) 20092, Italy
adg@crypto.lo.gy

Abstract. With physical attacks threatening the security of current cryptographic schemes, no security policy can be developed without taking into account the physical nature of computation.

In this paper we adapt classical reliability modeling techniques to cryptographic systems. We do so by first introducing the notions of *Cryptographic Key Failure Tolerance* and *Cryptographic Key Reliable Lifetimes*. Then we offer a framework for the determination of reliable lifetimes of keys for any cryptographic scheme used in the presence of faults, given an accepted (negligible) error-bound to the risk of key exposure. Finally we emphasize the importance of selecting keys and designing schemes with good values of failure tolerance, and recommend minimal values for this metric. In fact, in *standard environmental conditions*, cryptographic keys that are especially susceptible to erroneous computations (e.g., RSA keys used with CRT-based implementations) are exposed with a probability greater than a standard error-bound (e.g., 2^{-40}) after operational times shorter than one year, if the failure-rate of the cryptographic infrastructure is greater than 1.04×10^{-16} *failures/hours*.

Keywords: Key Lifetimes, Fault-Attacks, Dependability, Security Policies, Fault Tolerance, Reliable Lifetimes, Reliability Modeling, Side-Channels.

1 Introduction

The manifestation of faults at the user interface of a cryptographic module may jeopardize the security by enabling an opponent to expose the secret key material [9,12,13,14,27,20,15,16]. In fact, by failing to take into account the physical nature of computation, the current mathematical models of cryptography are unable to protect against physical attacks that exploit in a clever way the peculiarities inherent the physical execution of any algorithm [31,23]. Consequently,

---

[†] This work was completed during the summer 2003 while the author was a visitor in the Katholieke Universiteit Leuven, Dept. Elect. Eng.-ESAT/SCD-COSIC, Kasteelpark Arenberg 10, B-3001 Leuven-Heverlee, Belgium.

* A preliminary version of this paper appeared as a COSIC Technical Report.

L. Breveglieri et al. (Eds.): FDTC 2006, LNCS 4236, pp. 144–158, 2006.

one should not rely on the services delivered by today's cryptographic modules, if specific dependability guarantees are not satisfied. However, the possession of dependability attributes should be interpreted in a relative, probabilistic, sense [38,40]. Due to the unavoidable occurrence of *transient faults* or the presence of *dormant faults*, there will be always a non-zero probability that the system will fail, sooner or later.

In order to keep the risk of key exposure below a desired boundary ϵ, the use of error detection techniques in fault-tolerant cryptographic modules is necessary but not sufficient [39,5,6,8,7,26]. In fact, for standard error-bounds (2^{-40}, or also lower values), with typical fault rates and using fault-tolerant systems with high levels of coverage, the probability of a key exposure may exceed the desired error bound within very short mission times, depending on the number of incorrect cryptographic values necessary to perform the fault attack against a specific cryptographic scheme. We show that this is true also at *standard environmental conditions*, where examples of transient and dormant faults - potentially affecting both hardware and software components - are respectively: Single Event Upsets (SEUs) [22,21,34], and code defects with low activation probability, such as those described by Harvey in [24] for software implementation of the DFC block cipher. For instance, as will be shown in Sect. 3, cryptographic modules that implement cryptographic schemes especially susceptible to erroneous computations (e.g., RSA based on the residue number system [27,30]), will expose the key material with a probability greater than ϵ by exceeding the required reliability level after operational times so short, that the number of scenarios where these schemes find application in the presence of faults results to be remarkably limited. Trying to increase further the coverage of fault-tolerant systems is not the most viable solution, since the difficulty of obtaining statistical confidence for extremely low failure-rates would raise the costs of cryptographic modules, by requiring a much larger number of hours during the design and assessment phases. Moreover, modules implemented in *software* typically need to be executed on different hardware or software platforms, and their testing phases may be iterated, depending on the Software Development Life Cycle (SDLC) in use.

Therefore, we argue that a careful management of key-lifetimes can provide a sensible and pragmatic approach to protect against fault attacks at standard environmental conditions. In particular, since reliability is a function of time, key-lifetimes should be selected so that the key material will no longer be used when the effective reliability of the system falls below the level required to guarantee the accepted negligible risk of key exposure.

In this work, we adapt classical reliability modeling techniques to cryptographic systems. We do so by first introducing the notions of *Cryptographic Key Failure Tolerance* and *Cryptographic Key Reliable Lifetimes*. Then we offer a framework that enables to limit the risk of key exposure to a desired error-bound in the presence of faults, by modeling the reliability of typical cryptographic infrastructures and relating their failure rates, the failure tolerances of the cryptographic keys and the mission duration for the required reliability goals, to the lifetimes of keys. Using this framework, we provide guidelines both for the determination of reliable lifetimes of keys for any cryptographic scheme implemented in generic cryptographic modules, or for the selection of cryptographic infrastructures that can provide the required level of reliability, if specific lifetimes and schemes are desired. In fact, as long as the mathematical models of cryptography are not extended to the physical setting, reliability and security will remain strictly related. Consequently, security policies will have to be developed by carefully taking into account the peculiarities inherent in the physical execution of any algorithm.

Our framework is intended to be used together with the existing guidelines to the selection of cryptographic key sizes and lifetimes [17,29,28,35,37,18,25,32, 33,10,42], assuming one agrees with the formulated hypotheses of the prior works or with the explicit assumptions on which our recommendations are based. The existing guidelines should be considered complementary to this framework, as based on the analysis of the computational effort required to break cryptographic schemes by exhaustive search.

The major advantage of our approach, besides its simplicity, is that it allows to keep the risk of key exposure below an accepted error-bound using one or more cryptographic modules characterized by different failure rates.

Organization. The rest of the paper is organized as follows. We describe the model and introduce the notion of *Cryptographic Key Failure Tolerance* in Sect. 2. In Sect. 3 we extend the notion of *reliable life* to cryptographic keys and offer a first framework to model the risk of key exposure in the presence of faults and to compute upper bounds to the lifetimes of keys, by incrementally modeling the reliability of the following two cryptographic infrastructures: 1) single systems implementing cryptographic schemes tolerating a generic number of erroneous computations, 2) highly available cryptographic infrastructures characterized by a pool of independent systems providing service concurrently, using any cryptographic scheme, and sharing the key material. Sect. 4 will be devoted to provide examples of how to use the proposed framework. We discuss the consequences of our estimates and emphasize the importance of choosing cryptographic keys and designing cryptographic schemes with good levels of failure tolerance in Sect. 5. We conclude in Sect. 6.

2   The Model

The model consist of a cryptographic module containing some cryptographic secret. The interaction with the outside work follows a cryptographic protocol. On some rare occasions, the module is assumed to be affected by faults causing it to output incorrect values [14].

2.1   Key Points

In the presence of faults, the choice of cryptographic key lifetimes depends primarily on the following points:

I. Environmental conditions;
II. The failure tolerance of cryptographic keys (defined in Sect. 2.3) - 1st security parameter;
III. Accepted (negligible) risk of key exposure: the desired security margin - 2nd security parameter;
IV. Failure rates: the rate of occurrence for incorrect values at the cryptographic module user interface - 3rd security parameter;

2.2   Environmental Conditions and Passive Fault Attacks

We limit our analysis to the black-box scenario characterized by the occurrence and activation of faults *in standard environmental conditions*.

Assumption 1. Our main assumption is that the security of cryptographic modules will not be compromised by any deliberate or accidental excursions outside their normal operating ranges of environmental conditions. For instance, a cryptographic module has been designed according to today's security standards [19] to operate, or to respond, in a safe way also with widely varying environmental conditions. Or, the computing device can be simply kept in a controlled environment (e.g., a network-attached HSM working in a controlled data center).

The Threat Model. As the attacker does only observes failures as they are occurring, tries to exploit them in an opportunistic way, and does not deliberately induce faults, we call this kind of attack *Passive Fault Attacks*. For instance, a remote attacker may observe erroneous digitally-signed objects (e.g., CRLs, X.509 PKC, X.509 AC) stored in X.500 Directory Services [11]. We emphasize that, according to the second principle outlined by Anderson in [1], system designers should expect real problems to come from blunders in the system design and in the way it is operated. It is interesting to note how an opportunistic threat model characterize largely deployed systems, such as payment systems [2,3] and prepayment electricity meter systems [4].

All the estimates offered in this paper would be drastically modified if a modification of the environmental conditions can augment the occurrences of failures

Table 1. The Cryptographic Key Failure Tolerance of some cryptographic schemes

Crypto Scheme + Sec. Parameter(s)	Fault Model	$CKFT$	Author(s)	Year
Fiat-Shamir Id. Scheme $(t = n)$	~1bit	$O(n)$	*Boneh, et al.* [14]	1996
RSA (1024 bit)	1bit	$O(n)$	*Boneh, et al.* [14]	1996
Schnorr's Id. Protocol $(p = a, q = n)$	1bit	$n \cdot \log 4n$	*Boneh, et al.* [14]	1996
RSA+CRT	1bit	0	*Lenstra* [27]	1997
AES (n=128)	1bit	49	*Giraud* [20]	2003
AES (n=128)	1byte	249	*Giraud* [20]	2003
AES (n=128)	1byte	1	*Piret, et al* [36]	2003
KHAZAD	1byte	2	*Piret, et al* [36]	2003

(i.e., as happens in presence of active fault attacks). Hence, the framework provided in this paper is complementary to fault-diagnosis and tolerance techniques aimed at increasing the reliability of cryptographic systems.

2.3 Cryptographic Key Failure Tolerance

Definition 1. *Let B be a black-box implementing a cryptographic scheme S and containing a secret key K that is inaccessible to the outside world, and with the set of security parameter(s) P. The Cryptographic Key Failure Tolerance, $CKFT^m_{K_{(S,P)}} \in \mathbb{Z}^0_+$, is defined to be the maximum number of faulty values, occurring according to the fault model identified by the label 'm', that B can output through its cryptographic protocol before K gets exposed by a fault-attack[1].*

Whenever there is no ambiguity we will write f for $CKFT^m_{K_{(S/P)}}$.

Remark 1. In the presence of fault-attacks, the Cryptographic Key Failure Tolerance (CKFT) is a security parameter. As the value assumed by this metric increases, the probability of succeeding in a fault-attack within time T decreases. A quantitative estimate of this probability is provided in Sect. 3.

In Table 1 the failure tolerance of some cryptographic schemes is provided. For example, an AES-128 key can be exposed by 2 faulty ciphertexts while considering the 1byte fault model and the attack suggested by Piret and Quisquater in [36]. It should be noted how several cryptographic keys may be characterized by a common value of this metric. We denote the set of all cryptographic keys with failure tolerance f under the fault model m, C^m_f. Obviously, new fault attacks or improvements to already existing attacks can determine new failure tolerance values for a given set of keys. Hence, we will refer in a generic way to the $CKFT$ values. For instance, a beautiful refinement by Lenstra [27] to the first fault-attack on RSA used with Chinese Remainder Theorem (CRT) [12,13,14] caused the shifting of all RSA private keys used with the CRT from C^{1bit}_1 to C^{1bit}_0, where 1bit denotes the fault-model considering single faults affecting one bit at a time.

2.4 Accepted Error-Bound to the Risk of Key Exposure

This is the 2nd security parameter. It can assume every desired value in the interval $(0, 1)$. Typical values are 2^{-40} or lower.

2.5 Failure Rates

Throughout the rest of this paper, unless specified differently, we will refer to the failure rate, μ^m, as the rate of occurrence of incorrect values at the user interface of a given cryptographic module, while considering the fault model m.

---

[1] If the $CKFT$ of a a given key is equal to 0, then K do not tolerate *any* failure. Hence it is sufficient to *output* a single faulty value in order to expose the key material. This is the case of RSA private keys used by implementations based on the Chinese Remainder Theorem, under the fault models described in [27] and [41].

The failure rate is a security parameter. In fact, as will be shown in Sect. 3, as the failure rate increases the mean time to failure (MTTF) decreases, and consequently the probability of succeeding in a fault-attack within time T increases.

In Sect. 3, we model the failure rates of cryptographic infrastructures composed by multiple independent subsystems[2] providing service concurrently and characterized by different failure rates. Since failure rates of each component are strongly dependent, among other factors, either on the implementation details of cryptographic modules, or on each target fault model, we leave them as parameters. Therefore, the estimates of lifetimes are provided for a representative sample of failure rates in the range $(1 \times 10^{-15}, 1 \times 10^{-9})$, in *failures/hours*.

3   Cryptographic Key Reliable Lifetimes

In order to limit the risk of key exposure, it is necessary to limit the lifetime of the key so that the key material will no longer be used when the reliability of the computing system falls below the required level.

Definition 2. *Let B be a black-box implementing a cryptographic scheme S and containing a secret key $K \in C_f^m$. The* Cryptographic Key Reliable Lifetime, $CKRL_K^{\epsilon,m}$, *is defined to be the longest period of time elapsed from the activation of the key-material, t_R, after which the reliability of B, $R(t_R)$, has fallen below the level required to enforce the security margin ϵ, while considering the fault model identified by m.*

It is easy to extend the notion of CKRL to multiple target fault models by computing this quantity for each fault model being considered, and taking the smallest lifetime estimate as the upper bound to the lifetime of the cryptographic credential: $CKRL_K^{\epsilon,\mathbf{M}} = \min\left(CKRL_K^{\epsilon,m}\right)$ for all $m \in \mathbf{M}$ where $\mathbf{M}$ is the set of target fault models.

3.1   Estimation Methodology

Given $\mathbf{M}$, the accepted error-bound ϵ, and the failure tolerance value that characterize a generic key $CKFT_{K_{(S,P)}}^m$, we first determine the reliability level $R(t_R)$ necessary to enforce the security margin. Then, by modeling the reliability of specific infrastructures, we determine the final failure rate μ_{Infr}^m for each fault model $m \in \mathbf{M}$. The resulting values are used to compute respective reliable lifes of the infrastructure t_R^m, or the mission durations for the required reliability level. The smallest mission duration is the upper bound to the lifetime of the key $K_{(S,P)}$, $CKRL_K^{\epsilon,\mathbf{M}}$.

---

[2] We consider two subsystems to be independent if electrically isolated from each other, using separate power supplies and located in separate chassis. The subsystems can share common data objects and cryptographic keys.

150   A. De Gregorio

3.2 Single Cryptographic Modules Implementing a Generic Cryptographic Scheme

Let T be a random variable representing the time of occurrence of faulty values at the user interface of the computing system. Let $F(T)$ be the distribution of T. Typically, computing systems are assumed to fail according to the exponential distribution. This distribution, being characterized by constant failure rates, is consistent with the *Assumption 1*.

In particular, we use the two-parameter exponential distribution. Its probability density function (pdf) is given by,

$$f(T) = \mu e^{-\mu(T-\gamma)}, \quad f(T) \geq 0, \quad \mu \geq 0, \quad T \geq 0 \text{ or } \gamma \tag{1}$$

The location parameter γ, enables the modeling of those systems that can manifest incorrect values at their user interface only after γ time units (e.g., hours) of operation.

From (1) follows that the two-parameter exponential cumulative density function (cdf) and the exponential reliability function are respectively:

$$Q(T) = 1 - e^{-\mu(T-\gamma)} \tag{2}$$

$$R(T) = 1 - Q(T) = e^{-\mu(T-\gamma)}, \quad 0 \leq R(T) \leq 1 \tag{3}$$

Equations (2) and (3) give respectively the probability of failure, and the reliability of the system. The system is considered to be functioning as long as the key material has not been exposed (i.e., as long as the number of failures is less than or equal to f) with a probability greater than ϵ. Hence, the cryptographic key can be viewed as a pool of $f+1$ of identical, independent and *non-repairable* sub-systems each characterized by a generic failure rate μ, under the fault model m^3. The components of the pool provide service concurrently. As soon as a failure occurs the number of sub-systems in the parallel pool decreases by one unit. The pool fails (i.e., the key gets exposed) when no sub-systems remains in service. Given the accepted risk of key exposure ϵ:

$$R(T) = 1 - \prod_{i=1}^{f+1} Q_i(T) \geq 1 - \epsilon \tag{4}$$

The sub-systems are identical, hence:

$$R(T) = e^{-\mu(T-\gamma)} \geq 1 - \sqrt[f+1]{\epsilon} \tag{5}$$

Therefore, the key lifetime for $K_{S,P}$, $L(K_{S,P})$, must be:

$$L(K_{S,P}) \leq CKRL_K^{\epsilon,m} = t_R = \gamma - \frac{\ln(1 - \sqrt[f+1]{\epsilon})}{\mu^m} \tag{6}$$

---

[3] Cryptographic keys that do not tolerate any failure at all, C_0^m, can be viewed as a single *non-repairable* system with failure rate μ^m, under the fault model m.

Table 2. Upper Bounds to Key Lifetimes for typical failure rates, with an accepted error-bound $\epsilon = 2^{-40}$ and $\gamma = 0$. Failure rates are expressed in *failures/hours*; upper bounds to key lifetimes are expressed in *hours*.

C_f^m $\downarrow$	μ_0^m 1×10^{-15}	μ_1^m 1×10^{-14}	μ_2^m 1×10^{-13}	μ_3^m 1×10^{-12}	μ_4^m 1×10^{-11}	μ_5^m 1×10^{-10}	μ_6^m 1×10^{-9}
$f=0$	9.09×10^2	9.09×10^1	9.09×10^0	9.09×10^{-1}	9.09×10^{-2}	9.09×10^{-3}	9.09×10^{-4}
$f=1$	9.54×10^8	9.54×10^7	9.54×10^6	9.54×10^5	9.54×10^4	9.54×10^3	9.54×10^2
$f=2$	9.69×10^{10}	9.69×10^9	9.69×10^8	9.69×10^7	9.69×10^6	9.69×10^5	$9.69e \times 10^4$
$f=3$	9.77×10^{11}	9.77×10^{10}	9.77×10^9	9.77×10^8	9.77×10^7	9.77×10^6	9.77×10^5
$f=4$	3.91×10^{12}	3.91×10^{11}	3.91×10^{10}	3.91×10^9	3.91×10^8	3.91×10^7	3.91×10^6
$f=5$	9.89×10^{12}	9.89×10^{11}	9.89×10^{10}	9.89×10^9	9.89×10^8	9.89×10^7	9.89×10^6
$f=6$	1.92×10^{13}	1.92×10^{12}	1.92×10^{11}	1.92×10^{10}	1.92×10^9	1.92×10^8	1.92×10^7
$f=7$	3.17×10^{13}	3.17×10^{12}	3.17×10^{11}	3.17×10^{10}	3.17×10^9	3.17×10^8	3.17×10^7
$f=8$	4.70×10^{13}	4.70×10^{12}	4.70×10^{11}	4.70×10^{10}	4.70×10^9	4.70×10^8	4.70×10^7
$f=9$	6.45×10^{13}	6.45×10^{12}	6.45×10^{11}	6.45×10^{10}	6.45×10^9	6.45×10^8	6.45×10^7
$f=10$	8.38×10^{13}	8.38×10^{12}	8.38×10^{11}	8.38×10^{10}	8.38×10^9	8.38×10^8	8.38×10^7
$f=11$	1.04×10^{14}	1.04×10^{13}	1.04×10^{12}	1.04×10^{11}	1.04×10^{10}	1.04×10^9	1.04×10^8

In case there are multiple fault models to consider, it is possible to estimate the reliable lifetime of the same key by taking the smallest mission time, given every possible faul model in $\mathbf{M}$ (i.e., computing the reliable life given the biggest failure rate: μ_{max}^m, $m \in \mathbf{M}$).

Table 2 provides upper bounds to key lifetimes for a number of representative failure rates affecting systems using keys characterized by a *CKFT* value in the interval $(0, 11)$, $\epsilon = 2^{-40}$, and $\gamma = 0$. Failure rates are expressed in *failures/hours* and upper bounds to key lifetimes (i.e., CKRL) are in *hours*.

3.3   Highly Available Cryptographic Infrastructures

It is straightforward to extend the modeling of the risk of key exposure to highly available cryptographic infrastructures. Consider a pool of l different and independent cryptographic modules (i.e., failing independently), each characterized by its own failure rate μ_l^m, that provides service using a common generic key characterized by a failure tolerance of $CKFT_{K_{(S,P)}}^m$. For example the key material may be stored in a shared secure device, or replicated among the l modules. Moreover we assume the following:

Assumption 2. All cryptographic module present in the pool start to provide service simultaneously (i.e., $\gamma_1 \approx \gamma_2 \approx \ldots \approx \gamma_l$).

Similarly to single cryptographic modules, the infrastructure is considered to be functioning as long as the cryptographic key has not been exposed (i.e., as long as the number of failures is less than or equal to $CKFT_{K_{(S,P)}}^m$) with a probability greater than ϵ. It should be noted that in this scenario the failures of each module should be considered to be *cumulative*. In fact, by affecting a shared resource (i.e., the cryptographic key), each failure affects also the residual lifetime of the remaining units in the pool. For example, assuming that the infrastructure is using a cryptographic key that does not tolerate any failure, it is sufficient a single faulty output to compromise the service provided by the entire infrastructure. Hence, the pool of cryptographic modules should be modeled as a *series of systems*.

$$R_{HA}(T) = \prod_{i=1}^{l} R_i(T) = e^{-\sum_{i=1}^{l} \mu_i^m (T-\gamma)} \tag{7}$$

Equation (7) gives the reliability of the series of cryptographic modules present in the pool. This is equivalent to reliability of a system with failure rate $\mu_{HA} = \sum_{i=1}^{l} \mu_i^m$. Using (6) is possible to compute the reliable life of the key $K_{(S,P)}$ used by the considered highly available cryptographic infrastructure:

$$L(K_{S,P}) \leq CKRL_K^{\epsilon,m} = t_R = \gamma - \frac{\ln(1 - \sqrt[f+1]{\epsilon})}{\sum_{i=1}^{l} \mu_i^m} \tag{8}$$

Remark 2. **Scaling-Out May Be a Hazard**
Obviously, the number l of cryptographic modules present in this typical high-availability configuration (i.e., active-active model) affects one of the security parameters, since it increases the risk of exposure of cryptographic credentials. In fact, as the final failure rate gets higher, the MTTF gets smaller; hence, decreasing the reliable life of the whole HA system. Consequently, the use of cryptographic modules with very low failure rates becomes *especially critical* when its necessary to design highly available cryptographic infrastructures. In Fig.1 the required reliability goals necessary to limit the risk of key exposure to $\epsilon = 2^{-40}$ are shown for either a single cryptographic module with $\mu_{single}^m = 1 \times 10^{-15}$ *failures/hours*, or a pool of 10 independent and identical cryptographic modules with $\mu_{HA}^m = \sum_{i=1}^{10} \mu_{single}^m$, providing service concurrently using a common cryptographic credential with a CKFT value in the interval $(0,9)$.

4   Using This Framework

4.1   Estimating Upper Bounds for Cryptographic Key Lifetimes

Suppose one needs to select the lifetime of a cryptographic key that belongs to C_1^m (i.e., has cryptographic failure tolerance 1). Suppose also that is necessary to guarantee a risk of key exposure less than or equal to $\epsilon = 2^{-40}$ using a cryptographic infrastructure with failure rate $\mu_{Infr}^m = 1 \times 10^{-11}$ *failures/hours*. Using (8), or looking at the row of a precomputed table (e.g., Table 2) for the failure tolerance 1, one finds that the key lifetime should not exceed *10 years*. This is only the upper bound. Additional considerations, related to the specific cryptographic scheme and to the application context, may obviously decrease the selected lifetime. We emphasize, however, that there are cases when the

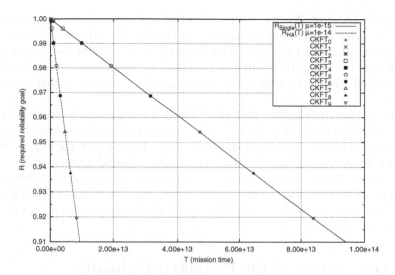

Fig. 1. Reliability goals for CKFT values in the internal (0,9), with Pr. Key Exposure $\epsilon = 2^{-40}$. Mission times are expressed in hours.

CKRL value is well *below* any recommended lifetime for the given credential. For instance, any cryptographic key in C_0^m in presence of a failure rate $\mu^m = 1 \times 10^{-15}$ *failures/hours* has a reliable life no longer than 9.09×10^{-2} *hours*, if the desired security margin is equal to 2^{-40}.

4.2 Selecting Dependable Cryptographic Infrastructures

It is straightforward to use Table 2 (or equation (7)) also to look up the failure rate that is necessary to guarantee the accepted negligible risk of key exposure, given a required key lifetime and cryptographic scheme. Suppose one needs to choose a cryptographic infrastructure among a number of alternatives, each characterized by *different costs*. The entire system must be able to use a cryptographic key with failure tolerance 9 and a lifetime of 4 years, while keeping the risk of key exposure below 2^{-128}. Expressing the failure rate as a function of the reliable life from equation (7) one finds that is sufficient to select an infrastructure characterized by a failure rate not greater than 4×10^{-9} *failures/hours*.

4.3 Scaling-Out Cryptographic Infrastructures

Suppose now that one wants to provide a cryptographic service with an infrastructure characterized at the initial stage by a pool of l cryptographic devices and needs to scale-out it, without changing the key material and guaranteeing a risk of key exposure not greater than 2^{-40}.

If the number h of additional sub-system that will be added in the future, and the respective failure rates μ_h^m, are known *a priori*, and there is a required lifetime, it is possible to use Table 2 to look up the column with failure rate

$\sum_{i=1}^{l} \mu_i^m + \sum_{j=1}^{h} \mu_h^m$ to find the first level of failure tolerance f_{min}, characterized by an error bound greater than or equal to the desired one. In this scenario,
the cryptographic key must be characterized by a level of failure tolerance greater
than or equal to f_{min}. It is worth to note that these are conservative estimates,
since here all the $l + h$ components are assumed to start their operation simultaneously.

If the failure rates of the additional sub-systems are not known at the time
the initial nodes are deployed and it is necessary to use a cryptographic scheme
with failure tolerance f, it is possible to lookup the row f of Table 2, to find the
first failure rate μ_{max}^m, characterized by an error bound greater than or equal
to the desired lifetime of keys. In this second scenario, the final failure rate of
the cryptographic infrastructure $\sum_{i=1}^{l+h} \mu_i^m$ must be less then or equal to μ_{max}^m.
Hence, the sum of the failure rates of the additional sub-systems needs to be:
$\sum_{j=1}^{h} \mu_j^m \leq \mu_{max}^m - \sum_{i=1}^{l} \mu_i^m$.

5   Consequences of the Presented Estimates

According to equation (8), in order to achieve a reliable life long at least one year,
while requiring $\epsilon = 2^{-40}$, cryptographic keys that do not tolerate any erroneous
computation (i.e., C_0^m) must be used on a cryptographic infrastructure that fail
with a rate lower than $\mu^m = 1.04 \times 10^{-16}$ $failures/hours$. The required rates
decreases further when lower error-bounds are desired.

These are certainly very low rates. Although it is possible to design highly
reliable cryptographic modules, the costs necessary during the design and assessment phases and the still low reliable life strongly limits the number of scenarios
where keys especially susceptible to erroneous computation may find application.
Unfortunately, this is the case of RSA keys used with CRT-based implementations [27,14]. The same considerations applies for keys in C_1^m (e.g., AES keys,
see Table 1) at failure rates beyond 9.54×10^{-5} $failures/hours$.

In today's cryptographic applications (e.g., e-commerce and bank secure web
servers, smart IC cards) it is common to find RSA keys used with CRT-based

Table 3. Effective risk of key exposure for credentials in C_0^m. The estimates are computed for a number of typical lifetimes (in years) and failure rates ($failures/hours$). The
exponents are rounded up to the nearest integer.

T $\downarrow$	μ_0^m 1×10^{-15}	μ_1^m 1×10^{-14}	μ_2^m 1×10^{-13}	μ_3^m 1×10^{-12}	μ_4^m 1×10^{-11}	μ_5^m 1×10^{-10}	μ_6^m 1×10^{-9}
1	2^{-36}	2^{-33}	2^{-30}	2^{-26}	2^{-23}	2^{-20}	2^{-16}
2	2^{-35}	2^{-32}	2^{-29}	2^{-25}	2^{-22}	2^{-19}	2^{-15}
3	2^{-35}	2^{-31}	2^{-28}	2^{-25}	2^{-21}	2^{-18}	2^{-15}
4	2^{-34}	2^{-31}	2^{-28}	2^{-24}	2^{-21}	2^{-18}	2^{-14}
5	2^{-34}	2^{-31}	2^{-27}	2^{-24}	2^{-21}	2^{-17}	2^{-14}
10	2^{-33}	2^{-30}	2^{-26}	2^{-23}	2^{-20}	2^{-16}	2^{-13}
20	2^{-32}	2^{-29}	2^{-25}	2^{-22}	2^{-19}	2^{-15}	2^{-12}

implementation characterized by lifetimes long months, or often *years*. These lifetimes are selected without modeling the risk of key exposure in the presence of faults. Therefore it is interesting to estimate this risk for cryptographic credentials with $CKFT = 0$. The probabilities are furnished in Table 3 for typical lifetimes and failure rates, using (6) and (8). The exponents are rounded up to the nearest integer. The estimates shows hazard rates that are likely beyond those initially predicted without considering dependability metrics.

In the next section we emphasize the importance of choosing keys with a good CKFT values, by offering estimates of minimal values of this metric necessary to enable the selection of key lifetimes long enough for any real application scenario.

5.1   On the Importance of Good CKFT Values

Let T_{max} a maximum desirable key lifetime (i.e., the maximum lifetime of a key for any real application scenario). From (6) and (8) follows that the minimum value of CKFT required to guarantee a desired ϵ using a cryptographic infrastructure with failure rate μ^m, is given by:

$$CKFT_{min}^m = \lceil \ln_{Q(T_{max}-\gamma)} \epsilon - 1 \rceil \qquad (9)$$

In Table 4 we provide the minimal CKFT values for a number of error-bounds and failure rates, and with $T_{max} = 200 years$.

Table 4. Minimal CKFT required to enable the selection of CKRL long up to $T_{max} = 200$ *years*, for a number of ϵ and μ. $\gamma = 0$.

ϵ $\downarrow$	μ_0^m 1×10^{-15}	μ_1^m 1×10^{-14}	μ_2^m 1×10^{-13}	μ_3^m 1×10^{-12}	μ_4^m 1×10^{-11}	μ_5^m 1×10^{-10}	μ_6^m 1×10^{-9}
2^{-40}	1	1	1	2	2	3	4
2^{-64}	2	2	2	3	4	5	6
2^{-80}	2	3	3	4	5	6	8
2^{-128}	4	4	5	6	8	10	13
2^{-256}	8	9	11	13	16	20	27

6   Conclusions

As long as the mathematical models of cryptography are not extended to the physical setting [31,23], reliability and security will remain strictly related. Consequently, security policies will have to be developed by carefully taking into account the peculiarities inherent the physical execution of any algorithm. In this paper we have offered a first framework that enables to bound the risk of key exposure in the presence of faults, by modeling the reliability of typical cryptographic infrastructures and relating their failure rates, the failure tolerance of the cryptographic keys, and the accepted (negligible) error-bound, to the lifetimes of keys.

Acknowledgments. The author would like to thank Bart Preneel for his determinant support and valuable comments, anonymous reviewers for providing helpful feedback, and all the people at COSIC for their great hospitality.

References

1. R. J. Anderson, *Liability and Computer Security: Nine Principles*, in Proceedings of the Third European Symposium on Research in Computer Security, Lecture Notes In Computer Science, Vol. 875, Springer-Verlag, pp. 231-245, 1994.
2. R. J. Anderson, *Why Cryptosystems Fail*, in Proceedings of the 1st ACM Conference on Computer and Communications Security, pp. 215-227, 1993.
3. R. J. Anderson, *Why Cryptosystems Fail*, in Communications if the ACM, November, 1994.
4. R. J. Anderson, S. Bezuidenhout, *On the Security of Prepayment Metering Systems*, to appear.
5. C. Aumüller, P. Bier, W. Fischer, P. Hofreiter, J.P. Seifert, *Fault Attacks on RSA with CRT: Concrete Results and Practical Countermeasures*, Lecture Notes in Computer Science, Vol. 2523, Springer-Verlag, pp. 260-275, 2002.
6. G. Bertoni, L. Breveglieri, I. Koren, P. Maistri, and V. Piuri, *Error Analysis and Detection Procedures for a Hardware Implementation of the Advanced Encryption Standard*, in IEEE Transactions on Computers, Vol. 52, No. 4, pp. 493-505, ISSN 0018-9340, April, 2003.
7. G. Bertoni, L. Breveglieri, I. Koren, P. Maistri, and V. Piuri, *On the Propagation of Faults and Their Detection in a Hardware Implementation of the Advanced Encryption Standard*, in Proc. Int'l Conf. Application-Specific Systems, Architectures, and Processors (ASAP '02), pp. 303-312, 2002.
8. G. Bertoni, L. Breveglieri, I. Koren, and V. Piuri, *Fault Detection in the Advanced Encryption Standard*, in Proc. Conf. Massively Parallel Computing Systems (MPCS '02), pp. 92-97, 2002.
9. E. Biham, A. Shamir, *Differential Fault Analysis of Secret Key Cryptosystems*, Lecture Notes in Computer Science, Vol. 1294, Springer-Verlag, 1997.
10. M. Blaze, W. Diffie, R. Rivest, B. Schneier, T. Shimomura, E. Thompson, and M. Wiener, *Minimal Key Lengths for Symmetric Ciphers to Provide Adequate Commercial Security*, Report of *ad-hoc* panel of cryptographers and computer scientists, January 1996. Available via http://www.crypto.com/papers/.
11. S. Boeyen, T. Howes, P. Richard, *Internet X.509 Public Key Infrastructure LDAPv2 Schema*, Internet Engineering Task Force, RFC 2587, June 1999. Available via http://www.ietf.org/rfc/rfc2587.txt.
12. D. Boneh, R. A. DeMillo, R.J. Lipton, *On the Importance of Checking Computations*, Lecture Notes in Computer Science, Vol. 1233, Springer-Verlag, pp.37-51, 1997
13. D. Boneh, R. A. DeMillo, R.J. Lipton, *On the Importance of Checking Cryptographic Protocols for Faults*, in Lecture Notes in Computer Science, Vol. 1233, Springer-Verlag, pp. 37-51, 1997.
14. D. Boneh, R. A. DeMillo, R.J. Lipton, *On the Importance of Eliminating Errors in Cryptographic Computations*, in Journal of Cryptology, Vol. 14, no. 2, Springer-Verlag, pp. 101-119, 2001.
15. M. Ciet, M. Joye, *Elliptic Curve Cryptosystems in the Presence of Permanent and Transient Fault*, Cryptology ePrint Archive, Report 2003/028, 2003, available via http://eprint.iacr.org/2003/028.

16. E. Dottax, *Fault Attacks on NESSIE Signature and Identification Schemes*, report NES/DOC/ENS/WP5/031/1 of the NESSIE Project, 2002, https://www.cosic. esat.kuleuven.be/nessie/reports/phase2/SideChan_1.pdf.

17. ECRYPT - European Network of Excellence in Cryptology, *ECRYPT Yearly Report on Algorithms and Keysizes (2004)*, D.SPA.10, Revision 1.1, 17 March 2005. http://www.ecrypt.eu.org/documents/D.SPA.10-1.1.pdf.

18. ETSI, SR 002 176 V1.1.1 Special Report, *Electronic Signatures and Infrastructures (ESI); Algorithms and Parameters for Secure Electronic Signatures*, March 2003.

19. Federal Information Processing Standards Publication 140-2, Security Requirements for Cryptographic Modules.

20. C. Giraud, *DFA on AES*, Cryptology ePrint Archive, Report 2003/008, 2003, available via http://eprint.iacr.org/2003/008.

21. P. Graham, M. Caffrey, J. Zimmerman, P. Sundararajan, E. Johnson, C. Patterson, *Consequences and Categories of SRAM FPGA Configuration SEUs*, in Proc. of Military and Aerospace Applications of Programmable Logic Devices (MAPLD 2003), September 9-11, 2003.

22. R. K. Iyer, I. Lee, *Measurement-Based Analysis of Software Reliability*, in M. Lyu, Editor, Handbook of Sofware Reliability Engineering, pp. 303-358, IEEE Computer Society Press and McGraw-Hill, 1996.

23. Y. Ishai, A. Sahai, D. Wagner, *Private Circuits: Securing Hardware against Probing Attacks*, 23rd Annual International Cryptology Conference, Santa Barbara, California, USA, August 17-21, 2003, Lecture Notes in Computer Science, Vol. 2729, Springer-Verlag, ISBN 3-540-40674-3.

24. I. Harvey, *The DFC Cipher: an attack on careless implementations*, presented at the Rump Session of Second AES Candidate Conference (AES2), March 22-23, 1999.

25. B. Kaliski, *TWIRL and RSA Key Size*, RSA Laboratories Technical Notes, Revised May 6, 2003.

26. R. Karri, W. Kaijie, P. Mishra, and K. Yongkook, *Fault-Based Side-Channel Cryptanalysis Tolerant Rijndael Symmetric Block Cipher Architecture* in Proc. Defect and Fault Tolerance in VLSI Systems (DFN '01), pp. 418-426, 2001.

27. A. K. Lenstra, *Memo on RSA signature generation in the presence of faults*, Available at: http://cm.bell-labs.com/who/akl/rsa.doc.

28. A. K. Lenstra, *Unbelievable security. Matching AES security using public key systems*, Proceedings Asiacrypt 2001, Lecture Notes in Computer Science, Vol. 2248, pp. 67-86, Springer-Verlag, 2001.

29. A. K. Lenstra and E. R. Verheul, *Selecting Cryptographic Key Sizes*, Journal of Cryptology, Vol. 14, No. 4, pp. 255-293, 2001.

30. A. J. Menezes, P. C. van Oorschot, S. A. Vanstone. *Handbook of Applied Cryptography*, CRC Press, ISBN: 0-8493-8523-7, October, 1996.

31. S. Micali, L. Reyzin, *Physically Observable Cryptography*, In Cryptology ePrint Archive: Report 2003/120, http://eprint.iacr.org/2003/120.

32. NESSIE Consortium, *Portfolio of Recommended Cryptographic Primitives*, February 27, 2003. Available via http://www.cryptonessie.org/.

33. NIST, *Special Publication 800-57: Recommendation for Key Management*, Part 1: General Guideline. Draft, January 2003, Available at: http://csrc.nist.gov/CryptoToolkit/tkkeymgmt.html.

34. E. Normand, *Single Event Upset at Ground Level*, IEEE Transactions on Nuclear Science, Vol. 43, No. 6, December, 1996.

35. H. Orman, P. Hoffman, *Determining Strengths For Public Keys Used For Exchanging Symmetric Keys*, Internet Engineering Task Force, RFC 3766/BCP 86, April 2004. Available via http://www.ietf.org/rfc/rfc3766.txt.

36. G. Piret, J.J. Quisquater, *A Differential Fault Attack Technique against SPN Structures, with Applications to the AES and KHAZAD*, in C. Walter, C. K. Koç, C. Paar, editors, Fifth International Workshop on Cryptographic Hardware and Embedded Systems (CHES 2003), Lecture Notes in Computer Science, Vol. 2779, pp. 291-303, Springer-Verlag, 2003.

37. RSA Labs, *A Cost-Based Security Analysis of Symmetric and Asymmetric Key Lengths*, RSA Labs Bulletin #13, Available at http://www.rsasecurity.com/rsalabs/.

38. SQUALE Consortium, *Dependability Assessment Criteria*, January 1999, http://www.newcastle.research.ec.org/squale/SQUALE4.pdf.

39. A. Shamir, *Method and Apparatus for protecting public key schemes from timing and fault attacks*, U.S. Patent Number 5,991,415, November, 1999; also presented at the rump session of EUROCRYPT'97.

40. K. S. Trivedi. *Probability and Statistics with Reliability, Queueing, and Computer Science Applications - Second Edition*, John Wiley and Sons, New York, 2001, ISBN number 0-471-33341-7.

41. D. Wagner, *Cryptanalysis of a provably secure CRT-RSA algorithm*, in the Proceedings of ACM Conference on Computer and Communications Security 2004, pp. 92-97.

42. L. C. Williams, *A Discussion of the Importance of Key Length in Symmetric and Asymmetric Cryptography*, Available via http://www.giac.org/practical/gsec/Lorraine Williams GSEC.pdf.

A Comparative Cost/Security Analysis of Fault Attack Countermeasures

Tal G. Malkin[1], François-Xavier Standaert[1,2], and Moti Yung[1]

[1] Dept. of Computer Science, Columbia University
[2] UCL Crypto Group, Université Catholique de Louvain
{tal, moti}@cs.columbia.edu, fstandae@dice.ucl.ac.be

Abstract. Deliberate injection of faults into cryptographic devices is an effective cryptanalysis technique against symmetric and asymmetric encryption algorithms. To protect cryptographic implementations (*e.g.* of the recent AES which will be our running example) against these attacks, a number of innovative countermeasures have been proposed, usually based on the use of space and time redundancies (*e.g.* error detection/correction techniques, repeated computations). In this paper, we take the next natural step in engineering studies where alternative methods exist, namely, we take a comparative perspective. For this purpose, we use unified security and efficiency metrics to evaluate various recent protections against fault attacks. The comparative study reveals security weaknesses in some of the countermeasures (*e.g.* intentional malicious fault injection that are unrealistically modelled). The study also demonstrates that, if fair performance evaluations are performed, many countermeasures are not better than the naive solutions, namely duplication or repetition. We finally suggest certain design improvements for some countermeasures, and further discuss security/efficiency tradeoffs.

Keywords: Attacks and countermeasures in hardware and software.

1 Introduction

Fault attacks consist of forcing a cryptographic device to perform some erroneous operations, hoping that the result of that wrong behavior will leak information about the secret parameters involved. These techniques have been increasingly studied since the publication of Boneh, Demillo and Lipton in 1996 [9] in the context of public key cryptosystems, and its extension to the private key setting by Biham and Shamir [8]. They were improved thereafter by several different authors in various contexts (*e.g.* [7,17,27]). Two survey papers have recently described practical and algorithmic issues of these methods [3,13].

Countermeasures against fault attacks can be deployed in hardware or software and generally help circuits to avoid, detect and/or correct faults. Certain active protections use sensors and detectors to infer abnormal circuit behaviors. Passive protections such as randomization of the clock cycles or bus and memory encryption [10,14] may also be used to increase the difficulty of successfully attacking a device. However, in practice, most proposed schemes are

L. Breveglieri et al. (Eds.): FDTC 2006, LNCS 4236, pp. 159–172, 2006.

based on classical error-detecting techniques using space or time redundancies [5,6,16,20,19,21,22,23,32]. In this paper, we conduct a comparative study regarding these latest techniques, assessing their security and efficiency. We believe that while the original investigations are useful and inventive in many ways, the comparative perspective is valuable since it forces a more uniform and perhaps more realistic view of the effectiveness of the countermeasures, from both security and cost point of view. In particular, our findings underline that certain published countermeasures may not be sufficient to counteract fault attacks due to limited modelling (*e.g.* intentional malicious fault injection that are unrealistically modeled as random limited number of faults, more typical in non-malicious environments). We also point out that, if fair performance evaluations are conducted, many countermeasures are not better than the naive solutions, namely duplication or repetition. Finally, we discuss the resulting security *vs.* efficiency tradeoff in the general context of hardware implementations that our study implies.

The rest of this paper is structured as follows. Section 2 investigates error detection techniques based on the use of space redundancies, including parity checks and other codes. We discuss limitations of security models in certain countermeasure designs which lead to attacks and, when overcome, lead to efficiency overhead. Section 3 similarly discusses techniques based on repetition or duplication. We reveal certain design issues that need corrections and we essentially realize that these schemes tend to resemble the naive countermeasures. Our conclusions, outlining the usefulness of our comparative study are in Section 4.

2   Error Detection Techniques Using Space Redundancies

2.1   Description of a First Scheme

References [23,32] describe a solution for the low cost concurrent error detection in substitution-permutation networks. We briefly summarize the proposed schemes in this section. For clarity purposes, we target the AES Rijndael [11].

A round of an unprotected block cipher implementation is represented in Figure 1. **S** blocks, representing non-linear substitution boxes (*i.e.* SubBytes in Rijndael), are followed by a linear diffusion layer (*i.e.* ShiftRows and MixColumns in Rijndael) and a bitwise key addition. The basic purpose of the countermeasure is to add a parity bit to the scheme in order to track errors during the execution of the

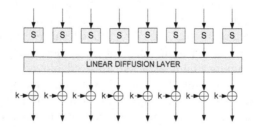

Fig. 1. Block cipher round without error check

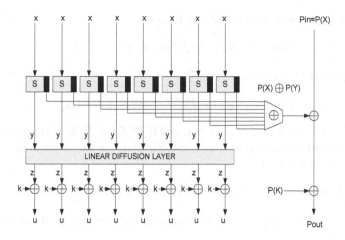

Fig. 2. Block cipher round with error check

algorithm. A single block cipher round with concurrent error check is represented in Figure 2 and the different steps of the error check are as follows.

1. **Computing the input parity.** The parity of the 128-bit input, denoted as Pin, is determined by a tree of XOR gates. This parity is computed once at the beginning of the algorithm.
2. **Parity modification according to the S-boxes.** An output bit is added to the S-boxes in order to implement the XOR of the parity of all S-boxes input bits with the parity of all S-boxes output bits, denoted as $P(X) \oplus P(Y)$. The value of this additional output bit can be determined from the truth table of the original S-box. It is represented as a black box in Figure 2.
3. **No parity modification according to the diffusion layer.** As detailed in [23,32], the linear substitution layer of Rijndael does not involve any modification of the previously defined parity. It is obvious for ShiftRows which only permutes the bytes of the state and does not affect their values. For MixColumn, it is observed that, due to the linearity of the transform, it does not alter the parity when the 32-bit columns are considered.
4. **Parity modification according to the key addition.** Since a 128-bit round key is bitwise XORed with the output of the diffusion layer, the input parity has to be modified by the parity $P(K)$.
5. **Output parity checking.** The parity of the actual outputs finally has to be compared with the modified input parity of the round.

According to the original paper, the proposed step-by-step parity modification overcomes the high diffusion of faults in block ciphers. Namely, a local fault detected within a processing step by parity checking of this processing step outputs will also be detected by comparing the modified parity of the round outputs. As an illustration of the technique, let us consider an input X with correct parity $P(X)$ and assume that a single bit fault occurs on this value of X, producing new intermediate values X^*, Y^*, Z^*, U^*.

First, the parity will be modified as follows:

$$Pout = P(X) \oplus P(X^*) \oplus P(Y^*) \oplus P(K)$$

Then, computing the output bits parity, we find:

$$P(U^*) = P(Z^*) \oplus P(K) = P(Y^*) \oplus P(K)$$

It is clear that the parities will only be equal if $P(X) = P(X^*)$, therefore allowing to detect the fault at the end of the round. Similarly, a single bit fault introduced after the S-boxes will cause:

$$Pout = P(X) \oplus P(X) \oplus P(Y) \oplus P(K) = P(Y) \oplus P(K)$$

This is because the parity $P(Y)$ is computed independently of the value of Y. Also, we have:

$$P(U^*) = P(Z^*) \oplus P(K) = P(Y^*) \oplus P(K)$$

Again the output parities will allow to detect the fault, and so will be for faults introduced after each processing unit of the block cipher. Although it is clear that multiple faults of even order will not be detected by such a scheme, the authors argue that, according to [26], the probability of 1-bit, 2-bit, 3-bit and 4-bit errors is respectively approximated by 85%, 10%, 3% and 1% in combinatorial logic circuits. It is therefore concluded that the error-correcting scheme allows to prevent most practical attackers, with a low hardware overhead.

2.2   Security of the Presented Scheme

Before discussing the presented countermeasure, let us first emphasize that, from an algorithmic point of view, the number of faults necessary to mount a successful attack has been dramatically reduced during the last years. In particular, it has been shown in [27] that the AES Rijndael can be corrupted with only two faulty ciphertexts. As a very straightforward consequence, a protection detecting only 85% of the injected faults is clearly not enough. Moreover, considering single-bit faults only is certainly not a conservative approach, as multiple-bit faults start to be a concern in very deep submicron technologies. Recent experiments have notably shown that high-energy ions can energize two or more adjacent memory cells in a circuit [15,28].

Anyway, in practice, it is unlikely that the mentioned experiments (*i.e.* evaluations of fault occurrences due to radiations effects) correctly model the behavior of a malicious insider. In particular, there are at least two parameters missing in the previous analysis, namely time and space localization, that may enhance the attacker capabilities to much more precision than unintended radiation effects.

Starting with time localization, it is clear that being able to induce a single-bit fault twice during a round function will simply bypass the previous countermeasure. Choosing the time at which the fault occur can be done by using side-channel information to monitor the progress of the algorithm. As present pulse generators allow to deal with high frequencies, it is virtually possible to insert a fault anytime during a cryptographic computation.

Similarly, being able to induce single faults in different nodes of an implementation also bypass a single-bit parity check. Choosing the location of the fault can be done if light [31] or electromagnetic [29] induction are considered. These techniques have been proven very efficient to force low cost faults in cryptographic devices. More expensive techniques are susceptible to be even more powerful.

As a consequence, the fault detection technique in Section 2.1 is practically insecure as soon as real attacker capabilities are considered. This discussion also suggests that resistance against faults attacks involve higher constraints than usually required for integrated circuits. In particular, multiple bit faults have to be taken into account, as well as space and time localization.

2.3   Description of Improved Schemes

From the previous descriptions, there are two basic reasons making the countermeasure in [23,32] susceptible to multiple-bit faults: (1) only one parity bit is used, (2) parity codes are linear. Both reasons involve simple extensions in order to improve the detection capabilities of the method. In this section, we discuss these improvements of the original scheme and their additional cost[1].

1. Using more parity bits is suggested and implemented in [5] in order to improve multiple-bit faults detection. Simple arguments allow to evaluate the effect of such a countermeasure if the faults are uniformly distributed. For example, let n be the number of parity bits used, the probability that a double fault affects twice the same parity bit is:

$$P = \frac{n}{\binom{n+1}{2}} = \frac{2}{n+1} \tag{1}$$

[5] proposes one parity bit per byte for Rijndael, which yields $P = 0.12$.

Again, from a simple probabilistic point of view, the proposed improvement is not sufficient to reject all attackers. Moreover, it is likely that multiple faults will not be uniformly distributed, as multiple-bit faults usually target adjacent memory cells. As a consequence, the probability of masked errors (*e.g.* double faults occurring in the same byte) will actually be higher than predicted.

Regarding the additional cost for AES implementations, the proposal involves more hardware overhead as there are more parity bits, but also because the parities are now affected by MixColumn, which involves the need of parity predictors for this transform as well. These overheads are summarized in Table 1.

---

[1] Note that making the parity checks only once a round does not affect the fault coverage. As suggested in Section 2.1, what is detectable inside the round is also detectable at its output. As a consequence, the use of more parity checkers only affects the detection latency and may not be considered as a relevant improvement.

Finally, let us remark that using pipelined implementations (*i.e.* dealing with multiple inputs in parallel) is another solution to decrease the probability of (1). Double masked errors then have to affect twice the same parity bit and text.

2. Using non linear robust codes is another solution proposed in [19,20,24] to obtain good resistance against single and multiple fault errors. For this purpose, the authors use a much more restricting fault model where faults are uniformly distributed throughout the circuit and the expected number of faults (*i.e.* fault multiplicities) is proportional to the number of gates in the circuit. Two proposals are actually considered.

In the first one [19], the AES Rijndael is divided into two blocks: linear and non-linear, where the non-linear block only consists in the multiplicative inverse of the Rijndael S-box. The non-linear code is simply represented in Figure 3 and computes the product of two inverses X and Y. In order to reduce the area overheads, it is proposed to check only a few bits (typically 2) of the result. Then, for the linear-part, every column of the AES is associated with an 8-bit

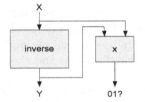

Fig. 3. Multiplicative inverse with error check

parity, namely the XOR between the 4 bytes of the column. It yields a 32-bit redundancy for the complete algorithm, which is computed independently, as the S-boxes parities in Section 2.1. The fault coverage of this scheme is contrasted. On the one hand, the non-linear part allows good detection of multiple faults, while low-order faults can clearly be masked because of the 2-bit comparison. On the other hand, the linear part suffers from the same problems as the previous linear schemes for the detection of higher-order faults. Globally, it is conjectured that the scheme only provides good error detection for faults with high multiplicities. The hardware overheads of the proposal are again summarized in Table 1. Note that [19] requires the S-box inverters and affine transforms to be implemented independently, while hardware implementations frequently combine both transforms in one single RAM block.

In the second proposal [20], a robust non-linear code is described, based on the addition of two cubic networks, computing $y(x) = x^3$ in $GF(2)^8$, to the previous linear scheme. The method allows to produce r-bit signatures to detect errors. It is shown that the fraction of undetectable errors is proportional to 2^{-2r}. Although the proposal offers a good fault coverage, its actual implementation is a real concern as the ratio throughput/area (a usual estimator of hardware efficiency) is decreased by a factor of two. As a consequence, the solution cost is somewhat comparable to duplication, which also has good non-linear properties and therefore provides good fault coverage. Note finally that non-linear robust codes have been additionally discussed in [24] and the question to know if they can lead to more efficient implementations is open.

2.4 Summary of the Results

We have investigated 5 recent countermeasures against fault attacks, based on the use of space redundancies. Those are summarized in Table 1. The first two ones use an unrealistic fault model, considering single faults only, and may not be considered as sufficient to protect against a malicious attacker. [5] proposes to use more parity bits to improve their fault coverage, but faults of even order may still be masked with non-negligible probability.

Table 1. Space redundancy based techniques

Ref.	Method	Sin. fault detection	Mul. fault detection	Area overhead	Delay overhead	Thr. overhead	Thr./Area overhead
[23,32]	single parity bit	yes	no	+7.4%	+6.4%	-	-
[5]	multiple parity bits $(n=16)$	yes	double faults masked with $P \propto \frac{2}{n+1}$	+20%	-	-	-
[19]	linear + non-linear codes	weak	good	+35%*	-	-	-
[20]	non-linear r-bit codes $(r=28)$	good, missed with $P \propto 2^{-2r}$	good, missed with $P \propto 2^{-2r}$	+77%	+15%	-13%	-51%

The last two ones use a much more restrictive fault model, but only [20] provides good error detection properties against faults of all multiplicities. For this last scheme, the hardware overhead is comparable to duplication, as the ratio throughput/area has been divided by two. Remark that the objective of this table is only to summarize the results, not to provide fair comparisons between the different proposals. As a matter of fact, the area overhead is a function of the hardware cost of the unprotected primitive and, for example, [19,20] are low cost architectures compared to the ones used in the parity code papers. As a consequence, their overhead in % are higher.

3 Error Detection Using Repetition and Duplication

The previous section underlined that error-detection techniques based on space redundancies become as expensive as duplication if realistic attackers are considered. As a consequence, it is natural to investigate how codes based on repetition or duplication can be used to improve the security of cryptographic devices. For this purpose, we start with some precisions about our model.

(1) We consider a n-bit block cipher, with q rounds independently implemented. (2) We assume that the error detection can be performed at three different levels: algorithm-level, round-level or operation level. Working at one level involves that the observed level is performed in at least one clock cycle, as its result has to be stored and compared. (3) In operation level detection schemes, we denote the number of operations considered per round as p. (4) The error detection latency only depends on the detection level. (5) Depending on the detection level, the codes have different non-linearity properties. However, as we perform n-bit comparisons, we assume that the error miss rate is 2^{-n} for all levels.

In general, the performance reduction in repetition or duplication schemes has two parts. One corresponds to the comparators required to check the validity of intermediate values. It is inversely proportional to the detection latency, as illustrated in Table 2, where τ denotes the timing function[2]. The other one corresponds to the repetition or duplication itself and directly affects the implementation throughput or area. Namely, repetition codes will cause a -50% reduction of the throughput while duplication will require +100% additional hardware. Regarding their detection properties, both solutions are not equivalent, as *repetition codes only allow to detect temporary (or soft) faults while duplication also allows to detect permanent (or hard) faults.*

Table 2. Latency *vs.* additional resources tradeoff

Latency	Additional 1-bit comparators
τ(Algorithm)	n
τ(Round)	nq
τ(Operation)	npq

While these solution may be straightforwardly implemented, the next sections show that certain particular contexts allow to obtain the effects of repetition or duplication for less than their usual cost.

3.1   Description of a First Scheme

Reference [16] describes a solution for the low cost concurrent error detection in involutional block ciphers, exploiting the involution property to check if the condition $f(f(x)) = x$ is respected through the cipher. The authors argue that the scheme achieves close to 0% time overhead. In this section, we show that:

1. The proposal can be improved by modifying the comparison scheme.
2. The proposal can be extended to non-involutional ciphers.
3. The proposal is actually a kind of repetition code.

---

[2] Remark that the registers needed to store intermediate values are not considered as hardware overhead. We show in the next section that, if well chosen, they can be combined with the original implementation registers.

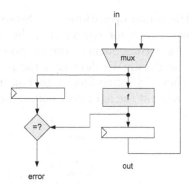

Fig. 4. Concurrent error detection for involutional functions [16]

The original error correction principle is represented in Figure 4. Reference [16] applies it to the Khazad block cipher [4], for which the non-linear and linear layer are involutional. First, let us observe that the area overhead can be straightforwardly reduced by changing the comparison scheme. Indeed, by comparing the function f's output with its following register output in place of with the multiplexor output, *we can avoid the comparison register.* It is represented in Figure 5, where we extend the scheme to a complete block cipher loop architecture.

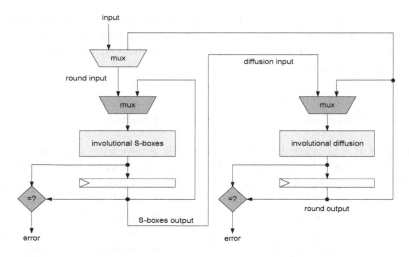

Fig. 5. Improved concurrent error detection for involutional rounds

Now, let us investigate the real time overhead of the countermeasure. For clarity purposes, we assumed that the work frequency was not affected by the comparison scheme. In Figure 5, we represented the original round operations in light grey and the overhead in dark gray. Removing the dark grey boxes, it is clear that the round can be performed in two clock cycles. It is basically a pipelined implementation dealing with two different plaintexts concurrently. Then, adding

168   T.G. Malkin, F.-X. Standaert, and M. Yung

the dark grey registers, the round operations (*i.e.* S-boxes and diffusion layer) will be used half the clock cycles for encrypting, the other half for checking the involution property. As a consequence, the proposed countermeasure will cause a -50% throughput overhead. We show that the proposed countermeasure is actually a repetition code, by extending it to non-involutional ciphers, as illustrated in Figure 6. Looking at the light grey boxes, the round is again divided

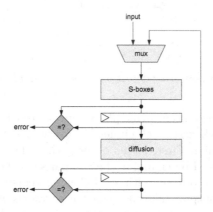

Fig. 6. Similar concurrent error detection for non involutional ciphers

into two operations and pipelined. Let us imagine an encryption mode where the same plaintext is encrypted twice and we add the comparison boxes. We can then detect errors as in Figure 5. The repetition is now obvious. The only differences between schemes 5 and 6 are:

1. The involutional scheme allows to detect permanent errors.
2. The involutional scheme needs two additional multiplexors.

At this point, it is not clear how the proposal can achieve a 0% time overhead and actually, this assumption is not generally true. However, considering the context of feedback encryption modes, the countermeasure of [16] becomes particularly interesting, as the pipeline cannot be used to deal with different plaintexts[3] but still allows to ensure error-proofness. Compared to a non-pipeline loop architecture, as usually required in feedback modes, we still require twice more clock cycles for one encryption, but it is likely that the clock frequency will be improved proportionally, so that the throughput will only slightly be affected. Note that this latter point is not a particular quality of the proposed technique, but a general rule in hardware design. A fair comparison of architectures for feedback encryption modes is represented in Figure 7, where we can clearly observe the tradeoff between the number of cycles increase for one encryption and the expected increase of clock frequency (because the critical path is reduced).

---

[3] It is mandatory to complete one plaintext encryption before starting the next one.

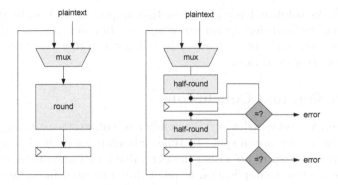

Fig. 7. Encryption with feedback, without and with error detection

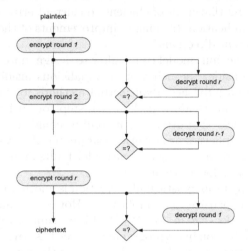

Fig. 8. Concurrent error detection using encryption/decryption designs

3.2 Another Proposal Equivalent to Repetition/Duplication

A very similar scheme has been presented in [21] for the concurrent error detection in symmetric block ciphers. It is based on exactly the same ideas as [16], in the more general context of non-involutional ciphers.

Basically, as the involutional property is not available, it is replaced by a design allowing to perform encryption and decryption. The error-detection principle is illustrated in Figure 8 and can be viewed as (1) duplication if the encryption and decryption blocks are independently implemented, or (2) repetition if the same hardware resources are used for encryption and decryption[4]. However, as in the previous section, the proposal gain particular interest in certain specific contexts. For example, if the cost of a decryption design is less than the one for

---

[4] For most algorithms, only a part of the resources can be shared between encryption and decryption. A perfect repetition scheme is only possible for involutional ciphers.

encryption[5], the solution has a lower cost than duplication. Also, in applications where encryption and decryption are necessary, but not concurrently, the actual performances will not be harmed by using the (otherwise unused) reverse operation for error detection.

4   Discussion and Conclusions

In this paper, we reviewed a certain number of countermeasures against fault attacks based on the use of space or time redundancies. It is shown that most of these countermeasures are either insecure, due to an unrealistic fault model, or their cost is close to duplication or repetition, excepted in certain particular implementation contexts (*e.g.* encryption with feedback, encryption/decryption designs). From an information theoretic point of view, this conclusion is close to the one in [25], stating that most of efficient concurrent error detection schemes exceed the cost of duplication. In general, improvements of these protections are possible in two different directions.

First, restricting the fault model could allow to design more efficient solutions, but it requires to consider the behavior of a malicious insider. Presently, only a few works have been published about actual methods for fault injections and more practical experiments are a preliminary step for such improvements. In particular, it is not clear that attacker capabilities could reasonably be reduced in terms of fault multiplicities or any other parameter. A conservative approach therefore requires to provide an equal security for faults of any multiplicity, with possible space and time localization.

Second, considering probabilistic fault detection is another usual alternative to design schemes less expensive than duplication. However, regarding the requirements of present attacks (*e.g.* in [27], Rijndael is corrupted with only two faulty ciphertexts), fault detection in cryptographic devices has particularly strong constraints. Therefore, this proposal has to be taken with care as faults have to be detected with high probability.

More specifically, this work:

1. Points out the unrealistic fault model used in certain recently proposed countermeasures [23,32].
2. Suggests that the actual cost of other countermeasures [19,20] are close to duplication if fair comparisons are performed.
3. Improves the comparison scheme of [16] and generalizes it from involutional block ciphers to all block ciphers.
4. Observes that countermeasures proposed in [16,21] are actual repetition codes used in a specific context.

As a consequence of these observations, theoretical solutions to the problem of fault attacks, as suggested in [12], no more appear as completely unpractical. Also, due to their good detection properties, non-linear robust codes, such as the ones in [19,20,24], would deserve further analysis to improve their hardware cost and see how better they can compare with duplication.

---

[5] This is very rarely the case in practice.

References

1. R. Anderson, M. Kuhn, *Tamper Resistance - a Cautionary Note*, in the proceedings of the USENIX Workshop on Electronic Commerce, pp 1-11, Oakland, CA, USA, November 1996.
2. R. Anderson, M. Kuhn, *Low Cost Attacks on Tamper Resistant Devices*, in the proceedings of the 5th International Workshop on Security Protocols, Lecture Notes in Computer Science, vol 1361, pp 125-136, Paris, France, April 1997, Springer-Verlag.
3. H. Bar-El, H. Choukri, D. Naccache, M. Tunstall, C. Whelan, *The Sorcerer's Apprentice Guide to Fault Attacks*, IACR e-print archive 2004/100, http://eprint.iacr.org, 2004.
4. P.Barreto, V.Rijmen, *The KHAZAD Legacy-Level Block Cipher*, Submission to NESSIE project, available from http://www.cosic.esat.kuleuven.ac.be/nessie/
5. G. Bertoni, L. Breveglieri, I. Koren, P. Maistri, V. Piuri, *Error Analysis And Detection Procedures for a Hardware Implementation of the Advanced Encryption Standard*, IEEE Transactions on Computers, vol 52, num 4, pp 492-505, April 2003.
6. G. Bertoni, L. Breveglieri, I. Koren, P. Maistri, *An Efficient Hardware-Based Fault Diagnosis Scheme for AES: Performance and Cost*, in the proceedings of DFT 2004, 9 pp, Cannes, France, October 2004.
7. I. Biehl, B. Meyer, V. Müller, *Differential Fault Analysis on Elliptic Curve Cryptosystems*, in the proceedings of Crypto 2000, Lecture Notes in Computer Science, vol 1880, pp 131-146, Santa Barbara, California, USA, August 2000.
8. E. Biham, A. Shamir, *Differential Fault Analysis of Secret Key Cryptosystems*, in the proceedings of Crypto 1997, Lecture Notes in Computer Science, vol 1294, pp 513-525, Santa Barbara, CA, USA, August 1997, Springer-Verlag.
9. D. Boneh, R. DeMillo, R. Lipton, *On the Importance of Checking Cryptographic Protocols for Faults*, in the proceedings of Eurocrypt 1997, Lecture Notes in Computer Science, vol 1233, pp 37-51, Konstanz, Germany, May 1997, Springer-Verlag.
10. E. Brier, H. Handschuh, C. Tymen, *Fast Primitives for Internal Data Scrambling in Tamper Resistant Hardware*, in the proceedings of CHES 2001, Lecture Notes in Computer Science, vol 2162, pp 16-27, Paris, France, May 2001.
11. J. Daemen, V. Rijmen, *"The Design of Rijndael. AES – The Advanced Encryption Standard,"* Springer-Verlag, 2001.
12. R. Gennaro, A. Lysyanskaya, T. Malkin, S. Micali, T. Rabin, *Algorithmic Tamper-Proof Security: Theoretical Foundations for Security Against Hardware Tampering*, in the proceedings of TCC 2004, Lecture Notes in Computer Science, vol 2951, pp 258-277, Cambridge, MA, USA, February 2004, Springer-Verlag.
13. C. Giraud, H; Thiebauld, *A Survey on Fault Attacks*, in the proceedings of CARDIS 2004, Toulouse, France, August 2004.
14. J.D. Golic, *DeKaRT: A New Paradigm for Key-Dependent Reversible Circuits*, in the proceedings of CHES 2003, Lecture Notes in Computer Science, vol 2779, pp 98-112, Cologne, Germany, September 2003.
15. K. Johansson, M. Ohlsson, N. Blomgren, P. Renberg, *Neutron Induced Single-Word Multiple-Bit Upset in SRAM*, in IEEE Transactions on Nuclear Science, vol 46, num 7, pp 1427-1433, December 1999.
16. N. Joshi, K. Wu, R. Karry, *Concurrent Error Detection Schemes for Involution Ciphers*, in the proceedings of CHES 2004, Lecture Notes in Computer Science, vol 3156, pp 400-412, Cambridge, Massachusset, USA, August 2004.

17. M. Joye, A.K. Lenstra, J.-J. Quisquater, *Chinese Remaindering Based Cryptosystems in the Presence of Faults*, Journal of Cryptology, vol 12, num 4, pp 241-246, 1999, Springer-Verlag.
18. T. Karnik, P. Hazucha, J. Patel, *Characterization of Soft Errors Caused by Single Event Upsets in CMOS Processes*, IEEE Transactions on Secure and Dependable Computing, vol 1, num 2, April 2004.
19. M. Karpovsky, K.J. Kulikowski, A. Taubin, *Differential Fault Analysis Attack Resistant Architectures For The Advanced Encryption Standard*, in the proceedings of CARDIS 2004, Toulouse, France, August 2004.
20. M. Karpovsky, K.J. Kulikowski, A. Taubin, *Robust Protection against Fault Injection Attacks on Smart Cards Implementing the Advanced Encryption Standard*, in the proceedings of DSN 2004, 9pp, Florence, Italy, June 2004.
21. R. Karri, K. Wu, P. Mishra, Y. Kim, *Concurrent Error Detection Schemes for Fault-Based Side-Channel Cryptanalysis of Symmetric Block Ciphers*, in IEEE Transactions on Computer-Aided Design, vol 21, num 12, pp 1509-1517, December 2002.
22. R. Karri, M. Gössel, *Parity-Based Concurrent Error Detection in Symmetric Block Ciphers*, in the proceedings of ITC 2003, pp 919-926, Charlotte, USA, September 2003/
23. R. Karri, G. Kuznetsov, M. Gössel, *Parity-Based Concurrent Error Detection of Substitution-Permutation Network Block Ciphers*, in the proceedings of CHES 2003, Lecture Notes in Computer Science, vol 2779, pp 113-124, Cologne, Germany, September 2003.
24. K.J. Kulikowski, M.Karpovsky, A. Taubin, *Robust Codes for Fault Attack Resistant Cryptographic Hardware*, in the proceedings of FDTC 2005, pp 2-12, Edinburgh, Scotland, September 2005.
25. S. Mitra, E.J. McCluskey, *Which Concurrent Error Detection Scheme ro Choose*, in the proceedings of the International Test Conference 2000, pp 985-994, October 2000, Atlantic City, NJ, USA.
26. V. Moshanin, V. Otscheretnij, A. Dmitriev, *The Impact of Logic Optimization on Concurrent Error Detection*, in the proceedings of the 4th IEEE International On-Line Testing Workshop, pp 81-84, July 1998.
27. G. Piret, J.-J. Quisquater, *A Differential Fault Attack Technique Against SPN Structures, With Applications to the AES and Khazad*, in the proceedings of CHES 2003, Lecture Notes in Computer Science, vol 2779, pp 77-88, Cologn, Germany, September 2003.
28. R. Reed, *Heavy Ion and Proton Induced Single Event Multiple Upsets*, in the proceedings of the IEEE Nuclear and Space Radiation Effects Conference, July 1997.
29. D. Samyde, S. Skorobogatov, R. Anderson, J.-J. Quisquater, *On a New Way to Read Data from Memory*, in the proceedings of the IEEE Security in Storage Workshop 2002, pp 65-69, Greenbelt, Maryland, USA, December 2002.
30. P. Shirvani, *Fault Tolerant Computing for Radiation Environments*, PhD Thesis, Center for Reliable Computing, Stanford University, June 2001.
31. S. Skorobogatov, R. Anderson, *Optical Fault Induction Attacks*, in the proceedings of CHES 2002, Lecture Notes in Computer Science, vol 2523, pp 2-12, Redwood City, CA, USA, August 2002, Springer-Verlag.
32. K. Wu, R. Karri, G. Kuznetsov, M. Goessel, *Low Cost Error Detection for the Advanced Encryption Standard*, in the proceedings of ITC 2004, Oct 2004.

Non-linear Residue Codes for Robust Public-Key Arithmetic

Gunnar Gaubatz[1,*], Berk Sunar[1,*], and Mark G. Karpovsky[2]

[1] Cryptography & Information Security Laboratory
Worcester Polytechnic Institute, Massachusetts, U.S.A
{gaubatz, sunar}@wpi.edu
[2] Reliable Computing Laboratory
Boston University, Masachusetts, U.S.A
markkar@bu.edu

Abstract. We present a scheme for robust multi-precision arithmetic over the positive integers, protected by a novel family of non-linear arithmetic residue codes. These codes have a very high probability of detecting arbitrary errors of any weight. Our scheme lends itself well for straightforward implementation of standard modular multiplication techniques, i.e. Montgomery or Barrett Multiplication, secure against active fault injection attacks. Due to the non-linearity of the code the probability of detecting an error does not only depend on the error pattern, but also on the data. Since the latter is not usually known to the adversary a priori, a successful injection of an undetected error is highly unlikely. We give a proof of the robustness of these codes by providing an upper bound on the number of undetectable errors.

Keywords: Robust arithmetic, non-linear residue codes, public-key cryptography, fault tolerance, error detection.

1 Introduction

In 1996 Boneh et al. demonstrated painfully how vulnerable straightforward implementations of public-key cryptographic algorithms are to a class of attacks now commonly referred to as "Bellcore attacks". In the following a simple and "low-cost" countermeasure was proposed by Shamir [1]. However, it was shown to be flawed by Aumüller et al. [2], since it does not protect all steps of the computation. More advanced protection schemes were proposed by Blömer et al. [3] and Yen et al. [4], and there exist claims that some of them can be broken, too [5], although this seems to be disputed.

Apart from Bellcore style attacks there exists another type of fault attack, which is aimed at common countermeasures to passive attacks. In order to prevent power and electro-magnetical analysis techniques, many VLSI implementations nowadays employ power balanced logic gate libraries, whose power consumption and hence electro-magnetic emanations are data-independent. New

---

* This work was supported through grants by the National Science Foundation and Intel Corporation.

L. Breveglieri et al. (Eds.): FDTC 2006, LNCS 4236, pp. 173–184, 2006.

fault attacks are aimed at introducing glitches into the circuit which cause such gates to 'loose balance', i.e. reveal data through power imbalances. This opens the door to various classical attacks on the circuit, like simple and differential power (SPA,DPA) and electromagnetic (SEMA,DEMA) analysis. All this demonstrates the urgent need for a truly robust error detection scheme.

A family of systematic non-linear error detecting codes, termed 'robust codes', was derived from systematic linear block codes in [6]. Their use in symmetric ciphers like the AES has been proposed in [7] and later refined in [8]. The robustness of these codes is due to the much more uniform error detection capabilities these codes offer, which is independent of the error multiplicity. Furthermore, the probability $Q(e)$ of an undetected error e does not only depend on the error pattern, but also on the data itself. In the case of a cryptographic key which is not known to the attacker a priori, a fault-injection attack is much more difficult to mount than with a linear encoding scheme. While robust codes work well with symmetric ciphers that employ only little more than table look-ups, XORs and byte-wise rotations, they are virtually unusable within the finite field arithmetic structure that forms the basis of most public-key algorithms.

During the early years of fault-tolerant computing, residue codes were proposed [9] as a means for checking arithmetic operations for errors, while preserving the integrity between operands and their check symbols. The check symbol in residue codes is computed as the remainder of the operand (or its complement) with respect to the check modulus, usually a prime. Several variations such as multi-residue and non-separate (AN) codes were also introduced early on. Designed for the purpose of detecting only sporadically occuring bit errors their arithmetic distance is limited to 2 or 3. Mandelbaum [10] introduced arithmetic codes with larger distance properties, however, with an unattractively large amount of redundancy. Unfortunately, due to the linear encoding scheme, standard arithmetic residue codes do not offer robustness properties, since any error pattern which itself is a codeword can not be detected, irrespective of the actual data.

We summarize our contributions in this paper as follows: We start by stating our assumptions about the fault model in section 2. In section 3, following the definition of robustness, we propose a new class of non-linear, systematic arithmetic residue codes, along with a proof of its robustness. We then use these codes to derive robust arithmetic primitives for performing digit-serial multi-precision arithmetic in a fault tolerant manner. In section 5 we use Montgomery modular multiplication as an example of how to implement field and ring arithmetic for public-key cryptography, that can be used in RSA and Diffie-Hellman like schemes as well as Elliptic Curve Cryptography over $GF(p)$. In the future we are planning to extend our analysis to include robust arithmetic in binary extension fields, i.e. for ECC over $GF(2^k)$, in order to provide a complete set of robust arithmetic operations for public key cryptography.

Our codes are attractive due to their data dependent and asymptotically low probability of missing errors. These properties make it nearly impossible for an adversary to successfully inject faults that are missed by the error detection network. A nice side-effect of encoding is that any arbitrary fault besides adversarial faults, e.g. one introduced by 'mother nature', is also handled automatically.

2 Adversarial Fault Model

An active side channel attack such as differential fault analysis (DFA) relies on the manifestation of injected faults as erroneous results which can then be observed at the output of the device. The error is therefore the difference between the expected output x and the observed output $\tilde{x} = x + e$. In the following we do not assume that the adversary is limited to any specific method of fault injection. The only assumption is that direct invasive access to the chip itself is prevented by some tamper-proof coating, a reasonable assumption, since this is a common practice, e.g. in the smart card industry.

However, even if the attacker should manage to remove the shielding and obtain direct access to the chip's surface [11], a successful fault analysis is still highly unlikely. Let us assume for a moment that he or she has the ability to toggle the state of an arbitrary number of bits with the required spatial and temporal resolution, i.e. reliably introduce an arbitrary error vector. Due to the data dependent probability $Q(e)$ of missing an error in the error detection network, the expected number of attempts to successfully introduce a non-detectable error is at least $\frac{1}{2} \min_{e \neq 0} \left(Q(e)^{-1} \right)$. For a sufficiently large digit size k (e.g. 32 bits), this number is on the order of several hundred million trials. While this number seems low enough to warrant an exhaustive trial and error process, such an attack can easily be defeated by a mechanism that detects an unusually large number of errors and simply shuts off the device. Only if the attacker has the capacity to read out the live state of the circuit and instantly compute an undetectable error vector the attack will be successful. We note that these are rather strong assumptions that require a high degree of sophistication and motivation.

When talking about errors as manifestations of faults, there are two principle ways of characterization. A logical error is a bitwise distortion of the data, usually modeled as the XOR of data and error, i.e. $\tilde{x} = x \oplus e$, while arithmetical errors admit the propagation of carries up to the range limit: $\tilde{x} = x + e \bmod 2^k$, where k is the width of the data path. The former is appropriate for storage dominated devices (register files, RAM, flip-flops, etc.), the arithmetic error model is more useful for arithmetic circuits such as adders and multipliers. For the remainder of this paper we will assume the latter, since it helps to simplify the analysis.

3 Robust Arithmetic Codes

As mentioned before, a class of non-linear systematic error detecting codes, so-called "robust codes", were proposed by Karpovsky and Taubin [6]. They achieve optimality according to the minimax criterion, that is, they minimize over all (n, k) codes the maxima of the fraction of undetectable errors $Q(e)$ for $e \neq 0$. While they are suitable for data transmission in channels with unknown characteristics, and also for robust implementation of symmetric-key cryptosystems with little arithmetic structure, they do not preserve arithmetic. We thus propose a new type of non-linear arithmetic code, based on the concept of arithmetic residue codes. We define robustness as follows:

Definition 1. *Let $C = \{(x,w)|x \in \mathbb{Z}_{2^k}, w = f(x) \in \mathbb{F}_p\}$ be an arithmetic single-residue code with a function $f : \mathbb{Z}_{2^k} \mapsto \mathbb{F}_p$ to compute the check symbol w with respect to the prime check modulus p of length $r = \lceil \log_2 p \rceil$ bits. A non-zero error $e \in \{(e_x, e_w)|e_x \in \mathbb{Z}_{2^k}, e_w \in \mathbb{Z}_{2^r}\}$ is masked for a message x, when $(x + e_x, w + e_w) \in C$, i.e. iff*

$$f\left((x + e_x \bmod 2^k)\right) = f(x) + e_w \bmod 2^r . \tag{1}$$

The error masking probability for a given non-zero error is thus

$$Q(e) = \frac{|\{x|(x + e_x, w + e_w) \in C\}|}{|C|} . \tag{2}$$

We call the code C robust, if it minimizes maxima of $Q(e)$ over all non-zero errors. Total robustness is achieved for $\max_{e \neq 0}(Q(e)) = 2^{-r}$. We also call C ϵ-robust if it achieves an upper bound $\max_{e \neq 0}(Q(e)) \leq \epsilon \cdot 2^{-r}$, where ϵ is a constant much smaller than 2^r.

In the following we propose a class of non-linear single-residue arithmetic codes C_p based on a quadratic residue check symbol, which achieves ϵ-robustness. Since in practice total robustness is hard to achieve, we will from now on refer to ϵ-robustness simply as robustness.

Theorem (Robust Quadratic Codes). Let C_p according to Definition 1, with $f(x) := x^2 \bmod p$. C_p is robust iff $r = k$ and $2^k - p < \epsilon$, and has the error masking equation

$$(x + e_x \bmod 2^k)^2 \bmod p = w + e_w \bmod 2^k \tag{3}$$

Proof. To prove robustness we proceed by proving an upper bound ϵ on the number of solutions of the error masking equation (3), as that directly translates into a bound on $Q(e)$. The modulo 2^k operator from the LHS of (3) stems from the limitation of the data path to k-bits. This limits the ranges of both the message and the message error to $0 \leq x, e_x < 2^k$. We can therefore remove the modulo 2^k operator by distinguishing between the two cases $x + e_x < 2^k$ and $x + e_x \geq 2^k$. Similarly, an error is masked only if the faulty check symbol $w < p$, so for $k = r$ we can distinguish between the three cases $w + e_w < p$, $p \leq w + e_w < 2^k$ and $2^k \leq w + e_w < 2^k + p$. This allows us to simplify the RHS of (3).

1. Solutions $x < 2^k - e_x$: An error (e_x, e_w) is masked iff

$$(x + e_x)^2 \bmod p = w + e_w \bmod 2^k$$

Simplifying the RHS we have the following three cases:

(a) If $w < p - e_w$, the error is masked iff

$$(x + e_x)^2 \bmod p = w + e_w \qquad (4)$$

If $e = (p, 0)$ eq. (4) has exactly $2^k - p$ solutions. For $e_x \neq p$ and $e_x \geq 2^k - p$ there exists at most a single solution; at most two solutions exist in the case of $e_x < 2^k - p$.

(b) If $p - e_w \leq w < 2^k$, the error will never be masked, since a check symbol $w \geq p$ will always be detected.

(c) For $w \geq 2^k - e_w$ the error will be masked iff

$$(x + e_x)^2 \bmod p = w + e_w - 2^k . \qquad (5)$$

Eq. (5) has at most two solutions.

2. Solutions $x \geq 2^k - e_x$: An error (e_x, e_w) is masked iff

$$(x + e_x - 2^k)^2 \bmod p = w + e_w \bmod 2^k$$

For the RHS we distinguish the following three cases:

(a) If $w < p - e_w$, the error is masked iff

$$(x + e_x - 2^k)^2 \bmod p = w + e_w \qquad (6)$$

Eq. (6) has at most two solutions, unless we have an error $e = (2^k - p, 0)$, in which case there are $2^k - p$ solutions.

(b) If $p - e_w \leq w < 2^k$, the error will never be masked, since a check symbol $w \geq p$ will always be detected.

(c) For $w \geq 2^k - e_w$ the error will be masked iff

$$(x + e_x - 2^k)^2 \bmod p = w + e_w - 2^k . \qquad (7)$$

Eq. (7) has at most two solutions.

$Q(e)$ is determined by the number of solutions to the error masking equation (3). A simple counting argument involving the cases above provides us with an initial, but somewhat weak bound:

There are at most $2^k - p + 2$ solutions to (3) for errors of the form $(p, 0)$ or $(2^k - p, 0)$, and at most 8 solutions for all other errors.

A tighter bound can be established by differentiating more precisely under which conditions two solutions can occur. We omit the proof here due to space restrictions and only give the result.

There are at most $2^k - p + 1$ solutions for errors of the form $e = (p, 0)$ or $e = (2^k - p, 0)$, and 4 solutions for all other error patterns.

We thus have $\max_{e \neq 0}(Q(e)) = 2^{-k} \cdot \max(4, 2^k - p + 1)$

We would like to point out that the transition from linear arithmetic to robust quadratic codes with the same parameters k, r and p results in a much more uniform distribution of the error detecting capability of the code. For example, for linear codes with $k = r$ there are double errors with $e_x = e_w$ such that $Q(e)$ is very close to 1, i.e. the errors cannot be detected. For robust quadratic codes with the same parameters, $Q(e)$ is close to zero for all e.

We now give an intuitive argument to show the existence of practical robust codes for cryptographic purposes with the help of the prime number theorem. The idea here is that for fault-tolerance in an adversarial situation, the probability of not detecting an error should be insignificantly small. As we saw from the proof, in the best case we have a probability of at most $Q(e) = 4 \cdot 2^{-k} = 2^{-k+2}$ of not detecting an error (assuming a uniform distribution of messages). Therefore, a $Q(e)$ that makes insertion of an error infeasible for an attacker, requires a sufficiently large digit size k and a prime p close enough to 2^k so that the difference does not increase $Q(e)$ too much. For example, for $k = r = 32$ the k-bit prime closest to 2^k is $2^{32} - 5$, thus bounding $Q(e)$ by $(2^k - p + 1) \cdot 2^{-k} = 3 \cdot 2^{-31}$. According to the prime number theorem the number of primes smaller than or equal to x is approximately $x/\ln x$, i.e. for our case $2^k/k$. Intuitively it thus seems reasonable to expect to find a prime within the interval $[2^k - k, 2^k)$. In Table 1 we give the distance of the primes closest to 2^k from below for practical values of k.

Table 1. Closest prime number distances from 2^k for practical values of k

k	17	18	19	20	21	22	23	24	25	26	27	28	29	30	31	32
$2^k - p$	1	5	1	3	9	3	15	3	39	5	39	57	3	35	1	5
k	33	34	35	36	37	38	39	40	41	42	43	44	45	46	47	48
$2^k - p$	9	41	31	5	25	45	7	87	21	11	57	17	55	21	115	59
k	49	50	51	52	53	54	55	56	57	58	59	60	61	62	63	64
$2^k - p$	81	27	129	47	111	33	55	5	13	27	55	93	1	57	25	59

4   Robust Arithmetic Operations

In the previous section we proved the robustness of quadratic codes for digits of size k bits. We now wish to apply them in a generalized framework for multi-precision arithmetic over the positive integers.

Due to the range limitation of the information bits to $0 \leq x < 2^k$, we need to handle any overflow resulting from arithmetic operations. This may be a carry bit generated by the addition of two k-bit operands, or the $2k$-bit result of a multiplication. The new digits that are created in this manner will need their own check symbols, which cannot be derived from the input operands' check symbols alone. Thus they need to be derived purely from the information bits of the new digits, creating a potential loophole for the insertion of an error. This can be avoided by re-computing the joint check symbol from the newly generated individual check symbols and comparing it to the output of the predictor. This

re-computation represents an integrity check which allows us bridge disconti-
nuities introduced by interleaving mixed modulus operations, here the check
modulus p and the implicit range limiting modulus 2^k. Once the integrity check
is in place we can perform standard arithmetic operations, and implementing an
algorithm like Montgomery's for modular arithmetic becomes straightforward.

In the following we show how this check may be implemented for various
arithmetic primitives. Let $(a, |a^2|_p)$ and $(b, |b^2|_p)$ denote encoded input operands
a and b, where $|x^2|_p$ is short-hand notation for $x^2 \bmod p$. We also introduce
mnemonics for these primitives, in order to tie them into a robust variant of the
digit serial Montgomery multiplication algorithm in the next section.

Addition (RADD and RADDC): RADD (Robust ADDition) and RADDC (Robust ADDition with Carry) compute the sum of the two input operands. This
is depicted in Figure 1. For reference, the operators $\oplus_p$ and $\otimes_p$ stand for addition and multiplication modulo p, respectively. The sum $c = a + b$ ($+c_{\text{in}}$)
may be larger than 2^k by at most a single bit. Let c_h denote this new carry,
and c_l the k-bit sum. The predictor computes the joint check symbol $|c^2|_p$ as
the sum of the check symbols and additional terms involving the operands:
$|c^2|_p = |(a + b + c_{\text{in}})^2|_p = ||a^2|_p + |b^2|_p + 2(ab + c_{\text{in}}(a + b)) + c_{\text{in}}|_p$. For error
detection we first create the check symbol for the k-bit sum $|c_l^2|_p$ (the check
symbol for the carry bit is the carry bit itself). Then we re-compute the joint
check symbol as

$$
\begin{aligned}
|c^2|_p^* &= |(c_h 2^k + c_l)^2|_p \\
&= \left| c_h \cdot |2^{2k}|_p + c_h \cdot |c_l|_p \cdot |2^{k+1}|_p + |c_l^2|_p \right|_p \\
&= \left| c_h \cdot |2^{2k} + c_l \cdot 2^{k+1}|_p + |c_l^2|_p \right|_p
\end{aligned}
\tag{8}
$$

If the check $|c^2|_p^* = |c^2|_p$ holds, then the result is deemed to be free from errors.
The resulting carry from both RADD and RADDC is held in a register local to
the addition circuit. If the following addition operation is RADDC, then that
carry is used for computation of the new sum. If it is RADD, then a zero carry
is used.

Multiplication (RMUL): The product of a and b and its joint check symbol
is $(c, |c^2|_p) = (a \cdot b, ||a^2|_p \cdot |b^2|_p|_p)$. However, the previous tuple is not a code
word, since c may exceed 2^k. We therefore split c into two halves c_h and c_l (cf.
Figure 2), both of which are within the desired range:

$$
c = c_h \cdot 2^k + c_l \quad 0 \le c_h, c_l < 2^k .
$$

We then compute the check symbols $|c_h^2|_p$ and $|c_l^2|_p$ separately, and establish
their integrity with the composite check symbol $|c^2|_p$:

$$
\begin{aligned}
|c^2|_p^* &= \left| (c_h \cdot 2^k + c_l)^2 \right|_p \\
&= \left| c_h^2 \cdot 2^{2k} + c_h \cdot c_l \cdot 2^{k+1} + c_l^2 \right|_p \\
&= \left| |c_h^2|_p \cdot |2^{2k}|_p + |c_h|_p \cdot |c_l|_p \cdot |2^{k+1}|_p + |c_l^2|_p \right|_p
\end{aligned}
\tag{9}
$$

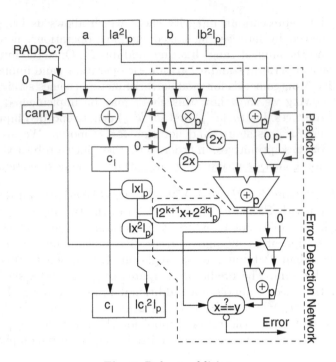

Fig. 1. Robust addition

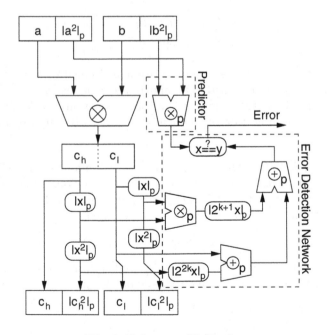

Fig. 2. Robust multiplication

Observe that the values $|2^{2k}|_p$ and $|2^{k+1}|_p$ are constant for a given implementation and that $|c_h|_p$ and $|c_l|_p$ are intermediate results from the computation of the separate halves' check symbols. Hence we have all the necessary ingredients to re-compute the joint check symbol as $|c^2|_p^*$ and compare it to the value obtained from the predictor. If the comparison passes we assume there were no errors.

Shifts, Subtraction, Logic Operations: We can apply similar re-computation techniques for other operations. Out of space considerations and since we do not need these other operations for the next section, we skip their details at this point.

Error Detection: The comparison between the predictor output and the re-computed joint check symbol is an easy target for an attack if carelessly implemented. We therefore require implementation as a totally self-checking circuit [12]. The same holds for any other integrity checks.

5   Robust Montgomery Multiplication

We now show how to apply our robust code in a digit serial Montgomery Multiplication scheme. A good overview over several variants of the Montgomery algorithm is given in [13]. In this example we will refer to the finely integrated operand scanning (FIOS) variant. It is the most suitable one for hardware implementations since it can be used in a pipelined fashion offering some degree of parallelization [14].

Algorithm 1. k-bit Digit-Serial FIOS Montgomery Multiplication

---

Require: $d = \{0, \ldots, 0\}$, $M_0' = -M_0^{-1} \bmod 2^k$
1: **for** $j = 0$ to $e - 1$ **do**
2:     $(C, S) \Leftarrow a_0 b_j + d_0$
3:     $U \Leftarrow S M_0' \bmod 2^k$
4:     $(C, S) \Leftarrow (C, S) + M_0 U$
5:     **for** $i = 1$ to $e - 1$ **do**
6:         $(C, d_{i-1}) \Leftarrow C + a_i b_j + M_i U + d_i$
7:     **end for**
8:     $(d_e, d_{e-1}) \Leftarrow C$
9: **end for**

In the following we require some basic familiarity on part of the reader with the way of how Montgomery multiplication works. To review briefly: the objective is to compute the modular product of two N-bit numbers with respect to the N-bit modulus M. Montgomery's algorithm requires the initial transformation of all operands into residues of the form $\hat{x} = xR \bmod M$ and some final transformation back $x = \hat{x}R^{-1} \bmod M$. Here R is the Montgomery radix, usually $2^{k \cdot e}$, where $e = \lceil N/k \rceil$ represents the number of digits per operand. Without loss of generality we assume that the transformation into the Montgomery residue system has already taken place and we operate entirely within the residue system, so in order to simplify notation we will refer to a residue $\hat{x}$ simply as x.

Algorithm 2. Robust Montgomery Multiplication

Require: $d = \{(0,0), \ldots, (0,0)\}$, $M_0' = -M_0^{-1} \bmod 2^k$

1: **for** $j = 0$ to $e - 1$ **do**
2:     **if** Check$((a_0, |a_0^2|_p), (b_j, |b_j^2|_p), (d_0, |d_0^2|_p), (M_0', |(M_0')^2|_p), (M_0, |M_0^2|_p))$ **then**
3:        $((T_1, |T_1^2|_p), (T_0, |T_0^2|_p)) \Leftarrow$ RMUL$((a_0, |a_0^2|_p), (b_j, |b_j^2|_p))$
4:        $(T_0, |T_0^2|_p) \Leftarrow$ RADD$((T_0, |T_0^2|_p), (d_0, |d_0^2|_p))$
5:        $(T_1, |T_1^2|_p) \Leftarrow$ RADDC$((T_1, |T_1^2|_p), (0,0))$
6:        $((-,-), (U, |U^2|_p)) \Leftarrow$ RMUL$((T_0, |T_0^2|_p), (M_0', |M_0'^2|_p))$
7:        $((T_3, |T_3^2|_p), (T_2, |T_2^2|_p)) \Leftarrow$ RMUL$((M_0, |M_0^2|_p), (U, |U^2|_p))$
8:        $(-,-) \Leftarrow$ RADD$((T_0, |T_0^2|_p), (T_2, |T_2^2|_p))$
9:        $(T_0, |T_0^2|_p) \Leftarrow$ RADDC$((T_1, |T_1^2|_p), (T_3, |T_3^2|_p))$
10:       $(T_1, |T_1^2|_p) \Leftarrow$ (carry, carry)
11:       **for** $i = 1$ to $e - 1$ **do**
12:          **if** Check$((a_i, |a_i^2|_p), (b_j, |b_j^2|_p), (d_i, |d_i^2|_p), (U, |U^2|_p), (M_i, |M_i^2|_p))$ **then**
13:            $(T_0, |T_0^2|_p) \Leftarrow$ RADD$((T_0, |T_0^2|_p), (d_i, |d_i^2|_p))$
14:            $(T_1, |T_1^2|_p) \Leftarrow$ RADDC$((T_1, |T_1^2|_p), (0,0))$
15:            $((T_4, |T_4^2|_p), (T_3, |T_3^2|_p)) \Leftarrow$ RMUL$((a_i, |a_i^2|_p), (b_j, |b_j^2|_p))$
16:            $(T_0, |T_0^2|_p) \Leftarrow$ RADD$((T_0, |T_0^2|_p), (T_3, |T_3^2|_p))$
17:            $(T_1, |T_1^2|_p) \Leftarrow$ RADDC$((T_1, |T_1^2|_p), (T_3, |T_3^2|_p))$
18:            $(T_2, |T_2^2|_p) \Leftarrow$ (carry, carry)
19:            $((T_4, |T_4^2|_p), (T_3, |T_3^2|_p)) \Leftarrow$ RMUL$((M_i, |M_i^2|_p), (U, |U^2|_p))$
20:            $(d_{i-1}, |d_{i-1}^2|_p) \Leftarrow$ RADD$((T_0, |T_0^2|_p), (T_3, |T_3^2|_p))$
21:            $(T_0, |T_0^2|_p) \Leftarrow$ RADDC$((T_1, |T_1^2|_p), (T_3, |T_3^2|_p))$
22:            $(T_1, |T_1^2|_p) \Leftarrow$ (carry, carry)
23:          **else**
24:            ABORT
25:          **end if**
26:       **end for**
27:       $(d_{e-1}, |d_{e-1}^2|_p) \Leftarrow (T_0, |T_0^2|_p)$
28:       $(d_e, |d_e^2|_p) \Leftarrow (T_1, |T_1^2|_p)$
29:     **else**
30:       ABORT
31:     **end if**
32: **end for**

The k-bit digit serial FIOS Montgomery algorithm (Alg. 1.) takes as its inputs the e-digit vectors a and b, and computes the product MM$(a,b) = a \cdot b \cdot R^{-1} \bmod M$. The value M_0' is pre-computed whenever the modulus changes. In terms of notation, a pair (C,S) represents the concatenation of two variables as the destination for the result of an operation. Furthermore, the variable C is slightly larger than the other variables, i.e. $k + 1$ bits. This is so to efficiently handle extra carries from the accumulation of C, d_i and the two products $a_i b_j$ and $M_i U$. The division by R is handled by the algorithm implicitly. For example, in line 4 the sum $(C,S) + M_0 U$ is assigned to (C,S), but in the following step S is dropped. This shift to the right by k bits, repeated e times, results in division by R. As one can easily verify, Algorithm 1. consists of only very basic addition and multiplication steps. We may therefore obtain a robust digit-serial Montgomery algorithm (Alg. 2.) simply by mapping all arithmetic steps to our robust arithmetic primitives introduced in the previous section. Additionally we insert intermediate checks during which we verify the integrity of operand values and their check symbols. This is indicated by a call to the pseudofunction Check$((x, |x^2|_p), \ldots)$. Although not indicated in the algorithm description, we further assume that the error signal generated by the the internal integrity check within the arithmetic primitives RADD, RADDC and RMUL, is also constantly evaluated. In the case of an error the algorithm is aborted with an exception.

Some comments about the robust algorithm: Algorithm 1. appears much shorter than Algorithm 2., since it combines multiple arithmetic operations into a single step. Also, while it handles carries implicitly using a larger width variable C, the robust algorithm is restricted to a digit size of exactly k bits. Thus, extra carry handling steps are required. In Alg. 2., line 6, the destination of the top half of the result is not assigned: $(-, -)$. This is equivalent to computing the result modulo 2^k, as in Alg. 1., line 3. A similar thing happens in Alg. 2., line 8, where the lower half of the result is dropped due to the implicit shift to the right. The point of performing the addition is purely to determine whether or not a carry is generated.

6 Conclusion

We have presented a novel systematic non-linear arithmetic code which is robust against adversarial injection of faults and statistically occurring random faults (soft-errors). Based on this code we have introduced arithmetic primitives for robust computation over encoded digits. We have further used the example of digit serial Montgomery modular multiplication to demonstrate how robust arithmetic can be deployed for fault-secure multi-precision public-key computations.

Quite naturally the robustness of our scheme adds overhead, which has a negative impact on performance. This is a price we have to pay for the non-linearity that enables robustness. In terms of critical path delay we estimate that multiplication incurs a performance hit of a little less than 100%, compared to a linear scheme, due to the re-computation of the quadratic check symbol. For addition, the absolut overhead is roughly the same, however, in terms of relative overhead it fares much worse. One of our aims for future research is to quantify more precisely the performance and area overhead, and compare a variety of system parameters, i.e. digit size k, check modulus p, degree of parallelism, etc. For example, for certain values of k there exist Mersenne prime check moduli, which enable very efficient implementations for check symbol computation.

Our scheme scales reasonably well, since once the digit size is determined, the complexity of the predictor and error detection networks remain constant. We would like to emphasize that we clearly prioritize robustness over performance. Given the increased vulnerability level of mobile and ubiquitous security devices, and the progress in adversarial fault analysis techniques, we believe that this is a sensible argument. For future research we aim to extend these codes to arithmetic in extension fields $GF(2^k)$, i.e. for use in elliptic curve cryptography, as well as give more concrete performance numbers, as mentioned above.

References

1. Shamir, A.: Method and apparatus for protecting public key schemes from timing and fault attacks. US Patent No. 5,991,415 (1999)
2. Aumüller, C., Bier, P., Fischer, W., Hofreiter, P., Seifert, J.P.: Fault attacks on RSA with CRT: Concrete results and practical countermeasures (2002)
3. Blömer, J., Otto, M., Seifert, J.: A new crt-rsa algorithm secure against bellcore attacks. In: CCS '03: Proceedings of the 10th ACM conference on Computer and communications security, New York, NY, USA, ACM Press (2003) 311–320
4. Yen, S., Joye, M.: Checking before output may not be enough against fault-based cryptanalysis. IEEE Trans. Comp. **49** (2000) 967–970
5. Wagner, D.: Cryptanalysis of a provably secure CRT-RSA algorithm. In: CCS '04: Proceedings of the 11th ACM Conference on Computer and Communications Security, New York, NY, USA, ACM Press (2004) 92–97
6. Karpovsky, M., Taubin, A.: New class of nonlinear systematic error detecting codes. IEEE Transactions on Information Theory **50** (2004) 1818–1820
7. Karpovsky, M., Kulikowski, K., Taubin, A.: Robust protection against fault-injection attacks of smart cards implementing the advanced encryption standard. In Simoncini, L., ed.: Proc. Int. Conf. Dependable Systems and Networks (DSN'04), IEEE Computer Society, IEEE Press (2004) 93–101
8. Kulikowski, K., Karpovsky, M., Taubin, A.: Robust codes for fault attack resistant cryptographic hardware. In Breveglieri, L., Koren, I., eds.: 2nd Int. Workshop on Fault Diagnosis and Tolerance in Cryptography (FDTC'05). (2005)
9. Rao, T., Garcia, O.: Cyclic and multiresidue codes for arithmetic operations. IEEE Trans. Inf. Theory **17** (1971) 85–91
10. Mandelbaum, D.: Arithmetic codes with large distance. IEEE Transactions on Information Theory **13** (1967) 237–242
11. Anderson, R., Kuhn, M.: Tamper resistance - a cautionary note. In: Proceedings of the Second Usenix Workshop on Electronic Commerce, USENIX Assoc., USENIX Press (1996) 1–11
12. Pradhan, D., ed.: Fault Tolerant Computing – Theory and Techniques. 1st edn. Volume 1. Prentice-Hall, New Jersey (1986)
13. Koç, Ç.K.., Acar, T., Kaliski, B.J.: Analyzing and comparing montgomery multiplication algorithms. IEEE Micro **16** (1996) 26–33
14. Gaubatz, G.: Versatile montgomery multiplier architectures. Master's thesis, Worcester Polytechnic Institute, Worcester, Massachusetts (2002)

Fault Attack Resistant Cryptographic Hardware with Uniform Error Detection

Konrad J. Kulikowski, Mark G. Karpovsky, and Alexander Taubin

Reliable Computing Laboratory, Boston University
8 Saint Mary's Street, Boston, MA 02215
{konkul, markkar, taubin}@bu.edu

Abstract. Traditional hardware error detection methods based on linear codes make assumptions about the typical or expected errors and faults and concentrate the detection power towards the expected errors and faults. These traditional methods are not optimal for the protection of hardware implementations of cryptographic hardware against fault attacks. An adversary performing a fault-based attack can be unpredictable and exploit weaknesses in the traditional implementations. To detect these attacks where no assumptions about expected error or fault distributions should be made we propose and motivate an architecture based on robust nonlinear systematic (n,k)-error-detecting codes. These code can provide uniform error detecting coverage independently of the error distributions. They make no assumptions about what faults or errors will be injected by an attacker and have fewer undetectable errors than linear codes with the same (n,k). We also present optimization approaches which provide for a tradeoff between the levels of robustness and required overhead for hardware implementations.

1 Introduction

Hardware implementations of cryptographic algorithms are vulnerable to malicious analyses that exploit the physical properties of the designs. These attacks which exploit the implementation specific weaknesses are known as Side-Channel Attacks (SCA). Information derived from the power consumption, electro-magnetic radiation, execution time, and behavior in the presence of faults of a device can all be used to drastically decrease the complexity of cryptanalysis. Mobile cryptographic devices such as smartcards and mobile computers are especially vulnerable since the physical hardware implementing the algorithms, and hence the side-channel information, is easily accessible.

The side-channel attacks of interest to this paper are Differential Fault Analysis (DFA) attacks. DFA attacks use the information obtained from an incorrectly functioning implementation of an algorithm to derive the secret information. DFA attacks were first proposed by Biham et al. [1] against hardware implementations of the Data Encryption Standard (DES). They have since been extended to other symmetric key algorithms, such as the Advanced Encryption Standard (AES) in [5-9].

Incorrect operation can result from faults within the circuit (permanent or transient) which may be due to natural effects or be maliciously induced. Faults can be injected

L. Breveglieri et al. (Eds.): FDTC 2006, LNCS 4236, pp. 185–195, 2006.
© Springer-Verlag Berlin Heidelberg 2006

into a circuit even in the presence of tamper resistant packaging by introducing the device to elevated levels of radiation or temperature, atypical clock rate, or incorrect voltage [3].

Current DFA protection methods for symmetric ciphers based on error-detecting codes use linear codes such as parity or repetition codes (e.g. duplication). These linear methods provide for good overall coverage but their error detecting capabilities depend on error distributions. The protection they provide is not uniform against all errors. Linear codes have areas of poor error coverage which can be exploited by an attacker regardless of how good the overall average protection is. In this paper we demonstrate a method of transforming from protection based on linear codes to protection based on non-linear robust codes which provide for more uniform error-detection coverage. This results in a drastic reduction of a number of undetected faults which can be exploited by an attacker. We also present optimization methods for design of robust smart cards which provide for a tradeoff between levels of robustness (uniformity of error coverage) and hardware overheads.

2   Current Protection Methods for Symmetric Ciphers

Several methods and architectures have been proposed for protecting symmetric key ciphers like AES against DFA attacks. These methods range in their granularity, protection they provide, and the overhead they require. One method proposed by several groups is based on linear error-detecting codes [11-12]. Hardware redundancy is added to the circuit to concurrently predict and verify a signature of the device. Usually very simple linear codes such as parity or duplication are used. The second method [10] exploits the symmetry and reversibility of private key algorithms. The method performs the encryption (or decryption) operations followed by their inverse decryption (or encryption). If no error was present in the operation, then performing the inverse operation should lead to the original data. The inverse and comparison can be performed on various granularities. This method usually requires large temporal overhead, since the inverse operation cannot be performed before the original computation is performed, or large hardware overhead to facilitate the verification on a finer granularity. The solutions based on linear codes can have smaller overheads but are efficient only if the errors are within the given distribution for which the codes were designed. We note that several recently published DFA attacks [5-9] require very few faults to be injected.

3   Attack Model

Attackers inject faults and observe errors which are manifestations of the faults at the output. In general, a fault produces useful information for analysis for a symmetric cipher only if an erroneous output can be observed by the attacker. The erroneous output is the expected output distorted by some error e ($e = x \oplus \tilde{x}$, where x is the expected output and $\tilde{x}$ is the observed distorted output, and $\oplus$ stands for componentwise XOR of binary vectors). In this model, detection and prevention of a fault attack is equivalent to determining if the output is distorted by an error (error detection) and suppressing the output to prevent analysis. Multiple faults have to be injected and observed for successful cryptanalysis so it is important to have the highest protection possible to detect the attack before it is successful and disable the device.

We do not limit the analysis to any method of fault injection but assume that tamper proof packaging is used so that the attacker does not have direct access to the chip surface. We assume that the attacker cannot precisely control the location of the injected faults and so the locations of the actual faults are randomly distributed within some given area of the chip. We assume that it is realistic for the attacker to have control over the multiplicity (number) of faults introduced. The multiplicity of faults can be controlled by manipulating the fault injection mechanisms such as the level of radiation, temperature, etc.

4 Limitations of Methods Based on Linear Error-Detecting Codes

Protection methods based on linear error-detecting codes do not provide for uniform level of protection against all possible faults but rather concentrate on a certain subclass of the possible faults. One of the most important criteria for evaluating the effectiveness of a protection method is not to consider the overall average protection the method provides, but rather focus on the size and type of the security holes which exist.

The three main criteria that are important for evaluating the effectiveness and practicality of a protection scheme are:

1. The number of undetectable output distortions or output errors
2. The maximum probability of missing an error or class of errors
3. Spatial and temporal overhead

Methods based on linear error-detecting codes do not provide optimum solutions with respect to the above criteria. For example, consider protection based on duplication where the hardware is doubled and the outputs of both copies are compared. If the copies match, then no error was assumed to have occurred. If an error affects an odd number of bits per a ($n = k + r$, $k = r$)-bit codeword (where k=number of information bits, r=number of redundant bits), then this protection scheme can detect those errors, and hence prevent an attack, 100% percent of the time. However, when errors are of an even multiplicity it is possible that the error will distort both copies in the same manner thus making the error undetectable. As an example, Figure 1 shows the percent of detectable errors as a function of error multiplicity (number of distorted bits) for 7-bit duplication ($k=r=7$).

Duplication is not robust; its detection capability depends largely on the multiplicity and type of the error. The scheme offers relatively poor protection for errors of even multiplicities. Although the overall probability of injecting an undetectable error (assuming all errors are equally likely) is 2^{-r}, which for the $k=r=7$ linear duplication example is $2^{-7} = 0.78\%$, it is deceiving to imply that the method provides for this level of protection. In addition to the overall average protection it is important to note the class of errors with the weakest protection level. As shown in Figure 1, for errors with multiplicity 2, the probability of successfully injecting an undetectable error increases by an order of magnitude.

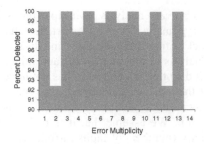

Fig. 1. Percent of errors detected for 7 bit linear duplication ($k=r=7$)

The above limitations shown for duplication are present in any protection scheme based on linear error-detecting codes. The classes of errors with lower probabilities of detection can serve as weak points for attack, regardless of how good the overall protection is.

The protection method proposed in this paper minimizes the size and weakness of the least protected areas under given limitations imposed by overheads. We propose a protection method based on a class of nonlinear systematic error-detecting codes called robust codes. Robust nonsystematic codes which provide equal probabilities of detection for all error distributions were presented in [15-16]. The methods in this paper are based on systematic robust nonlinear error detecting codes which are similar to those described in [4, 13]. We present a new construction of these codes which uses a multiplicative inverse as the nonlinear transformation. A method of reducing the hardware overhead while preserving much of the robustness is also presented.

These nonlinear codes are robust in terms of having the capability of providing equal protection against all errors. That is, for a completely robust code C the probability $Q(e)$ of missing an error e should be constant independently of an error, i.e.

$$Q(e) = \frac{|\{w \mid w \in C, w \oplus e \in C\}|}{|C|} = \text{Constant}, \ e \neq 0. \tag{1}$$

Where $w, e \in GF(2^n)$, $C \subseteq GF(2^n)$, $|C|$ is the number of codewords of the code.

Additionally, these codes for the same n and k have fewer undetectable errors than their linear counterparts. As we will see in the next section, for a systematic nonlinear (n,k) robust code the number of undetectable errors is 2^{k-r} versus 2^k for a linear code with the same length n and same number of redundant bits r. The construction and details of these robust codes are discussed in the next section.

5   Systematic Robust Codes

The binary robust codes presented in [4] were constructed using a cubic signature. In this paper we use inversion (multiplicative inverse in the field) as the nonlinear transformations for the signature. The same robust properties observed with the cubic are also observed with the robust codes which use inversion: data dependent error detection, reduction of the number of undetectable errors, and uniform distribution of the error-detecting power.

We will present now a formal description of these codes.

Let V be a binary linear (n,k) – code with $n \leq 2k$ and check matrix $H = [P \mid I]$ with $rank(P) = n - k = r$ over $GF(2)$. Code V can be made into a nonlinear systematic robust code C_V by taking the multiplicative inverse in $GF(2^r)$ of the r redundant bits:

$$C_V = \{(x,v) \mid x \in GF(2^k), v = (Px)^{-1} \in GF(2^r)\} \tag{2}$$

where 0^{-1} is defined to be 0.

For the code C_V, error $e = (e_x \in GF(2^k), e_v \in GF(2^r))$ is not detected for data $(x,(Px)^{-1})$ iff

$$(P(x \oplus e_x))^{-1} = (Px)^{-1} \oplus e_v \tag{3}$$

For linear codes an error is either always missed or never missed $(Q(e) \in \{0,1\})$, regardless of data to which the error occurred, and error detection depends only on the error pattern. For these nonlinear codes detection of errors depends not only on the error, as shown in (3), but also on the data to which the error occurred. For these robust codes there are additional classes of errors which are conditionally detected. There is also a redistribution of errors among the new classes of errors.

Table 1 summarizes this redistribution for nonlinear robust codes, C_V, when the data is assumed to be uniformly distributed. The redistribution differs depending on the number of redundant bits r. If the code has a signature where the multiplicative inverse is over $GF(2^r)$ where r is odd and $r > 2$, then there are 3 different classes of errors, identical to the nonlinear robust codes based on a cubic signature presented in [4]. When r is even and $r > 2$, there is an additional class of errors which are detected with probability $1 - 2^{-r+2}$.

Table 1. Redistribution of errors among the three classes for a linear and a robust code

detected with probability of	Number of errors		
	Linear	Robust with inversion (r is odd)	Robust with inversion (r is even)
0	2^k	2^{k-r}	2^{k-r}
1	$2^n - 2^k$	$2^{n-1} + 2^{k-1} - 2^{k-r}$	$2^{n-1} + 2^{k-1} - 2^{k-r} + 2^k - 2^{k-r}$
$1 - 2^{-r+1}$	0	$2^{n-1} - 2^{k-1}$	$2^{n-1} - 2^{k-1} - 2(2^k - 2^{k-r})$
$1 - 2^{-r+2}$	0	0	$2^k - 2^{k-r}$

As Table 1 shows, one very desirable consequence of the addition of inversion to create a robust code is the reduction in the number of undetectable errors. The number of undetectable errors is reduced from 2^k to 2^{k-r}. When $k=r$, all nonzero errors are detectable.

The codes described above are capable of providing almost uniform error detection coverage for all errors. For example, if instead of performing simple duplication, the redundant bits are the multiplicative inverse (in $GF(2^r)$) of the k-information bits, the detection profile is much more uniform. In contrast to Figure 1, Figure 2.a shows the $k=r=7$ robust duplication (codewords are in the form $\left(x, x^{-1}\right)$, $x \in GF(2^7)$).

The error detection is much more uniform independently of the type of error that is injected. This kind of error profile is more desirable for security applications, since it provides equal protection regardless of what type of errors are injected.

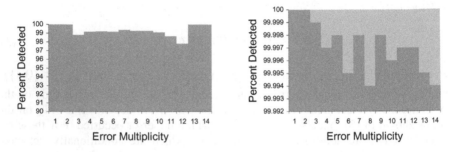

Fig. 2. Robust Duplication where $k=r=7$ a. detection for $M=1$, b. $M=2$ and $M=3$

Additionally, as Table 1 shows, for the robust codes there is a class of errors which are conditionally detected. That is, for these errors their detection depends on the data to which the error occurred, and each error in this class is missed for 2^{k-r+1} or 2^{k-r+2} messages. Unlike in the linear case where all errors are either always detected or always missed regardless of the message, the detection of these errors for robust codes is data dependent. If an error of this class is missed for one message, there is a very high probability that it will be detected by the next message. For example, for the robust duplication for any $k=r$, where r is odd, there are at most two messages for which an error is missed. So if the same error is present for three different messages, the error is guaranteed to be detected, regardless of what the error is. More precisely, if $k=r$ and all messages are different, then:

$$\max Q(e) = 2^{-r+1} \quad \text{after } M=1 \text{ message}$$

$$\max Q(e) = 2^{-r} \quad \text{after } M=2 \text{ messages}$$

$$\max Q(e) = 0 \quad \text{after } M=3 \text{ messages}$$

Figure 2.b shows the increased probability of detecting an error after $M=2$ and $M=3$ messages for the robust duplication where $k=r=7$.

For the case $k=r$ these systematic robust codes are optimum in terms of providing uniform level of protection against all errors [4]. We note that for any linear code there are always undetectable errors, so $\max Q(e) = 1$ regardless for how many messages the error is present.

6 General Architecture

The method of transforming protection based on a linear code to a more robust protection based on the systematic robust codes involves slight modification of the general linear error-detection architecture.

The general architecture used for protection with linear codes is presented in Figure 3. The architecture is composed of three major hardware components: original hardware, redundant hardware for predicting the r-bit signature v (which is a linear combination of components of the output x of the original device), and an error-detecting network (EDN).

The signature predictor contains the majority of the redundant hardware. The k bits of output of the original hardware and the r redundant output bits of the signature predictor form the $n=k+r$ extended output of the device. The extended output forms a codeword of the systematic (n,k) error-detecting code which can be used to detect errors in the original hardware or in the Predictor. It is the EDN which verifies, that the extended output of the device belongs to the corresponding code V, if it does not then the EDN raises an error signal. In a linear protection scheme the predicted r-bit signature v of the Predictor is a linear combination of the k-bit output of the original device. ($v = Px$, where P is a $(r \times n)$- check matrix for the linear (n,k) code V used for protection)

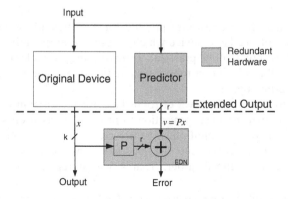

Fig. 3. General architecture for protection of hardware with error-detecting codes

With only a slight modification, the same architecture used for protection with linear error-detecting codes, can be used to provide protection based on the robust systematic nonlinear error-detecting codes presented earlier. The transformation only requires an addition of two copies of one extra component for multiplicative inverse in $GF(2^r)$.

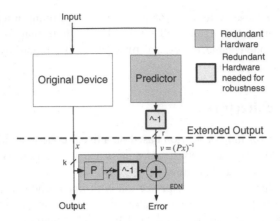

Fig. 4. Architecture for protection of hardware with robust error-detecting codes

The modified architecture is shown in Figure 4. The Extended Output of the device is now protected with the robust nonlinear code with the properties outlined above. An additional (and identical) multiplicative inverse is also needed in the EDN to verify the nonlinear signature. This transformation can be applied to any linear protection method regardless of what algorithm it is protecting.

7   Architectural Optimizations

The method for modifying an architecture based on linear codes into a robust architecture codes requires an overhead for computation of inverses in $GF(2^r)$, which is of the order $O(r^2)$.

Since large r may be necessary to provide for a sufficiently high error-detecting probability the use of one large device which takes the multiplicative inverse of all of the r-redundant bits might not be practical. Transforming an implementation protected by a linear code with $r=32$ into a robust systematic code would require several thousands additional 2-input gates.

It is possible to tradeoff the level of robustness for the amount of hardware overhead required to transform linear protection to protection based on systematic robust codes. Instead of taking one multiplicative inverse for all r-bit vectors, it is possible to divide the one large inversion into disjoint smaller inversions while retaining many of the robust properties outlined earlier. That is, we can replace multiplicative inverse in $GF(2^r)$ by t s-bit disjoint inverses in $GF(2^{\frac{r}{t}})$ to produce the nonlinear r bit output ($r = ts$).   Thus, instead of having two r-bit multiplicative inverses in $GF(2^r)$ for the whole design, there could be $2t$ inverses in $GF(2^{\frac{r}{t}})$ as it is presented in Figure 5 for $t=2$. Since the number of two input gates to implement the inverse is proportional to the square of the number of bits at its input, a modification

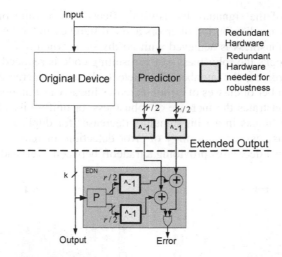

Fig. 5. Optimized architecture, the multiplicative inverse in split into $t=2$ separate modules

where $t=2$ would result in roughly 50% decrease of an overhead associated with the architecture based on robust codes. As a consequence this also results in a slight decrease in the level of robustness and an in introduction of errors which are detected with different probabilities.

The division of the nonlinear signature results in the creation of additional classes of errors which detected with different probabilities depending on the number of divided signatures they affect. To account for this division Table 1 has to be extended. Table 2 shows the redistribution of errors among the additional classes for t s-bit signatures if r is odd, a very similar table can be constructed for the case when r is even.

Table 2. Redistribution of errors as function of the number of blocks t of the signature when r is odd

#of blocks	\multicolumn{5}{c}{Number of errors missed with probability p}
	$p=1$ (undetectable)	$p=0$ (always detected)	$p=2^{-s+1}$	$p=2^{-2(s+1)}$	$p=2^{-i(s+1)}$
Linear	2^k	$2^{k+r}-2^k$	0	0	0
$t=1$ (robust)	N_1	N_2	N_3	0	0
$t<\dfrac{r}{2}$ (robust)	$(N_1)^t$	$\displaystyle\sum_{i=1}^{t}\binom{t}{i}N_2^{\,i}(2^s-N_2)^{t-i}$ $=(2^s)^t-(2^s-N_2)^t$	$tN_3(N_1)^{t-1}$	$\dbinom{t}{2}(N_3)^2(N_1)^{t-2}$	$\dbinom{t}{i}(N_3)^i(N_1)^{t-i}$
$t\geq\dfrac{r}{2}$	2^k	$2^{k+r}-2^k$	0	0	0

where $N_1 = 2^{\frac{k}{t}-s}$, $N_2 = 2^{\frac{k+r}{t}-1} + 2^{\frac{k}{t}-1} - 2^{\frac{k}{t}-s}$, $N_3 = 2^{\frac{k+r}{t}-1} - 2^{\frac{k}{t}-1}$

The splitting of the signature has several effects. Depending on the number of blocks, t, there is a redistribution of errors and a difference in the level of robustness. The maximum robustness is achieved with no divisions when $t=1$. With an increasing number of blocks the robustness of the resulting code is reduced. As the number of blocks, t, increases, the number of undetectable errors increases exponentially. Likewise, the number of classes of errors increases linearly as t increases.

Figure 6 demonstrates the increase of robustness, or uniformity of error coverage, as the number of blocks in a r-bit signature decreases for duplication where $k=r=8$. The level of robustness, or uniformity of error detection, increases as the number of signature divisions t decreases providing a tradeoff between overhead and robustness.

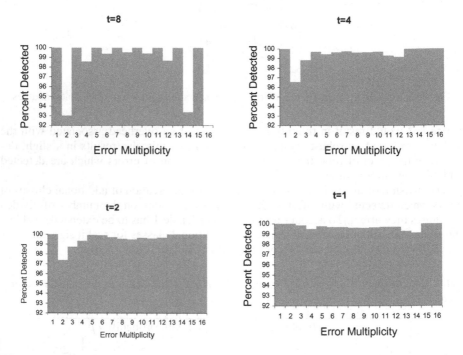

Fig. 6. The effect of splitting the r-bit signature into t disjoint inverses on robustness where $k=r=8$

8   Conclusions

The protection provided by linear error detecting codes is not uniform and is not suitable for cryptographic hardware which is susceptible to fault attacks. The level of protection they provide depends largely on the type of error that is considered. We presented a method of protection based on nonlinear systematic robust codes which can provide for uniform protection against all errors thus drastically reducing the probability that an attacker will be able to inject an undetected error. We also presented an optimization which allows for a tradeoff between the level of robustness and area overhead.

The construction of the presented robust codes was based on the use of a multiplicative inverse as the nonlinear transformation. The multiplicative inverse is a building block of the Sbox of the Advanced Encryption Standard. This inverse based construction of the codes might be useful in further reduction of overhead if the inversion hardware in AES can be used to produce the nonlinear signature.

References

1. Biham, E. and A. Shamir, "Differential fault analysis of secret key cryptosystems", CRYPTO 97, LNCS 1294, pp.513-525
2. FIPS PUB 197: "Advanced Encryption Standard", http://csrc.nist.gov/publications/fips/fips197/fips-197.pdf
3. Bar-El H., H. Choukri, D. Naccache, M. Tunstall and C. Whelan. "The Sorcerer's Apprentice Guide to Fault Attacks". Cryptology ePrint Archive, Report 2004/100. Available: http://eprint.iacr.org/2004/100.pdf
4. Karpovsky, M.G. and A. Taubin, "A New Class of Nonlinear Systematic Error Detecting Codes", *IEEE Trans Info Theory*, Vol 50, No.8, 2004, pp.1818-1820
5. Chen, C.N. and S.M. Yen. "Differential Fault Analysis on AES Key Schedule and Some Countermeasures". ACISP 2003, LNCS 2727, pp18-129, 2003.
6. Dusart, P., G. Letourneux, O. Vivolo, "Differential Fault Analysis on AES". Cryptology ePrint Archive, Report 2003/010. Available: http://eprint.iacr.org/2003/010.pdf
7. Giraud, C. "DFA on AES". Cryptology ePrint Archive, Report 2003/008. Available: http://eprint.iacr.org.
8. Blömer, J. and J.P. Seifert. "Fault Based Cryptanalysis of the Advanced Encryption Standard (AES)". Financial Cryptography 2003: pp. 162-181.
9. Quisquater, J.J. and G. Piret. "A Differential Fault Attack Technique against SPN Structures, with Application to the AES and KHAZAD". CHES 2003, LNCS 2779, pp 77-88, 2003.
10. Karri, R., K. Wu, P. Mishra, and Y. Kim. "Concurrent Error Detection of Fault Based Side-Channel Cryptanalysis of 128-Bit Symmetric Block Ciphers". *IEEE Trans. on Computer-Aided Design of Integrated Circuits and Systems*, Vol.21, No.12, pp. 1509-1517, 2002
11. Karri, R., G. Kuznetsov, M. Gössel. "Parity-Based Concurrent Error Detection of Substitution-Permutation Network Block Ciphers". *In Proc. of CHES 2003*. pp.113-124.
12. Bertoni, G., L. Breveglieri, I. Koren, P. Maistri and V. Piuri. "Error Analysis and Detection Procedures for a Hardware Implementation of the Advanced Encryption Standard". *IEEE Transactions on Computers*, vol. 52, no. 4, 2003
13. Karpovsky, M.G., K. Kulikowski, and A. Taubin, "Robust Protection against Fault-Injection Attacks of Smart Cards Implementing the Advanced Encryption Standard". Proc. Int. Conference on Dependable Systems and Networks (DNS 2004), July, 2004
14. Karpovsky, M.G., K. Kulikowski, and A. Taubin, "Differential Fault Analysis Attack Resistant Architectures for the Advanced Encryption Standard". Proc. World Computing Congress, Cardis, Aug., 2004
15. Karpovsky, M.G., P. Nagvajara, "Optimal Robust Compression of Test Responses," IEEE Trans. on Computers, Vol. 39, No. 1, pp. 138-141, January 1990.
16. Karpovsky, M.G., P. Nagvajara, "Optimal Codes for the Minimax Criterion on Error Detection," IEEE Trans. on Information Theory, November 1989.

Robust Finite Field Arithmetic for Fault-Tolerant Public-Key Cryptography[*]

Gunnar Gaubatz and Berk Sunar

Cryptography & Information Security Laboratory
Worcester Polytechnic Institute, Massachusetts, U.S.A
{gaubatz, sunar}@wpi.edu

Abstract. We present a new approach to fault tolerant public key cryptography based on redundant arithmetic in finite rings. Redundancy is achieved by embedding non-redundant field or ring elements into larger rings via suitable homomorphisms obtained from modulus scaling. Our approach is closely related to, but not limited by the exact definition of cyclic binary and arithmetic codes. We present a framework for system-designers that allows flexible trade-offs between circuit area and desired level of fault tolerance. Our method applies to arithmetic in prime fields and extension fields of characteristic 2 where it serves two mutually beneficial purposes: The redundancy of the larger ring can be used for error detection, while its modulus has a special low Hamming-weight form, lending itself particularly well to efficient modular reduction.

Keywords: Finite field arithmetic, public-key cryptography, fault tolerance, homomorphic embedding, modulus scaling, error detection, cyclic codes, arithmetic codes, idempotency.

1   Introduction

Finite field arithmetic over $GF(q)$ and $GF(q^k)$ has found many uses in cryptography, particularly in public key cryptography and for substitution functions in symmetric key algorithms like the AES. For quite some time before cryptographers discovered its usefulness, most of its applications were in coding theory. The high performance of many error correcting codes is due to the efficient arithmetic in binary extension fields. Real world implementations of cryptographic algorithms and protocols are rarely challenged by the computational resources of an attacker anymore. Key sizes of 128 bits for symmetric schemes and matching sizes for public key schemes offer sufficiently large security margins to withstand even huge leaps in the cryptanalytical progress. The real, tangible threat stems from side-channel attacks in which an attacker tries to use flaws in the implementation, rather than flaws in the algorithm. This threat is accelerated further through the growing adoption of embedded and ubiquitous security devices, e.g. smart cards, cryptographic tokens, etc. Several different classes of side-channel

---

[*] This work was supported by the National Science Foundation under grants No. NSF-ANI-0112889 (ITR) and No. NSF-ANI-0133297 (CAREER).

L. Breveglieri et al. (Eds.): FDTC 2006, LNCS 4236, pp. 196–210, 2006.

attacks have been identified and a variety of countermeasures have been proposed. Passive attacks such as power and electromagnetic analysis typically require a circuit designer to go to great lengths for balancing power consumption or shielding EM emissions from leaving the security perimeter. Other approaches use adaptive masking techniques for randomization and hence, de-correlation between the power signature and the secret information.

Active attacks are much more powerful than passive attacks, since they no longer confine the attacker into the role of an observer. Through the deliberate insertion of faults into the computation an adversary might cause the leakage of secret key information. The consequences of not employing at least an error detection scheme have been demonstrated vividly in [1]. Protecting against this class of attacks requires more than elaborate circuit tricks; it requires a mechanism for detecting modification of data, faulty behavior of the arithmetic circuit, or both. Just as traditional mission critical applications like avionics and systems working under harsh environmental conditions require fault tolerant design techniques, it becomes increasingly important for embedded security devices operating in a hostile environment.

In this paper we propose *scaled embedding* as a new approach to fault tolerant arithmetic for public key cryptography that is based in principal on two important classes of codes: arithmetic and binary cyclic codes. The former were designed with the intention of protecting integer arithmetic operations against faults, while applications of the latter can be found mostly in a communications setting, where they ensure the reliable transmission of data. Incidentally, the arithmetic structure of these codes is in principle the same as that of public key cryptographic schemes based on integer and binary polynomial rings and fields, in particular *Elliptic Curve Cryptography*. The theories of both classes of codes contain a significant amount of overlap, which suggests a unified treatment. It is possible and useful to view the encoding of operands along with their arithmetic operations as a ring homomorphism. It can be used to embed elements from the non-redundant ring or field $\mathcal{F}$ into a larger, redundant ring $\mathcal{R}$ by means of multiplication with a constant scaling factor. While this may not adhere to the strict definition of cyclic codes, a less stringent definition allows a more flexible choice of scaling factors, despite the absence of theory proving the robustness of this method. When robustness is required, one can always fall back on the special case of cyclic codes. Arithmetic operations executed in $\mathcal{R}$ preserve the operations that otherwise would have to be executed without redundancy in $\mathcal{F}$. This redundancy can be utilized in every step of the computation to detect errors caused either by transient faults due to circuit crosstalk and radiation, or by malicious fault insertion from an adversary. Our method serves two mutually beneficial purposes: The redundancy of the larger ring can be used for error detection, while its modulus has a form lending itself particularly well to efficient modular reduction. Our method constitutes a generalization of homomorphic embedding for fault tolerant arithmetic which contains arithmetic and binary cyclic codes as special cases. This generalization is what enables us to obtain a larger choice of parameters, thereby allowing flexible time-space trade-offs.

The remainder of this contribution is structured as follows. Following a summary of related work in Section 2 we provide definitions for ring and field homomorphisms in Section 3 and show how they can be applied to create redundant computational paths, particularly in the case of homomorphic embedding. The practical implications of our scheme become more apparent in Section 4 where we discuss issues pertaining to the implementation of different embedding functions, error detection strategies and the analysis of error coverage. The relationship of scaled embedding to the theory of cyclic codes is illustrated with more detail in Section 5, followed by concluding remarks.

2   Related Work

Early work on fault tolerant cryptography has either revolved around the use of simple parity prediction schemes or adapted traditional mechanisms like *triple modular redundancy (TMR)* and time redundancy for determining the correct result in the presence of errors. It seems, however, that most of the current effort is concentrated on *concurrent error detection (CED)* schemes for symmetric ciphers. Efforts to provide error detection capabilities to public key schemes based upon finite field arithmetic have so far only seen sporadic treatment. A common approach is augmentation of finite field multipliers over $\mathbb{F}_2^k$ with parity prediction capabilities [2,3]. These techniques, however, do not make use of the rich mathematical structures provided by finite rings and fields, which form the arithmetic foundation for many cryptographic schemes. Furthermore, their error detecting capabilities are mostly aimed at faults caused by *single event upsets* (SEU), e.g. due to background radiation, but not faults induced by an intelligent attacker.

A strategy that has not been explored yet is the use of *error detecting codes (EDC)* with arithmetic structure, specifically cyclic and arithmetic codes, upon which our approach is based. The main difficulty is that our purpose is not only to encode and decode data for transmission over a noisy channel. In viewing the computation itself as a noisy channel, we aim to compute with encoded operands while preserving the arithmetic structure. We thus propose to embed finite field elements into a larger ring via a suitable ring homomorphism, and to utilize the redundancy for error detection purposes. Embedding finite fields into larger rings has been used before, e.g. for the implementation of efficient finite field multiplier architectures based on redundant representation in cyclotomic rings [4]. The authors, however, have not explored the usefulness of this redundancy for fault tolerance. Our work on *scaled embedding* was motivated by earlier work on modulus scaling [5,6] and its connection to coding theory. In [6] a scaled modulus of special low Hamming-weight form was used to enable low-complexity modular reduction, but the redundancy was not used for error detection. By additionally scaling the operands with a constant factor, the information is spread out across an extended range of bits. This allows the detection of errors by simply dividing out that factor and checking for the remainder to be zero.

As mentioned earlier, cyclic codes may be used for fault tolerant arithmetic, albeit with some practical limitations. Most importantly, in the case of cyclic binary codes there is only a severely limited number of cryptographically significant fields, e.g. those suitable for elliptic curve cryptography, that can be embedded into the ring $GF(2)[x]/(x^n - 1)$. In order to avoid attacks based on Weil descent [7], a cautious implementor will want to select a field whose (irreducible) field polynomial is of prime degree k. The precise definition of a cyclic code, however, limits suitable field polynomials to those which are proper divisors of $x^n - 1 \bmod 2$. For fields with an extension degree in the range that is of interest for elliptic curve cryptography, i.e. $130 \leq k \leq 500$, there are exactly ten suitable choices, and each carries a large amount of redundancy, i.e. $n = 2k + 1$ as shown in Table 1. The situation is only slightly better with cyclic arithmetic codes which are defined in a similar way. In this case the field modulus and the amount of redundancy is determined by the integer factorization of $2^n \pm 1$.

We can increase the number of suitable parameters by taking an alternative viewpoint. By relaxing the notion that the code has to be strictly cyclic, we can find ring structures which can embed fields of nearly arbitrary cardinality, with flexible trade-offs between field size and amount of redundancy. We thus obtain a generalized interpretation in which arithmetic and binary cyclic codes constitute special cases. The generalized ring modulus can now take any form, preferably one of pseudo-Mersenne form $2^n \pm u$ $(x^n + u(x)$ in the binary polynomial case), where u is odd and of low weight (has small degree). Via factorization of the ring moduli we can obtain a broad range of suitable field and scaling factor parameters. For illustration we have included a selection of parameters in Tables 2, 3 and 4 in the Appendix.

3 Redundancy Through Ring and Field Homomorphisms

Our intention is to devise an error detection/correction scheme which utilizes the rich mathematical structure of the very foundation of public key cryptography: finite fields and rings. For this we want to use a transformation through which we introduce redundancy in our representation and thereby gain error detection/correction capabilities. We require the transformation $\phi : \mathcal{F} \to \mathcal{G}$ to map between the additive identities and preserve the addition and multiplication operations in rings $\mathcal{F}, \mathcal{G}$, i.e. for all $a, b \in \mathcal{F}$:

$$\phi(0) = 0 \ ,$$
$$\phi(a) \cdot \phi(b) = \phi(a \cdot b) \ \text{ and}$$
$$\phi(a) + \phi(b) = \phi(a + b) \ .$$

If these criteria are satisfied then ϕ is a *ring homomorphism*. Note, however, that the two conditions do not necessarily warrant the preservation of multiplicative inverses. Under a ring homomorphism we can develop two strategies for error detection/correction:

- If $|\mathcal{F}| \geq |\mathcal{G}|$ then $\phi(.)$ may be used to create an additional verifier datapath besides the original main datapath. It mimics all computations on the main datapath using the homomorphic representations initially generated through

$\phi(.)$ (cf. Fig. 1). At the end of all computations the result from the regular main datapath is run through $\phi(.)$ again and compared to the output of the verifier datapath. This type of strategy is similar to the one employed for parity prediction circuits, e.g. in [2]. We will not further elaborate on this strategy in this paper.

– If $|\mathcal{F}| < |\mathcal{G}|$ then we speak of *embedding* $\mathcal{F}$ into $\mathcal{G}$, and the difference in cardinality establishes the amount of redundancy present in the embedding. After mapping all operands from $\mathcal{F}$ to $\mathcal{G}$ via the homomorphism $\phi(.)$, all computation is carried out in $\mathcal{G}$. At the end of all computations the result is converted back to $\mathcal{F}$ via the inverse homomorphism $\phi^{-1}(.)$ (cf. Fig. 2).

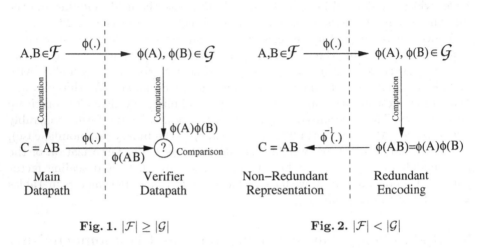

Fig. 1. $|\mathcal{F}| \geq |\mathcal{G}|$ Fig. 2. $|\mathcal{F}| < |\mathcal{G}|$

4 Homomorphic Embedding in Rings and Extension Fields

One may exploit the natural embedding provided by the field/subfield relationship of field extensions. For instance, we may carry out arithmetic in a finite field $\mathcal{F} = \mathrm{GF}(q^n)$ by embedding all operands into an extension $\mathcal{G} = \mathrm{GF}((q^n)^m)$. This method has the advantage of carrying the same field operations, i.e. addition, multiplication, inversion. To construct such an embedding we need a function mapping elements from $\mathcal{F}$ to $\mathcal{G}$, i.e. an injective map $\phi : \mathcal{F} \mapsto \mathcal{G}$. However, having both the domain and the range of the mapping to be fields may prove to be too restrictive. As an alternative we may define the mapping from a field $\mathcal{F} = \mathrm{GF}(q^n)$ to a ring $\mathcal{R}$ which offers more flexibility in choosing suitable parameters. As described in the previous section the function $\phi(.)$ needs to be a homomorphism and preserve the addition and multiplication operations.

Consider the case when $\mathcal{F} \subset \mathcal{R}$. Embedding works by mapping any element $a \in \mathcal{F}$ via a ring homomorphism $\phi : \mathcal{F} \mapsto \mathcal{R}$ onto an element $\phi(a) \in \mathcal{R}$. Therefore we can carry out all arithmetic operations originally defined for $\mathcal{F}$ in $\mathcal{R}$ instead. At the end of the computation it will be required to use the inverse homomorphism $\phi^{-1} : \mathcal{R} \mapsto \mathcal{F}$ to transform the result back to the field. In the following we will explicitly define homomorphisms to make our approach more vivid. We investigate two different methods for embedding: *Basic* and *Idempotent* scaled embedding. Both methods tie into the theory of cyclic codes for certain parameter selections, but can also be seen as a generalization of the concept without making claims about any sort of minimum distance metric. We discuss this link to coding theory further in Section 5. We would like to point out that both methods apply equally well to integer *and* polynomial rings. For sake of simplicity, however, we will refrain from making explicit distinctions in notation throughout the remainder of this paper, unless such a distinction is required.

As pointed out before, scaled embedding is closely related to modulus scaling, which was applied in [6] to obtain a modulus of pseudo-Mersenne form, leading to efficient modular reduction. The redundancy introduced by the scaled modulus allows us to implement an error detection scheme. Naïve direct embedding $\phi(a) = a$, however, does not provide error detection capabilities, since there is no way to distinguish errors from data. *Scaled embedding* on the other hand multiplies operands by a generator value g, which may be distinct from the modulus scaling factor s. It effectively partitions the ring $\mathcal{R}$ into cosets, of which only one contains valid codewords. Error detection can therefore be based upon checking for membership in the right coset. With respect to the choice of a suitable modulus scaling factor we strive to achieve two goals:

1. To select the resulting ring large enough to have sufficient redundancy for error detection purposes, i.e. an amount proportional to the length of the scaling factor, i.e. $\log_2 s$.
2. To obtain a ring modulus $m = p \cdot s$ for which an efficient reduction technique exists. This helps to offset some of the overhead in complexity that we incur from the redundancy.

If the field $\mathcal{F}$ and its associated modulus (prime integer or irreducible polynomial) p are determined by the application, then the choices for a suitable scaling factor might be limited. If, however, the value of the modulus is not fixed, then one can choose a suitable pair (s, p) based on the required levels of security (modulus size) and redundancy. The computationally most efficient moduli in (pseudo-)Mersenne form have very small Hamming-weight, e.g. less than 5. Therefore, in order to find such a pair we let $m = 2^n \pm u$, with u small and $n = \lceil \log_2 p + \log_2 s \rceil$, be the preferred ring modulus and find a suitable field by way of factorization. Depending on the size of n factorization might take a long time, especially in the case of finding suitable prime fields.

For polynomial moduli the ideal form is a binomial $m(x) = x^n \pm 1$, as in cyclic codes, but other moduli $x^n \pm u(x)$ with small degree $u(x)$ are also conceivable. When $u(x) = 1$ then the reduction of partial products, e.g. during the shifting step of bit-serial multiplication, becomes trivial since the shift with reduction can be simplified to a bit rotation due to the equivalence $x^{n+1} \equiv 1 \bmod p(x)$. The factorization of binomials is well studied, and there exist many efficient methods. What we are looking for specifically are large irreducible factors of prime degree.

This is important mainly for applications in elliptic curve cryptography due to the vulnerability of composite degree fields to a class of attacks based on Weil descent [7].

4.1 Basic Scaled Embedding

Once we have found suitable parameters for the modulus and its scaling factor, we can encode the input operands by means of multiplication with the generator value g. For basic scaled embedding this is the same value as the modulus scaling factor s, i.e. $g = s$. The function $\phi_s(a) = g \cdot a$ maps an element a from $\mathcal{F}$ to $\mathcal{R}$. It provides error detection capabilities since all valid elements of $\mathcal{R}$ must be proper multiples of g. Note that while the mapping preserves addition, it does not preserve regular multiplication, i.e.

$$\phi_s(a \cdot b) = g \cdot a \cdot b \neq \phi_s(a) \cdot \phi_s(b) .$$

However, by re-defining[1] the multiplication operation such that it implicitly eliminates the extra scaling factor, $\phi_s(.)$ becomes a ring homomorphism with respect to $+$ and $\cdot / \star$ operations, i.e. $\phi_s(a \cdot b) = \phi_s(a) \star \phi_s(b)$.

Definition 1. *Let $A = \phi_s(a)$ and $B = \phi_s(b)$ denote the elements found by mapping a and $b \in \mathcal{F}$ to the ring $\mathcal{R}$. We re-define multiplication in the ring $\mathcal{R}$ as $A \star B = ((g \cdot a \cdot g \cdot b)/g) \bmod m = \phi_s(a \cdot b)$, where division by g occurs strictly before modular reduction by m.*

Therefore, multiplications in $\mathcal{R}$ are implemented using the $\star$ operation instead of regular ring multiplication, while addition in the ring remains the same. Since the value for g is constant for a specific modulus, division may be implemented more efficiently than in the general case. Algorithms for division by constants have been treated, for example, in [8].

Error Detection. As mentioned earlier, detection of errors can be based on checking for membership of an operand in a specific coset of the ring $\mathcal{R}$ by means of computing the remainder modulo g. A value of zero indicates that the operand is likely to be free of errors. We have to use caution here, because quite naturally our scheme can not detect error patterns that are proper multiples of g. We apply a relatively simple error model to determine the error coverage of this method: We assume that errors only occur as additive terms on input operands and that the operation itself is fault-free. Consequently, the output is the sum of the correct result and another additive error term related to the input errors and the operation. While such an error model may be rather simple, we would like to make a point for its validity in the context of fault-insertion attacks. From an adversarial point of view, the most accessible targets with high probability of success for introducing an error are storage elements like registers and SRAM memory cells. A glitch attack on such a bistable device, e.g. using optical fault induction with a focussed laser beam [9], is able to cause an error regardless of

---

[1] We use a different symbol here to prevent confusion.

the exact point in time during which it is carried out (with respect to the clock interval). A glitch in a combinational part of a circuit will manifest itself as an error, only if it reaches the next register in time for the next clock edge and if it does not significantly violate setup and hold time requirements.

We will now determine the conditions under which we can detect errors. Let $A = \phi_s(a)$, $B = \phi_s(b) \in \mathcal{R}$ denote the fault-free input operands of the multiplication operation $A \star B$ and C the fault-free result.

$$C = A\star B = (A\cdot B)/g \pmod{m} = ((g\cdot a\cdot g\cdot b)/g) \pmod{m} = g\cdot a\cdot b \pmod{m}$$

Furthermore let C' denote the result in the presence of additive error terms e_A, $e_B \in \mathcal{R}$ on the inputs:

$$
\begin{aligned}
C' &= (A + e_A) \star (B + e_B) \\
&= (g^2 \cdot a \cdot b + g(a \cdot e_B + b \cdot e_A) + e_A \cdot e_B)/g \pmod{m} \\
&= C + a \cdot e_B + b \cdot e_A + \frac{e_A \cdot e_B}{g} \pmod{m} \\
&= C + e_C
\end{aligned}
$$

Here $e_C \in \mathcal{R}$ is the resulting error on the output. Certain errors can be detected immediately during the division step of the $\star$ multiplication procedure, i.e. if the remainder $C' \bmod g \neq 0$, which means that $g \nmid e_A \cdot e_B$. There are two other non-trivial cases of potentially undetectable errors:

1. A one-sided error, e.g. $e_A = 0$, $e_B \neq 0$. Then $e_C = a \cdot e_B \bmod m$, which is not detectable if $g|e_C$.
2. A two-sided error $e_A, e_B \neq 0$. Now we have $e_C = a\cdot e_B + b\cdot e_A + \frac{e_A\cdot e_B}{g} \bmod m$. The error is undetectable iff $g|e_C$.

The procedure for error detection is based on modular reduction of the operands with respect to the scaling factor g and checking for a non-zero remainder. Here it can be performed outside of the critical path of the computation. As long as there is no error in any of the previous operations, the result can immediately be used as the input for subsequent operations, while an error check is performed in parallel. The major problem we face with basic scaled embedding is the division step that is intrinsic to the $\star$ multiplication, since it adds to the critical path. Division is notoriously complex in hard- and software implementations unless the divisor is a constant of special form, which is not usually the case. In the next section we present a modification to the basic scaled embedding idea, which completely avoids the division step of $\star$ multiplication.

4.2 Idempotent Scaled Embedding

The division step of $\star$ multiplication in the basic scaled embedding scheme is required because both operands contain a multiplicative factor g which results in a square factor g^2 for the product. One way to avoid the extra g is to perform multiplication with only one scaled input, the other unscaled, but this introduces a host of other problems. First we would loose error detection capabilities in the unscaled operand, and secondly the product of two results from previous multiplications would again require division.

The solution is to find a scaling factor that is idempotent with respect to the scaled modulus, i.e. $g \equiv g^2 \bmod m$. A class of non-separate arithmetic codes known as AN codes use the same encoding principle as scaled embedding and suffer from the same problem of an extra residue of the generator value. In [10] Proudler introduced a class of idempotent AN codes that preserve addition *and* multiplication in the ring. These codes can therefore be used to form a ring homomorphism $\phi_i(.)$ that avoids division altogether. A critical flaw of idempotent AN codes is, however, that a one-sided error, i.e. one that only appears in one of two input operands, will be masked in a multiplication with the other error-free operand due to the distributive law:

$$A' = \phi_i(a) + e_A$$
$$B = \phi_i(b)$$
$$A' \cdot B = (g \cdot a + e_A)(g \cdot b) \quad (\bmod\ m)$$
$$= g^2 \cdot a \cdot b + g \cdot b \cdot e_A \quad (\bmod\ m)$$
$$= \phi_i((a + e_A)b)$$

This flaw can be compensated for by extending from idempotent AN to idempotent AN+B codes. These were also introduced in [10] and like AN codes derive their names from the encoding procedure. In addition to being scaled by the generator value g, a constant term c is added to the operands during encoding. AN+B codes exist whenever the ring modulus $m = p \cdot s$ and $\gcd(p, s) = 1$. Then we can construct the values g and c idempotent with respect to the modulus m as follows:

$$g = (s^{-1} \bmod p)\, s \tag{1}$$
$$c = (p^{-1} \bmod s)\, p \tag{2}$$

where

$$g^2 \equiv g \quad (\bmod\ m)\ , \tag{3}$$
$$c^2 \equiv c \quad (\bmod\ m)\ \text{ and} \tag{4}$$
$$g \cdot c \equiv 0 \quad (\bmod\ m)\ . \tag{5}$$

Unlike AN codes, AN+B codes are no longer addition preserving. In the presence of a heterogeneous mix of addition and multiplication operations it is therefore necessary to convert[2] operands back and forth between codes. Luckily this is a rather trivial exercise since both codes share the same generator g. We can re-define multiplication to implicitly handle the conversion steps by adding the

---

[2] Note that conversion is only necessary at the boundary between heterogeneous operations like addition and multiplication. It can be omitted for homogeneous operations like modular exponentiation, which are based exclusively upon multiplication.

constant term c to each operand before multiplication and subsequently subtracting it from the result. The difference to ordinary multiplication in the ring is indicated through the use of the $\star$ symbol:

Definition 2. *Let $A = \phi_i(a)$ and $B = \phi_i(b)$ denote operands embedded in $\mathcal{R}$, where $\phi_i(x) = g \cdot x \bmod m$. Then addition in the ring is defined as usual and multiplication is re-defined as*

$$
\begin{aligned}
A \star B &= (g \cdot a + c) \cdot (g \cdot b + c) - c \quad (\bmod\ m) \\
&= g^2 \cdot a \cdot b + c \cdot g(a + b) + c^2 - c \quad (\bmod\ m) \\
&= \phi_i(a \cdot b) = g(a \cdot b) \quad (\bmod\ m)
\end{aligned}
$$

due to the equivalences defined in (3), (4) and (5).

We can thus define an idempotent ring homomorphism with respect to $+$ and $\star / \cdot$ operations as

$$
\begin{aligned}
\phi_i(0) &= 0, \\
\phi_i(a) + \phi_i(b) &= \phi_i(a + b) \quad \text{and} \\
\phi_i(a) \star \phi_i(b) &= \phi_i(a \cdot b) \ .
\end{aligned}
$$

Now a one-sided error e_A will not be masked anymore, provided that $s \nmid e_A$:

$$
\begin{aligned}
A' \star B &= (g \cdot a + c + e_A)(g \cdot b + c) - c \quad (\bmod\ m) \\
&= g(a \cdot b) + e_A(g \cdot b + c) \quad (\bmod\ m) \\
&\equiv e_A \bmod s
\end{aligned}
$$

Once all computations have been performed the non-redundant result needs to be converted back from the ring to the field via the inverse homomorphism $\phi_i^{-1}()$. This is achieved through modular reduction of the result with respect to the field modulus p.

We now have an efficient method for embedding a field into a larger ring with meaningful redundancy that we want to use for error detection purposes. Since valid code words need to be proper multiples of the generator value $g \equiv 0 \bmod s$, an error check can be performed by computing the remainder of a division by s. An additive error e_R on the result will be detected as $e'_R = e_R \bmod s$, if it is not evenly divisible by s. Hence, if $e'_R = 0$, the result can be assumed free of errors with high probability. There may, however, be cases in which an error e_A remains undetectable. In the following we establish the probability of this happening.

Error Detection. We apply the same error model as before, which assumes that errors only occur at the input operands. In the presence of additive error terms we can model system behavior for addition as

$$
A' = A + e_A\ , \quad B' = B + e_B
$$
$$
A' + B' = g(a \cdot b) + (e_A + e_B) \bmod m
$$
$$
e_{R+} = e_A + e_B \tag{6}
$$

and for multiplication as

$$A' \star B' = (g \cdot a + e_A + c) \cdot (g \cdot b + e_B + c) - c \bmod m$$
$$= g(a \cdot b) + e_A(g \cdot b + c) + e_B(g \cdot a + c) + e_A \cdot e_B \bmod m$$
$$e_{R\star} = e_A(g \cdot b + c) + e_B(g \cdot a + c) + e_A \cdot e_B \bmod m . \tag{7}$$

From the reduction modulo s we obtain the detectable portion of the error term. In the case of addition (6) this is $e'_{R+} = e_A + e_B \bmod s$. A faulty result is undetectable if $e_A \equiv -e_B \bmod s$. For simplicity we assume that the errors e_A and e_B are independent and identically distributed random variables from uniform. Thus the probability of an undetectable error is $1/s^2$.

An error occurring during multiplication will produce the term $e'_{R\star} = e_A + e_B + e_A \cdot e_B \bmod s$ which we obtained through application of the equivalences $g \equiv 0 \bmod s$ and $c \equiv 1 \bmod s$ to (7). We can find the probability of an undetectable error during multiplication using the following lemma:

Lemma. Let X, Y be two independent and identically distributed random variables uniform over $[0, s-1]$ and let the event $A = \{(X = x, Y = y) : x + y + x \cdot y \equiv 0 \bmod s\}$. Then the probability of A occurring is $\Pr[A] = \Phi(s)/s^2$, where $\Phi()$ denotes the Euler totient function.

Proof. We can rewrite the event A as follows: $A = \{(X = x, Y = y) : y = f(x)\}$, where $f(x) = -x \cdot (x + 1)^{-1} \bmod s$. The function $f(x)$ will only be defined if the inverse of $x + 1$ exists. For any given modulus s this is the case only for $\Phi(s)$ choices in the range $0 \le x < s$. Hence, $f(x)$ is defined and has a value with probability $p_R = \Phi(s)/s$. Y takes on a specific value y with probability $p_L = 1/s$. The joint probability of the event A occurring is therefore $p = p_L \cdot p_R = \Phi(s)/s^2$, due to the independence of X (and hence $f(X)$) and Y.   □

Here the event A stands for the occurrence of an undetectable error at the output of the multiplier. It is easy to see that the best error coverage can be obtained when the modulus scaling factor s is composite and large. We would like to re-iterate that the error detection mechanism requires a full modular reduction by s, which in the general case does not have a suitable special form as the scaled modulus m. While this might be conceived as a drawback, it should be noted that checking for errors can be done outside of the critical path (in hardware) or at regular intervals (software realization), while the main computation continues operation. As a matter of fact, the regular field modulus p does not in general have a suitable special low Hamming-weight form either, such that the overhead due to error detection is easily offset by the efficient reduction modulo $m = s \cdot p$.

4.3   Error Correction Using Algorithm-Based Fault Tolerance

Quite naturally one would like to build an arithmetic architecture with the ability to also correct errors that occur during computation. For cyclic codes syndrome decoding allows the correction of the most likely error pattern. It does not, however, give good results in the presence of burst errors, as they would likely occur if an adversary tries to influence the computation.

A different approach is the use of algorithm-based fault tolerance. The principal idea here is to keep the input operands available until the computation has finished and an error check determines a valid result. If the error check fails, the computation can be repeated until a valid result is available. Alternatively, if the computation fails repeatedly, an alarm can be signaled and the operation canceled. The advantage of this method is clearly its robustness in the presence of transient burst errors. It does not matter which of all possible errors covered under a specific syndrome triggered the detection, when the computation can simply be repeated. Another advantage is the relatively low overhead that is required, which is mostly caused by the storage elements necessary to keep backup copies of operands. A potential disadvantage is that the method does not degrade gracefully, meaning that permanent faults due to stuck-at-0/1 errors can not be compensated for. Circuit defects thus render this method completely useless and do not help, for example, to increase the yield of circuit production.

5   Relation to Cyclic Codes

We have frequently mentioned the relation of our scaled embedding method of fault tolerance to the theory of arithmetic and binary cyclic codes. Principally, these codes constitute special cases of our generalized method. The advantage of using cyclic codes for embedding is that we can make statements about the worst-case minimum distance (design distance) of codewords based on the BCH theorem given as follows:

Theorem (BCH bound). Let C be a q-ary (n, k) cyclic code with generator polynomial $g(x)$. Let m be the multiplicative order of q modulo n (GF(q^m) is thus the smallest extension field of GF(q) that contains a primitive nth root of unity). Let α be a primitive nth root of unity. Select $g(x)$ to be a minimal-degree polynomial in GF$(q)[x]$ such that $g(\alpha^b) = g(\alpha^{b+1}) = \ldots = g(\alpha^{b+\delta-2}) = 0$ for some integers $b \geq 0$ and $\delta \geq 1$. $g(x)$ thus has $(\delta - 1)$ consecutive powers of α as zeros. $\Rightarrow$ The code defined by $g(x)$ has minimum distance $d_{\min} \geq \delta$.

The design distance δ given by this theorem, however, is not necessarily a tight bound that gives the true minimum distance. The most serious disadvantage of cyclic codes, as mentioned briefly in the related works section, is the small number of suitable parameters that allow the embedding of finite fields applicable to elliptic curve cryptography. These fields require an irreducible polynomial of prime degree. Cyclic codes are defined as the principal ideals generated by the divisors of $x^n - 1 \bmod q$. For $q = 2$, which is a frequent choice due to the ease of implementation with logic circuits, the number of useful parameters (n, k) for which the factorization of this binomial yields irreducible polynomials of prime degree k is vanishingly small for useful sizes of k. In the range $130 < k < 500$, which represents typical elliptic curve cryptography operand sizes, there are only ten instances which fulfill the requirements. In all cases the redundancy exceeds the field size by more than 100%. Table 1 lists the design distances for suitable pairs (n, k).

Table 1. Cyclic codes with prime degree irreducible divisors in the range $100 < k < 500$

n	263	359	383	479	503	719	839	863	887	983
k	131	179	191	239	251	359	419	431	443	491
δ	8	9	9	13	9	11	11	9	9	11

6   Conclusion

We have presented a novel scheme for fault-tolerant finite field computation with applications in public-key cryptography. Our method of scaled embedding is practical and allows designers of cryptographic systems to add fault tolerance with moderate resource overhead. It provides adequate protection against transient faults of either random or adversarial nature. The latter is of particular importance, due to the continuing success of fault-insertion attacks on cryptographic embedded systems. The close relation to binary and arithmetic codes with arithmetic structure (which constitute special cases of our method), coupled with our initial error coverage analysis is indicative of our scheme's robustness. A more detailed analysis, however, is desirable and therefore the subject of ongoing research.

References

1. Boneh, D., DeMillo, R., Lipton, R.: On the importance of checking cryptographic protocols for faults. In Fumy, W., ed.: Advances in Cryptology - EuroCrypt'97. Volume 1233 of Lecture Notes in Computer Science., Heidelberg, Springer (1997) 37–51 Proceedings.
2. Reyhani-Masoleh, A., Hasan, M.: Error detection in polynomial basis multipliers over binary extension fields. In Kaliski, Jr., B., Koç, Ç. K.., Paar, C., eds.: Cryptographic Hardware and Embedded Systems CHES 2002. Volume 2523 of Lecture Notes in Computer Science., Heidelberg, Springer (2002) 515–528 4th International Workshop, Redwood Shores, CA, USA.
3. Reyhani-Masoleh, A., Hasan, M.: Towards fault-tolerant cryptographic computations over finite fields. ACM Transactions on Embedded Computing Systems **3** (2004) 593–613
4. Wu, H., Hasan, M., Blake, I., Gao, S.: Finite field multiplier using redundant representation. IEEE Transactions on Computers **51** (2002) 1306–1316
5. Walter, C.: Faster modular multiplication by operand scaling. In Feigenbaum, J., ed.: Advances in Cryptology - CRYPTO '91: Proceedings. Volume 576 of Lecture Notes in Computer Science., Heidelberg, IACR, Springer (1992) 313–323
6. Öztürk, E., Sunar, B., Savaş, E.: Low-power elliptic curve cryptography using scaled modular arithmetic. In Joye, M., Quisquater, J.J., eds.: Workshop on Cryptographic Hardware and Embedded Systems–CHES 2004. Volume 3156 of Lecture Notes in Computer Science LNCS., Springer (2004) 92–106
7. Gaudry, P., Hess, F., Smart, N.P.: Constructive and destructive facets of weil descent on elliptic curves. Journal of Cryptology **15** (2002) 19–46
8. Parhami, B.: Computer Arithmetic: Algorithms and Hardware Designs. Oxford University Press (2000)

9. Skorobogatov, S., Anderson, R.: Optical fault induction attacks. In Kaliski, Jr., B., Koç, Ç. K.., Paar, C., eds.: Cryptographic Hardware and Embedded Systems - CHES 2002. Volume 2523 of Lecture Notes in Computer Science., Berlin, Heidelberg, New York, Springer-Verlag (2002) 2–12
10. Proudler, I.: Idempotent AN codes. In: IEE Colloquium on Signal Processing Applications of Finite Field Mathematics, London, IEE, IEE (1989) 8/1–8/5

Appendix

For practical purposes we present a selection of useful parameters for scaled embedding. In all three tables the parameter n refers to the size in bits, respectively degree, of the scaled modulus $m = p \cdot s$, while the parameter k is indicative of the size (degree) of the field modulus of $\mathcal{F}$ to be embedded in the ring. Finally, the amount of redundancy due to the scaling factor s is quantified by the difference $n - k$. Table 2 provides parameters for prime field embedding, while Tables 3 and 4 give parameters suitable for embedding binary extension fields.

Table 2. Factorizations of $m = p \cdot s = 2^n + u$, with $k = \lceil \log_2 p \rceil$ and $n - k = \lceil \log_2 s \rceil$

n	k	u	n-k	n	k	u	n-k	n	k	u	n-k	n	k	u	n-k
300	160	1	140	203	168	-3	35	206	177	3	29	229	203	1	26
205	161	1	44	261	168	-1	93	200	180	-3	20	256	206	1	50
211	162	3	49	208	171	3	37	221	181	-1	40	233	208	1	25
236	162	1	74	227	172	-1	55	223	184	1	39	241	217	-1	24
239	162	-1	77	205	173	3	32	259	184	-1	75	248	227	1	21
232	163	1	69	210	173	3	37	233	186	-1	47	251	232	1	19
209	166	-3	43	202	174	-3	28	210	193	-3	17				

Table 3. Factorizations of $p \cdot s = x^n + x + 1$, with prime $\deg(p) = k$ and $\deg(s) = n - k$

n	k	n-k	n	k	n-k	n	k	n-k	n	k	n-k
173	163	10	482	269	213	475	359	116	862	443	419
190	163	27	419	277	142	662	359	303	786	449	337
202	163	39	495	277	218	456	367	89	831	457	374
264	163	101	587	311	276	728	373	355	920	461	459
209	179	30	605	311	294	407	379	28	630	463	167
235	191	44	470	313	157	401	389	12	760	463	297
308	191	117	355	337	18	626	389	237	618	467	151
334	191	143	446	337	109	724	389	335	577	479	98
239	193	46	544	337	207	492	397	95	748	491	257
306	211	95	604	337	267	559	397	162	763	503	260
390	211	179	669	337	332	623	397	226	764	503	261
371	239	132	578	349	229	715	401	314	849	503	346
391	239	152	590	349	241	458	409	49	957	503	454
452	251	201	674	349	325	827	419	408	553	521	32
412	263	149	468	353	115	746	443	303	779	521	258

Table 4. Factorizations of $p \cdot s = x^n + x^2 + 1$, with prime $\deg(p) = k$ and $\deg(s) = n - k$

n	k	n-k		n	k	n-k		n	k	n-k		n	k	n-k
235	167	68		291	251	40		381	373	8		765	457	308
283	179	104		383	269	114		473	389	84		823	457	366
199	181	18		321	281	40		463	401	62		785	463	322
207	199	8		417	281	136		617	409	208		965	487	478
319	199	120		543	281	262		477	431	46		675	503	172
405	223	182		295	293	2		521	431	90				
357	229	128		341	293	48		471	433	38				
281	233	48		509	317	192		615	457	158				

DPA on Faulty Cryptographic Hardware and Countermeasures

Konrad J. Kulikowski, Mark G. Karpovsky, and Alexander Taubin

Reliable Computing Laboratory, Boston University
8 Saint Mary's Street, Boston, MA 02215
{konkul, markkar, taubin}@bu.edu

Abstract. Balanced gates are an effective countermeasure against power analysis attacks only if they can be guaranteed to maintain their power balance. Traditional testing and reliability methods are used primarily only to ensure the correctness of the logical functionality and not the balance of a circuit. Due to the hardware redundancy in balanced gate designs, there are many faults which can imbalance a balanced gate without causing logical errors. As a result, traditional testing and reliability methods and architectures are unable to test and verify if a gate is completely defect and fault-free and hence balanced. Our simulations show that a few faulty balanced gates can make a circuit as vulnerable to power analysis attacks as a completely imbalanced implementation. This vulnerability opens the possibility of new methods of attacks based on a combination of fault and power attacks. A solution to the vulnerability based on a built-in differential self-balance comparator is presented.

1 Introduction

Cryptographic algorithms are vulnerable to attacks which exploit the physical characteristics of their hardware implementations. The formal security models of cryptographic algorithms assume that information about the intermediate data during computation (encryption, decryption, etc.) is not available to an adversary. An adversary with access to intermediate data can drastically decrease the complexity of cryptanalysis. Examining the power consumption or behavior in the presence of faults of a device can provide such information to an attacker. Efficient methods for performing power analysis and fault analysis attacks have been developed which can analyze the side-channels and extract useful information which can be used to aid in cryptanalysis.

To prevent such attacks several countermeasures have been proposed which aim to reduce or eliminate the amount of information which can be inferred about intermediate data in a hardware implementation of a cryptographic algorithm. Traditionally, the power and fault attacks and their countermeasures have been considered and developed separately. One of the most effective countermeasures against power analysis attacks is based on the use of specially designed balanced gates for which the power consumption is equal for all data and all transitions of the gate. Several such gates have been previously presented (SABL [1], DyCML [2], BSDT [3], WDDL [4], Replication Gates [5]). The proposed fault attack countermeasures have been based on adding redundancy to the device, usually in the form of error-detecting codes, to detect errors in the logical values of the processed data (i.e. [6-8]).

L. Breveglieri et al. (Eds.): FDTC 2006, LNCS 4236, pp. 211–222, 2006.

Balanced gates and error-detecting codes are effective countermeasures for their respective attacks if the side-channels are considered separately. The details of the proposed countermeasures and a joint consideration of both power and fault side-channels raises several practical security limitations of the approaches. There are several major limitations and potential problems with the current power and fault countermeasures which stem from the redundancy associated with balanced gate designs when power and fault attacks are considered together.

All the currently known balanced gate designs require considerable hardware re-dundancy and overhead to ensure balanced computations (2.5 to 10x area overhead over standard synchronous static-CMOS implementations). Much of this redundant hardware is not directly associated with the logical or Boolean function of the gate; it is present to ensure power balance during computations. The additional consideration of data independent power consumption means that a gate's primary functionality is no longer limited just to its logical or Boolean function. The power balance of the gate is just as important. Weaknesses in the present balanced gate designs exist due to the redundancy of the gate; there exist many internal transistor level faults which will not affect the Boolean function of the gate but will affect the balance of the gate.

There are a number of methods to ensure proper Boolean functionality of circuits in all stages of the device's lifecycle. Techniques for post manufacturing testing, built in self-test (BIST), and on-line testing have been developed and are available for a variety of applications. While the methods which ensure proper Boolean functionality and hence provide reasonable protections against traditional fault attacks are mature, there are practically no developed architectures, methods, or techniques for testing and verification of the other crucial component of a gate's functionality: its balance.

The inability to ensure proper balance functionality during the lifecycle of a device creates a serious security weakness. The security of the cryptographic devices is dependent on the balance of the circuit. Without methods to test or verify this balance no guarantees can be made about the security. Moreover, the lack of built-in self balance test (BISBT) opens a possibility of combined fault and power attacks. The addition of a few imbalances, either from natural effects or from malicious tampering, can make it possible to perform established power analysis attacks even on protected devices.

The next section analyzes some proposed balanced gate designs and shows that faults can easily be manifested in a circuit which can imbalance the proposed gates without changing the gate's functionality. The effects of a few imbalances in a circuit are analyzed. The proposed countermeasures and research avenues for developing BISBT techniques and architectures are examined.

2   Vulnerabilities of Existing Balanced Gates

The additional constraint of data independent power consumption translates to more complex and more elaborate gate designs than the traditional minimal static CMOS gate implementations. The additional structures necessary to meet the balance re-quirements create redundancy with respect to the structures which are necessary for the Boolean functionality. Indeed, all current balanced gate designs are based on dual-rail return-to-zero (RTZ) signaling protocols which have an inherent hardware overhead. The two respective functions of a balanced gate are mostly separate and correct operation of one of the functionalities does not imply the correctness of the other functionality.

Examples of two balanced gates styles which demonstrate this redundancy and partial separation of functionalities are pictured in Figure 1. The two gate styles represent the two ends of a spectrum of the approaches to balanced gate design. The first, (Figure 1A) proposed by Jaffe et al. in [5], balances gates with the use of standard unsecured static CMOS gates to create a larger balanced gate. Approaches such as this one have very large overheads but also have an advantage in that existing standard-cell libraries can be used reducing the development costs. The other end of the spectrum is exemplified with the SABL gate, (Figure 1B) proposed by Kris Tiri et al. in [1]. The SABL gate is a much more compact, highly specialized implementation but requires a custom dedicated standard-cell library or a completely custom design flow. Both of these implementations have redundancy which is not directly associated with the Boolean functionality of the gate.

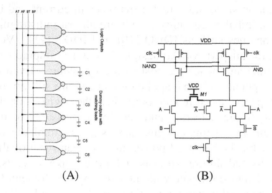

(A)   (B)

Fig. 1. (A). Balanced NAND gate proposed by Cryptographic Research (B). SABL AND-NAND gate with enhanced special DPDN

The first balanced gate design, shown in Figure 1A, requires a 700% hardware redundancy to achieve balance. The gate combines a dual-rail design with additional gates which are used to balance the internal switching characteristics of the sub-gates. In the resulting balanced gate the bottom 6 sub-gates of the larger balanced gate shown in Figure 1A are only used for balancing purposes and are not connected to logical outputs of the gate. The SABL gate, Figure 1B, has a similar, but smaller, redundancy. Specifically, transistor's M1 function is to discharge all the internal capacitance of the whole gate for every cycle of operation and has no direct Boolean purpose.

If the implementations can be guaranteed to be 100% reliable, then this hardware redundancy in itself is not a problem. The complications with such arrangements arise when the reality of physical devices, the imperfect manufacturing methods, and the adaptability of an active attacker are considered.

The fact that real devices are not perfect and not completely reliable has been a crucial consideration in standard circuit and system level design. Through the years a vast number of techniques and architectures have been developed to test and verify a device's functionality throughout its complete life-cycle. Methods for testing and verification for on-line and post manufacture are all indispensable to today's digital devices to ensure reliability and correct operation. Testing and fault hardening is of even more importance where the correct functionality of the device is crucial to the safety or security of a system. However, virtually all of the developed testing and reliability methods have been based around ensuring and verifying the correct functionality of the Boolean function of the device. Testing and reliability measures for the power functionality, in terms of power balance, have not been previously considered and there are neither developed methods nor architectures for ensuring balanced computations. Manufacturing a component for a critical application without verification and built-in reliability measures is unthinkable for standard Boolean circuits considering process yields and reliability of devices which are only declining as a result of scaling.

Aside from performing a full differential power analysis (DPA) attacks or other statistical analysis [9] on a manufactured circuit there have been no known methods for balance verification since the actual differences in current and behavior of a balanced circuit and an imbalanced faulty circuit are almost indistinguishable by normal current testing techniques such as IDDQ [10] and IDDT [11]. Verification by performing an attack for all parts of the designed circuit is impractical due to the dramatic increase in time and hence the cost of the procedure. Even if the drastic cost increase can be acceptable for some applications there are still no methods or mechanisms to ensure proper balanced functionality once the device is deployed.

Relying only on Boolean testing and reliability measures to detect defects and faults is not adequate. In existing designs there is not a complete overlap between the structures necessary for the balanced-power and Boolean functionality of a gate. As a result there are faults and failures (transistor failures, open circuits, wire shorts, etc) which can easily imbalance the gate without affecting the Boolean functionality. This non-overlapping functionality can be drastic as in, for example, the gate in Figure 1A where over 75% of the hardware of the gate is used only for balancing purposes. For that implementation it means that a fault is over three times more likely to affect the balance functionality than the Boolean functionality of the gate. About 75% of faults would not be detected if only the traditional Boolean off-line testing and on-line self-error- detecting methods based on error-detecting codes are used. A similar effect is also present in the SABL gate style shown in Figure 1B. Although the percentage of faults which can imbalance but not affect the logical function of the gate is smaller it is still not comparable to the reliability measures for key life-time requirements for cryptographic algorithms which are on the order of 2^{-40} [12].

Even with the optimized gates such as the SABL gate, there is still the need for additional methods and considerations which will ensure balance at a comparable level to that of the logical functionality. The problem of weakened security due to undetectable failures is a real threat. Without a guaranteed level of balance no precise estimates can be given about the security of the device (in terms of power analysis attack resistance). A couple of faults can easily imbalance a circuit making power analysis attacks easier than the original design seemed to ensure.

The next section will show an example of the realistic nature of such weaknesses in the balanced SABL gate implementations.

3 Effects of Failures on Imbalance and Power Analysis Attacks

To demonstrate the effects of faults on balanced gates and their consequence on power analysis attacks faulty versions of the SABL style gates were simulated. The resulting imbalances were measured and compared to the non-faulty gates. To illustrate how a few imbalance-causing faults can affect a DPA attack was simulated on a substitution box (Sbox) of the Data Encryption Standard (DES) implemented with both normal and faulty SABL [1] gates.

The SABL gate represents the state-of-art for synchronous balanced gate designs. It is a compact and optimized dynamic implementation which has a high level of balance and small level of redundancy. Despite the optimized design the gates still have areas of redundancy which are only used for balancing purposes. Using a simple fault model, the gate can easily be imbalanced without affecting the logical output of the gate.

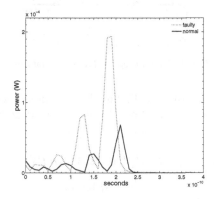

Fig. 2. Absolute power imbalance of a correctly functioning and a faulty SABL AND/NAND gate during the evaluation phase

For the properly functioning SABL AND/NAND gate implemented in a 0.18um technology assuming equal output load capacitances on both data output rails there is relatively little temporal difference in the gate's power signature. Figure 2 shows the absolute imbalance of the gate with respect to time where the magnitude of the curve represents the value of the instantaneous power consumption for the four possible input combinations.

To imbalance the gate pictured in Figure 1B, the gate VDD voltage of the M1 transistor was removed simulating a simple open circuit fault. As a consequence of the disabled transistor the effective internal balance of the gate is reduced to that of a normal differential dynamic gate. By disabling the M1 transistor, practically all the benefits of using a sense-amplified balanced design are removed. The effective absolute power imbalance of the gate is effectively more than doubled. The injected fault has no effect on the logical output of the gate. The gate continues functioning correctly in all respects except its balance. Many other more drastic faults can be envisioned which could create larger power imbalances.

Full analog SPICE simulations were performed on a Sbox of DES to evaluate the impact a small number of faulty gates can have on power analysis attacks. The circuit is a small component of a complete symmetric cryptosystem. The Sbox is usually the circuit component which is targeted for power analysis attacks. The simulation circuit, shown in Figure 3, is composed of 137 two-input OR, AND, and XOR gates. It has a 10-bit text input , a 6-bit secret-key input and a 4-bit output. The Sbox1 combinational circuit was automatically synthesized from a table specification using Design Compiler from Synopsys. The circuit was simulated on the transistor level (schematic level, pre layout) using the analog Spectre simulator from Cadence for all of the 1024 input combinations and fixed key input. The power consumption of the circuit was recorded and then analyzed by performing a Differential Power Analysis attack.

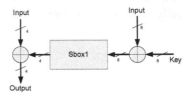

Fig. 3. Circuit used for DPA simulations

The DPA attack was performed by finding the measured power and hypothesis correlation on the 4-bit output of the Sbox by using the Pearson's correlation coefficient $C(M,P)$:

$$C(M,P) = \frac{\mu(M,P) - \mu(M)\mu(P)}{\sqrt{\sigma^2(M)\sigma^2(P)}} \qquad (1)$$

where P is the set of predictions, M is the set of recorded power measurements, $\mu(X)$ is the mean of the set X and $\sigma^2(X)$ is its variance. The Pearson's correlation coefficient gives a measure of the data dependence of the power consumption. A survey of correlation methods and attacks on S-boxes can be found in [13].

In comparing the security of vulnerability of balanced gate designs the most common method has been to determine the number of necessary power measurements for disclosure of the secret key. Since the simulations performed are only on a small circuit with a very limited number of inputs and no additional circuitry which would create noise and etc. we used a new comparison approach.

An important practical aspect in considering the feasibility of a power attack is to evaluate the required capability of an attacker which is necessary for a successful attack. An important capability consideration is the required sophistication of the measuring equipment or rather the required minimal precision for estimation of a power consumption which is necessary to have a successful attack. The necessary precision was used as a comparison metric. All simulations and all the data were recorded with the maximum level of precision of the simulator. After all the power data was recorded the precision of the measurements was incrementally reduced until the attack was no longer successful. The reduction of precision was based the following formula:

$$rp = np - np \bmod(precison) + precision * rand() \qquad (2)$$

where *rp* are the reduced precision measurement, *np* are normal precision measurements, *precision* is the maximum assumed precision capability of the attacker, and *rand()* is a random number from the interval [-1,1].

Table 1. Minimum required measurement precision for a successful DPA attack for normal and faulty implementations of the DES Sbox

Implementation	Min required measurement precision for successful DPA
Normal	$5.5 \times 10^{-4} W$
Four Gates Faulty	$11.2 \times 10^{-4} W$
All Gates Faulty	$11.6 \times 10^{-4} W$

The consequences on the required precision of the measurements for all input combinations for the normal and faulty Sbox test circuits are shown in Table 1. The results shown in Table 1 provide for a relative comparison of the results of faults within the circuit. It should be noted that the absolute precision values might not completely reflect the precision required for an actual physical attack on a complete circuit. The simulation results are based on ideal measurements from a small test circuit. Actual attacks and measurements would be subject to noise of additional power consumption of the extra circuitry, timing uncertainty in measurements, as well as additional capacitive and inductive effects from packaging and probing materials. These effects would certainly reduce the capacity to perform successful attacks. In physical attacks it should be expected that the absolute values of the minimum precision required should be lower (more precision would be required) than the table suggests. However, the relative value of the minimum precision should still be accurate and provide for an accurate relative comparison of the effects of faults on power analysis.

The first row in Table 1 represents results from simulations performed on the normal non-faulty SABL implementation. This value is used as a relative reference point for comparison. The absolute minimum precision measurement value required for successful DPA analysis was slightly more than four times the imbalance of a normal SABL AND gate (Figure 2). This absolute value of the necessary precision reflects the fact that four Sbox outputs were targeted for the attack and hence it was their driving gates whose combined imbalance was observed in Table 1. For the second result in Table 1, the four output gates of the 137 2-input gates which make up the Sbox were made faulty by making the gate terminal of the M1 transistor disconnect from VDD. The effective imbalance of the faulty gates was doubled as shown in Figure 2. Although only a small fraction of the gates were imbalanced, the necessary minimum precision necessary for a successful attack more than doubled. The minimum precision required for the attack increased proportionately to effective imbalance of the individual gate. Moreover as the last row of Table 1 indicates, the effect of just a few imbalanced gates on the required precision of DPA was almost equal to that of the implementation in which all the gates are faulty. The implementation in which all the gates were faulty is roughly equivalent to an unprotected normal implementation based on differential dynamic logic.

The above results demonstrate the criticality of considering faults on balanced gates. As the results suggest, only a few imbalanced gates are enough to make a protected implementation be as vulnerable to DPA analysis as an unprotected implementation. In compact implementations, for example in some sensor network applications, the datapath widths are kept at a minimum to meet the required maximum instantaneous power requirements. In such implementations where the datapath can be as small as 8 bits, a single fault which causes an imbalance can be enough to reveal a complete key and completely compromise the security of the device.

4   Countermeasure Strategies

The experimental results from the previous section confirm that the inability to verify and check balanced computation can create serious holes in the security of even "protected" cryptographic devices. Architectures and methods for detecting imbalance need development. Detection of imbalances is a difficult paradigm shift in that it requires an exact consideration of an analog continuous functionality, the power consumption of the device, in hardware which is optimized for digital processing. Some possible countermeasures are considered next.

One of the least invasive methods to combat the problem would be to redesign the balanced gates so that all internal faults which can cause imbalances will also cause logical faults. This would allow the use of existing error detection architectures and techniques which are already a standard requirement on secured hardware for the prevention of fault analysis attacks. If successful, this approach would greatly simplify the additional design tasks since after one redesign, everything else would involve "standard" considerations. However, due to the large difference between Boolean and balance functionalities the chances of success of this approach are small as exemplified in the designs of current balanced gates which are unable to meet this requirement.

Another possible approach is to adapt existing analog based techniques used in testing. In architectures based on IDDQ and IDDT Built-in Self Test approaches the circuit is tested by measuring its current or power consumption while it performs predetermined computations. The current is then compared with a stored reference value. Any differences (exceeding a selected threshold) from the predetermined signature can mean faults within the circuit. One disadvantage of this approach is the inherent complexity of performing comparisons with a stored reference value. To detect imbalances the built in test circuits needs to record, digitize and compare the power signatures to a stored reference value (threshold for current consumption) with a high level of accuracy. The necessary precision translates into large and precise Analog to Digital (AD) converters which require substantial amount of hardware. Thus the approach is only suitable for larger designs where one current sensor is used for a large portion of the circuit. Even more problematic is the fact that since the current and power consumptions of circuits vary depending on temperature, process variability and voltage levels the thresholds used for comparing good and bad circuits needs to be quite lax. As a result mostly catastrophic or short circuit faults in the original and redundant parts of the device can be tested in this manner and the sensitivity needed to determine if some gates are only out of balance is beyond the capabilities of the method.

A possible solution to the problem which overcomes the drawbacks of the previously mentioned approaches is based on modifying some of the concepts present in IDDQ testing. The solution also exploits the symmetry which is present in many cryptographic hardware implementations. The approach is based on a number of distributed analog voltage or current comparators whose detection capability can be propagated into a conventional digital alarm signal (which can be used to disable the device). The details of this approach, which will be referred to as a built-in differential self balance test (BISBT), are discussed in the remainder of this section.

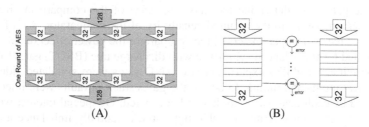

Fig. 4. (A) Datapath of one Round of AES is divided into four separate parallel slices. (B) Subdivision of parallel slices with an analog comparator to check for equal power consumption.

Many of the encryption algorithms, especially symmetric key algorithms such as the Advanced Encryption Standard (AES) [14], have lots of symmetry in their structure. In AES-128 (AES with a 128 bit key) for example, the 128 bit parallel datapath of each round of the algorithm is divided into four 32-bit independent and parallel slices each of which is composed of exactly the same hardware (Figure 4). (These parallel slices are also internally divided into smaller parallel slices.) The data along the complete 128-bit datapath is generally synchronized and all slices perform the exact same functions but on different data. If the circuits of the slices are implemented with truly balanced gates which are functioning correctly then the power consumption of all the respective slices should be practically equal even if the circuits are processing different data. **More importantly, the power consumption of the two circuits which are processing different data will be the same only if their implementations are balanced.**

The proposed differential balanced comparison approach exploits the above mentioned property of balanced design by partitioning the parallel slices of the data path so that a small analog comparator can be used to compare the current consumption of two equal circuit components from respective slices (Figure 4b). The comparator should have a suitable maximum difference threshold upon which a latch in the comparator is set to indicate an imbalanced operation. This error signal can be, in the case of asynchronous fine-grained balanced gate implementations [15, 16], used to stall the pipeline thereby providing a distributed protection mechanism without a single point of failure.

This approach allows a distributed protection because the balance check is not based on an absolute stored reference value but on a low cost comparison. The comparison operation generally requires much smaller hardware since neither AD converters nor memory is needed. Additionally, since the method is based on a comparison of power of two equal circuits which are on the same chip the method is not sensitive to temperature and manufacturing variability which is a large problem with reusing normal IDDQ or IDDT testing methods. Both of the compared circuits will be subjected to the same temperature fluctuations. Likewise, because the small circuits can be grouped locally within a chip, they will by subject only to the local manufacturing process variability effects. Finally, one of additional benefits is that such protection is that it is continuously active whenever the module operates; there would be no need for a special test cycle.

The critical requirement of this method is best possible balance of gates. The balance of the gates will determine the maximum size of the comparison circuits, the maximum granularity, and the required sensitivity of the comparator. As a first order evaluation of the critical parameters of the comparator the power effect details of faults was examined for the balanced symmetric with discharge tree (BSDT) gates [3].

For the initial feasibility experiment two AND gates were simulated side by side with identical inputs and timing. In one of the gates stuck-at faults were injected. The current used by each gate was recorded and compared. Of special interest were those faults which were logically undetectable but could potentially imbalance a gate. An exhaustive set of stuck at faults was injected into one of the gates. The gates were simulated for all possible input combinations. Example current comparison curves of normal and faulty gates for two logically undetectable faults are shown in Figure 5. All of the injected faults produces large differences in the temporal power signatures which are easily identifiable by a current comparison. The internal undetectable faults in the functional block produced large differences in the current consumption of the AND gates. Most faults resulted in a shift and amplitude difference of the current curves which are easily recognizable in the power. The current differences needed to be observed by a comparator are on the order of $5 \times 10^{-4} A$, which is two orders of magnitude larger than the normal imbalance of a gate. As was shown in [3] the maximum temporal current difference of a balanced BSDT-style AND gate was no more than $6 \times 10^{-6} A$ in post layout simulations.

Additionally, the power fault simulations show that this method can also serve as a natural compliment to traditional built-in reliability measures since it is able to detect many faults or errors which cause logical errors. For example, faults which created an invalid value on the dual-rail output of the BSDT gate (11) also resulted in large temporal current differences which can be detected by a comparator.

Based on the initial experiments, it should be practical to place a differential current comparator for partitions of 50 to 60 gates. If a comparator can be on the order of 40 transistors then the overhead will be lower than a traditional BIST architecture. Many of the physical design components, such as current sensors and differential amplifiers, have been developed for IDDQ BIST architectures and can potentially be adapted for this application but many challenges remain in fine tuning the methods to achieve the necessary sensitivity and speed.

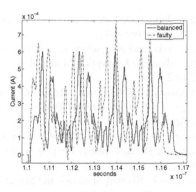

Fig. 5. The effect of a logically undetectable fault in the functional block on power where dotted and solid lines are for the faulty and normal AND gate respectively

5 Conclusions

As the approaches and architectures for balanced gate designs mature many practical considerations need to be addressed. Reliability and balance preserving fault tolerance will be of critical importance. As it has been shown in this paper, a small number of faults can potentially make power analysis attacks feasible even on protected devices. Due to the redundancy of balanced gates these faults might not create logical errors and hence would not be detected by traditional voltage level testing and reliability measures. A possible solution method was described which exploits the symmetry of cryptographic hardware and the operation of balanced gates.

Acknowledgements

This work was partially supported by a grant from OmniBase Logic Inc.

References

1. Tiri, K., M. Akmal, and I. Verbauwhede. A Dynamic and Differential CMOS Logic with Signal Independent Power Consumption to Withstand Differential Power Analysis on Smart Cards. 28th European Solid-State Circuits Conference (ESSCIRC 2002), pp. 403-406, September 2002
2. Mace, F., F. X. Standaert, J.J. Quisquater, J.D. Legat, A Design Methodology for Secured ICs Using Dynamic Current Mode Logic, Lecture Notes in Computer Science, Volume 3728, Aug 2005, Pages 550 - 560
3. MacDonald, D.J., A Balanced-Power Domino-Style Standard Cell Library for Fine-Grain Asynchronous Pipelined Design to Resist Differential Power Analysis Attacks. Master of Science Thesis. 2005, Boston University: Boston, availabe at http://reliable.bu.edu/Projects/MacDonald_thesis.pdf.
4. Tiri, K. and I. Verbauwhede, A Logic Level Design Methodology for a Secure DPA Resistant ASIC or FPGA Implementation. Design, Automation and Test in Europe Conference (DATE 2004), pp. 246-251, February 2004.

5. Jaffe, J., P. Kocher, and B. Jun, "Hardware-level mitigation and DPA countermeasures for cryptographic devices" US Patent 6654884.
6. Karpovsky, M., K. Kulikowski, and A. Taubin. Differential Fault Analysis Attack Resistant Architectures for the Advanced Encryption Standard. in Proc. World Computing Congress, CARDIS, pp. 177-192, 2004.
7. Kulikowski, K., M. Karpovsky, and A. Taubin. Robust Codes for Fault Attack Resistant Cryptographic Hardware. in Fault Diagnosis and Tolerance in Cryptography, 2nd International Workshop. 2005. Edinburgh.
8. Karri, R., G. Kuznetsov, and M. Gossel. Parity-Based Concurrent Error Detection of Substitution-Permutation Network Block Ciphers. Lecture Notes in Computer Science, Volume 2779, Sep 2003, Pages 113 - 124
9. Coron, J.S., D. Naccache, and P. Kocher, Statistics and Secret Leakage. Trans. on Embedded Computing Sys. 3, 3 (Aug. 2004), 492-508.
10. Rajsuman, R., Iddq testing for CMOS VLSI. Proceedings of the IEEE, 2000. 88(4): p. 544-568.
11. Su, S.-T., R.Z. Makki, and T. Nagle, Transient power supply current monitoring - A new test method for CMOS VLSI circuits. Journal of Electronic Testing, 1995. 6(1): p. 23-43.
12. Gregorio, A.D. Cryptographic Key Reliable Lifetimes: Bounding the Risk of Key Exposure in the Presence of Faults. in FTDC. 2005.
13. Canovas, C. and J. Clediere, What do S-boxes Say in Differential Side Channel Attacks?, in IACR e-Print archive. 2005/311.
14. FIPS PUB 197: Advanced Encryption Standard, http://csrc.nist.gov/publications/fips/fips197/fips-197.pdf.
15. Smirnov, A., A. Taubin, and M. Karpovsky. An Automated Fine-Grain Pipelining Using Domino Style Asynchronous Library. in ACSD 2005: Fifth International Conference on Application of Concurrency to System Design. 2005.
16. Kulikowski, K., A. Smirnov, and A. Taubin. Automated Design of Cryptographic Devices Resistant to Multiple Side-Channel Attacks. in Cryptographic Hardware and Embedded Systems (CHES), 2006.

Fault Analysis of DPA-Resistant Algorithms

Frederic Amiel[1], Christophe Clavier[1], and Michael Tunstall[2]

[1] Gemalto, Security Labs,
Avenue des Jujubiers, La Ciotat, F-13705, France
{frederic.amiel, christophe.clavier}@gemalto.com
[2] Smart Card Centre, Information Security Group,
Royal Holloway, University of London,
Egham, Surrey TW20 0EX, UK
m.j.tunstall@rhul.ac.uk

Abstract. In this paper several attacks are presented that allow information to be derived on faults injected at the beginning of cryptographic algorithm implementations that use Boolean masking to defend against Differential Power Analysis (DPA). These attacks target the initialisation functions that are used to enable the algorithm to be protected, allowing a fault attack even in the presence of round redundancy. A description of the experiments leading to the development of these attacks is also given.

1   Introduction

The use of collisions to find and exploit a fault at the beginning of an algorithm has appeared in several papers. In [7] a method of exploiting faults in the early rounds of a DES implementation is described. This detailed a complex attack where faults were injected in the early rounds of DES, and the fault injected was then derived by finding a message that would naturally give the same ciphertext. This information was then used to derive information on the key.

A trivial case of this type of attack is given in [3] where a known bit of the first XOR in AES is assumed to be forced to zero. If the ciphertext changes then this bit would have been a 1; if the ciphertext remains the same then the bit is a 0. This would break an AES implementation with a mere 128 executions with successful fault injections. However, modifying bits in such a manner requires too much precision to be practical. We refer to this type of attack as Collision Fault Analysis (CFA).

Some variations of these types of attack will be presented that can be implemented against AES on embedded devices. A simple byte-wise implementation of the attack presented in [3] will be described. Several other, more complex, attacks that take advantage of DPA countermeasures to derive information on the key are also detailed. Implementations of some of these attacks, conducted under controlled conditions, are described. A similar attack will also be described, using the DES as an example, where the initialisation of randomised S-boxes are faulted. It will be demonstrated that the simplest version of this attack is by combining the modification of S-box values with differential fault analysis [2].

L. Breveglieri et al. (Eds.): FDTC 2006, LNCS 4236, pp. 223–236, 2006.

The experiments implementing these attacks using glitches on the power supply or clock are also given.

The paper is organised as follows. Section 2 discusses an attempt at implementing a bytewise version of the attack described in [3], and the changes to the attack that needed to be made. Section 3 describes the most popular method for protecting algorithms against DPA attacks. Section 4 describes a possible attack against the first XOR in the AES. Section 5 gives an attack against the key masking process used to initialise the key. Section 6 describes the first attack found using this method. Section 7 details how the countermeasure proposed for the attack described in Section 6 can be circumvented, and proposes a different attack. More complete countermeasures are given in Section 8, followed by the conclusion.

2   Another Trivial Case

Another trivial CFA based attack is a bytewise implementation of the attack given in [3]. If a fault is injected so that a byte of the output becomes zero during the first AddRoundKey function a similar attack can be implemented. All the possible combinations of message bits corresponding to the modified byte can be tested and the algorithm executed again for each value. This process is stopped once a collision is found with the faulty ciphertext. This will give a message with an intermediate state where the fault was injected that is naturally equal to 0. This means that the message byte found is equal to 0 after being XORed with the corresponding key byte. This message byte will therefore be equal to the corresponding key byte.

This requires 16 faulty ciphertexts to be generated, and a search of 2^8 with the targeted device to find each key byte giving a total search time of 2^{12}.

This attack was attempted with several different microprocessors with different methods of fault injection. Varying from glitches on the Vcc to laser light injection. No successful implementation of this attack was achieved.

In [11] faults are demonstrated that enable a **for** loop to be terminated before it has finished all of its iterations. If the memory where the result of the XOR between the message and the key is stored has not been used, it has a high chance of being 00 or FF depending on the logical representation of the physical state. If this attack is applied to the key XOR an attack can be implemented by changing one byte of the output to zero and generating the corresponding ciphertext. Then two bytes etc. as in Table 1, as originally proposed in [2].

This can be achieved with 15 successful faults. The first byte of the key can then be found by searching through the 2^9 (i.e. 2^8 values for XX and 2 possible values for the rest of the bits depending on the logical representation of the physical state) possible key values that could produce C_{15}. Once the first key byte is known the second key byte can be found with a further 2^8 AES executions using C_{14}. This can be continued with 2^8 AES executions for each subsequent byte, for a total of 2^{13} AES executions to derive the entire key.

Table 1. The Biham-Shamir Attack

Input	AES Key	Output
$M \rightarrow$	$K_0 =$ XX XX XX XX XX XX XX XX XX XX XX XX XX XX XX XX	$\rightarrow C_0$
$M \rightarrow$	$K_1 =$ XX XX XX XX XX XX XX XX XX XX XX XX XX XX XX 00	$\rightarrow C_1$
$M \rightarrow$	$K_2 =$ XX XX XX XX XX XX XX XX XX XX XX XX XX XX 00 00	$\rightarrow C_2$
$M \rightarrow$	$K_3 =$ XX XX XX XX XX XX XX XX XX XX XX XX XX 00 00 00	$\rightarrow C_3$
$\vdots$	$\vdots$	$\vdots$
$M \rightarrow$	$K_{14} =$ XX XX 00 00 00 00 00 00 00 00 00 00 00 00 00 00	$\rightarrow C_{14}$
$M \rightarrow$	$K_{15} =$ XX 00 00 00 00 00 00 00 00 00 00 00 00 00 00 00	$\rightarrow C_{15}$

The basic attack (memory content set to '0') was been implemented on an 8-bit smart card microprocessor using a glitch as fault injector by scanning the entire loop that copies the AES key from Non-Volatile Memory (NVM) to a temporary working RAM buffer at the beginning of AES execution (just before the AddRoundKey function). This produced 127 different faulty ciphertexts (whereas 15 different ones were expected), giving as a result the 22 possible keys listed below in base 16 by searching though the results in a bytewise fashion:

```
00000000000000000000000000000000
FE000000000000000000000000000000
FEDC0000000000000000000000000000
FEDCBA0000000000000000000000000000
FEDCBA98000000000000000000000000
FEDCBA9876000000000000000000000000
FEDCBA987654000000000000000000000
FEDCBA987654320000000000000000000
FEDCBA987654321000000000000000000
FEDCBA987654321001000000000000000
FEDCBA987654321001230000000000000
FEDCBA987654321001234500000000000
FEDCBA987654321001234567000000000
FEDCBA987654321001234567890000000
FEDCBA9876543210012345 6789ABCDEF
FEDCBA987654321001234567 89ABCD00
FEDCBA98765432100123456789ABCDCD
FEDCBA98765432100123456789AB0000
FEDCBA98765432100123456789AB00EF
FEDCBA98765432100123456789AB00AB
FEDCBA98765432100123456789ABEF00
FEDCBA98765432100123456789AB5300
```

Due to desynchronisation effects and the exhaustive scanning of the copy loop, some unexpected faulty ciphertexts are produced. In the possible keys it can be seen that there are several possible values for the last two bytes, which makes the attack slightly more complicated than originally supposed but it still remains practical. The correct key during these experiments was:

FEDCBA98765432100123456789ABCDEF

3   Secure Algorithm Implementations

Implementations are made secure against DPA [9] and related attacks by masking the data being manipulated with a random value. The data is then manipulated in such a way that the value present in memory is always masked with the same random. An example of this sort of implementation can be found in [1], based on ideas proposed in [4].

The size of the random is generally limited as S-boxes need to be randomised before the execution of the random so that the input and output values of the S-box leak no information. This is done using an algorithm such as Algorithm 1, where the notation $(\cdot)_x$ denotes values of base x i.e. $(s_0, s_1, s_2, \ldots, s_n)_x$ containing S broken into words of size x.

Algorithm 1. Randomising S-Box Values

Input: $S = (s_0, s_1, s_2, \ldots, s_n)_x$ containing the S-box, $\mathbf{R}$ a random $\in [0, n]$, and r a random $\in [0, x)$.

Output: $RS = (rs_0, rs_1, rs_2, \ldots, rs_n)_x$ containing the randomised S-box.

for $i \leftarrow 0$ **to** n **do**
    $rs_{(i \oplus \mathbf{R})} \leftarrow s_i \oplus r$
end

return RS

As shown, the random used for masking the input data can be no larger than n, and the random used for the output value can be no larger that x. In the case of AES both $\mathbf{R}$ and r will be one byte, which means that the random mask used during the calculation is likely to be one byte. This is more problematic for DES as the input and output have a different size, and the bitwise permutations add complexity, but the principal remains the same.

4   Attacking the First XOR

At the beginning of AES the algorithm conducts an XOR between the message and the key before the first ByteSub function. This will happen as shown in Algorithm 2.

As in Section 2 faults are used that enable a **for** loop to be ended before it would normally do so. If Algorithm 2 is attacked in this way so that the loop only runs to 14, rather than 16, two bytes will not be written to KM i.e. two bytes will be untouched. This means that physically these bytes will be set to 0, but the algorithm will take the value as $\mathbf{R}$ due to the masking.

Algorithm 2. The First XOR

Input: $M = (m_1, m_2, m_3, \ldots, m_{16})_{256}$ containing the message,
   $K = (k_1, k_2, k_3, \ldots, k_{16})_{256}$ containing the key masked with $\mathbf{R}$ a random
   byte.
Output: $KM = (km_1, km_2, km_3, \ldots, km_{16})_{256}$ also masked with $\mathbf{R}$.

for $i \leftarrow 1$ **to** 16 **do**
   $km_i \leftarrow m_i \oplus k_i$
end

return KM

By searching through the 2^{16} possible values for m_{15} and m_{16}, it will be possible to find a collision where $k_{15} \oplus m_{15} \oplus \mathbf{R} = 0$ and $k_{16} \oplus m_{16} \oplus \mathbf{R} = 0$ i.e. $m_{15} \oplus \mathbf{R} = k_{15}$ and $m_{16} \oplus \mathbf{R} = k_{16}$, and therefore $m_{15} \oplus m_{16} = k_{15} \oplus k_{16}$. It is not important what values km_{15} and km_{16} become, but they do need to be the same value. If the value of the memory becomes FF, for example, it can still be assumed to be 00 and the error can be taken up in the value of $\mathbf{R}$.

This in itself only reduces the keyspace from 2^{128} to 2^{120}. The attack can be continued by repeating the attack with three bytes of the key being left uninitialised by Algorithm 2. The same method can then be used to derive $k_{14} \oplus k_{15}$ with the same amount of work as $k_{15} \oplus k_{16}$.

For each fault injected the attacker needs to search through 2^{16} different values to determine the message values that enable information on the key to be derived. This needs to be done with the smart card under attack so the attack process will be lengthy.

In DPA-resistant algorithms it is usual to do as much as possible in a random order, as this is an additional countermeasure to that described in Section 3. The loop given in Algorithm 2 would therefore take one of the 120, i.e. $\binom{16}{2}$, different orders possible to XOR the message with the key. This is so that the data being manipulated from one execution to another will occur at different points in time which is primarily a DPA countermeasure.

If a random order is implemented and the last two bytes are not assigned these will be two random bytes in the buffer. To find a collision an attacker will have to search through the 2^{23} possible messages. The random involved will be different each time so two pairs, e.g.

$$k_i \oplus m_i \oplus \mathbf{R},\ k_j \oplus m_j \oplus \mathbf{R},\ \text{and}$$
$$k_j \oplus m_j' \oplus \mathbf{R}',\ k_k \oplus m_k \oplus \mathbf{R}'$$

These pairs cannot be directly related to each other. However, if they have one message byte in common it is possible to change the random mask so that they become the same by XORing the two values together i.e.:

$$k_j \oplus m_j \oplus \mathbf{R} \oplus k_j \oplus m_j' \oplus \mathbf{R}' = m_j \oplus \mathbf{R} \oplus m_j' \oplus \mathbf{R}'$$

As m_j and m'_j are known values these values can be removed from this value with an XOR, leaving $\mathbf{R} \oplus \mathbf{R}'$. This value can be applied to $k_k \oplus m_k \oplus \mathbf{R}'$ so that it becomes $k_k \oplus m'_k \oplus \mathbf{R}$. This then gives:

$$m_i \oplus \mathbf{R} = k_i$$
$$m_j \oplus \mathbf{R} = k_j$$
$$m_k \oplus \mathbf{R} = k_k$$

This process can then be repeated until information is derived on every byte of the key. This then leaves an exhaustive search of 2^8 to find the value of $\mathbf{R}$ and therefore the key.

In order to be able to find collisions the attacker needs to generate a dictionary of 2^{23} entries. These values depend on the key so they need to be generated with the device under attack, which is prohibitively large for devices such as smart cards that use relatively slow communication protocols. To form an idea of the amount of time required to create a dictionary a smart card with a DPA-resistant AES was timed. It took the smart card approximately 149 milliseconds to create one dictionary entry. The whole dictionary will therefore require around 14.5 days to create.

This is an advantage over the version that does not use a random order, as the dictionary can be generated once and used numerous times. As the fault injected will not always do what is expected this may help speed up the overall attack process. In the first version of this attack each search of 2^{16} will require around 3 hours with the test card used.

The implementation conditions of the attack are the same as those described in Section 2 with two exceptions. The implementation used was DPA resistant and the timing of the glitch injection was fixed as the random order provided the temporal variation. The key was known *a priori* so the dictionary was generated with a computer rather than with the smart card.

By conducting faults using glitches on the Vcc for less than one hour, 118 faulty ciphertexts were obtained. Amongst these, 72 unique collisions were extracted. The information in these 72 collisions was compiled to find 31 unique keys i.e. no linear relationship between any of the 31 keys. This process took approximately 10 minutes on a standard PC.

Only one 16-byte key candidate was expected, but 31 were produced showing that some fault injections have produced some collisions not related to the key values. However, the number of keys produced can easily be tested to determine the correct key, requiring $31 \times 2^8 = 2^{12}$ AES executions.

As mentioned above, generating 2^{23} ciphertexts with a smart card takes a prohibitively long time to generate. This can be reduced by only generating a certain amount of the dictionary and conducting more fault attacks to generate the data required to derive the key.

For example, if a dictionary of size 2^{19} was generated, which would take around 21 hours with the test card, faulty ciphertexts could be generated until a collision was found. It would be expected that 1 in 2^4 faulty ciphertexts would be present in the dictionary. An attacker would therefore need 16 times as much data compared to the attack described above, but as only a few faulty ciphertexts are required to realise the attack this is an efficient option.

5   Attacking the Key Masking

Before the key can be used by the algorithm in the fashion described in Section 3 the random value, **R**, that is applied to the S-boxes needs to be applied to the key. The key values are usually stored XORed with a random value of the same size as the key. This is because this random is a static value for one card as it is stored in the EEPROM and is diversified from one card to another. This mask needs to be removed, and replaced with **R** without the key being manipulated. This process is shown in Algorithm 3. Again, this happens in a random order rather than as shown.

Algorithm 3. Masking the Key

Input: $KR = (kr_1, kr_2, kr_3, \ldots, k_{16})_{256}$ masked with a random
$\qquad R = (r_1, r_2, r_3, \ldots, r_{16})_{256}$, **R** a random byte.
Output: $K = (k_1, k_2, k_3, \ldots, k_{16})_{256}$ masked with **R**.

for $i \leftarrow 1$ **to** 16 **do**
$\qquad k_i \leftarrow kr_i \oplus \mathbf{R}$
$\qquad k_i \leftarrow k_i \oplus r_i$
end

return K

A similar attack can be envisaged against this process to that shown in Section 4. If only one byte is initialised by this loop the the resulting memory will be predominately set to zero. Again, the algorithm will take this value as being **R**, which gives 2^{20} possible ciphertexts that need to be generated before the attack is conducted. As this attack changes key bytes this dictionary can be generated by a PC as the values are not dependent on the rest of the key.

This attack can be repeated until enough information is derived about the key to enable an exhaustive search to take place. The expected number of faulty ciphertexts needed to derive each byte in this way can be calculated by using the coupon collectors test given in [8]. In the case of AES this would require 50 ciphertexts to derive the whole key.

The implementation conditions of the attack are the same as that described in Section 2. The same software implementation was run on the same smart card.

The precomputation of the dictionary was generated in a matter of minutes on a standard PC. Unlike the attack described in Section 2 the dictionary does not dependent on the value of the secret key used, so the dictionary generated would be valid for any secret key value.

After attacking the implementation for approximately one hour around 60 collisions were generated from faulty ciphertexts. After acquiring these ciphertexts the *a posteriori* processing was trivial as no incorrect hypotheses were produced by the collisions found.

6   Modifying Known S-Box Values

If the S-box values are created as shown in Algorithm 1, the order in which the S-box is constructed is therefore known (as i is incremented from 0 to 63). A fault attack can then be constructed around the modification of known S-box values.

The first S-box value of the first S-box is modified by a fault and the algorithm executed with a message for which the ciphertext is known. If the ciphertext is not equal to the known ciphertext then this S-box value was used by the algorithm; if it stays the same the S-box value was not used anywhere in the algorithm. All 64 values of the first S-box can each be changed in this manner and the algorithm executed. After which, all the S-box entries used from the first S-box will be known for a given message.

The expected number of S-box entries used per DES execution can be calculated using the solution to the classical occupancy problem, as described in [10], giving a value of 14.3. Therefore, if the attack is repeated for each S-box a list of around 14 different values will be given for the number of entries used in each S-box.

If these values are taken as possible hypotheses for the S-box entries used in the first round, the index values of the S-box entries can be turned into hypotheses on the first subkey. To do this, the index values simply need to be XORed with the relevant message bits. This will produce slightly under 2^{31} hypotheses for the first subkey leading to a total exhaustive search of 2^{39} to find the entire DES key.

In order to reduce the size of the exhaustive search the attack can be repeated with a different message. The intersection of the two keyspaces will contain the first subkey. This provides $14.255 \times (14.255/64) = 3.18$ different hypotheses per S-box, which gives 2^{13} hypotheses for the first subkey, leading to a total exhaustive search of 2^{21} keys.

In practice, embedded implementations of DES are unlikely to have the 512 S-box values necessary for DES written separately in memory. These are generally compressed to optimise the amount of memory required by the DES implementation.

One way of achieving this is to store the data on 256 bytes where the odd numbered S-boxes are stored in the high nibbles and the even numbered S-boxes are stored in the low nibbles. This corresponds to the attack implementation detailed below and all further discussion will assume this is the case. There are several other ways in which the S-box data could be compressed, but is not considered to be something an attacker needs to know before conducting an attack, as all the possible combinations can be attempted until the correct one is found.

The number of key hypotheses generated by implementing this attack against a DES using compressed S-boxes is shown in Table 2 for different numbers of messages used. As can be seen, this is more efficient than modifying 1 S-box value as information on 2 boxes can be gained at once i.e. less faults are required to derive the key.

Table 2. The hypotheses generated by attacking a compressed S-box

Messages	Hypotheses per S-box pair	Hypotheses for the first round key	Total Keyspace
1	25.3	2^{37}	2^{45}
2	10.0	2^{27}	2^{35}
3	3.97	2^{16}	2^{24}
4	1.57	2^{5}	2^{13}

In attempting to implement the attacks described in [2], it was observed that when the duty cycle[1] of the clock given to the smart card was too small an incorrect ciphertext was produced. This was on a different chip to that used in the previous attacks on the initial functions of the actual algorithm. Further study revealed that if the duty cycle was below 15% data written to certain areas of the chip's memory would then be written incorrectly.

This attack could therefore be implemented against a smart card using this effect. As mentioned above, the S-boxes were written in a compressed format to save memory, so this needed to be taken into account. The attack was conducted with three different messages, followed by a small exhaustive search to find the key. The entire attack took 45 minutes using tools created specifically for this purpose.

This attack can be further optimised by analysing the faulty ciphertexts generated by the modified S-boxes. It should be apparent from the ciphertext if a faulty S-box values has been used in the fifteenth or sixteenth round. As the aim is to try and derive hypotheses on the first subkey these ciphertexts provide no information. Ciphertexts where the faulty S-box is used in the last round can be considered to be equivalent to the S-box value not being used. If the faulty value is used in the fifteenth round no information is provided as the detection of this event is subject to false positives (as described in Section 7) and a different message needs to be used to provide information on this S-box value.

The countermeasure for this specific attack is to randomise the order in which the S-boxes are randomised. This applies to the order in which the S-boxes are treated, and to the order in which the S-box elements are masked. The data masking can be done as shown in Algorithm 4, which adds no extra time to the algorithm implementation. The counter i is XORed with a random before being used so the order in which the S-box elements are treated is unknown.

If just the order in which the S-boxes are treated is randomised an attack could be envisaged based on searching for S-box elements that never change the ciphertext when modified. This is because the information about which index value has been changed will be present. If the same S-box element is repeatedly changed, but after numerous executions with the same message the ciphertext never changes, it can reasonably be assumed that this index value does not

---

[1] The duty cycle is the amount of time that a voltage is applied to the clock pin compared to the time no voltage is applied e.g. a standard clock will have a duty cycle of 50%.

Algorithm 4. Randomising DES S-Box Values

Input: $S = (s_0, s_1, \ldots, s_{63})_{16}$ containing the S-box, **R** a random $\in [0, 63]$, and r a
random $\in [0, 15]$.

Output: $RS = (rs_0, rs_1, \ldots, rs_{63})_{16}$ containing the randomised S-box.

for $i \leftarrow 0$ to 63 do
$\quad rs_i \leftarrow s_{(i \oplus \mathbf{R})} \oplus r$
end

return RS

---

represent a key hypothesis for any part of the first subkey. The expected number
of executions required to be sure of this information is 22 (given by the coupon
collectors test as defined in [8]). The randomisation of the order of treatment
would therefore render the attack much slower. 1408 fault injections would be
required to treat every S-box value for a given message, this would give an
expected number of hypotheses of 55.5 per S-box and a total key search of $2^{54.3}$
possibilities. A total of 10 different messages would be required to bring the
expected key search to $2^{39.5}$ which is more possible. The amount of fault attacks
required may make this amount of fault injections unrealistic if the effect of the
fault is not deterministic.

The attack presented in this section require a high degree of precision, as
information is derived from a fault having occurred and then not having an
effect on the ciphertext. This was possible due to the manner in which the fault
was injected, but is unlikely to be possible with other fault injection methods.
A fault is generally expected to be successful with a certain probability when it
is applied to a chip [3], in this case the probability of success was equal to 1.

7   Modifying Unknown S-Box Values

If an S-box element can be modified, but the attacker does not know which
element has been modified (i.e. Algorithm 4 is used), the attack described in
Section 6 will not work. Nevertheless, an attack can be used by implementing
the algorithms given in [2,6].

If one S-box value is modified and used in round 15, and only in round 15,
then the ideas described in [2] will apply. The modification of 1 S-box look-up
in the fifteenth round will, on average, change the entry value for 3.2 different
S-boxes in the sixteenth round, providing differential across these S-boxes for
key hypothesis testing.

The advantage of this attack over the attack described in Section 6 is that the
effect of the desired fault can be seen in the ciphertext. The fault can be detected
by calculating the differential of the S-box output in the fifteenth round, which
can be done by observing the ciphertext. If only one nibble in this value is not
equal to zero, then there is a high probability that the corresponding S-box value
was only used in the fifteenth round. The probability that this event occurs is
$\left(\frac{63}{64}\right)^{15} \frac{1}{64} = 0.0123$.

This probability is high enough that an attacker can conduct the attack numerous times until the desired event is observed. Some key information can then be derived and the process repeated.

There is a possibility that the S-box is used in the fourteenth round and that this will yield a value that will be detected as a S-box value used in the fifteenth round. This occurs when the modification in the fourteenth round produces a 1 bit fault (all the output bits go to different S-boxes). There are 4 possible values among the 15 possible faults that will produce this effect. Half of these values will modify more than one S-box in the fifteenth round, i.e. they will span two S-boxes due to the expansion permutation. This leaves only two possible values from the fifteen possible faults. The probability of a false positive is therefore $\frac{2}{15} \left(\frac{63}{64}\right)^{15} \frac{1}{64} = 0.00165$.

The probability of a false positive is relatively high when compared to the probability of the event that will enable the attack. Approximately 1 in 7 detections will be false positives. However, as described in [6], the false hypotheses introduced by these false positives will not have a major effect on the success of the attack.

As detailed in Section 6, S-box values are usually stored in a compressed state so an attacker may be forced to modify several S-box entries at once. If two S-box entries are modified the probability of one of the values being used in the fifteenth round is $2 \left(\frac{63}{64}\right)^{15} \frac{1}{64} \left(\frac{63}{64}\right)^{16} = 0.0192$.

This is more efficient than modifying 1 S-box value as the probability of the S-box value being used in the fifteenth round is higher. This probability will change following the method of S-box compression, but only the case under study is analysed.

The probability of one S-box value being used in the fourteenth round and causing a false positive can be calculated as before. If two modified S-box values are used in the fourteenth round this can also provoke a false positive if two one-bit errors are caused and these bits are used in the same S-box without being reproduced by the expansion permutation in the fifteenth round. This probability was derived by simulating all the possible combinations as $89/147456$. The overall probability of a false positive is therefore $2\frac{2}{15} \left(\frac{63}{64}\right)^{15} \frac{1}{64} \left(\frac{63}{64}\right)^{16} + \frac{89}{147456} \left(\left(\frac{63}{64}\right)^{15} \frac{1}{64}\right)^{2} = 0.00256$.

The probability of a false positive given that a detection has occurred is about the same ($\approx 2/15$) given that the event has been detected for both implementations. The implementation using a compressed S-box will provide results quicker as the desired event occurs with a higher probability.

This attack was implemented on the same chip as the attack described in Section 6 because the fault used was ideal for modifying the S-box values as they were created. The first attempt at this attack was against a DES implementation that just used data masking and constructed S-boxes using Algorithm 4. The tools conducting the attack waited until at least 1 differential had been found across each S-box before conducting an exhaustive search of the hypotheses derived from the fault injection. The tools found the key after 8 minutes.

A second attempt was conducted with the addition of random delays in hardware and software, so that a fault would be produced with a lower probability. The same tools took 20 minutes to derive the key.

This attack was easier to implement than the attack described in Section 6, as only one fault injection position was needed to attack a random S-box entry. In the previous attack it was necessary to shift the position of the fault injection for each new fault injection attempt.

In the case of an implementation using compressed S-boxes it would be logical to use the event of both faulty S-box values being used in the fifteenth round. As previously, this can be observed by looking for two nibbles with a non-zero differential in the ciphertext. This information can be combined with the event of one nibble having a differential in the ciphertext. The probability of this occurring is $2 \left(\frac{63}{64}\right)^{15} \frac{1}{64} \left(\frac{63}{64}\right)^{16} + \left(\left(\frac{63}{64}\right)^{15} \frac{1}{64}\right)^2 = 0.0193$.

As previously, there is a chance of a false positive. In this case the events of one or two modified S-box values being used in the fourteenth round could potentially simulate one or two changed values in the fifteenth round. If one S-box value is changed in the fourteenth round the probability that two values are modified in the fifteenth round is $1/5$, if two values are changed in the fourteenth round the probability that two values are changed in the fifteenth round is $914609/29491200$. Again, these were derived by simulating all the possible combinations. The probability of a false positive is therefore $2\frac{2}{15} \left(\frac{63}{64}\right)^{15} \frac{1}{64} \left(\frac{63}{64}\right)^{16} + \frac{89}{147456} \left(\left(\frac{63}{64}\right)^{15} \frac{1}{64}\right)^2 + 2\frac{1}{5} \left(\frac{63}{64}\right)^{15} \frac{1}{64} \left(\frac{63}{64}\right)^{16} + \frac{914609}{29491200} \left(\left(\frac{63}{64}\right)^{15} \frac{1}{64}\right)^2 = 0.00640$.

The probability of getting useful information remains approximately the same as when only one modified S-box is considered, but the probability of a false positive is 2.5 times greater. The data acquired will therefore be much more noisy and will increase the amount of time required to conduct the attack. There is therefore little interest in conducting the attack in this manner.

8   Countermeasures

There are several countermeasures that can be used to protect an algorithm against this type of attack. As has been described above, randomisation of the algorithm is not an efficient countermeasure against this fault attack.

Random Delay: If a high degree of precision is required the attack could be slowed to the point where an attacker will not believe the attack is possible. This applies to both hardware and software random delays. A study of the effect of random delays on DPA is given in [5], similar effects will be seen when this is used against fault attacks.

Checksums: If S-boxes need to be constructed in RAM they need to be protected by a checksum. The simplest method of achieving this would be to XOR all the values together after the table has been created i.e. after the table has been written to memory. This has the added advantage of removing the randomisation, as the amount of entries in the S-box will be an even number. Nevertheless, this is not adequate to defend against the attacks described above. If the checksum is on 1 byte an attacker could modify several values and have a probability of $1/256$ of having a valid checksum. A second checksum calculated in a different manner could remove this problem, as the second checksum can be chosen such that there is no fault that will allow both checksums to remain valid.

Redundancy: It is already known that it is advisable to repeat the first 2 or 3 rounds of a secret key algorithm to protect against attacks like [7]. The initial functions can be repeated and the memory contents verified, in the same way that rounds of an algorithm are repeated to ensure no exploitable faults can be injected. However, this is prohibitively time consuming especially for the construction of S-boxes.

Memory Randomisation: All "work" areas of RAM used can be filled with independent random values before the start of the algorithm. The feasibility of the attack would then rest on the quality of the random values used. If, for example, an LFSR was used to generate these values it may be possible to predict the value of one byte if the previous byte is known. This could mean that the attack described in Section 4 is still possible with very little change i.e. the end search would be 2^{16} rather than 2^8 because an attacker would have to exhaust the possible initial values of the random used.

9   Conclusion

Several different attacks where faults were used to generate faults at the beginning of a secure implementations of AES and DES were presented. The implementations of some of these attacks have been briefly described. The algorithms were chosen because the source code for several different implementations was already available.

These attacks are generic attacks and can be considered to apply to any secret key implementation. These attacks show that DPA countermeasures are not an intrinsic barrier against fault attacks and that depending on round redundancy is not sufficient to achieve a secure implementation on smart cards.

Acknowledgements

The authors would like to thank Pascal Moitrel and Christophe Mourtel who designed and built the hardware mentioned in this paper, which enabled us to implement the attacks described above. The work described in this paper has been financially supported by the European Commission through the IST Program under Contract IST-2002-507932 ECRYPT.

References

1. M.-L. Akkar and C. Giraud. An implementation of DES and AES secure against some attacks. In Ç. K. Koç, D. Naccache, and C. Paar, editors, *Cryptogaphic Hardware and Embedded Systems — CHES 2001*, volume 2162 of *Lecture Notes in Computer Science*, pages 309–318. Springer-Verlag, 2001.
2. E. Biham and A. Shamir. Differential fault analysis of secret key cryptosystems. In B. S. Kaliski Jr., editor, *Advances in Cryptology — CRYPTO '97*, volume 1294 of *Lecture Notes in Computer Science*, pages 513–525. Springer-Verlag, 1997.
3. J. Blömer and J.-P. Seifert. Fault based cryptanalysis of the advanced encryption standard (AES). In R. N. Wright, editor, *Financial Cryptography — FC 2003*, volume 2742 of *Lecture Notes in Computer Science*, pages 162–181. Springer-Verlag, 2003.
4. S. Chari, C. S. Jutla, J. R. Rao, and P. Rohatgi. Towards approaches to counteract power-analysis attacks. In M. Wiener, editor, *Advances in Cryptology — CRYPTO '99*, volume 1666 of *Lecture Notes in Computer Science*, pages 398–412. Springer-Verlag, 1999.
5. C. Clavier, J.-S. Coron, and N. Dabbous. Differential power analysis in the presence of hardware countermeasures. In Ç. K. Koç and C. Paar, editors, *Cryptographic Hardware and Embedded Systems — CHES 2000*, volume 1965 of *Lecture Notes in Computer Science*, pages 252–263. Springer-Verlag, 2000.
6. C. Giraud and H. Thiebeauld. A survey on fault attacks. In Y. Deswarte and A. A. El Kalam, editors, *Smart Card Research and Advanced Applications VI — 18th IFIP World Computer Congress*, pages 159–176. Kluwer Academic, 2004.
7. L. Hemme. A differential fault attack against early rounds of (triple-)DES. In M. Joye and J.-J. Quisquater, editors, *Cryptographic Hardware and Embedded Systems — CHES 2004*, volume 3156 of *Lecture Notes in Computer Science*, pages 254–267. Springer-Verlag, 2004.
8. D. Knuth. *The Art of Computer Programming*, volume 2, Seminumerical Algorithms. Addison–Wesley, third edition, 2001.
9. P. Kocher, J. Jaffe, and B. Jun. Differential power analysis. In M. J. Wiener, editor, *Advances in Cryptology — CRYPTO '99*, volume 1666 of *Lecture Notes in Computer Science*, pages 388–397. Springer-Verlag, 1999.
10. A. Menezes, P. van Oorschot, and S. Vanstone. *Handbook of Applied Cryptography*. CRC Press, 1997.
11. D. Naccache, P. Q. Nguyễn, M. Tunstall, and C. Whelan. Experimenting with faults, lattices and the DSA. In S. Vaudenay, editor, *Public Key Cryptography — PKC 2005*, volume 3386 of *Lecture Notes in Computer Science*, pages 16–28. Springer-Verlag, 2005.

Java Type Confusion and Fault Attacks

Olli Vertanen

University of Kuopio, Department of Computer Science,
Microkatu 1, 70210 Kuopio, Finland
vertanen@cs.uku.fi

Abstract. Virtual machines executing high level languages are nowadays found even in small secure embedded systems. We have studied properties of the Java virtual machine and the Java virtual machine language under certain fault attacks. Focused glitching attacks may enforce type confusion situations. Defensive Java virtual machine is prosed as a counter-measure.

Keywords: Java, Java Card, type confusion, fault attacks, embedded systems.

1 Introduction

Recently, high level language virtual machines (HLL VMs) have established themselves in small embedded devices, e.g. mobile phones [1], smart cards [2] and even sensor networks [3]. Advantage of the HLL VMs is high density of the translated code, which makes transferring code over communication lines economical. The use of high level languages also aims at easier programmability and shorter application management cycles than in traditional embedded application development. On the other hand, virtual machines always introduce performance degradation compared to native code execution.

Some embedded devices, especially smart cards, are designed to store and process data in a secure manner. It can even be claimed that the existence of smart cards is solely justified by their ability to "keep secrets". This implies that the HLL VM on the device must also be secure. The product as a whole, the hardware and software, must be designed to be tamper-resistant.

Java is a common language in HLL VM systems. It is generally considered as a secure language because it is strongly typed, enforces boundary checks for arrays, does not use pointers or pointer arithmetics, variables are initialised before they are used, and the language contains access modifiers for classes, methods and fields. Naturally, the compiled Java code, the bytecode (also called Java virtual machine language, JVML), must preserve these properties. Thus, the bytecode is checked for correctness before it is executed. This checking is done by a bytecode verifier.

However, verification introduces a *time of check, time of use* (TOCTOU) condition, because the code is checked well before it is used. The fact that the verification process is very memory intensive may cause a vulnerability. In small

L. Breveglieri et al. (Eds.): FDTC 2006, LNCS 4236, pp. 237–251, 2006.

systems, it is not necessarily possible to run the verifier *on-device* but the verification must be done *off-device*. So, there is a significant cap, in space and time, between checking and using the code.

Fault attacks may also turn TOCTOU condition over to a vulnerability. Faults have proven to be a very powerful way to break secure systems. Several authors [4,5,6,7,8,9] have shown that, by introducing transitive faults into a system, it is possible to change program's run-time behaviour. With sophisticated equipment the fault may be focused on a particular instruction in memory or a particular value on the system bus. This, in effect, means that the executed program is not the same as the verified one.

To counter fault attacks normal fault tolerance schemes can be used. In some environments a *defensive Java virtual machine* (dJVM) [10,11], a VM that does 'on-the-fly verification', can be one possibility to prevent execution of fraudulent Java code.

In this paper, we study properties of the Java bytecode and the Java virtual machine in presence of fault attacks. Inspired by the earlier work, we present some scenarios how fault attacks can be utilised in order to produce type confusion, i.e. circumvention of the Java type system, in Java programs. The scenarios are based on previous observations of processors behaviour under attack (e.g. [5]).

The rest of the paper is organised in the following way. In Section 2 we review some known attack techniques, both logical and fault attacks. In Section 3 we take a look how combining fault attacks with valid but intentionally malicious bytecode can break Java's type system. In Section 4 we reason, whether these attacks designed on basis of Java bytecode can be applicable on real systems. Finally, we discuss about counter-measures to proposed attacks.

2   Types of Attacks

Attacks against secure systems can be classified by their objectives or by their means [12]. The purpose may be to attack privacy, integrity or availability of the system or data. The means describe how to technically implement an attack. We use following classification for the means:

1. Physical attacks: Direct tampering of the hardware, for example, optically reading the ROM, or micro-probing the system bus.
2. Fault attacks: Affecting the system behaviour via an injected physical fault. Source of the fault can be voltage or system clock manipulation, external radiation (X-ray, laser beam, electromagnetic field, white light) or temperature variation. To be useful, faults have to be transient and repeatable.
3. Observation attacks: Information retrieval by observing an unusual information channel, e.g. power consumption, or instruction timing. These attacks are often called side-channel or covert channel attacks.
4. Malicious code: Affecting the system behaviour by illegitimate programs like Trojan horses, viruses or worms. Malicious code may be injected into a system as result of buffer overflow or other logical fault.

The means are ordered here by descending degree of physical interference needed to launch the attack. In order to achieve the ultimate goal these techniques can be mixed. Faults can be used to open a side-channel, or malicious code can be used to find out the right point of execution for a fault. Here we focus primarily on malicious code and fault attacks.

2.1   Basic Type Confusion Attacks

We are primarily concerned about embedded devices which are fully accessible to the attacker. If the system is on a single chip, like smart card, accessing physically the hardware requires special equipment. It is impossible to change the ROM or system software. But if the attacker can freely install Java programs, can the secrets in the memory be exposed?

Java overcomes many traditional security problems. Java programs cannot directly access the hardware or address arbitrary memory. Programs run on a virtual hardware – the Java Virtual Machine. Programs also run in a constrained environment called sandbox. Type safety is one cornerstone of the Java language security and the verifier is the key defender in the front line. If this defence breaks (i.e. the code is not verified or the code can be changed after the verification) then security can be broken. Also, flaws in the language implementation can open up opportunities for attackers.

Buffer overflows are a common way to break systems. The basic idea is that the target program contains an unchecked buffer which will overflow if the input to the program is long enough. Program code can be placed to the overflowing part of the input and change the running program. A stack overflow typically injects some executable code to the stack area and then overwrites the return address on the stack in order to get the injected code executed. Similarly, a heap overflow overwrites a buffer in the heap memory area.

The Java type system and run-time checks should prevent buffer overflow attacks. Some cases have been reported, but those typically exploit bugs in parts that are written in some native language [13] and are external to the JVM.

However, similar attacks are possible. In order to emulate a stack overflow attack in Java, we must first be able to place the attack code somewhere. Second, we must learn the physical address of the code, and third, we must be able to replace a return address on stack with the address of the attack code. A normal byte-array might be a good place to store the injected code, but the second and third requirements are trickier. Language constraints of the bytecode must be circumvented. We now present principles of the attack. The details are always environment dependent.

The JVM operates with references, not with direct addresses. Originally, after compilation, references are symbolic and resolved during linking of the application. The actual run-time representation of references is implementation dependent. A reference can be, for example, an indirection to a handle of an object, an offset within a object or it can be a direct pointer to a memory area. The last one is interesting: For performance reasons direct references are desirable, and in the case of a class methods and class variables (static methods and variables) even very likely in implementations[14].

To learn the address of a static variable, a *type confusion* can be used. The principle of type confusion is very simple and also commonly used in weakly typed languages like C. Figure 1 shows a example of a method that casts an address to an integer. This is against Java's typing rules and the method does not compile. The bytecode has to be handcrafted and does not pass verification.

Java:

```
private int illegalCast(Object ref)
{
  return ref;
}
```

bytecode:

```
aload_0    ; push reference to stack
ireturn    ; return as integer
```

Fig. 1. Illegal casting from reference to integer

To change the return address on the stack the method in Figure 2 can be used. It assumes that return address is just on the top of the stack when method is invoked.

Java:

```
private void goWild(int goHere, int dummy)
{
  // some fill instructions here ..
  return;
}
```

bytecode:

```
istore_1   ; pop return address and store it to dummy
iload_0    ; push address 'goHere' to stack
return     ; 'return' to address goHere
```

Fig. 2. Jump into an array

Depending on the environment there are alternative ways to perform the steps of the attack. For example, in some virtual machines the address of an object can be derived from the return value of the .hashCode() method [9]. In Java Card environment [15] (Java Card is a special Java release for memory constraint devices) user may infiltrate physical memory references to the bytecode. In this environment a part of the linking task is done off-line in order to minimise the amount of meta-data and the size of the binary file (converted applet file, CAP file). The CAP file has a special `RefLocation` table. It lists all code offsets with variable references that should be resolved during the applet loading. If the applet installer trusts this table and does not check the integrity of `RefLocation` table, the attacker can write direct physical addresses into the method code and 'resolve' the variable references manually.

Often it suffices for an adversary to dump out a memory location in order to expose private information. This might be possible if buffer boundaries can be overrun. Forgery of the size of an array is possible by forging the type of the array elements. For example, the `baload` bytecode (byte array element load, hexadecimal 0x33) retrieves an element of one byte. If the instruction is forged to `iaload` (integer array element load, hexadecimal 0x2e), the program can access memory outside the actual array memory area. This kind of confusion has been already applied in Java Card environment [16]. Of course, this attack can be used for writing into memory as well.

These scenarios are eliminated if an on-device verifier can be used. However, not all devices can embody a verifier. The verification can be run off-device, but then there exists a risk that verified programs are modified. To counter that threat the compiled class-files can be digitally signed. That, in turn, needs utilisation of some cryptographic mechanisms, key-management system etc. In principle, the whole tool-chain (compilers etc.) must be trusted. The overall system gets complex and there still remains risk for insider attacks.

2.2   Glitching

Methods of generating faults are numerous. Currently, various glitching techniques are most practical. A glitch can be a variation in the clock signal, fluctuations in the power line or a change in the external electric field around the processor. Glitches make some of the flip-flops inside the processor temporarily adopt a wrong state. Glitching attacks require physical access to the target, and therefore can be applied to small ubiquitous embedded devices such as smart cards, sensors in senor networks or car electronics.

Several types of effects of glitches have been reported [17]. For example branch instruction may be ignored or by-passed, run-time loops can be extended or reduced, and CPU may execute completely different instruction. Also values on the data bus can be changed.

To design a successful attack careful searching of values for glitch variables (amplitude, frequency, duration, timing etc.) and a lot of re-iteration is needed. Power analysis can be applied to focus glitches to a correct point in the program flow. Analysis can recognise power profile of certain instructions and fault can be applied when program reaches certain point of execution.

Bar-El et.al [5] reported on successful experiments where glitching and power analysis was combined. They dropped the power line to ground voltage for a few nanoseconds and it made the processor to *"skip number of instructions"* in the instruction flow and resume normal execution after some microseconds. Also data manipulation was possible this way. They also noted that "value of data could be corrupted while the interpretation of instructions was left unchanged".

In addition, it can be noted that so called single event upsets (SEUs) [18] have become an increasing problem. This is mainly because of the decreased feature size and smaller voltage safe-margins in the current chips. Less energy than before is needed to disturb transistors. SEUs can flip transistors logical state to the opposite, so the effect may resemble the one of fault-attacks. The main difference is that SEUs are generated by energetic particles from the space or from the chip's packaging material. These particles bring external energy into transistor gates and change change the direction of hole or electron flow. So, SEUs have a random nature and are in that sense less critical to the systems security than fault attacks which are carefully targeted.

3   Combined Attacks

As noted earlier, successful attacks often combine different techniques. In this section we take a look how malicious code and fault induction can be used together in order to break Java's type system.

An successful example of this kind of attack was reported in [9]. In that experiment the Java code itself was valid and accepted by the Java verifier. On the other hand the code was crafted so that a memory error easily led to circumvention of the type system. Even when the applet was run inside a normal Java sandbox, the attacker was able to break the sandbox protection and run arbitrary code in most of the cases. In this case, faults were random bit flips and were generated by heating up RAM chips with a standard 50W spotlight bulb. At certain temperature memory chip began malfunction. The most notable conclusion of the experiment was that letting an attacker to choose the program to run is fatal to the system security.

We now present a hypothetical scenario that will use focused faults and techniques presented in [5]. The basic idea of the attack is following:

1. Program an applet that is legal and passes the verifier. It must be programmed so that, if some lines of the bytecode is bypassed, the code can be used as an attack.
2. Analyse the power curve of the applet and locate the place where critical instruction lie on the curve.
3. Apply a voltage or power glitch (or combination) attack. Reiterate 2 and 3 until desired effect is observed.

The Java code and the corresponding bytecode (of the method `main()`) is presented in Figures 3 and 4 respectively. The valid version of the code just prints out one byte. If lines from B5 to B7 can be jumped over, a reference to the static variable `a1` will be stored to `b` (on line B8) and later loaded for loop termination check at B12. The effect of the glitch will be the same if we would change line A14 of the source code to `byte b[]= a1;`. Class `BogusArr` has just one field `length` and that mimics the length field of arrays. The result is that arbitrary memory context can be dumped out. To tune the attack, suitable glitch parameters can be searched and also bytes can be added to code between line B5 and B7.

```
A1  public class Attack
A2  {
A3    public static class BogusArr
A4    {
A5      int length;
A6    }
A7
A8    static BogusArr a1 = new BogusArr();
A9
A10   public static void main()
A11   {
A12     a1.length = 0x8000;
A13     BogusArr a2 = a1;
A14     byte [] b = new byte[1];
A15     for (int i=1; i<b.length; i++)
A16         System.out.print(b[i]);
A17   }
A18 }
```

Fig. 3. Java source of the combined attack

Similar scenarios can be generated. An interesting application for 'jumping over instructions' glitches could be bypassing `checkcast` bytecodes. Java compiler generates a `checkcast` bytecode instruction from each casting expression in the program code (figure 5 illustrates the placement of the operation in the bytecode). The operator should check assignment compatibility in the run-time. The verifier notices `checkcast` bytecode and trusts the run-time system to do the ultimate decision. If we can bypass the check using a glitch, the type system is broken, and attack programs can be programmed direct in Java with no need to play with the bytecode representation.

To further illustrate vulnerability of the JVM in the presence of faults we assume that the adversary can manipulate the program counter register either by changing the offset in a branch instruction or by directly affecting the register itself. The idea is to program the code in a way that all instruction operands are also valid bytecodes. When the PC value is corrupted, the virtual machine executes totally other code that was intended.

Figure 6 shows a simplified version of this attack. The method `illegalCast` originally returns integer value 42. But 42 (hexadecimal 2a) is also the opcode of `aload_0` instruction. If the first byte of the method can be skipped, the method returns a reference to the object it took as a parameter.

As a final note to this section we point out that semantics of some bytecode instructions are very complex. Implementations of these bytecodes consist

```
B1    getstatic #2
B2    sipush  2048
B3    putfield #3
B4    getstatic #2
B5    astore_0         ; assign top of stack to a2
B6    iconst_1         ;
B7    newarray byte    ;
B8    astore_1         ; assign top of stack to b
B9    iconst_1
B10   istore_2
B11   iload_2
B12   aload_1
B13   arraylength
B14   if_icmpge 40
B15   getstatic #4
B16   aload_1
B17   iload_2
B18   baload
B19   invokevirtual #5
B20   iinc 2, 1
B21   goto B11
B22   return
```

Fig. 4. Bytecode of the combined attack. Skipping lines B5 to B7 causes a type confusion situation.

Java:

```
    ClassA a;
    ClassB b;

    a = (ClassA)b;
```

bytecode:

```
    aload b
    checkcast #ClassA
    astore a
```

Fig. 5. Checkcast is used to check assignment compatibility of the top of the stack variable with the class given as instruction operand

of sub-operations that are not visible to instruction level. These operations are often security critical like array boundary checks (e.g. in `baload` and `iaload` instructions) or null pointer checks (in every instruction referencing a class instance). Also, firewall checks in the Java Card environment must be embedded in the implementations of bytecodes accessing objects [15]. These sub-operations might be a good targets for "instruction skip attacks".

Java 1:

```
    private int illegalCast(Object ref)
    {
      return 42;
    }
```

bytecode 1:

```
    bipush 42       0x10 0x2a
    ireturn         0xac
```

bytecode 2:

```
    aload_0;        0x2a
    ireturn;        0xac
```

Java 2:

```
    private int illegalCast(Object ref)
    {
      return ref;
    }
```

Fig. 6. PC shift attack: The original method (Java 1) always returns an universal answer 42. Bytecode 1 shows the corresponding symbolic (left column) and binary (right column) formats. Bytecode 2 presents the scenario when the byte 0x10 has been skipped. Java 2 is the resulting high level code – a reference is illegally casted to an integer

4   Execution of Java Bytecode

We have presented some simple scenarios how to break Java's type system using focused glitching attacks. In this section, we take a look how applicable the attacks would be in a running system. In order to take advantage of the method, the adversary must know how each bytecode instruction maps to native instructions, and where are the boundaries of separate bytecode implementations in the native code.

Java virtual machines come in many flavours. Table 1 summarises various approaches to execute Java bytecode. The main reason for the diversity is to find ways to improve performance in different environments. The JVML is still generally considered as an interpreted language. A switched interpreter consists of an instruction dispatcher loop. In the loop bytecode is fetched and passed to the subroutine that implements the bytecode. When the subroutine exits, control is handed back to the interpreter loop, next bytecode is fetched etc.. The structure is the most simple one, but dispatching causes significant overhead. In a direct threading interpreter bytecodes of a program are replaced by addresses to bytecode implementations. Dispatching is done in the end of each subroutine by a direct jump to next implementation. This removes the dispatcher loop. The inline threading scheme further drops dispatching overhead by creating dynamically groups of bytecode implementations from basic blocks of the program.[19]. Dispatching is needed only after every basic block, but bytecode boundaries are still very clear and distinct during the execution.

Table 1. Different ways to implement Java bytecode execution

1. Interpreted	a. switched
	b. direct threading
	c. inline threading
2. Compiled	a. just in time (JIT)
	b. ahead of time (AOT)
	c. selective dynamic compilation (Hotspot)
3. Hardware	a. hardware translation
	b. Java processor
	c. co-processor

Interpreted code always suffers from performance penalties due to dispatching compared to compiled code. In case of Java, the stack architecture adds another source of poor performance on register machines. Also, some sub-operations of JVML instructions (e.g. array boundary checks), could be optimised, but the JVML presentation inhibits it (that is: operations are not visible at the bytecode level). To make better use of underlying architecture and modern optimisation techniques the JVML must be compiled.

Just-in-time compilation (JIT) [20], or dynamic compilation, suits well with a mobile and dynamic language like Java. A JIT compiler translates a method from bytecode to native code at the moment when the method is invoked. JIT compiler has the advantage over traditional compilers that it can make use of run-time information of the program. Heavily optimising JIT compiler requires a lot of resources from the target machine: The compiler itself is a large program, requires a fair amount of processing time, and also the resulting executable is bigger than the original bytecode. For example, the Jikes RVM uses, while compiling, three different intermediate formats, and performs optimisations after each transformation from one format to another [21]. Because there is a compilation overhead a the first time method is executed, significant performance gain over interpretation is achieved only after several runs of the method. Different optimisation and instruction scheduling schemes may split execution of one bytecode instruction to several distinct locations in the final code.

In embedded systems a JIT compiler will very likely not fit into memory, and a different approach must be considered. Traditional compilation, which can be called ahead-of-time compilation (AOT) in contrast to JIT, is an alternative although some dynamic features of the language are lost. If the system has fixed set of programs and is not designed extensible, AOT compilation may suffice and the compiler can feature significant optimisations [22].

Dynamic compilation strategies special to embedded systems has also been proposed. Resource requirements can be kept small if only performance critical parts (hotspots) are compiled and compiler is kept simple. For example, E-Bunny [23] is a selective one-pass compiler that uses precompiled codelets and generates stack-based code. The resulting native code has thus similar structure than the original bytecode. Deville and Grimaud [24] use a simple intermediate language to facilitate on-device compilation. The language maps each bytecode to a pre-implemented method, which also preserves bytecode boundaries in the native code.

Java on hardware may be implemented with an extension to instruction set architecture (ISA) (Jazelle [25]), with a pure Java ISA processor (picoJava [26]) or as a co-processor (MOCA-J [27]). The first approach is also know as hardware translation [28]. It adds a special unit in the front of the processor's instruction path. The unit translates bytecodes to sequences of microcode which are fed into execution. The most complex bytecodes are implemented with an interpreter routine. As bytecodes are fetched in sequence the bytecode boundaries are visible also in the final code. Co-processor solution is similar, and is used with co-processor aware JVM.

PicoJava's ISA contains more than 300 instruction. Most of the ISA are implemented hardwired or in microcode. Only a group of 30 very complex instructions need operating system support. An interesting detail is that the JVM specification define only 226 bytecodes. The additional instructions are for coping with the real hardware, and for performance optimisations.

Instruction folding was the most important optimisation introduced by the picoJava. Folding groups several bytecode instructions to a single instruction (also called super-instruction). The main purpose of folding is to mitigate access inefficiency in stack machines. Folding has been recently proposed to other environments as well [29][30].

Java resolves identifiers dynamically, which is slow. One optimisation is to replace a bytecode with another version (so called quick-instructions) [31] when an identifier is resolved. It means that the code changes its appearance during the execution.

As a conclusion to the discussion in this section we can notice that mapping from a JVML instructions to native instructions can be 1:1, 1:N (one bytecode corresponds to many native instructions), N:1 (many bytecodes form a single native instruction as in case of folding and super-instructions) or N:M (boundaries may be blurred because of optimisations). One must also notice that same sequence of bytecodes may map to several alternative native code sequences because of the execution or optimisation techniques used. So, the actual attack based on the scheme presented in the previous section will after all be heavily platform specific in spite of the universal nature of the bytecode. In small embedded systems the executed code is generated from to bytecode in a straight-forward way, and the implementation of the attack will be easier than in heavily optimising environments.

To find the correct point of execution to attack is thus difficult if the original bytecode of the target program is not know. If the adversary can load programs into the target hardware the task will be a lot easier. The behaviour of the JVM in question can be learnt by observing some physical property (electrical emission, power curve etc.). By bracketing the interesting points of the program with easily observable events, as presented in [32], the adversary can observe the characteristics of the bytecodes she is interested in, and pick up the right moment to launch the attack.

5   Counter-Measures

Defence against faults depends on the required protection policy. The policy how to deal with faults can be defined as prevention, detection or tolerance. Trying to prevent faults (with physical shields etc.) can be successful only if the causes of faults are known in advance. If the purpose is to prevent unauthorised information disclosure, it suffices to detect faults, and halt computation directly afterwards. If integrity of data is the concern, the detection mechanism should combined with a transaction mechanism. If availability of the system must be guaranteed then fault tolerance methods with significant redundancy must be applied.

There are basically three choices to place protection mechanism: to hardware external to computing logic, as part of logic circuits or in software. The first choice must target specific physical phenomenas (e.g. detectors for temperature, power, etc.) causing faults while the second and the last ones react on the consequences of faults. Basically, redundancy in circuit level (dual-rail encoding [8]), in hardware blocks, or in time can be used. Software mechanisms typically use redundancy in time, for example computing same value twice and comparing the result.

A good overview of fault protection techniques can be found in [5] and [33] .

As the source of the vulnerabilities presented in this paper is the 'time of check, time of use' condition created by the verifier, we propose solving the problem by removing this TOCTOU situation. It can be done by doing the verifier checks at the moment of use. This approach is called defensive Java virtual machine. The dJVM enforces the language constraints during program execution. It would not guarantee fault free operation, but merely program execution according to rules given to Java language.

For example, the attack situation in figure 4 would be detected and the execution halted at line B13, because of a type conflict. If the lines B5 to B7 in the bytecode had been jumped over, then the local variable 1 (of the current method) would contain a reference to class BogusArr (not to byte[] as in untampered code). Thus, on line B13 we would apply arraylength instruction to type BogusArr, which is against language constraints.

The dJVM would make bytecode verifier obsolete, because it implements same functionality. On the other hand, the dJVM would introduce severe penalties in memory consumption (type information has to be stored to stack) and especially in performance. Also one should note, that pure software dJVM would be just a set of new checking instructions that could be bypassed (like `checkcast` operation). So, a dJVM without hardware assistance cannot be a solution.

6 Discussion and Further Work

We have presented some simple scenarios how to break Java's run-time type system using fault attacks. Earlier work has demonstrated how to enforce type confusion situation with random bit flips. We propose using focused faults with programs specially designed for attacks.

In the Java run-time environment the verifier checks that instructions follow all language constraints. The check is done well before the code is executed, and the time cap can be exploited by the adversary. We propose using defensive virtual machine that would close the cap and do the verification on the fly. Attack counter-measures come never free, so also the dJVM is intrinsically resource demanding. The actual cost, in terms of time and memory, is not yet known, and our future work is focused on the study of feasibility, implementation and optimisation of the dJVM for embedded devices.

References

1. Lawton, G.: Moving Java into mobile phones. Computer **35**(6) (2002) 17–20
2. Baentsch, M., Buhler, P., Eirich, T., Hring, F., Oestreicher, M.: JavaCard – from hype to reality. IEEE Concurrency **7**(4) (1999) 36–43
3. Levis, P., Culler, D.: Maté: a tiny virtual machine for sensor networks. In: ASPLOS-X: Proceedings of the 10th international conference on Architectural support for programming languages and operating systems, New York, NY, USA, ACM Press (2002) 85–95
4. Naccache, D.: Finding faults. IEEE Security & Privacy (2005) 61–65
5. Bar-El, H., Choukri, H., Naccache, D., Tunstall, M., Whelan, C.: The sorcerer's apprentice guide to fault attacks. http://www.gemplus.com/smart/rd/publications/pdf/BCN_04sor.pdf In: Workshop on Fault Diagnosis and Tolerance in Cryptography. (2004)
6. Anderson, R., Kuhn, M.: Low cost attacks on tamper resistant devices. In: Security Protocols, 5th International Workshop. Volume 1361 of LNCS., Springer-Verlag (1997) 125–136
7. Skorobogatov, S., Anderson, R.: Optical fault induction attacks. In: Cryptographic Hardware and Embedded Systems Workshop (CHES-2002). Number 2523 in LNCS, Springer-Verlag (2002) 2–12
8. Moore, S., Anderson, R., Cunningham, P., Mullins, R., Taylor, G.: Improving smart card security using self-timed circuits. In: ASYNC '02: Proceedings of the 8th International Symposium on Asynchronus Circuits and Systems, Washington, DC, USA, IEEE Computer Society (2002) 211
9. Govindavajhala, S., Appel, A.W.: Using memory errors to attack a virtual machine. In: Proceedings of 2003 IEEE Symposium on Security and Privacy. (2003) 154–165
10. Stärk, R., Schmid, J., Börger, E.: Java^{TM} and the Java^{TM} Virtual Machine, Definition, Verification, Validation. Springer-Verlag (2001)

11. Cohen, R.M.: The defensive Java virtual machine specification version 0.5. Technical report, Computational Logic Inc., Austin, Texas (1997)
12. Ravi, S., Raghunathan, A., Chakradhar, S.: Tamper resistance mechanisms for secure, embedded systems. In: VLSID '04: Proceedings of the 17th International Conference on VLSI Design, Washington, DC, USA, IEEE Computer Society (2004) 605
13. Hoglund, G., McGraw, G.: Exploiting Software, How to break code. Addison-Wesley (2004)
14. Venners, B.: Inside the Java Virtual Machine. 2nd edn. McGraw-Hill (2000)
15. Sun Microsystems Inc. Palo Alto, California: Java Card 2.2 Run-Time Environment (JCRE) Specification. (2002)
16. Witteman, M.: Java card security. Information Security Bulletin **8** (2003) 291–298
17. Kömmerling, O., Kuhn, M.G.: Design principles for tamper-resistant smartcard processors. In: USENIX Workshop on Smartcard Technology (Smartcard'99). (1999) 9–20
18. Dodd, P.E., Massengill, L.W.: Basic mechanims and modeling of single-event upset in digital electronics. IEEE Transactions on Nuclear Science **50**(3) (2003) 583–602
19. Gagnon, E.: A Portable Research Framework for the Execution of Java Bytecode. PhD thesis, School of Computer Science, McGill University, Montreal (2002)
20. Aycock, J.: A brief history of just-in-time. ACM Comput. Surv. **35**(2) (2003) 97–113
21. Alpern, B., Attanasio, C.R., Barton, J.J., Burke, M.G., Cheng, P., Choi, J.D., Cocchi, A., Fink, S.J., Grove, D., Hind, M., Hummel, S.F., Lieber, D., Litvinov, V., Mergen, M.F., Ngo, T., Russell, J.R., Sarkar, V., Serrano, M.J., Shepherd, J.C., Smith, S.E., Sreedhar, V.C., Srinivasan, H., Whaley, J.: The Jalapeño virtual machine. IBM System Journal **39**(1) (2000)
22. Schultz, U.P., Burgaard, K., Christensen, F.G., Knudsen, J.L.: Compiling Java for low-end embedded systems. In: LCTES '03: Proceedings of the 2003 ACM SIGPLAN conference on Language, compiler, and tool for embedded systems, New York, NY, USA, ACM Press (2003) 42–50
23. Debbabi, M., Gherbi, A., Ketari, L., Talhi, C., Yahyaoui, H., Zhioua, S.: A synergy between efficient interpretation and fast selective dynamic compilation for the acceleration of embedded Java virtual machines. In: PPPJ '04: Proceedings of the 3rd international symposium on Principles and practice of programming in Java, Trinity College Dublin (2004) 107–113
24. Deville, D., Grimaud, G.: On board compiling in the very small. In: Construction and Analysis of Safe, Secure, and Interoperable Smart Devices: International Workshop, CASSIS04. (2004)
25. Porthouse, C.: High performance Java on embedded devices, Jazelle^{TM} technology: ARM^{TM} accelerator technology for the Java^{TM} platform, white paper, http://www.arm.com/pdfs/JazelleWhitePaper.pdf (2004)
26. McGhan, H., O'Connor, M.: PicoJava: A direct execution engine for Java bytecode. Computer **31**(10) (1998) 22–30
27. NanoAmp Solutions Inc: The MOCA-J Accelerator: Memory Oriented Coprocessor Accelerator for the J2ME^{TM} Platform. http://www.nanoamp.com/MOCA-J%20ProductBrief.pdf (2004)
28. Radhakrishnan, R., Bhargava, R., John, L.K.: Improving Java performance using hardware translation. In: ICS '01: Proceedings of the 15th international conference on Supercomputing, New York, NY, USA, ACM Press (2001) 427–439

29. Oi, H.: Instruction folding in a hardware-translation based Java virtual machine. In: CF '06: Proceedings of the 3rd conference on Computing frontiers, New York, NY, USA, ACM Press (2006) 139–146

30. Azevedo, A., Kejariwal, A., Veidenbaum, A., Nicolau, A.: High performance annotation-aware JVM for Java Cards. In: EMSOFT '05: Proceedings of the 5th ACM international conference on Embedded software, New York, NY, USA, ACM Press (2005) 52–61

31. Lindholm, T., Yellin, F.: The Java Virtual Machine Specification. The Java^{TM} Series. Addison-Wesley Professional (1997)

32. Chaumette, S., Sauveron, D.: An efficient and simple way to test the security of Java Cards^{TM}. In: Security in Information Systems, Proceedings of the 3rd International Workshop on Security in Information Systems, WOSIS. (2005) 331–341

33. Mitra, S., Seifert, N., Zhang, M., Shi, Q., Kim, K.S.: Robust system design with built-in soft-error resilience. Computer **38**(2) (2005) 43–52

Author Index

Lecture Notes in Computer Science

For information about Vols. 1–4160

please contact your bookseller or Springer

Vol. 4205: G. Bourque, N. El-Mabrouk (Eds.), Comparative Genomics. X, 231 pages. 2006. (Sublibrary LNBI).

Vol. 4204: F. Benhamou (Ed.), Principles and Practice of Constraint Programming - CP 2006. XVIII, 774 pages. 2006.

Vol. 4203: F. Esposito, Z.W. Raś, D. Malerba, G. Semeraro (Eds.), Foundations of Intelligent Systems. XVIII, 767 pages. 2006. (Sublibrary LNAI).

Vol. 4202: E. Asarin, P. Bouyer (Eds.), Formal Modeling and Analysis of Timed Systems. XI, 369 pages. 2006.

Vol. 4201: Y. Sakakibara, S. Kobayashi, K. Sato, T. Nishino, E. Tomita (Eds.), Grammatical Inference: Algorithms and Applications. XII, 359 pages. 2006. (Sublibrary LNAI).

Vol. 4199: O. Nierstrasz, J. Whittle, D. Harel, G. Reggio (Eds.), Model Driven Engineering Languages and Systems. XVI, 798 pages. 2006.

Vol. 4198: O. Nasraoui, O. Zaiane, M. Spiliopoulou, B. Mobasher, B. Masand, P. Yu (Eds.), Advances in Web Minding and Web Usage Analysis. IX, 177 pages. 2006. (Sublibrary LNAI).

Vol. 4197: M. Raubal, H.J. Miller, A.U. Frank, M.F. Goodchild (Eds.), Geographic, Information Science. XIII, 419 pages. 2006.

Vol. 4196: K. Fischer, I.J. Timm, E. André, N. Zhong (Eds.), Multiagent System Technologies. X, 185 pages. 2006. (Sublibrary LNAI).

Vol. 4195: D. Gaiti, G. Pujolle, E. Al-Shaer, K. Calvert, S. Dobson, G. Leduc, O. Martikainen (Eds.), Autonomic Networking. IX, 316 pages. 2006.

Vol. 4194: V.G. Ganzha, E.W. Mayr, E.V. Vorozhtsov (Eds.), Computer Algebra in Scientific Computing. XI, 313 pages. 2006.

Vol. 4193: T.P. Runarsson, H.-G. Beyer, E. Burke, J.J. Merelo-Guervós, L. D. Whitley, X. Yao (Eds.), Parallel Problem Solving from Nature - PPSN IX. XIX, 1061 pages. 2006.

Vol. 4192: B. Mohr, J.L. Träff, J. Worringen, J. Dongarra (Eds.), Recent Advances in Parallel Virtual Machine and Message Passing Interface. XVI, 414 pages. 2006.

Vol. 4191: R. Larsen, M. Nielsen, J. Sporring (Eds.), Medical Image Computing and Computer-Assisted Intervention – MICCAI 2006, Part II. XXXVIII, 981 pages. 2006.

Vol. 4190: R. Larsen, M. Nielsen, J. Sporring (Eds.), Medical Image Computing and Computer-Assisted Intervention – MICCAI 2006, Part I. XXXVVIII, 949 pages. 2006.

Vol. 4189: D. Gollmann, J. Meier, A. Sabelfeld (Eds.), Computer Security – ESORICS 2006. XI, 548 pages. 2006.

Vol. 4188: P. Sojka, I. Kopeček, K. Pala (Eds.), Text, Speech and Dialogue. XIV, 721 pages. 2006. (Sublibrary LNAI).

Vol. 4187: J.J. Alferes, J. Bailey, W. May, U. Schwertel (Eds.), Principles and Practice of Semantic Web Reasoning. XI, 277 pages. 2006.

Vol. 4186: C. Jesshope, C. Egan (Eds.), Advances in Computer Systems Architecture. XIV, 605 pages. 2006.

Vol. 4185: R. Mizoguchi, Z. Shi, F. Giunchiglia (Eds.), The Semantic Web – ASWC 2006. XX, 778 pages. 2006.

Vol. 4184: M. Bravetti, M. Núñez, G. Zavattaro (Eds.), Web Services and Formal Methods. X, 289 pages. 2006.

Vol. 4183: J. Euzenat, J. Domingue (Eds.), Artificial Intelligence: Methodology, Systems, and Applications. XIII, 291 pages. 2006. (Sublibrary LNAI).

Vol. 4182: H.T. Ng, M.-K. Leong, M.-Y. Kan, D. Ji (Eds.), Information Retrieval Technology. XVI, 684 pages. 2006.

Vol. 4180: M. Kohlhase, OMDoc – An Open Markup Format for Mathematical Documents [version 1.2]. XIX, 428 pages. 2006. (Sublibrary LNAI).

Vol. 4179: J. Blanc-Talon, W. Philips, D. Popescu, P. Scheunders (Eds.), Advanced Concepts for Intelligent Vision Systems. XXIV, 1224 pages. 2006.

Vol. 4178: A. Corradini, H. Ehrig, U. Montanari, L. Ribeiro, G. Rozenberg (Eds.), Graph Transformations. XII, 473 pages. 2006.

Vol. 4177: R. Marín, E. Onaindía, A. Bugarín, J. Santos (Eds.), Current Topics in Artificial Intelligence. XV, 482 pages. 2006. (Sublibrary LNAI).

Vol. 4176: S.K. Katsikas, J. Lopez, M. Backes, S. Gritzalis, B. Preneel (Eds.), Information Security. XIV, 548 pages. 2006.

Vol. 4175: P. Bücher, B.M.E. Moret (Eds.), Algorithms in Bioinformatics. XII, 402 pages. 2006. (Sublibrary LNBI).

Vol. 4174: K. Franke, K.-R. Müller, B. Nickolay, R. Schäfer (Eds.), Pattern Recognition. XX, 773 pages. 2006.

Vol. 4173: S. El Yacoubi, B. Chopard, S. Bandini (Eds.), Cellular Automata. XV, 734 pages. 2006.

Vol. 4172: J. Gonzalo, C. Thanos, M. F. Verdejo, R.C. Carrasco (Eds.), Research and Advanced Technology for Digital Libraries. XVII, 569 pages. 2006.

Vol. 4169: H.L. Bodlaender, M.A. Langston (Eds.), Parameterized and Exact Computation. XI, 279 pages. 2006.

Vol. 4168: Y. Azar, T. Erlebach (Eds.), Algorithms – ESA 2006. XVIII, 843 pages. 2006.

Vol. 4167: S. Dolev (Ed.), Distributed Computing. XV, 576 pages. 2006.

Vol. 4166: J. Górski (Ed.), Computer Safety, Reliability, and Security. XIV, 440 pages. 2006.

Vol. 4165: W. Jonker, M. Petković (Eds.), Secure, Data Management. X, 185 pages. 2006.

Vol. 4164: Z. Horváth (Ed.), Central European Functional Programming School. VII, 257 pages. 2006.

Vol. 4163: H. Bersini, J. Carneiro (Eds.), Artificial Immune Systems. XII, 460 pages. 2006.

Vol. 4162: R. Královič, P. Urzyczyn (Eds.), Mathematical Foundations of Computer Science 2006. XV, 814 pages. 2006.

Vol. 4161: R. Harper, M. Rauterberg, M. Combetto (Eds.), Entertainment Computing - ICEC 2006. XXVII, 417 pages. 2006.